Grey Area

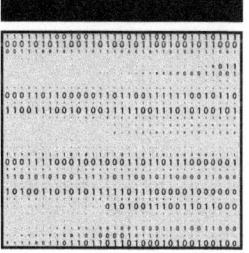

Grey Area

Dark Web Data Collection and
the Future of OSINT

Vinny Troia, PhD

WILEY

Published by John Wiley & Sons, Inc., Hoboken, New Jersey.

Published simultaneously in Canada.

For general information on our other products and services or for technical support, please contact our Customer Care Department within the United States at (800) 762-2974, outside the United States at (317) 572-3993 or fax (317) 572-4002.

Wiley also publishes its books in a variety of electronic formats. Some content that appears in print may not be available in electronic formats. For more information about Wiley products, visit our web site at www.wiley.com.

Library of Congress Cataloging-in-Publication Data

Names: Troia, Vinny, author. | John Wiley & Sons, publisher.
Title: Grey area : dark web data collection and the future of OSINT / Vinny
  Troia, PhD.
Description: Hoboken : John Wiley & Sons Inc, [2026] | Includes
  bibliographical references and index.
Identifiers: LCCN 2025032300 | ISBN 9781394357277 (paperback) | ISBN
  9781394357291 (adobe pdf) | ISBN 9781394357284 (epub)
Subjects: LCSH: Open source intelligence. | Dark Web.
Classification: LCC JF1525.I6 T76 2026
LC record available at https://lccn.loc.gov/2025032300

Cover Design: Wiley
Cover Image: © Nikelser/Getty Images

Printed and bound by CPI Group (UK) Ltd, Croydon, CR0 4YY
C9781394357277_270825

Allison Nixon
@nixonnixoff

As policy we don't accept tips from cybercriminals nor do we ever cultivate source relationships with them

To Allison (and everyone who shares her ideology), thank you for the motivation to write this book.

Additionally, in 2022, I was invited by SANS to deliver the keynote address at their 2024 OSINT Summit—an honor offered nearly two years in advance.

Following the announcement, SANS received significant backlash from parts of the cybersecurity community—ultimately canceling my keynote citing "negative feedback from the community regarding my practices."

This book exists, in part, as a response to that criticism. It was written to demonstrate—clearly and unapologetically—how those same "practices" can strengthen the posture of the intelligence community and have directly supported our national security.

Acknowledgments

This book would not have been possible without the contributions of several individuals across the private sector and intelligence communities. Thank you for sharing your time, insights, and experiences to help make this book happen.

Your willingness to speak candidly about the evolution of open-source intelligence, the role of commercial and publicly available data, and the operational realities of working in this space brought depth and credibility to every chapter.

This book reflects a unique moment in time where public and private intelligence efforts are colliding in ways we've never seen before. Your contributions helped me capture that shift—not through theory, but through real-world experience.

I would like to thank the following people for their willingness to walk the line between what can be said and what needs to be said.

- Andrew Roberts
- Bryan Seeley
- Charles Finfrock
- Dennis Eger
- Eliot Jardines
- Jason Barett
- Jeff Tieges
- Kristin Wood
- M. Scott Koller
- Melissa Stivaletti
- Randy Nixon
- Sue Gordon
- William Usher

I would also like to thank:

Sue Gordon—Our conversations were among the most insightful and grounding parts of this journey. Your thoughtful words shaped a foreword that was deeply moving. It's been a privilege and an honor to know you—I'm truly grateful for our time together and look forward to many more conversations ahead.

Dallas and the team at Mandiant, who played a critical role in shaping the investigative narrative.

Finally, this story wouldn't be what it is without the contributions—intentional or not—of two individuals:

- Connor Riley Moucka (aka Catist, aka Waifu, aka ellyel8)
- John Erin Binns (aka irdev)

Your actions and communications were pivotal in the events that unfold during the latter half of this book. While your methods were criminal, our communications helped shape a very important narrative setting the tone for this entire book.

And of course, to my amazing wife and daughter, to whom none of this would be possible were it not for your continued love and support.

About the Author

Vinny Troia, PhD, is the founder and head of Shadow Nexus, a St. Louis–based firm specializing in providing dark web data and open-source intelligence (OSINT) the U.S. intelligence community and national security organizations. With deep expertise in cyber threat intelligence, data breach investigations, and underground marketplace analysis, Troia has become a recognized voice in the cybersecurity space.

He is frequently cited by national media outlets for his insight into dark web activity, corporate data breaches, and cyber threats with national security implications. His work bridges the gap between technical operations and actionable intelligence, helping organizations understand and respond to emerging risks in real time.

Troia holds a PhD in Information Assurance and Cybersecurity from Capella University.

You can connect with him on LinkedIn at linkedin.com/in/vinnytroia or visit his personal site at vinnytroia.com.

About the Technical Editor

Espen Ringstad is the founder of multiple cutting-edge OSINT companies, known for tracking threat actors across the darkest corners of the Internet. With a sharp investigative mind and a taste for high-stakes digital manhunts, he's built tools and teams that uncover what others miss. Whether mapping extremist networks or exposing hidden adversaries, Espen operates where intelligence meets innovation—and is always one step ahead.

Contents at a Glance

Contents

Foreword

If 1947 never happened—if the intelligence community didn't exist and we were starting clean today, without the legacy systems or institutional baggage—what would we build?

If we were truly starting clean, we wouldn't be arguing over whether open-source information is valid. We'd begin with a single assumption: The world already knows everything.

Then we'd look around and say, *"If the world already knows everything, how do I make sense of it? How do I create advantage from it?"*

Because intelligence is fundamentally about advantage. It's not about knowing everything—it's about how we use what we know to create advantage. If the world already knows everything, then you need to know a little more, a little sooner, and put it together a little differently.

What distinguishes intelligence analysis from smart opinion is the underlying craft that makes fundamentally uncertain information actionable by accounting for that uncertainty. New tradecraft will need to be developed to address the uncertainty—and the bias—present in open information.

I am confident, however, that the combination of data volume and new technologies will move us closer to this goal and may even reveal the holy grail of "intent," which has long been the near-exclusive purview of human collection.

That's where open-source information is a game changer. It gets us closer to understanding intent, faster than traditional collection ever could. That can't be optional. And why would it be? The information is everywhere. If we're not incorporating it, we're not doing our jobs as intelligence professionals. Yet right now, we still treat open information as something we bring in—like an outsider—and that's backwards.

Data should drive the system. Not the other way around.

It will help if the intelligence community reconsiders its approach to secrecy and risk. Secrecy was a modality in a world where we were hunters—where what we found, only we knew. We are now in a world of gatherers—a world where secrecy is no longer as important as speed to insight.

We also need to rethink the risk of loss in this modern world; doing so will likely drive us to reimagine many of our approaches to perfection, loss, and sharing—so intelligence has the reach and impact the changing world demands.

That reimagining leads directly to a broader shift—from secrecy to speed—which means we need to stop asking whether OSINT is real and start asking, "how do we know what we need to know, given the landscape we're in? What becomes possible when we start treating the world's open data as part of the intelligence picture?"

Then I think the conversation we'd be having—the one we *should* be having—is this: how do you build tradecraft around information everyone can see?

Because if the world knows everything, then how do you operate in a world where you must be who you are?

That question changes everything. It changes the entire analytic craft, because you not only have to understand the nuances of the information—you must also understand how others perceive it, and be ready for people to manipulate it once they know you're using it.

That's the fundamental paradigm shift.

Because it's not just about collecting and using open information—it's about understanding what changes when you no longer get to hide. That's the work. That's the next layer: reconciling two truths—the tradecraft we've spent generations refining, and the availability of data we never built systems to process.

I believe this is an inflection point—*OSINT is the biggest opportunity intelligence has had in decades.*

Back in the early Cold War, the Soviets and Chinese took advantage of our open society while limiting what information we could see and collect. Now, open source finally gives us the same opportunities our early adversaries had—when we were the only open society and they were closed.

Adapting to this opportunity isn't just a technical shift—it's a mindset one. We need to stop treating open information as a hardship—because it's not. With the right application of this intelligence, we could be in our heyday.

We've never had access to this much data—to this volume of information. The only thing that can hold us back is our refusal to change.

We have the craft. We have the sources. We have the modalities. Now we need to adapt—to the world as it is, not as it was.

We must evolve so we can—once again—create movement advantage and knowledge advantage in this very different world.

That's the challenge. That's the opportunity. Let's not waste it.

—Susan M. Gordon
Former Principal Deputy Director of National Intelligence

Introduction

Grey Area: Dark Web Data and the Future of OSINT explores the critical intelligence value of information found on the dark web—whether it comes from hacked, breached, or leaked (HBL) datasets, or is extracted directly from the criminals responsible for them. While the subject matter may carry a negative association, the purpose of this book is quite the opposite: to show how dark web–derived intelligence—especially publicly available (PAI) and commercially available information (CAI)—is rapidly becoming the backbone of modern intelligence operations.

It also tells the story of how a human intelligence (HUMINT) network built around known cybercriminals helped uncover and ultimately stop one of the largest data breaches in history. This book is about defining—and reframing—the boundaries of ethical and legal collection practices, and how that evolving *grey area* is reshaping the future of OSINT and national security.

This book is not theoretical. It's meant to be practical, operational, and directly usable by professionals across the intelligence and cybersecurity fields. Whether you're a government analyst, OSINT practitioner, or an independent investigator, the goal is the same—to give you the tools, context, and clarity needed to work effectively with dark web data—and use it for good.

What Does This Book Cover?

Part I provides the foundation—a field guide to navigating dark web forums, data markets, and legal grey zones. You'll learn how these underground markets operate, how threat actors establish trust, and how to evaluate a potential deal—often with practical guidance informed by the U.S. Department of Justice.

This section explores where to acquire data, how to interact with threat actors safely, and how to stay within legal bounds. From pseudonym creation to operational compartmentalization, these chapters offers real-world practices for working in sensitive online environments.

It also brings clarity to the often-misunderstood concept of Publicly Available Information (PAI)—breaking down what's considered "fair game" and what crosses the line from an intelligence collection standpoint. You'll hear directly from senior voices in the intelligence community (IC) who define these boundaries and explain their operational implications.

To ground this theory in reality, I walk through real-world examples—data leaks from the Brazilian Nuclear Authority, Shanghai National Police, MBDA missile systems, and Russia's Institute for Nuclear Research—each highlighting how hacked, breached, and leaked (HBL) data can inform OSINT operations and mission outcomes.

Part II is all about open-source intelligence (OSINT) and how the data discussed in Part I can be used to enhance real-world intelligence collection. I begin by examining the evolution of OSINT within the intelligence community (IC), tracing how the discipline has matured—and where it's headed—through direct interviews with professionals across the Department of Defense (DoD) and broader IC. This section highlights the growing strategic role OSINT plays in reshaping how the IC approaches modern collection.

I also explore how dark web HBL data is actively leveraged in investigations. Through real-case studies, I show how disparate data points—such as leaked credentials, Telegram activity, and historical forum posts—can be assembled into cohesive profiles to identify known cybercriminals and uncover digital footprints.

Part II concludes with a topic too often overlooked: the use of OSINT in combating child sexual abuse material (CSAM) and human trafficking. Using live case examples, I examine how open-source tools and dark web intelligence can work together to support victim protection efforts and disrupt criminal networks in meaningful ways.

Part III is the most technical- and hands-on-section of this book, with every example grounded in real datasets sourced from the dark web. It opens with a look at disinformation risks and explores how to validate large datasets at scale, including how to use artificial intelligence (AI) to assess the integrity of a breached database containing Chinese national ID records.

This part also tackles the realities of data cleaning and transformation. You'll learn how to normalize invalid or unstructured data from Iranian, Chinese, and Russian breaches—converting foreign-language, inconsistent formats into structured, ingestible intelligence products.

Next, I explore the practical integration of AI and large language models (LLMs) in OSINT workflows. Through a case study involving a breach of an Iranian ride-hailing platform, I demonstrate how AI can dramatically accelerate analysis—flagging anomalies, identifying baseline behaviors, and surfacing operational insights that would otherwise take days or weeks to uncover.

From there, I shift from systems-based data to people-based intelligence. The final chapter explores the fundamentals of human intelligence (HUMINT)—specifically, how to elicit valuable information from individuals without triggering suspicion. From calibrated questions and false prompts to ego manipulation and rapport-building, this chapter breaks down the psychological tradecraft behind successful digital elicitation, and introduces key concepts in persona development and OPSEC—including how to build and maintain credible online identities.

Finally, through the lens of operational intelligence and national security, **Part IV** unpacks what is arguably one of the most significant data breaches in recent memory—the Snowflake hack—and the role I played through its identification and investigation under the alias *Reddington*.

Reddington

For those unfamiliar, *Raymond Reddington* is a fictional character from *The Blacklist*, portrayed by James Spader—a top-tier criminal turned FBI informant who operates in the shadows while sitting at the top the agency's most wanted list. The name felt fitting. In the cybercrime underground, many assume I work with the FBI. And in certain corners of the security community, many would argue that my methods are enough to put me on a target list of my own.

But the reality looks different.

Part IV follows my work under the alias Reddington—not as a criminal or an informant, but as an investigator—showing what modern HUMINT really looks like in practice, and how that intelligence led to the discovery of a data breach that impacted hundreds of organizations across industries and borders.

If not for my direct engagement with known cybercriminals, there's no telling how many more Snowflake customers would have been breached—or which nation-state might have purchased the data that, according to the DOJ, posed a "substantial risk to national security and public safety."

The discovery of what would become the only data breach in history delayed due to national security concerns wasn't the result of passive scraping. It came from a live human intelligence network—relationships built through targeted, real-time interaction.

The Snowflake story begins with the earliest signals—how the breach came to light, including my direct communications with the hackers behind it. Anchored by official court records, this text weaves together chat logs, personal notes, and intrusion analysis to build a full picture of how the investigation unfolded from the inside out.

Next, I shift focus to Snowflake itself—how we traced the source of the stolen data, and how we identified additional victims. This is where the investigation pivots from isolated victim cases to a systemic compromise.

I also provide a full analysis of the breach mechanics: how the hackers maintained persistent access, the tooling they deployed, and how they operationalized infostealer logs at scale to target Snowflake customers. In some cases, I include excerpts from interactions with the victim organizations to illustrate the rapid timeline and how quickly events were unfolding in real time.

The section closes with the story of Connor Moucka—also known as Catist, Waifu, ellyel8, and several other aliases—including the details of his unmasking and arrest.

This is where the book shifts from theoretical warnings about why some people choose not to engage with threat actors, to real-world proof of the value these relationships can provide—when managed with intention, tradecraft, and a clear operational goal.

Now let's turn the spotlight to the featured guests—whose insight and involvement were critical to bringing this story to life.

Introducing the Guest Experts

This book is shaped by the voices of some of the most respected figures in the national security and intelligence community. Their firsthand experiences, hard-won insights, and candid reflections are woven throughout the chapters that follow. Each guest has also contributed a short personal narrative—written in their own voice—capturing the professional journey and perspective they brought to our conversations.

The following narratives are in alphabetical order.

Jason Barrett
IC OSINT Executive, ODNI

The views and opinions provided herein are my own and do not necessarily represent the views of the Office of the Director of National Intelligence or of the United States. (See also 5 C.F.R. § 2635.807(b).)

I have worked in the IC for 22 years. I started out as a long time all-source analyst at DIA and the National Counterterrorism Center and led the creation of ODNI's senior analytic service, and held a variety of staff roles including being the presidential daily briefer for the national security advisor, as well as the senior executive assistant to the Director of National Intelligence.

I was also the Chief of the FBI's China and North Korea Cyber Intelligence Unit and have served in joint terrorism task forces in Manhattan and in Chicago.

I currently serve as the IC's Open Source Intelligence (OSINT) Executive at the Office of the Director of National Intelligence (ODNI). My role oversees the synchronization and coordination of OSINT efforts across the IC, with responsibilities including developing resource and investment plans, establishing policies and standards, and implementing new frameworks for acquiring and utilizing publicly and commercially available information.

Dennis Eger
Senior Open Source Advisor, INSCOM

I spent nearly 33 years in the Army, all of it in military intelligence. I came up as an all-source analyst and, toward the end of my career, served as a senior advisor to the Army G-2. That's when OSINT really entered my portfolio. Around 2018, my boss at the time—a three-star general—flagged that things were starting to stir in the open-source space. Not a tidal wave, but enough momentum that leadership wanted someone tracking it. He told me, "I need this in your portfolio." And that's how I stepped into it.

Up to that point, we didn't really talk about OSINT as a distinct discipline—it just wasn't part of the language coming up through the ranks. But in that senior role, I began to see where the Army was trying to go, especially in terms of building out training pipelines. It was early days, and the focus was mostly on preparing the workforce, but I saw the potential. When I retired in 2020, I applied for a civilian position focused on OSINT and was fortunate to be selected. That let me carry the mission forward and stay involved as the Army began taking OSINT more seriously—not just as a capability, but as a core part of how we fight and understand the information environment.

Charles Finfrock
Former Case Officer and HUMINT Operator, CIA

I spent 18 years with the CIA as a case officer, with most of that time overseas in places like the Middle East. My job was to recruit and manage human sources, both in the field and later back at headquarters.

Now I run a private company that supports the intelligence community and federal law enforcement by delivering training on ubiquitous technical surveillance—how data is passively and actively collected, how targeting is conducted across digital and physical domains, and how to detect, disrupt, and mitigate those threats.

On the private sector side, we support a wide range of corporate clients with specialized services. We run enhanced due diligence for executive hires and M&A activity, helping clients understand who they're really dealing with before a signature hits the page. We conduct scam, fraud, and impersonation investigations, especially where reputation, brand integrity, or customer safety is at risk.

Susan M. Gordon
Former Principal Deputy Director of National Intelligence

I am a career intelligence officer. I started out as a weapons systems analyst, then moved over to spacecraft development, and eventually returned to lead analytic units. That mix gave me a unique perspective on tools we were using—and, more importantly, the ones we weren't. That's what opened the door to figuring out how to reach Silicon Valley, and what ultimately laid the foundation for what eventually became *In-Q-Tel*. I'm pretty proud of that—25 years later, not many things in government still stand up like that.

After a brief eight-year hiatus as my role as a mom, I returned to the CIA—this time to the science and technology division within the Office of Special Activities, which built tools for covert action. That was my first real taste of ops.

From there, I moved into the Information Operations Center—still technical, but fundamentally operational—and that taught me a whole new set of lessons around risk.

I later became the Director of Support, which was a breathtaking opportunity. I was asked to figure out what "cyber" meant for the agency. After a few days, I came back with a single key question: how does the CIA do its work in a digital environment? That is, how does an organization built for analog secrets operate effectively in a digital, data-saturated world?

And here's where the story takes a turn. When you do something truly transformative—something that actually changes how things work—you tend to get buttered off the island. So I got the opportunity to work at NGA, which changed me as much as anything in my career.

First, it was a combat support agency, which is fundamentally different than strategic intelligence. That's where I was pulled into the revolution happening in commercial space and what it meant to operate successfully in the open. That's also where I learned how to talk about intelligence openly—to audiences that cared, and that, frankly, *were* the threat surface.

Later, I became the Principal Deputy Director of National Intelligence—the senior career intelligence officer in charge of the whole community—during a time when we were grappling with some profound challenges. We had an emergent China and the need to realign resources. And we were coming out of the long counterterrorism tunnel and realizing: the whole world had changed while we were fighting that fight. We were now in a digital world.

For the last five years, I've been working on national security from the outside—with the people who are, in many ways, the real decision-makers now. If I had to boil it all down: I took a whole series of jobs I didn't know how to do. But somewhere along the way, I became the person you called if you wanted something *done*.

And I do think I'm good at that.

When you're good at doing things, you tend to be less dogmatic about how they were done before and more willing to adapt to the environment you're in.

Eliot Jardines

Former Assistant Deputy Director of National Intelligence, ODNI
Founder, OSINT Foundation

I joined the Army at 17—mostly to pay for college—and ended up serving in both active duty and reserve roles. Early on, I was in a reserve unit assigned to the intelligence school at Fort Huachuca, where we developed curriculum for the basic and advanced intelligence officer courses. Around 1992, the Army started paying attention to this new thing called open-source intelligence. Our unit got tasked with creating a block of instruction and writing a fully unclassified OSINT handbook.

That handbook took off. That eventually led me to start one of the first moderated discussion groups for OSINT. People assumed I was some greybeard expert, not a 20-something living at home, but I rolled with it. That visibility got me tapped for deployments, including starting an OSINT cell in Germany during the Balkans war. When I returned from deployment, DIA brought me back on active duty to manage OSINT contracts, and in the late 1990s, I founded one of the first OSINT-focused companies—then sold it in 2005.

When ODNI stood up, I took on a leadership role as the Assistant Deputy Director of National Intelligence for Open Source. I didn't build the Open Source Center, but I was responsible for its oversight, direction, and funding. I've spent much of my career trying to professionalize OSINT—whether it was through standing up programs, defining standards, or pushing back when definitions got twisted. Today, I serve as Director of Operations for the OSINT Foundation, where we're building the career paths, certifications, and professional infrastructure the discipline's always needed.

M. Scott Koller
Privacy and Data Security Attorney, Clark Hill PLC

The views expressed in my quotes or comments are provided for general educational and informational purposes only and do not constitute legal advice. My statements do not create an attorney-client relationship, and readers should consult with their own legal counsel regarding any specific legal questions or concerns. Any opinions expressed are my own, and not necessarily those of Clark Hill.

I am a privacy and data security attorney specializing in data breach response and cybersecurity compliance. I advise clients across various industries on how to manage legal and operational risks associated with data collection, storage, and technology systems. My work includes guiding organizations through data security incidents, coordinating with law enforcement, and responding to regulatory investigations.

I regularly assist clients with incident response planning, cybersecurity training, and practical strategies for navigating complex compliance requirements. My experience spans key data protection frameworks, including the Gramm-Leach-Bliley Act (GLBA), HIPAA, the California Consumer Privacy Act (CCPA/CPRA), Payment Card Industry Data Security Standard (PCI DSS), and a range of state and international privacy laws.

Randy Nixon
Director, Open Source Enterprise, CIA

My career at the CIA began in 1991 as a student intern, followed by five years of active duty in the U.S. Army, where I served primarily in the Balkans. I returned to the Agency in 1999 and focused on military analysis, leading efforts across multiple conflict zones and unstable regions during a period of rapid global change.

Over the years, I've worked to bridge emerging technologies with mission needs. As the lead of the Digital Futures team within the Directorate of Digital Innovation, I focused on leveraging private-sector innovation to solve complex intelligence challenges—laying the groundwork for deeper integration of open-source capabilities across the Agency.

Today, I serve as the Director of the Open Source Enterprise (OSE) within the CIA's Directorate of Digital Innovation. I lead the Agency's efforts to harness publicly and commercially available information at scale, integrating open-source intelligence into core analytic and operational workflows. My focus is on making OSINT not just relevant—but indispensable—to how we meet today's national security threats.

Andrew Roberts
Former OSINT Integration Center Chief, DIA

I spent over 35 great years at the Defense Intelligence Agency, from 1984 to 2019. My career included intelligence engagement with nearly every facet of the Defense Intelligence Enterprise (DIE) and much of the intelligence community (IC). In my final six years, I was lead for the open-source intelligence (OSINT) effort in DIA and across the broader DIE, as well as serving as vice chair for the IC National Open Source Committee (NOSC). That role gave me the opportunity to collaborate with remarkable colleagues at the CIA, NGA, NSA, and a range of non-DoD components. I was also proud to have worked with the fine people in our Combatant Commands and Service intelligence components.

I concluded my tenure at the DIA as the first Chief of the OSINT Integration Center (OSIC). Along with the help of a great team, we stood up what is now the central hub for OSINT coordination across the Defense Department. We collectively worked to institutionalize OSINT as a core intelligence discipline, integrate commercial data streams into military decision-making, and foster collaboration across the entire intelligence ecosystem.

After a brief stint at RAND, I began service in 2021 at the Institute for Defense Analyses (IDA) as a senior Research Staff Member. I once again have the opportunity to work with a diverse set of great colleagues who care deeply about the security of our country, the defense of our constitution, and keeping our citizens safe.

This is my shared legacy.

Bryan Seeley
U.S. Marine (Ret.), Hacker

I'm a former U.S. Marine, ethical hacker, and cybersecurity expert with a mission-driven approach to protecting digital infrastructure. After the attacks of 9/11, I enlisted in the Marine Corps as a linguist, specializing in signals and human intelligence, with overseas deployments to Iraq and Kuwait. My military experience shaped a lifelong commitment to service—and to defending others, both on and off the battlefield.

I first gained international attention after exposing critical security vulnerabilities that allowed me to wiretap both the FBI and the Secret Service—legally, and with the intent to demonstrate the flaws before adversaries could exploit them. Unlike most hackers, I've always used my skills to protect—I'm a Marine. We protect.

Some call me a digital vigilante. I call it doing the right thing. My work has directly influenced policy changes at major tech platforms, and I regularly speak to global audiences about cyber threats, fraud prevention, and digital safety.

Melisa Stivaletti
Director, Open Source Intelligence, Guidehouse

I'm the Director of Open Source Intelligence (OSINT) at Guidehouse and have spent nearly 18 years working across the U.S. Government in the OSINT discipline. Over the course of my career, I've held roles within the Office of the Director of National Intelligence, DIA, CIA, the Department of the Army, and NGA—each of which shaped my deep commitment to advancing open source as a core intelligence capability.

I'm a certified Project Management Professional (PMP) with an MS in Public Policy and a BA in International Relations. I am also currently finishing my PhD in Public Policy. I also serve as the Chair of the Emerging Professionals in the Intelligence Community (EPIC) Committee and as a liaison member to the Intelligence Committee of the Armed Forces Communications and Electronics Association (AFCEA). Through my professional work and community leadership, I'm passionate about mentoring the next generation of intelligence professionals and pushing the OSINT field forward.

Jeff Tiegs
Lt Col, Delta Special Forces (Ret.),
CEO, Skull Games

I'm a retired Lieutenant Colonel from the U.S. Army. I spent close to 26 years in uniform, most of that within Special Operations. I ended my career at 1st Special Forces Operational Detachment-Delta— what most people know as Delta Force.

My background is in counter-terrorism (CT) and counter-insurgency (COIN). Two mission sets that often conflict—CT is rapid-cycle, surgical. You identify a target, take action, and start pulling threads to dismantle the network. It's a 24-hour clock. COIN is slower, more political, more layered. I operated in both environments.

As I moved toward retirement, I was looking for a new enemy to pursue. I was looking for a way to ensure that I continue to find passion and purpose. I'm a soldier. I've always been a soldier, but it really isn't my identity. I take it either one step forward or back, then my job is always the same—I'm a protector.

I felt a calling to look at sex trafficking, specifically domestic sex trafficking, and even more specific to that would be online commercial sex trafficking.

Now with Skull Games, our goal is to turn publicly available information into leads that law enforcement can act on.

Kristin Wood

Former Deputy Chief of Innovation and Technology, OSC, CIA
CEO & Co-Founder, August Interactive

I spent over 20 years at the CIA, serving in the Director's area and across three of the Agency's directorates. My career spanned five wars and included leading teams through high-consequence analysis, field operations, and the integration of open-source innovation and technology. One of the most meaningful parts of my time at the CIA was delivering the Presidential Daily Brief (PDB), providing critical intelligence to the President and senior national security leaders.

I closed out my CIA career as the Deputy Director for Innovation and Technology at the Open Source Center. That's where I became a true believer in the power of open-source information. I came to see that the most valuable insights often lived outside traditional classified channels—buried in datasets and signals the government wasn't collecting on its own.

After leaving the Agency, I joined Grist Mill Exchange, a government-focused data marketplace that brought together hundreds of commercial data providers into one platform—making OSINT more accessible, affordable, and usable for mission partners. Today, I'm the CEO and co-founder of August Interactive, a deep-tech gaming studio focused on building personalized, immersive games with purpose. I believe the future of gaming and extended reality is about more than entertainment—it's a critical part of our economic, educational, and social infrastructure.

William Usher

Senior Director of Intelligence, SCSP
Former Executive, CIA

I'm the Senior Director for Intelligence at the Special Competitive Studies Project. Our mission is to make recommendations on how the United States can remain competitive—particularly in artificial intelligence and other emerging technologies—amid intensifying geostrategic competition with the People's Republic of China, Russia, Iran, North Korea, and others.

I joined SCSP two years ago after spending 32 years at the CIA. Back then, most of my career was spent as an all-source intelligence analyst. I served in managerial and executive roles. As an analyst, I worked on a broad range of accounts and issues, including global energy markets and East Asia. I later led Agency units that focused on the Near East and on Eurasia.

Underground Field Guide

In This Part

If you're new to this space or if you're continuing from my last book, *Hunting Cyber Criminals*, you'll need a baseline before you dive into the deep end. This section is designed to give you that foundation.

What follows is a mix of personal experience, investigative reporting, and technical insight that frames the broader open-source intelligence (OSINT) story that this book is here to tell. I start with a summary of a saga involving a group of hackers who spent years trying to derail my work and reputation. That chapter closes the loop on that particular journey, and more importantly, it clears the runway for what comes next.

From there, I begin mapping the underground economy built entirely on stolen user accounts—how it works, who profits from it, and what fuels its continued growth. Chapter 3 opens up the world of dark web forums: what they are, how to access them, and what you'll find once you're inside. It also includes practical guidance for navigating those spaces safely, with legal context drawn directly from U.S. Department of Justice opinions.

Finally, Chapter 4 brings you to the core of the OSINT conversation: what is "publicly available information," and what are the legal and operational boundaries around collecting and using it? If you're going to understand open-source intelligence, you need to start by understanding what counts as fair game.

This section sets the foundation. The rest of the book builds from here.

Where We Left Off

This chapter lays the foundation—not just for the book, but for the credibility behind it. It reconnects readers to the aftermath of my previous work, *Hunting Cyber Criminals*, and closes the loop on the years-long campaign by both threat actors and journalists to discredit and disrupt everything that followed.

From being name-dropped in ransomware notes to having my identity spoofed in the Federal Bureau of Investigation (FBI) email system hack, I include this chapter as a reminder that working with and exposing cybercriminals comes with real-world consequences—including targeted harassment, swatting attempts, and even bomb threats.

It also marks the rise and fall of Conor Fitzpatrick (aka Pompompurin), former admin of a major dark web marketplace, and introduces a new class of adversary: groups like Scattered Spider ("The Com"), known not just for their digital intrusions, but for crossing the line into real-world intimidation and coercion.

Where to Start?

My last book, *Hunting Cyber Criminals*, followed a specific hacking group known as The Dark Overlord (TDO).

For some quick background: over the past six years, the hackers behind TDO have repeatedly aligned themselves with prominent groups like GnosticPlayers, ShinyHunters, and most recently, Pompompurin—using those affiliations to obscure their own involvement. Their M.O. was simple: install lesser-known (and often more gullible) hackers into high-visibility roles designed to absorb the fallout, while the real operators stayed safely in the shadows.

My previous book laid out in detail the technical sophistication of this hacking group and their consistent strategy of using public fall guys to shield their core operations.

Since publishing that book and subsequent investigative reports, I've had the unique honor of seeing my name regularly mentioned across dark web forums and Telegram channels and even embedded in ransomware notes sent to victim organizations.

I feel like a reasonably good personal measure of success in any given topic is when people care enough about you to make you into a meme. Whether they like you or not, it signifies that people are noticing what you do. And that's pretty much what happened.

The important point to note is that all these hackers were actively involved in massive data breach campaigns, high visibility in the hacking scene, and deep involvement with *BreachForums*, one of the largest underground communities of its kind.

Following my last book, they all made it their mission to discredit me. This had the unfortunate effect of muddying the waters a bit when it comes to my work.

For example, in 2020, ZDNet reported that a user had accessed and wiped the data from more than 15,000 Elasticsearch servers—belonging to thousands of organizations, globally—leaving only a single message in their wake: "If you want your data back, contact Vinny Troia of Night Lion Security."[1] People were not amused.

So before I get into the meat of the book, there are some lingering issues I want to address.

Addressing Past Aspersions

I've come to accept that my work on the dark web tends to polarize people in the security industry. Some respect the approach. Others view me as no different than the criminals I'm investigating. And that divide isn't limited to analysts and practitioners—a number of reporters have made their stance just as clear.

When Security Researchers Pose as Cybercriminals, Who Can Tell the Difference?

In 2018, a prominent cybersecurity journalist published an article that essentially compared my actions to the cybercriminals who regularly leak stolen data on dark web forums. The article accused me of operating under aliases that advertised the sale of stolen data across major marketplaces.

Without getting into semantics, I'll concede most of what was written was accurate. That said, there's one critical detail that was deliberately left out of the story—but one that completely changes the narrative: *Every action I took was sanctioned by law enforcement.*

Smoke and Mirrors

A few years later, the same reporter chose to write another story about my nefarious online activities, this time claiming that I had publicly leaked a database belonging to `verifications.io`, which purportedly contained personal information on several hundred million people.

The article, which quoted the text from the published database listing, stated, "This release contains 69 of 70 of the original verifications.io databases, totaling 200+ million accounts."

I will concede and state that all of this is completely accurate—but it's not quite the whole story.

As I explore in future chapters, infiltrating closed cybercriminal circles often requires offering something of value. The Department of Justice (DOJ) guidance acknowledges this reality explicitly:

---

[1] https://www.zdnet.com/article/a-hacker-has-wiped-defaced-more-than-15000-elasticsearch-servers/

It may be easier for an undercover practitioner to extract information from sources on the forum who have learned to trust the practitioner's persona, but developing trust and establishing bona fides as a fellow criminal may involve offering useful information, services, or tools that can be used to commit crimes.[2]

It's a slippery slope, no doubt, but the devil is in the details. Let's go back to that quote: "This release contains *69 of 70* of the original verifications.io databases."

Can you guess which database contained all the actual PII?

Spoiler alert: It's the one that was never released. The only thing published was a bunch of random server analytics and a database labeled "bounced_emails," consisting of several hundred million outdated or invalid email addresses.

It looked convincing enough to accomplish my goal, which was entirely the point. *It was a carefully controlled move, designed to establish credibility without crossing the line.*

Data Viper

The last in an attempt to publicly discredit me involves the showcasing of data claimed to have been stolen from my original threat intelligence platform, Data Viper.

The announcement of the hack coincided (almost to the day) with the release of my threat intelligence report on The Dark Overlord. What an amazing coincidence.

The information was published to an anonymous zine (see Figure 1.1), which contained an advanced copy of the report and my book. Maybe it's just me, but the blog seemed to be written by someone who was clearly angry with me.

Figure 1.1: Screenshot of the hack zine.

---

[2] https://www.justice.gov/criminal/criminal-ccips/page/file/1252341/

Yes, my platform was hacked. What wasn't so obvious was that the entire incident was a staged *honeypot*—a deliberate trap designed to lure in attackers. And while that may sound convenient, or even a little unbelievable, I literally documented how I would do it in my last book.

Finding admin credentials buried in application programming interface (API) documentation isn't exactly rare, especially when you're dealing with overseas developers who aren't paid enough to care about security. So when I intentionally planted those credentials in my public application documentation, no one questioned it. They took the bait.

> **NOTE** For those interested in the full details, including the Internet Protocol (IP) address attribution and the technical server logs from the incident, you can view the full report here: `https://nightlion.com/blog/2021/data-viper-honeypot-hack/`.

It was a simple plan—and it worked. I'll admit, there was some collateral damage I didn't anticipate, but in the end, it was worth it. The honeypot allowed me to tie IP addresses used to access my systems to multiple threat groups, including GnosticPlayers, ShinyHunters, and NSFW (better known as The Dark Overlord).

Of course, actions like these come with consequences. Even if they ultimately served a greater purpose, they made me a target.

Around the time this was all happening, RaidForums was the primary hub for data thieves and cybercriminals. But in 2022—not long after this article dropped—RaidForums was seized and taken offline by law enforcement.

Its replacement came quickly: BreachForums, run by a new admin who would become infamous in his own right—Pompompurin.

Pompompurin

Conor Brian Fitzpatrick (see Figure 1.2), aka Pompompurin, was the admin of BreachForums, one of the largest online marketplaces of hacked and stolen data.

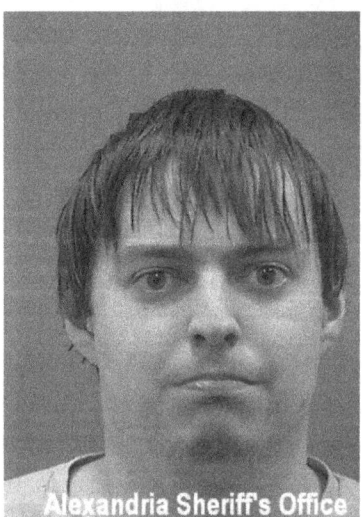

Figure 1.2: Conor Brian Fitzpatrick aka Pompompurin.

In addition to being the site's admin, he spent most of his free time trying to torment me.

During his reign as admin, Fitzpatrick (Pompompurin) was responsible for several notable hacks (mostly against me). There is one I feel is worth mentioning, because it directly relates to the work published in my last book.

The 2021 FBI Email Hack

On November 12, 2021, the FBI's official domain (`fbi.gov`) was compromised and used to send tens of thousands of legitimate-looking emails about an urgent cybersecurity threat: me.

The emails read:

Subject: Urgent: Threat actor in systems

Our intelligence monitoring indicates exfiltration of several of your virtualized clusters in a sophisticated chain attack. We tried to black hole the transit nodes used by this advanced persistent threat actor, however there is a huge chance he will modify his attack with fast flux technologies, which he proxies through multiple global accelerators. **We identified the threat actor to be Vinny Troia,** *who is believed to be affiliated with the extortion gang* **The Dark Overlord**. *We highly recommend you check your systems and IDS monitoring. Beware this threat actor is currently working under inspection of the NCCIC, as we are dependent on some of his intelligence research we cannot interfere physically within 4 hours, which could be enough time to cause severe damage to your infrastructure.*

Stay safe,
U.S. Department of Homeland Security | Cyber Threat Detection and Analysis | Network Analysis Group

Because these emails originated from an official `fbi.gov` server, they appeared completely legitimate. This capability could have been used to send any number of harmful messages, including sending very real looking phishing campaigns, or even to start a fake international news hoax.

Instead, Fitzpatrick decided to act his age and burn this one-time resource in order to send out thousands of messages stating that I was a part of the same group who I had investigated in my previous book. If for nothing else, I appreciated the nod for my hard work.

Within a few hours, the FBI and Cybersecurity and Infrastructure Security Agency (CISA) identified the offending server and took it offline, but not before tens of thousands of people received this email.

Pom's Sudden Change in Attitude

Sometime in December, 2022, all of these attacks came to a screeching halt. Something changed in Pom. Aside from becoming more distant and not as readily available online, he also became slightly more pleasant.

I remember asking him for help with a particular matter and mentioned that I would owe him–and would be happy to repay the favor someday. His response was, "It's ok. I've harassed you enough".

That's the exact moment I knew he had been caught.

Fitzpatrick's Role in BreachForums

On March 24, 2023, Fitzpatrick was officially arrested at his home in Peekskill, New York. At the time of his arrest, Pompompurin controlled the largest online marketplace dedicated to buying, selling, and distributing illicit tools and stolen data.

The following is a summary of BreachForums, and Pom's role as the administrator of that forum, taken directly from the official court documents:[3]

> BreachForums included a "Marketplace" section that was dedicated to the buying and selling of hacked or stolen data, tools for committing cybercrime, and other illicit material, including a "Leaks Market" subsection. Some of the items that were often sold in this section included bank account information, Social Security numbers, other personal identifying information (PII), and login information for compromised online accounts, such as usernames and passwords to access accounts with service providers and merchants.
>
> This information included names and contact information for approximately 200 million users. More recently, on March 9, 2023, a BreachForums user with the moniker "denfur" posted a message revealing the PII of tens of thousands of U.S. citizens. The message included a link to download a file containing names, dates of birth, Social Security numbers, employment information, and health insurance information compromised from a health insurance exchange.
>
> BreachForums also supported additional sections in which users posted stolen or hacked data and discussed tools and techniques for hacking and exploiting that information, including in the "Cracking," "Leaks," and "Tutorials" sections.

Confirming His Role as a Patsy

In 2021, I published an investigative report documenting why I believe Pompompurin was one of the core members of The Dark Overlord group. I received some backlash from the community regarding my analysis when Pom was identified as Fitzpatrick.

To be clear, I always believed Pom was nothing more than the next in a long line of patsies. The details provided in my writeup could *only* have been fed to him by the very person I believed were pulling his strings.

> **NOTE** You can read the full writeup here: `https://nightlion.com/blog/2021/pompompurin-fbi-email-hack//`.

Having spoken with Pom many times, I don't personally believe he had the technical skill to pull off the hacks attributed to him. The most obvious question then becomes, how does someone with virtually no reputation and minimal technical skill suddenly become the admin of one of the most high-profile hacking forums in history?

A simple and extremely plausible explanation is that the real operators behind BreachForums were the same people who *installed* him as a public-facing admin.

Of course, I can't know for sure. It's just a theory.

Then again, in the official court document released by The United States Court for the Eastern District of Virginia, Fitzpatrick pleaded guilty to several crimes including running the cybercrime forum BreachForums.

---

[3] `www.courtlistener.com/docket/67597382/united-states-v-fitzpatrick/`

In the court documents, Fitzpatrick stated,[4]

> *During the subsequent interview, FITZPATRICK admitted that he is the user of the Pompompurin account. He also admitted that he owns and administers BreachForums and previously operated the Pompompurin account on RaidForums.*
>
> *He stated that after RaidForums was seized by law enforcement, **he was approached by individuals who thought he would be competent enough to run a similar site. Fitzpatrick stated that he agreed to do so.***

I love being right. Unfortunately, Pom's numerous pranks against me signaled other, more dangerous, hacker groups to get involved.

Introducing The Com

The Com (aka Scattered Spider) is a collection of (mostly) U.S.-based hackers that are well known for escalating to attacks of physical violence. They play a pivotal role in the last section of this book, when I discuss the Snowflake hacks.

My introduction to The Com occurred very unexpectedly.

One night, I heard several loud pops outside my house. I didn't realize what it was until morning, when I was taking my daughter to school and realized that someone had re-configured my car windows (see Figure 1.3).

Figure 1.3: Photo of my car following the incident.

This incident was the first in many similar situations, including several unsolicited packages being sent to my house, a few visits by the local SWAT team, and even a bomb threat at my daughter's school (see Figure 1.4).

This unfortunately prompted me and my family to move to a new home and uproot our lives. Now, we purchase nothing using our real names. Our house and utilities were purchased under an untraceable LLC. Credit card, insurance, auto bills, and everything else are sent to their own unique mailing addresses.

---

[4] https://www.justice.gov/usao-edva/file/1300536/dl?inline

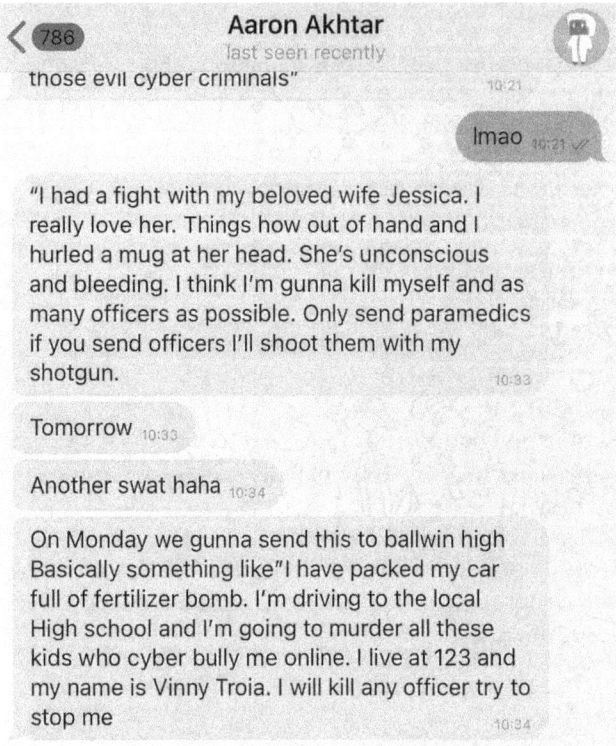

Figure 1.4: Message sent to Pom regarding my swatting.

Within a month or two, the credit bureaus will start picking up all of the different addresses as a primary residence—it's a great way to muddy the waters if you are trying to hide your true location.

All in a day's work, I suppose. But now the game has changed for me. I no longer focus on actor attribution. I have devoted my time to perusing something greater: supporting our national security.

Summary

This chapter bridges the timeline gap between my last book, *Hunting Cyber Criminals*, and this book. During that time, we saw the fall of RaidForums and the rise of BreachForums, led by Conor Brian Fitzpatrick, aka Pompompurin, the person responsible for (among other things) the 2021 FBI email hack. And discussed the events leading up to his arrest in 2023.

This chapter also introduced The Com, including their inclination to escalate hacks into physical violence. This included several successful swatting attempts against me, the destruction of my wife's car, and calling in a bomb threat to my daughter's elementary school.

With the background story out of the way, the next chapter begins setting the stage for the OSINT data collections by providing a wholistic look at a booming underground cybercrime economy.

A Cybercrime Economy of Stolen Data

This chapter looks at an ecosystem of cybercrime fueled by the buying and selling of hacked data. If you're already in the cybersecurity or threat intelligence field, you can probably skim through this chapter, as it is mostly background information and context for newer readers. The topics introduced in this chapter, including dark web forums, infostealers, Subscriber Identity Module (SIM) swapping, and The Com, set the stage for the story in the rest of this book.

For more seasoned readers, this chapter also includes an interesting commentary by blackhat hacker DonJuji on his methods for developing unique password combinations to steal user accounts.

The Stolen Account Black Market

In 2020, *Forbes* and Fox News ran a story detailing a billion-dollar black market based on buying and selling stolen Fortnite and Roblox gaming accounts.[1] The article was based on research provided in my original intelligence report, "The Fortnite Underground Cybercrime Economy."

> **NOTE** You can download the original report here: `https://nightlion.com/blog/2020/`
> `fortnite-cybercrime-economy-report/`.

---

[1] `https://www.foxnews.com/tech/fortnite-black-market-part-of-billion-dollar-hacker-economy-report-claims`

The premise of the underground economy is simple: Hackers seek out and steal video game accounts loaded with unique or hard-to-get items. Those accounts are cataloged and resold for a premium through any number of online marketplaces.

For example, the game Fortnite enables players to earn or buy "skins," which enable them to change the appearance of their character. (Skins are essentially costumes for your video game character.) These skins can often be very difficult, time-consuming, or costly to attain. The image in Figure 2.1 shows an example of a user's Fortnite skin.

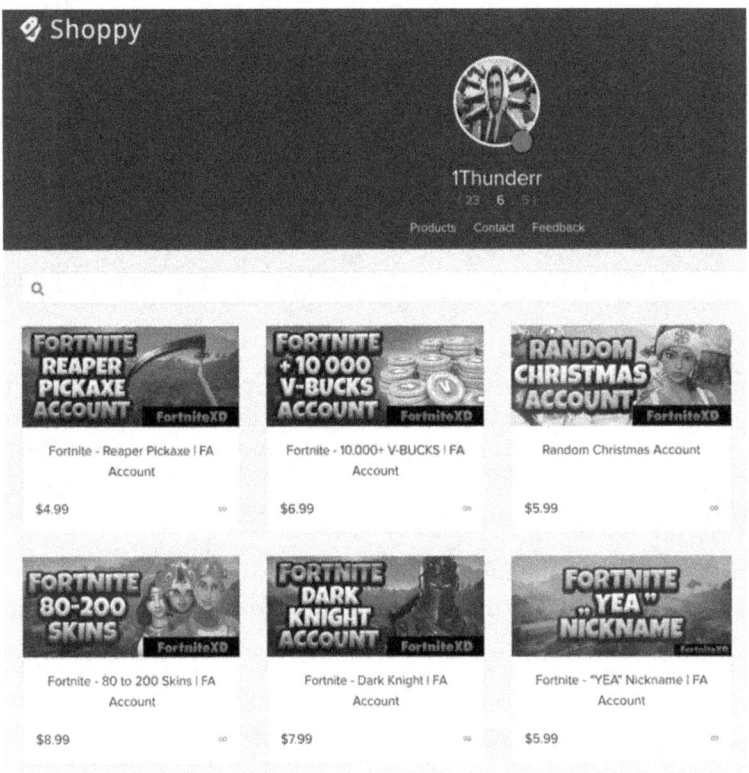

Figure 2.1: Screenshot from Shoppy.gg, where user @1Thunderr sells access to stolen Fortnite gaming accounts.

The more valuable the skin, the more money the hacker can make by reselling the stolen account on the black market.

At the height of the *Forbes* article, Fortnite accounts were being hacked and sold in bulk over private Telegram channels, with some selling for as much as $10,000.[2]

The accounts could also be purchased via clear websites like Shoppy.gg, an online marketplace primarily used as a place to buy and sell illicit digital products.

---

[2] https://www.forbes.com/sites/daveywinder/2020/08/27/heres-how-fortnite-hackers-make-1-million-a-year-epic-games-passwords/

At the time of the report, some of the higher-end Fortnite, Roblox, and Minecraft account brokers were clearing $400,000 per year … and that's just for stolen video game accounts.

Multiply that number by all the different online sites and services with logins that can potentially be stolen and resold. If there's a way to purchase an account for substantially less than retail value, chances are, you can find it on one of these markets.

Figure 2.2 is from another marketplace on Shoppy.gg that caters to the sale of a variety of different stolen accounts.

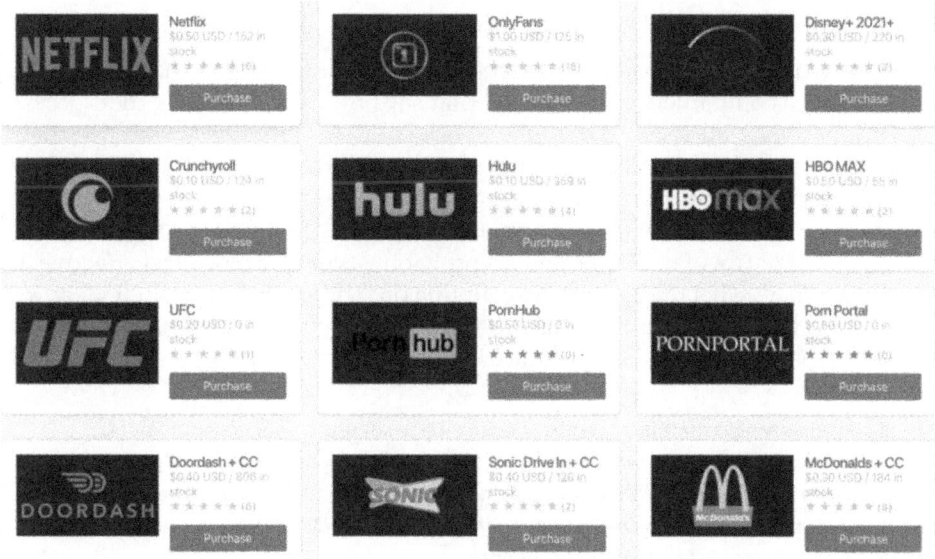

Figure 2.2: Screenshot from Shoppy.gg showing stolen account sales.

Stolen account sales are a huge business. Companies like Netflix and Hulu have attempted to crack down on the use of hacked or reused accounts by implementing security measures that limit the number of logins per account, or even that limit account logins to specific regional locations. Even with these added security measures, however, the stolen account markets continue to thrive.

How Are Hackers Accessing These Accounts?

Hackers gain access to sites like the ones previously shown by using username/password combinations ("combos") taken from different data breaches. Every time you hear about a company being hacked, the stolen data often contains usernames and passwords that are typically stolen in the millions. Those passwords are then resold to other hackers who will try to use them to log into other websites.

Now be honest for a second. How often do you use the same password on multiple accounts? Is your Netflix password the same as your Hulu password? If one of those companies is hacked and that password is exposed, now all of your other accounts are suddenly at risk.

Hackers will reuse those combos on every site they can think of in order to gain access. In some cases (usually with video game accounts), hackers will also try to access the email address associated with the account. And if you happen to use the same password for your email account and your online gaming account, the hacker will change both, so you have no way to regain access by resetting your password.

Stealing Accounts in Bulk

Do you know anyone who has had their Facebook or Instagram account hacked? These hacks are usually accompanied by a message that says they can buy back their access for $400. This happens quite a bit, because people use the same password for their Facebook account that they do on some other service, and the account didn't have any sort of multifactor authentication (MFA) set up to block the login.

Considering the hassle involved in re-creating a new account or trying to contact Facebook to regain control of your account, it's probably faster and more cost effective to just pay the $400. That's what the hackers are counting on. These types of account-takeover extortions are done in bulk, and the hackers probably control tens of thousands of accounts. Those $400 payments add up quickly.

> **NOTE** If you already have multifactor authentication (MFA) set up on your critical accounts, this won't be an issue for you … but what about your kids? Are their accounts properly protected? Most kids would be devastated if someone hacked and took over their video game accounts. It is worthwhile to ensure their accounts are protected with some type of MFA. A very easy way to do this is to just link their accounts to your phone number.

With the amount of money criminals are making, the stolen account market only keeps growing. I was introduced to the sheer enormity of this underground black-market eco-system by hacker DonJuji, which is why I asked him to provide additional context and his own viewpoints on this subject.

HACKER TIP: DONJUJI

The credential-stuffing scene, or "the cracking scene," has been growing since around 2016. I first got into the password-cracking scene around 2019, when it seemed to explode due to the release of a simple automated login tool, called Black Bullet.

For only $50, Black Bullet let you search for free accounts on any site you wanted, including Netflix, Google, Hulu, Fortnite, and even crypto accounts.

Using Black Bullet was incredibly simple. A user could create and load a config file, which was pretty much just a coded list of target URLs, a list of proxies, and a simple credential list (formatted like `email:password` or `username:password`). The software would then run anywhere between 5 and 100 concurrent login threads (per second), testing for valid accounts.

Black Bullet could also be custom configured to "capture" digital assets like Fortnite skins and other account objects. Depending on the service and the amount of data to be captured, attackers could easily verify and capture up to 50,000 accounts per minute.

The desired "captured assets" often consisted of digital assets like Fortnite skins, subscription status details (e.g., is this Netflix account premium or free), and crypto balances.

The availability of this software and the necessary password combo lists on forums like Nulled.to enabled users with little to no technical skill to make anywhere between $500 and $50,000 per week.

It's clear that login combos (i.e., combinations of usernames and passwords) are the key to this entire market, the origins of which can be traced back to any number of major data breaches. But that doesn't answer the question of *how* these criminals are able to access any of the data stolen from these breaches.

Accessing Breached Data

Online hacking forums like BreachForums and Nulled.to (recently seized by law enforcement) act as the central hub for the sale and publication of stolen databases. Hackers and key hacking groups—like ShinyHunters, Pompompurin, and Intel Broker—account for a vast majority of data breaches involving stolen user data. In other words, a handful of high-profile actors are directly responsible for fueling this entire criminal supply chain of stolen accounts.

Thanks to their efforts, complete databases of consumer information and password combos are stolen and sold to private buyers, only to be repurposed and used to hack more individual consumer accounts. They eventually make their way to being used in attacks targeting corporate employees.

Databases stolen and collected over the past 10 years are the basis for marketplaces like BreachForums, which now host billions of password combos and sensitive account details that are posted publicly and can be downloaded completely free of charge (see Figure 2.3). The current count of BreachForums' "Official Leaks" section shows more than 16 billion accounts publicly available for free consumption.

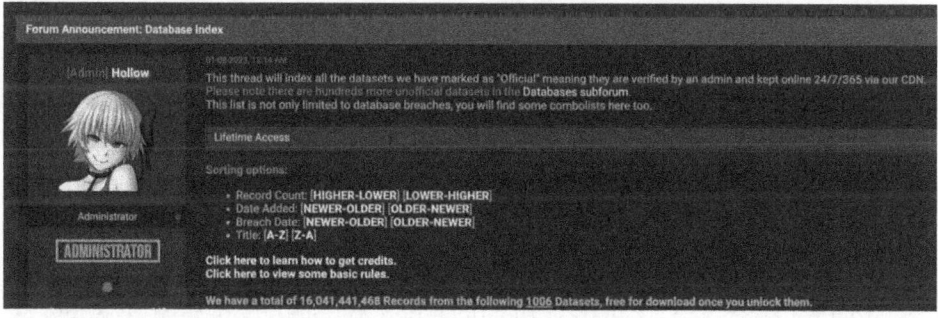

Figure 2.3: Screenshot from BreachForums.

The 16 billion records found in the public leaks section of BreachForums date back more than 10 years. While the passwords included in these databases might seem fairly worthless considering their age, they can actually still be quite useful.

> **NOTE**   It's good practice to know which of your accounts are now considered publicly accessible and are actively available on these marketplaces. A great free resource to check is www.haveibeenpwned.com (HIBP), operated by Troy Hunt. This site enables you to enter your email address and check to see if, when, and where your email or phone number has been spotted in a breach.

The Art of Password Guessing

You reading might be smirking and thinking, "I change my password all the time, so I don't have anything to worry about."

Sure, many of the passwords found in old data breaches are outdated and not useful anymore, mostly because people eventually change them, and newer breached databases typically contain passwords that are heavily encrypted. Unfortunately, most people don't sway far from their original password ideas, making their "new" passwords not that difficult to guess.

When it comes to finding information about people, there are countless open-source resources (and public data breaches) that can be used to collect a seemingly unlimited amount of data points on users.

One way to build profiles of targets is by connecting similar data points across different informational sources, and reused passwords are one of the best ways to do this.

A username from one data breach might give hackers a unique password that will connect them to an email address found in a different breach. Reused passwords are a notoriously easy way to form connections between seemingly unrelated data points since because everyone will, inevitably, reuse one or more of their passwords.

For example, if they are researching a user who has a somewhat unique password (e.g., Brown2Cows1s), searching that password across other data breaches will often lead to new usernames, email addresses, and other data points that they had not previously discovered.

Matching passwords between accounts is just the start of the process for cyber criminals, who are typically ahead of the curve when it comes to their tactics. Security teams spend their days trying to keep hackers out of their systems, while hackers spend their days figuring out new methods to circumvent the systems that were just put in place to block them.

Cyber criminals and fraudsters are required to stay at the bleeding edge of technology if they want to continue hacking and stealing accounts, so why not learn from the best?

Building Password Lists with ProParser

I've known DonJuji for many years. I consider him to be one of the best and most successful account hackers of our time. One of the things I find most impressive about Juji is his ability to guess passwords and hack into accounts, simply by making slight modifications to old passwords based on commonly available information.

His methods of accessing accounts were so successful that he developed and sold his own software, ProParser, a black-market tool designed to help others steal accounts by creating entirely new lists of account login combinations (see Figure 2.4).

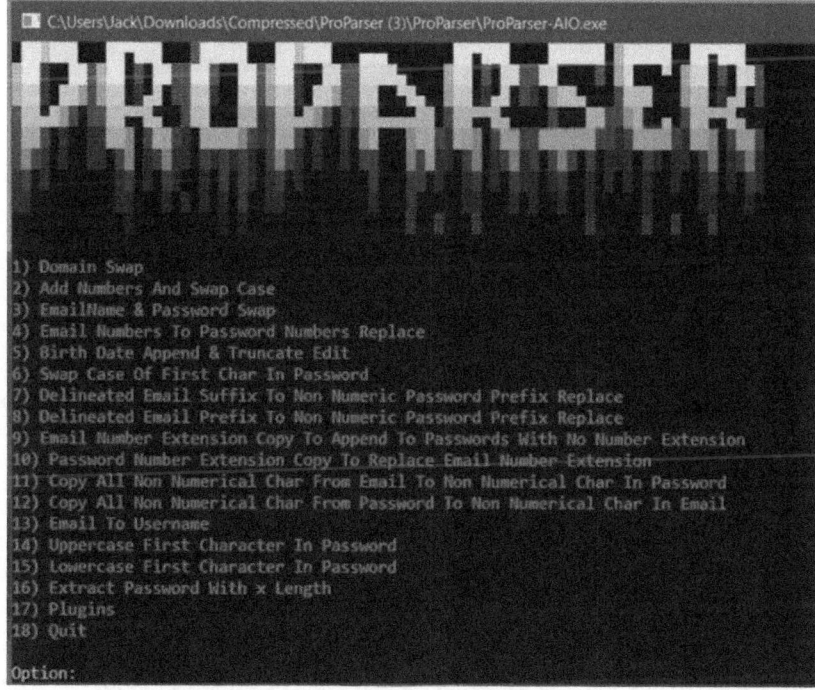

Figure 2.4: Screenshot of DonJuji's ProParser software.

ProParser worked by chopping up specific elements of a user's data points and then combining those elements with combinations of the more common traits exhibited by people when creating new passwords.

I asked Juji to share some insights into how he developed ProParser, and how it was so successful at guessing people's passwords.

HACKER TIP: DONJUJI

When looking for new passwords, the first and easiest approach is to swap the case of the first letter in the password. For example, password22 becomes Password22, and so on.

Next, you can start looking at other fields within a user's compiled profile, such as their birth data. This information won't always be available in a single data breach, so you need to do your research by gathering as much information as possible about your targets. A simple password like "baseball" combined with a person's year of birth becomes "baseball1995." That's easy enough.

Next, many people use special characters in their passwords. Knowing which one can come down to guessing ... but most people will use the same special character across all their passwords. So once you connect their email address to other known hacked passwords, it's usually just as simple as looking to see which character they have used in the past (e.g., #, !, $, and so on).

The next step involves separating known words and numbers by their preferred special character. A password of "baseball1995" can turn into a few different possibilities like "baseball#1995" or "Baseball#1995." People keep things simple, so the character will appear after the word.

(continues)

HACKER TIP: DONJUJI (CONTINUED)

It's worth noting that most people will use the same numbers in their email address or usernames as they do in their password. This is very important.

Someone with the username "internetlover906" might have a similar email address with the same username. If looking for new email addresses matches for your user, the first thing you can try is `internetlover906@*.com`. That will most likely turn up some new matches with additional data points you can use.

Next, the user may have used the password "Football" in a previous data breach. From that, you can extrapolate new combinations for username, emails, and passwords by transferring the number to the password.

Starting with the common word "football," you can try new combinations by capitalizing the password and transferring the numbers from the username to the password. Now you have user `internetlover906@gmail.com`, and a password of Football906, or Football#906.

People are simple, and they want their passwords to be as simple as possible, which is why a large number of passwords have similar elements and patterns, like "!123" or "!123!".

I compiled large lists of those common passwords add-ons, which I also try appending to existing passwords to create even more potential password combos to try. In this case, it would be useful to try logging into the test account with email: `internetlover906@gmail.com` using password "Football!123!".

They sound simple, but you wouldn't believe how effective these methods are. These methods were so effective that I decided to create my own tool called DonJuji's ProParser. The core of it only consisted of a few lines of code, but it sold for $1,000 per copy because it was a way for account hackers to come up with their own lists of completely unique password combos.

It was all guess work, but it turned out to be extremely effective and ended up selling really well on a number of cracking forums like Nulled.to.

NOTE   Comedian Michael McIntyre breaks down some of these common traits in a funny video called, "You Should Probably Change Your Password." Google it.

Password guessing is an impressive skill, but based on a system that requires you to have a starting point of people's passwords. And like with all things related to technology, there comes a point where old methods stop being useful. Today, with the vast majority of data breaches containing encrypted passwords, criminals needed a new way to get that baseline of information. Enter *infostealers*.

Infostealers

An *infostealer* is a type of malware that steals information. Infostealers capture any relevant user information, such as login details (i.e., usernames and passwords), browser cookies, search history, financial information, and even complete keystrokes, with the more recent infostealers being designed to target and steal cryptocurrency keys.

Being able to steal browser cookies is an important part of infostealers, because it enables the hackers to access websites that a user has already logged into, without the need to enter a password—and in some cases, without having to verify the login using MFA (because, thanks to the browser cookie, the user is already logged in).

> **NOTE** Think of it like this: When you log into Facebook from your computer's web browser, that browser stores a cookie so the next time you go back to Facebook, you won't have to log in again. The infostealer steals that cookie, enabling a hacker to load it into their own browser, so when they go to Facebook, they are already logged in as you.

Today, infostealers come in many shapes and sizes. For as little as $100/month, fraudsters can rent existing infostealer code and use it to create their own custom malware packages. The rental fee often comes with a nicely designed control panel, enabling the admin to log in and see the data as it's being collected in real time.

Infostealers aren't just used by low-level cyber gangs. Deploying infostealer malware can be the first step in a carefully executed plan to infiltrate an organization or carry out some form of cyber espionage.

As the compromised data is collected, it can be sold via an individual user account or in bulk via any number of online marketplaces and Telegram groups.

The most common ways infostealers are deployed include spamming users with phishing emails to bait them into clicking on a malicious link or visiting a malicious website. Another method for easy malware distribution is through pirated software, where users willingly download and install stolen software that has been modified to bypass the copy protection. Those modifications usually include the installation of malware.

A Condensed Infostealer History Lesson

Before moving forward with this story, this section takes a step back and looks at some basic history of well-known malware and infostealers that end up playing an important role in the latter part of this book.

Emotet

Emotet is a malware variant that appeared around March 2017. Its origins can be traced to the Business Club; a cybercriminal group whose activity began circa 2008. Emotet was discovered in 2014 as a banking trojan designed to specifically target clients of banks in Western Europe. Emotet's original functions were to initiate automatic fraudulent bank transfers from compromised bank accounts.

In 2015, Emotet evolved into a modular trojan, enabling it to retrieve stored system passwords (specifically those stored in web browsers). The malware could also steal contact lists as well as content and attachments from emails. It was designed to spread through an infected network using Server Message Block (SMB) vulnerabilities and recovered passwords.

Thanks to its modular structure, Emotet has continued to morph and evolve, adding advanced capabilities including an installation module, banking module, and Distributed Denial of Service (DDoS) module. Emotet has proven to be difficult to combat because of its "worm-like" features that enable it to borough its way through internal networks.

TrickBot

TrickBot is one of the oldest and most well-known strains of info-stealing malware. Discovered in 2016, its typical deployment methods involve the use of spam and malicious phishing techniques.

TrickBot isn't a traditional infostealer, because it doesn't solely focus on accessing information found in web browsers. While TrickBot *does* steal credentials and user passwords, it is much more sophisticated than a traditional infostealer. I suppose you could call it a *malware loader*, which is to say that it's a type of delivery system designed to load additional strains of malware.

TrickBot is typically found in links or attachments from malicious emails or office documents that contain malicious macros. Once launched, the malware will proceed to use other known tools (e.g., Mimikatz) to steal the credentials of other users who might be connected to the same corporate network. The credentials are then sent back to a command-and-control server and are recycled and used in additional attacks.

Malware-as-a-Service

As the years progressed, info-stealing malware improved and eventually gave way to a new business model: malware-as-a-service (MaaS). Among the most successful in the MaaS family is Redline Stealer, which is still a cornerstone in the arsenal of cybercriminals.

This approach of using MaaS enables even the least-experienced threat actors to launch sophisticated attacks at a relatively low cost. By purchasing a software license from the malware's developers, attackers gain access to the core malware library, future updates, and even a customer support portal.

Some variants go even further, bundling additional features like botnets for carrying out large-scale denial of service (DOS) attacks, or computer hijacking for mass cryptocurrency mining, providing cybercriminals with an all-in-one toolkit for launching their own illicit campaigns.

By 2024, Redline, alongside other prominent families, had dominated the infostealer threat landscape, accounting for roughly 64 percent of all compromised devices globally.

Now that you understand *how* the information is being stolen, the next section looks at what exactly *is* being stolen.

Anatomy of Stealer Logs

Figure 2.5 is an example of a single infostealer log that can be purchased or downloaded free of charge on any number of telegram channels.

Figure 2.5 shows several files stolen from a victim's computer and made available to the person downloading the data. Infostealers can capture a significant amount of information, including:

- Cookies and credential data (e.g., usernames and passwords)
- Session information and browser session cookies to hijack sessions
- Browser data, including autofill information, saved credit cards, browsing history, bookmarks, and downloaded files
- Lists of running system processes, installed software, and detected corporate domains
- Keystroke logs, which include captured text typed by the user from chats, emails, or login prompts

```
   4096 Mar 12 05:42 .
 221184 Mar 12 05:38 ..
   4029 Mar  1 18:38 blossomry.txt
   8894 Mar  1 18:38 Brute.txt
    165 Mar 12 05:36 Chrome
   8967 Mar  1 18:38 Clipboard.txt
   4096 Mar 12 05:36 Cookies
      6 Mar 12 05:41 Discord
     78 Mar 12 05:36 Edge
    222 Mar 12 05:36 GoogleAccounts
   4029 Mar  1 18:38 InstalledSoftware.txt
  12055 Mar  1 18:38 [          @gmail.com] [messages 0] [IL]_NCFYTbU.txt
 694131 Mar  1 18:38 Outlook_Good_Cookies.txt
   9263 Mar  1 18:38 Passwords.txt
  12186 Mar  1 18:38 Processes.txt
  16279 Mar  1 18:38 Software.txt
      6 Mar 12 05:41 Telegram
     75 Mar 12 05:36 Wallets
   4029 Mar  1 18:38 wvqbjqinaiepetuvzzj.txt
.sy/                                        HFMJ_2025_03_01T15_76_41_
```

Figure 2.5: A screenshot of an infostealer folder listing for a single account.

- Clipboard history, which often include passwords that are copy/pasted, documents, images, and other sensitive text
- Crypto accounts, credit card information, banking details, and other financial information

> **NOTE** Newer infostealer malware can even go as far as stealing one-time password OTP (OTP) tokens. At Schmoocon in 2025, security researchers illustrated how modern infostealer malware can steal browser plugin settings, which can include web-based OTP tokens.
>
> Using minimal effort, the researchers were able to successfully re-create a user's OTP codes by installing the same extension listed in the infostealer logs, then copying the secret key stored inside the browser extension settings.

Once a user is infected with an infostealer, their life becomes an open book to anyone on the market willing to pay a small fee to access their data.

Now that we understand what and how information is being stolen, let's shift our attention to where it is being sold.

Stolen Account Markets

This section dives into the seedy marketplaces of the data black market, where stolen accounts and infostealer logs are bought and sold in bulk. The lifecycle of these accounts begins with the data being stolen by malware, then sold or distributed into one of these markets. From there, the data is purchased and reused to carry out further attacks.

As discussed in the previous section, hackers can purchase this data to apply simple algorithms to match the new data points to information collected in older breach data, in order to create new packages of information that can then be resold on different (lower-tier) markets.

Genesis Market

Genesis Market was one of the most notorious marketplaces for buying and selling stolen packages of account credentials. Genesis was taken down in 2023, but not before it provided access to information stolen from millions of compromised computers and victim accounts across every type of website imaginable, including Amazon, eBay, Facebook, PayPal, and pretty much any other website you can think of.

Genesis Market was extremely simple to use, enabling hackers to filter lists of victims by country or a specific site they wanted to access. Figure 2.6 is a sales listing for three compromised computers. For only $40, someone could purchase these accounts and gain access to a person's Instagram, Twitter, Facebook, and more.

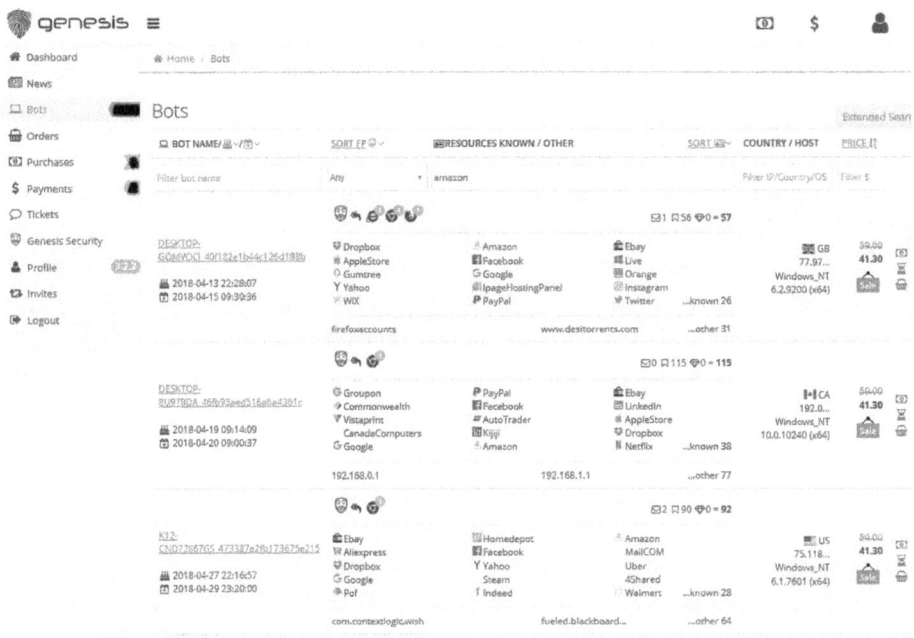

Figure 2.6: A screenshot of Genesis Market.

Genesis Market customers who purchased access to a system also had the ability to load the victim's authentication cookies automatically into their own web browser, enabling them to effectively bypass a website's authentication without the need for MFA.

Another feature of Genesis Market is that customers retained access to an infected system and were provided updates to it in real time. In other words, if a user of an infected system created a new online account, those credentials would be automatically stolen and sent to the Genesis customer's web portal.

The following excerpt is from an ad posted by Genesis Market on a popular cybercrime forum.

> *You can buy a bot with a real fingerprint, access to email, social networks, bank accounts, payment systems! You also get all previous digital life (history) of the bot—most services won't even ask for login and password and identify you as their returning customer. Purchasing a bot kit with the fingerprint, cookies, and accesses, you become the unique user of all his or her services and other websites. The other use of our kit of real fingerprints is to cover up the traces of your real Internet activity.*

The Fall of Genesis Market

On April 5, 2023, after five years of operation, Genesis Market was shut down. The U.S. Justice Department issued the following statement:

> *Working across 45 of our FBI Field Offices and alongside our international partners, the Justice Department has launched an unprecedented takedown of a major criminal marketplace that enabled cybercriminals to victimize individuals, businesses, and governments around the world.*
>
> *Since its inception in March 2018, Genesis Market has offered access to data stolen from over 1.5 million compromised computers around the world containing over 80 million account access credentials. Account access credentials advertised for sale on Genesis Market included those connected to the financial sector, critical infrastructure, and federal, state, and local government agencies. Genesis Market was also one of the most prolific initial access brokers (IABs) in the cybercrime world. IABs attract criminals looking to easily infiltrate a victim's computer system.*

Worth noting, Genesis Market had prided itself on the security of its users. Yet, the DOJ said its investigators were able to access the site's user database, which contained the purchase and activity history of its more than 59,000 members. That data ultimately helped them uncover the true identities of many of the site's prominent users.

After the fall of Genesis Market, several new markets appeared in its place, with the most prominent being Russian Market. To date, Russian Market is by far the biggest underground marketplace of infostealer logs.

OGUsers

Last (but not least) on the list of marketplaces is OGUsers (see Figure 2.7). OGUsers is technically more of a forum but also acts as a marketplace dedicated to buying, selling, and trading stolen accounts. In operation for at least eight years, it currently has hundreds of thousands of active users.

OGUsers was initially formed as a way to purchase hard-to-get, or "OG," social media accounts. These accounts are typically single name accounts or only have a few characters in the name (e.g., `Instagram.com/vinny` or `Instagram.com/og`).

These accounts are extremely valuable, and in many cases were so old (and unused) that the original owner never bothered to update their (now public) password. All it would take was to identify the email address associated with the account, find a common password, and the account was theirs.

Figure 2.7: The OGUsers logo.

However, this kind of account theft has become much harder (but not impossible). Improved security measures now block access or transfers unless the attacker can pass MFA. These increased security measures gave rise to a new forum of hacking that allowed users to easily bypass MFA, known as *SIM swapping*.

SIM Swapping

A subscriber identity module (SIM) card is a small physical chip or virtual device in a phone that links that phone to a specific phone number. *SIM swapping* is a form of hacking that reassigns a phone number to another phone. It typically involves tricking someone at the phone company into transferring a victim's phone number to a new phone. Once the SIM card is reassigned to the hacker's phone, they are free to request password resets to any user account tied to that phone number.

To date, OGUsers is still in operation and is the primary hangout for many known (and up and coming) SIM swappers. There is one particular story involving members of OGUsers that will illustrate the dangers of these attacks as well as the mentality of people involved in committing them.

SIM Swapping and OGUsers: A Cautionary Tale

In 2020, Jordan K. Milleson, 21, and Kyell A. Bryan, 19, were arrested for hijacking social media and bitcoin accounts using a mix of SIM swapping and "vishing" (or voice phishing) attacks. According to the court documents, the two youths were able to access internal wireless company tools that allowed them to reassign SIM numbers to other mobile devices.

The indictment states that the group would set up phishing websites designed to resemble legitimate wireless employee portals. The boys then emailed or called employees at that company, tricking them into logging into fake web portals designed to steal their passwords. Once the employee passwords were captured, the hackers were free to log into the wireless network's internal systems.

With access to the company's internal tools, the hackers could easily reassign customer phone numbers to their own devices, enabling them to intercept the phone calls and text messages used to send account reset codes for email, social media, and crypto accounts.

In theory, the hackers could have swapped the numbers away from the devices late at night while the victims slept, requested the verification codes, accessed the accounts, then ported the numbers right back before anyone noticed.

If they'd had a little more patience—or a little less ego—they probably could've kept the crypto without ever getting caught.

"Don't Break the Law When You're Breaking the Law"

More specifically, if you get into a business dispute with your partner after stealing thousands of dollars' worth of crypto, don't settle it by calling the cops on him, claiming he just murdered his father.

Well, according to the indictment filed on June 26, 2019, that's exactly what happened. The statement published by DOJ reads as follows:

> Bryan called the Baltimore County Police Department and falsely reported that he, purporting to be a resident of the Milleson family residence, had shot his father at the residence.
>
> During the call, Bryan, posing as the purported shooter, threatened to shoot himself and to shoot at police officers if they attempted to confront him.[3]

A *SWAT attack* is a tactic used by many juvenile (or sadistic) hackers, who will attempt to send law enforcement or a SWAT team to your house to create a potentially life-threatening situation. If the police believe the person in the house has murdered someone or is an active threat, there is always the chance that something will go wrong, and the person being swatted could be shot in the process.

Sadly, this same thing was perpetrated on me (twice) by members of The Com, a group that sets the stage for the rest of this story.

The Com aka Scattered Spider

The Com, more recently referred to as Scattered Spider, is a notorious group of cybercriminals from North America and the UK known for carrying out social engineering and SIM swapping attacks with an extremely high level of skill and sophistication.

In May 2024, the Cybersecurity and Infrastructure Security Agency (CISA) and the Federal Bureau of Investigation (FBI) issued a public warning highlighting the growing threat posed by the group due to their high success rate in targeting some of the largest companies in the country.

Operating since about 2022, The Com is a very loosely knit organization akin to a terrorist cell. Members connect on forums like OGUsers, forming independent groups that collaborate and compete. These hackers often gather in chat rooms and private forums, boasting about their exploits and pushing each other to take bolder actions.

More experienced group members tend to seek out and recruit younger, more aspiring hackers on gaming communities like Roblox and Minecraft, leveraging them to perform high-risk tasks.

---

[3] https://www.secretservice.gov/newsroom/releases/2021/10/defendant-who-stole-more-16000-cryptocurrency-and-orchestrated-swat

High Level of Sophistication

The group's core tactics focus on using credential harvesting and SIM swapping attacks. In its early days, the group would typically deploy ransomware following a successful infiltration. However, a recent report by Mandiant suggests the group is now focused primarily on data theft and extortion.

Mandiant's research indicates that members of Scattered Spider employ aggressive pressure tactics to obtain victim credentials. These tactics range from threats of *doxing*—exposing personal information—to intimidation involving physical harm against victims and their families, or even leveraging compromising material to coerce compliance.

In multiple cases, members of Scattered Spider have shown success at gaining initial access to privileged employee accounts using social engineering techniques that targeted overseas corporate help desks.

As part of their process, the group members meticulously research personally identifiable information (PII) on their victims, constructing detailed profiles that enable them to more easily bypass user verification questions.

To help put this in perspective, one successful tactic used across multiple victims involved calling the support help desk and pretending to be an employee who just got a new phone and needed a manual MFA reset code. A common pretext includes traveling on a personal trip without having access to their corporate laptop, making an urgent reset necessary.

The help desk employee would need to verify the employee's identity by asking for details like date of birth, Social Security number (SSN), and even the names of their manager or coworkers—all of which they readily have available because of their initial research.

This type of victim research and long-term planning yields a very high success rate, demonstrating a degree of sophistication that, until recently, was mostly associated with state-sponsored hacking groups.

Telework and the Rise of Supply Chain Attacks

Traditional passwords have become less effective as people and organizations moved toward requiring MFA to access critical applications. This trend of organizations adopting better security practices was interrupted in 2020 thanks to the COVID-19 pandemic.

During the pandemic, employees were required to work from home, which was a massive change from the traditional model of people going to work in offices. Thus, adopting better security practices needed to happen quickly.

The rapid shift to adapt to a new remote workforce forced some organizations to scale back some of their security practices to accommodate remote employees and keep their businesses operating smoothly.

For example, many companies now have policies enabling employees to remotely access internal systems from personal devices, while also permitting personal account use on work devices. To be honest, this was already beginning to happen, but COVID-19 accelerated it.

Most people are far less careful with what they install and access on their personal devices. This lack of caution opens the door to scenarios where an employee's personal device is infected (or targeted) with malware, which is then used as a gateway to pivot into a corporate network. This is what's known as a *supply-chain attack*.

A supply-chain attack occurs when a threat actor targets a less secure element within an organization's supply chain (e.g., a third-party vendor, contractor, or service provider) to gain unauthorized access to the primary organization's network.

A typical remote work scenario will involve an employee accessing restricted intranet or internal networks by using a corporate virtual private network (VPN). A VPN connection, by definition, creates a secure tunnel between the employee's workstation and the corporate network.

However, say a remote developer is working on a project using their personal laptop. In order to publish their work, they need to access the corporate network, which is possible by using their work credentials to access the VPN client.

Now let's also say that the employee's personal laptop also happens to be infected with infostealer malware, because they decided to download and install pirated software, which is how a majority of malware is spread. The infostealer malware hasn't only grabbed the employee's credentials, which can be used later to log into other systems, but the employee has essentially just punched a hole in the organization's corporate defense, providing a literal straight line for the malware to spread to other systems in the network.

Breaching the outer perimeter of a company's defense is typically regarded as the most difficult part of hacking into any system. Once inside, it's significantly easier to move around and find more flaws to exploit. With one careless move, an unsuspecting employee can tear down an entire organization's outer defense and enable the hackers right in.

It's impressive when you consider the level of effort that goes into planning and executing these attacks. But that's not the most notable part of this group. Before I end this chapter, I would like to discuss one last and very important element of The Com.

Violence-as-a-Service

The Com has gained a significant amount of notoriety for using physical violence against its victims, and against members of their own community. TylerB and Sosa are two high-profile group members who were also subjected to attacks of physical violence.

Tyler Buchanan (aka TylerB), the suspected head of Scattered Spider, was arrested in 2024. At the time of his arrest, the 22-year-old British citizen possessed Bitcoins worth $27 million USD, which he had acquired from a series of successful SIM swapping attacks.

Noah Michael Urban (aka Sosa and King Bob), 19, was also arrested in 2024 for stealing nearly $800,000 USD from five victims between 2022 and 2023. Sosa used similar SIM swapping techniques for each of his victims in order to compromise their email and financial accounts. Sosa was also alleged to be involved in the 2023 MGM Grand ransomware attacks. TylerB and Sosa's success made them targets, both by law enforcement and by rival SIM swapping gangs.

Brickings are one of many "violence-as-a-service" offerings available for sale on any number of cybercrime forums or Telegram channels. Listed as classified ads, this service is exactly what it sounds like—someone is hired to visit an address and toss a brick through the person's window. Other common jobs involve tire slashings and drive-by shootings. In my case, someone was hired to take a baseball bat to my car's windshield.

If that isn't bad enough, sometimes things can get really out of hand. In 2022, a video was published online showing attackers throwing a brick through an address associated with Sosa's parent's home in Florida.

This event preceded a junior member of Sosa's crew being *kidnapped and held for ransom*. Captors held a gun to his bloodied head while forcing him to record a video message pleading with his crew to pay a $200,000 USD ransom in exchange for his life. Luckily, he escaped the incident without much further damage.

Another case involved a 21-year old man from New Jersey who was arrested and charged with stalking in connection to these violence-as-a-service jobs. He was arrested for firing a handgun into a Pennsylvania home and helping to torch another residence with a Molotov cocktail—all in the name of stolen cryptocurrency.

While a number of key members have been arrested, Scattered Spider lives on as one of the largest and most notorious hacking groups in the United States.

Summary

This chapter provided a deep dive into the cybercrime economy built around the theft, resale, and abuse of digital account credentials.

The chapter explained how stolen login credentials—obtained via massive data breaches or info-stealing malware—are aggregated and repurposed into marketable digital products, and how something as seemingly trivial as hacked Fortnite or Netflix accounts can balloon into a billion-dollar industry.

This chapter also explored the infrastructure of cybercrime, detailing how forums like BreachForums and marketplaces like Genesis and OGUsers fuel this black market. It also traced the rise of infostealers like Redline and TrickBot and highlighted the increasingly blurred lines between cybercrime and real-world violence through SIM swapping and "violence-as-a-service" tactics popularized by groups like Scattered Spider (aka The Com).

Now that I've covered the core background topics, the next chapter shifts focus to the dark web forums—the epicenter of these criminal ecosystems.

Dark Market Forums

This chapter acts as a field guide to navigating dark web forums, stolen data marketplaces, and the legal grey zones that surround them. In it, you'll learn how these markets operate, how sellers establish trust, and what to look for when evaluating a potential deal—all with operating guidance from the U.S. Department of Justice.

This chapter also breaks down the lifecycle of Hacked, Breached, or Leaked (HBL) data—from breach to extortion, from private sales to public listings—and discusses why some of the most valuable datasets never make it to the forums at all.

Data Marketplaces

In 2020, the U.S. Department of Justice (DOJ) published a document titled "Legal Considerations When Gathering Online Cyber Threat Intelligence and Purchasing Data from Illicit Sources."[1] It addresses questions posed by information security practitioners who gather information and purchase data from *dark market forums*— places where illegal activities regularly occur—as part of their daily cybersecurity activities.

In short, accessing a dark web forum, or stolen data marketplace, doesn't violate any laws. Technically, neither does downloading the information that's publicly posted to those forums.

Getting access to most forums is actually quite easy and doesn't require you to enter anything more than a username, password, and email address for verification. However, accessing the more private forums and chat groups usually involves some form of referral or vetted entry. Gaining access to these types of forums might often require showing a willingness to contribute by doing something illegal.

---

[1] https://www.justice.gov/criminal/criminal-ccips/page/file/1252341/

For this type of scenario, the DOJ report states:

Forums operated by criminal actors may require proof that someone seeking access to the forum has bona fide criminal intent. For instance, the forum operator may require the purchase or delivery of malware or stolen personal information. As explained below, complying with such requests may place a practitioner in legal jeopardy.

When private parties join or participate in these online forums to collect information for lawful purposes, the line between gathering threat intelligence and engaging in criminal activity can be hard to discern. It may be easier for an undercover practitioner to extract information from sources on the forum who have learned to trust the practitioner's persona, but developing trust and establishing bona fides as a fellow criminal may involve offering useful information, services, or tools that can be used to commit crimes.

Whether a crime has occurred usually hinges on an individual's actions and intent. A practitioner must avoid doing anything that furthers the criminal objectives of others on the forums. Even though the practitioner has no intention of committing a crime, assisting others engaged in criminal conduct can constitute the federal offense of aiding and abetting.

In sum, a security practitioner should take care to avoid taking any action that would assist others in the commission of a crime or agreeing that a crime should occur.

Accessing these forums can often provide a wealth of information and, for the purposes of this chapter, access to a whole new world of open-source data.

Now let's turn our attention toward these markets and what data you might acquire data from them.

Anatomy of an Underground Data Purchase

There are a number of forums and online communities, each catering to its own unique group of people (e.g., breach data, ransomware, initial access, SIM swapping). These forums offer access to purchasing data that is often freshly compromised, or not openly distributed. To date, BreachForums is the largest forum for downloading and purchasing stolen data.

Figure 3.1 is a screenshot of the "leaks market" on BreachForums, where anyone can browse and ultimately purchase any of the data listed for sale.

Like any product purchase, buying data requires a mutual understanding—a meeting of the minds. Two parties must come together and agree on terms. In the underground economy, this often occurs over encrypted chat channels. Once the deal is spelled out (or more specifically, typed out), the information is handed off to a guarantor, the *middleman*, who oversees the transaction. If a seller refuses to use a middleman, it's almost always a red flag, as they're likely trying to run a scam.

Most dark market forums operate with an eBay-style reputation system. Meaning that every seller has a visible feedback score, earned through their ratings of previous transactions.

Figure 3.2 is one example of such a system: a user named "NanC" is offering data stolen from a Thai jewelry store. The screenshot shows that the seller has a reputation score of 511, which is incredibly high. Feedback is gained through successful transactions.

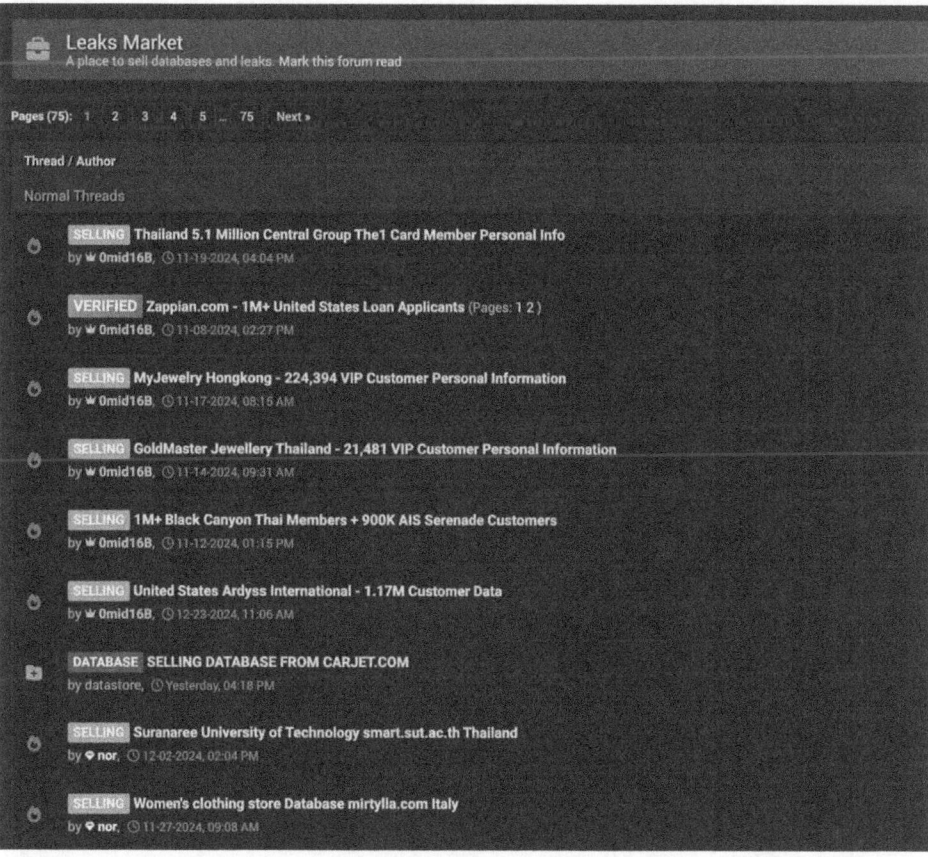

Figure 3.1: The BreachForums leaks market.

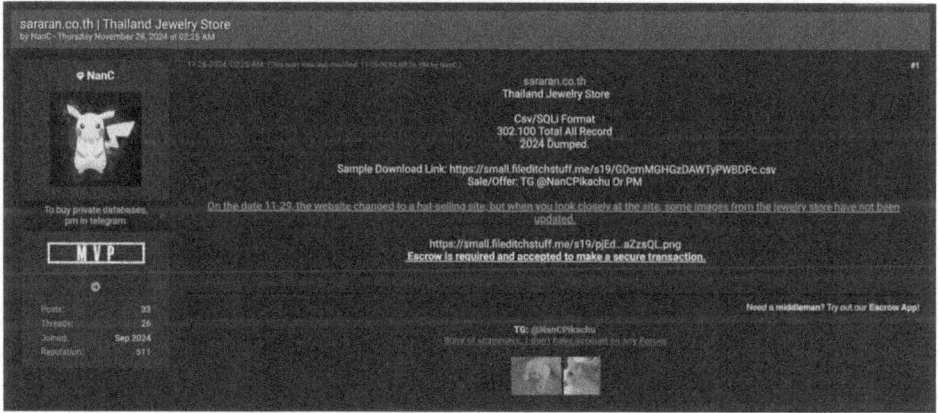

Figure 3.2: A listing for stolen data for sale from a Thailand jewelry store.

A reputation score this high isn't simply handed out—it's earned through dozens, if not hundreds, of successful deals. Someone with such a high score has bought/sold numerous items and is typically considered "trustworthy" in this type of scenario.

Once a deal is in motion, the buyer transfers cryptocurrency—usually bitcoin (BTC) or Monero (XMR)—to the middleman (sometimes referred to as the guarantor). Once the funds are confirmed, the seller is required to deliver the data to the buyer.

At this point, the buyer has a set period of time (as defined in the deal terms) to inspect and verify the data. If everything checks out, the buyer notifies the middleman, who then releases the funds to the seller, minus a 5 percent transaction fee.

If there's a dispute, the middleman becomes the arbiter, who makes a decision on whether the original terms are followed or a refund is granted. They review the sale's original terms, examine any evidence submitted, and then decide whether the data delivered matched the description. If not, the funds are returned or held from being delivered to the seller, depending on the outcome.

Some forums also have public dispute mechanisms. If the buyer believes they've been scammed, they can post about it in a dedicated "Scam Reports" section. Being listed here is often a death sentence for sellers—their accounts are banned, and their registration details are exposed. For vendors with high-reputation scores, that kind of exposure is a serious deterrent. An account with a 500+ reputation score takes time to build, and most high-reputation sellers won't risk the lowering of their scores by pushing junk data.

That being said, caution is always warranted. A strong reputation doesn't always eliminate risk—it just lowers it.

Purchasing Stolen Data

The Department of Justice (DOJ) offers some context for accessing or purchasing hacked, breached, or leaked (HBL) data, but they stop short of providing concrete legal guidance. The DOJ acknowledges that many firms now monitor dark web markets for mentions of their brand, employees, or customers. Some take it further, actively scanning for signs of stolen data that might confirm a breach.

In practice, most organizations outsource their dark web monitoring. Countless threat intelligence vendors offer services that continuously scan dark web forums, Telegram channels, and marketplaces for keywords tied to their clients. The entire process is reactive by nature, but the reality is that most victims learn that they've been breached once they find out their data is being sold on one of these forums.

Once that happens, a company may have a legitimate reason to buy back their stolen data. Sometimes it's about validation: confirming what was actually taken. A victim of a breach might need to purchase the data as a means of verifying if a breach is real. (Because in many instances, victims have no way to tell if anything was actually stolen.) But in many cases, the goal is containment. Victims may negotiate to buy back the data in exchange for the seller pulling it off the market and agreeing not to resell it to others.

Now, you're likely thinking, why would anyone trust a hacker to hold up their end of the deal? It's a fair question. As crazy as it sounds, this is the one area where you *can* trust data thieves. In this world, *reputation is everything* and trust matters.

When it comes to buying and selling stolen data.

Reselling data is considered a serious violation in most dark web communities. On some forums—like the Russian marketplace Exploit—getting caught double-dipping (i.e., reselling the same data) can get you banned outright.

However, it's more than just that. For sellers, reputation is the one thing that signals credibility in a market full of scams and imposters. Established vendors guard it closely, knowing that a single misstep could tank their sales. Established vendors guard it closely for fear of jeopardizing their future sales.

When it comes to repeat data thieves, stealing and selling data is their tradecraft—it's their livelihood—and the last thing they want is to give themselves a bad name, or even worse, get blacklisted and be unable to sell on a site.

But what are the actual legalities involved within buying stolen (aka HBL) data?

Legal Considerations

Does the purchasing of stolen data break laws, even if the data you're purchasing is your own? Does interacting with a criminal constitute a crime? Here, the DOJ provides some additional guidance on the matter:

Purchasing another party's stolen information without permission can raise questions about the purchaser's intent that invites investigative scrutiny to determine the purchaser's motive.

The type of stolen data being sold will also determine whether any criminal statutes prohibit it from being purchased. Many of the federal criminal statutes associated with the type of stolen data that tends to be sold in dark markets—e.g., passwords, account numbers, and other personally identifiable information—only apply if there is intent to further another crime: for instance, an intent to use the information to defraud. For this reason, a purchaser of the stolen data who lacks a criminal motive is unlikely to face prosecution under those statutes.

Knowingly purchasing another party's stolen data without that party's authorization can pose some legal risk. It is much more likely to raise questions about the purchaser's motives and result in scrutiny from law enforcement and the legitimate data owner, particularly if a trade secret is involved.

Although the response is somewhat vague, the report does state that it ultimately comes down to the person's motives. The report also states that there is no inherent crime in purchasing stolen data if there's no intent to commit further crimes.

If this is a path you decide to go down for whatever reasons, here is some helpful guidance.

Stolen Data Lifecycle

Stolen databases tend to follow a predictable lifecycle. Once a breach occurs and the data is exfiltrated, the hacker usually takes one of two routes. Some hackers will attempt *extortion*—reaching out to the victim organization and offering a chance to buy back the data in exchange for a promise not to leak or sell it to others.

The method of contact varies, based on the actor's sophistication. Some approach the company directly, while others post samples or ransom notes on forums like BreachForums or Exploit, hoping to bait a response.

Most companies, however, don't engage with hackers directly. If they choose to respond at all, they'll typically do it through an intermediary, which is often a law firm or a professional ransom negotiator (e.g., Reddington). But if the threat actor can't make contact or receives no response, the next move is usually to monetize the data through its resale.

At this point, two paths emerge: private sale or public listing.

In a private sale, the data never sees the light of day. It isn't posted to any forum, and more often than not, it never hits the headlines. These are the quiet deals—the ones that circulate among closed circles and vetted brokers. This is where the most valuable, sensitive, and operationally relevant data lives.

Getting access to those private channels isn't about scraping marketplaces, it's about relationships. These deals require direct lines to trusted sellers, and that kind of access isn't bought. It's earned over time, through reputation, consistency, and a deep understanding of how these ecosystems work.

In contrast, a public listing is just that—a listing that's openly marketed on known forums. These are the leaks that get picked up by researchers, media, and watchdogs. They're louder, riskier for the actors, and often less lucrative, but typically easier to move. The releases don't hear about? Those are the ones that often hold the most value.

Before we dive into purchasing, here's more legal guidance from the Department of Justice (DOJ) on accessing these marketplaces:

> *If a practitioner becomes an active member of a forum and exchanges information and communicates directly with other forum members, the practitioner can quickly become enmeshed in illegal conduct, if not careful.*
>
> *It may be easier for an undercover practitioner to extract information from sources on the forum who have learned to trust the practitioner's persona, but developing trust and establishing bona fides as a fellow criminal may involve offering useful information, services, or tools that can be used to commit crimes. Engaging in such activities may well result in violating federal criminal law.*
>
> *Whether a crime has occurred usually hinges on an individual's actions and intent. A practitioner must avoid doing anything that furthers the criminal objectives of others on the forums. Even though the practitioner has no intention of committing a crime, assisting others engaged in criminal conduct can constitute the federal offense of aiding and abetting.*
>
> *In some criminal forums, participants may be required to establish their criminal bona fides by assisting in a criminal act or furnishing proof that they have committed a prior offense. Do not provide any valid, useful information that can be used to facilitate a crime. Doing so could result in civil or criminal liability.*

Marketplace Data Listings

BreachForums is—*or was*—the largest online marketplace for buying and selling stolen data. I say *was* because there's a high probability it will be offline again by the time this book is published. These forums tend to have a short half-life.

Regardless, most stolen databases eventually surface on BreachForums. The purpose of posting a database for sale is usually obvious: The hacker wants to make money. But, in some cases, that post is more tactical. It's not just about finding a buyer; it's about applying pressure.

A seasoned seller will often price the data reasonably to attract interest from multiple buyers, creating a sense of urgency to buy. That attention can also have a secondary effect: drawing the victim organization into the conversation. The hacker's goal might actually be to prompt the company into negotiating a buyback to remove the listing.

This tactic is particularly effective when journalists are watching, which they often are. Enough reporters now monitor dark web forums that high-profile breaches often make their way into the mainstream media. And once a company sees its name trending next to the words *data breach*, the pressure to clean it up quickly intensifies.

However, not every post shows that level of finesse. Take the example shown in Figure 3.3, where a BreachForums sales thread from a user named "Sp1d3r" (who I talk about in Part IV of this book) was offering data stolen from QuoteWizard (a subsidiary of LendingTree) for $2 million USD.

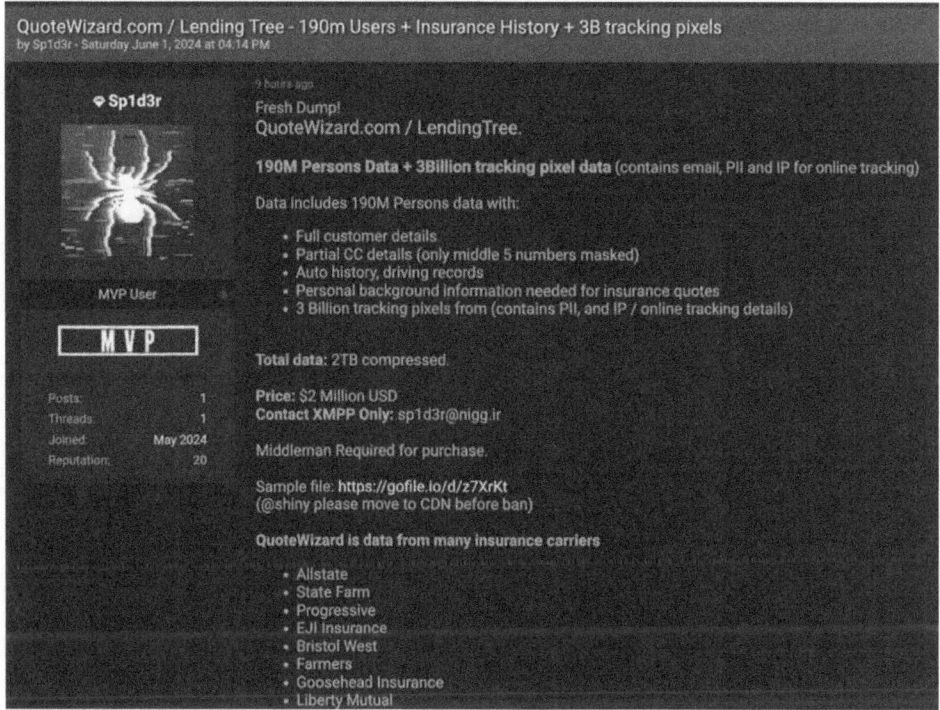

Figure 3.3: BreachForums post of Lending Tree data.

The $2 million price tag alone reveals a lot. It's a dead giveaway that the seller is inexperienced, or in this case, disconnected from reality. Veteran actors understand the market. A post like this would not attract serious buyers and only draw ridicule.

Figure 3.4 shows another example from around that same time frame by a different user, WhiteWarlock (who not surprisingly turned out to be the same person). It shows his post on Exploit forum selling a database of Santander Bank for approximately $2 million USD.

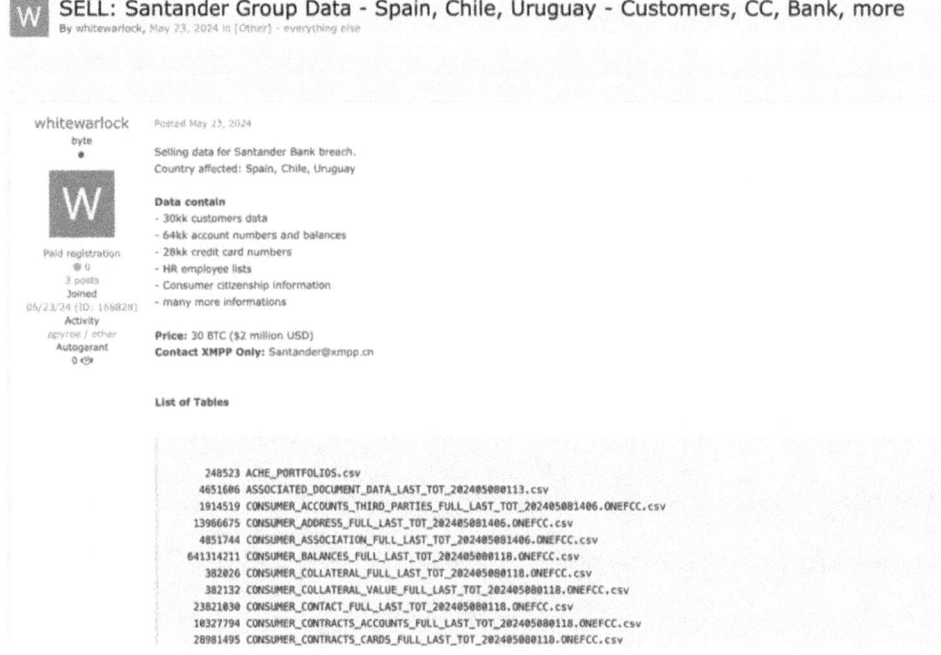

Figure 3.4: The Santander Bank data post.

Stolen databases are never sold for this much. I don't think there has been a database in history that has sold for more than a few hundred thousand dollars. This user posted these data sales threads in order to get the attention of the news media in an attempt to force the organization into paying their extortion.

Spoiler alert: This approach didn't work out for him.

In both cases, the data happened to be extremely valuable. One of the breaches made international news headlines. However, $2 million is a lot of money, and neither organization was willing to pay that much.

Legal Guidance on Data Buybacks

Assuming you're an organization that legitimately wants to buy back its own data, or you have a legitimate reason to be purchasing the data, here is some additional guidance from DOJ:

> *Practitioners engaged in these sorts of intelligence gathering activities should remain mindful that their communications and actions are occurring in the context of an online site that exists to facilitate criminal conduct and with individuals who may be planning*

to commit crimes. The practitioner should avoid providing any true, accurate, or useful information that could advance such crimes.

Negotiating with anonymous parties engaged in selling stolen property or security vulnerabilities on the dark web creates substantial risk of producing an array of undesirable outcomes: the seller may take the purchaser's payment without producing the promised data; may breach the agreement by selling copies of the data to others; may not have possession or control of all copies of the stolen data and, therefore, be unable to stop it from being further disseminated; may use the proceeds to fund more crimes; or may even produce a trojanized version of the data or vulnerability intended to compromise the purchaser's systems.

Still, some organizations may be willing to assume these risks because, on balance, they anticipate that there will be commensurate benefits. For instance, they may only seek to obtain a copy of their stolen data so they can assess the nature and scope of a previously undetected data breach and patch their networks to avoid further loss. Also, cybersecurity firms may be able to use the stolen information to create intelligence reporting that others can use to protect their networks better.

Purchasing one's own stolen data—or, in the case of a cybersecurity firm, the data of a party that authorizes the purchase of its stolen data—raises legal concerns that warrant consideration. At the outset, federal prosecutors have not typically brought charges against parties who merely attempt to purchase their own stolen data or buy a security vulnerability.

Purchasing another party's stolen information without permission or authority can raise questions about the purchaser's intent that invite investigative scrutiny to determine the purchaser's motive.

To manage this risk, upon recognizing that the purchased data contains information that it does not have the right to possess, the purchaser should promptly sequester it and not further access, review, or use it. The purchaser should then either immediately contact law enforcement and provide it with the data and/or inform the actual data owner, to the extent it can be determined, that it is in possession of its data.

Everything in this space carries some level of risk. And dealing with criminals opens the door to any number of additional and likely unplanned scenarios. If you do decide to venture down this path, consider the following basic principles to help you along the way.

Spotting Gimmicks and Scammers

Whatever your intentions are, no one likes to get scammed. Luckily, most scammers seem to share the same sets of tricks.

Always Use a Middleman

The very first (and last) red flag in any dark web transaction is a buyer or seller refusing to use a middleman. That alone should end the conversation. Seriously, there should not be any discussion past this point.

Personally, there are maybe a handful of people I'll deal with directly—and those relationships took time to build. Even with them, if I suggested using a middleman, they wouldn't object. That's how real actors behave.

So, if someone says, "I don't need a middleman"—that's it. Game over. Walk away. I don't care how tempting the offer looks, how urgent it feels, or how much you *want* what's being sold. You are being scammed.

Any respectable seller knows the value of their data, and as such, wants to give you the proper opportunity to validate it before they are paid. Anyone not willing to offer this time to validate their product is, I promise you, trying to steal your money.

The flip side is even more obvious. Figure 3.5 is a screenshot that I acquired from someone else. In this situation, there is a person interested in spending $30,000 to *purchase* a data product, but stating no middleman is needed.

Deleted Account
$30,000, no middleman needed. I wouldn't buy it if your results have a lot of errors

Figure 3.5: A screenshot of a scammer.

Let's think about this. Would you blindly send someone you don't know $30,000 in unrecoverable crypto on the off chance that they won't just run away with the money?

That's silly. This type of scenario where the person is a buyer not wanting to use a middleman typically turns into a different style of scam. In these situations, the buyer will typically change the terms of the deal at the end and try to only purchase a very small subset of the data (usually saying their boss needs proof of the full dataset).

Don't do this. Scammers do this to acquire unique samples of a data they can scam others by pretending they are the original seller. Get it? Since they have a piece of the data not in the publicly posted sample, they must be the original seller, right?

Regardless, the key takeaway here is simple: If anyone tells you there's no need for a middleman it's because they are warming you up for whatever scam they're trying to pull. Don't waste your time. Just walk away.

A Middleman Should Be Backed by a Forum

This scenario is actually really annoying because it won't get tossed at you until right before the deal starts. Meaning you've wasted all of that time working on a deal for nothing.

Throughout the process, the buyer will agree to use a middleman. Then when you finally both reach an agreement on terms, they tell you that they will only use *their* middleman.

Their standard response is usually that the BreachForums or Exploit middleman is "no good for them because they don't trust them." At this point, they'll usually recommend a "huawei guarantor" or some other random person that only operates on Telegram.

The reason you want to use a middleman backed by a forum is, again, due to the trust factor. If an admin of a major forum rips you off, you'll have recourse. You can shout it on their forum, and it will damage their credibility, causing them to eventually lose money. It's not a good business model for them. If a user insists on using a Telegram middleman or some other random foreign middleman, just sigh and move on.

Don't "Buy Direct" from a Third-Party Site

There are some forums and Telegram channels that link to very low priced data purchased "direct on their website" (see Figure 3.6).

Figure 3.6: Example site selling fake breached data.

For any number of reasons, don't waste your time with this. Just ask yourself this question: What do you think will happen when you send $825 in crypto to a random website? It's not like you can dispute the charge on your credit card.

Also, the prices listed in this figure for some of these are extremely low for what they are offering. You should always know that getting something *cheap* usually means it will cost you more in the long run.

You Get What You Pay For

Congratulations! You found that one dataset you've been trying to find for months, and amazingly, you found it on the Telegram channel being offered for an extremely reasonable price. Can you guess why?

What you are actually buying is the sample data wrapped around millions of generated lines of data. Generating fake data is extremely easy to do once you have an initial sample set to work from.

Hackers can use simple Python scripts to generate random names or numbers to make the data look real. I cover this in much greater detail in Chapter 10 when I really dive into data validation as a tradecraft.

If a database is that hard to find, don't expect to find it for a reasonable price, and certainly not on a public Telegram channel.

Verify with a News Story

This isn't always the case, but 99 percent of the time, any legitimate sale of breach data should correspond with a related news event. If a company's data is being leaked or sold, there's usually a paper trail like an announcement, a disclosure, or at minimum, media coverage.

In some cases, it's entirely possible that no public reporting exists yet, most likely because the victim organization hasn't realized they've been compromised. When that happens, you'll need to rely on your judgment, the reputation of the broker, and indicators from the data itself.

However, if you're dealing with brokers who operate out in the open—on public forums or Telegram channels—there should typically be a news story. Otherwise, vendors that sell private data collections don't operate in public spaces. If there isn't a corresponding news story with whatever you are buying, assume it's suspicious.

A great example of a Telegram scammer is @AresLeaks. What's unique about this scammer is that the data posted on his channel is extremely unique and, by design, very appealing. The databases listed in his channel can't be found anywhere else, but can be purchased direct from his website, where you can only pay in crypto.

Figure 3.7 shows the announcement of the sale of 19M records from the Iran Ministry of Justice. However, there isn't a single news story about this breach. If something like this was real, there would either be a news story or it wouldn't be advertised in this fashion.

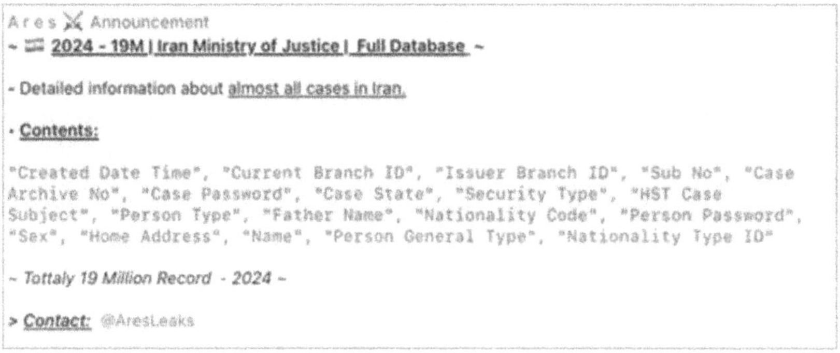

```
Ares ✗ Announcement
~ ▨ 2024 - 19M I Iran Ministry of Justice I Full Database  ~

- Detailed information about almost all cases in Iran.

· Contents:

"Created Date Time", "Current Branch ID", "Issuer Branch ID", "Sub No", "Case
Archive No", "Case Password", "Case State", "Security Type", "HST Case
Subject", "Person Type", "Father Name", "Nationality Code", "Person Password",
"Sex", "Home Address", "Name", "Person General Type", "Nationality Type ID"

~ Tottaly 19 Million Record - 2024 ~

> Contact: @AresLeaks
```

Figure 3.7: Telegram message of @aresleaks.

As shown in Figure 3.8, AresLeaks is supposedly selling top secret Russian Federal Security Service (FSB) documents.

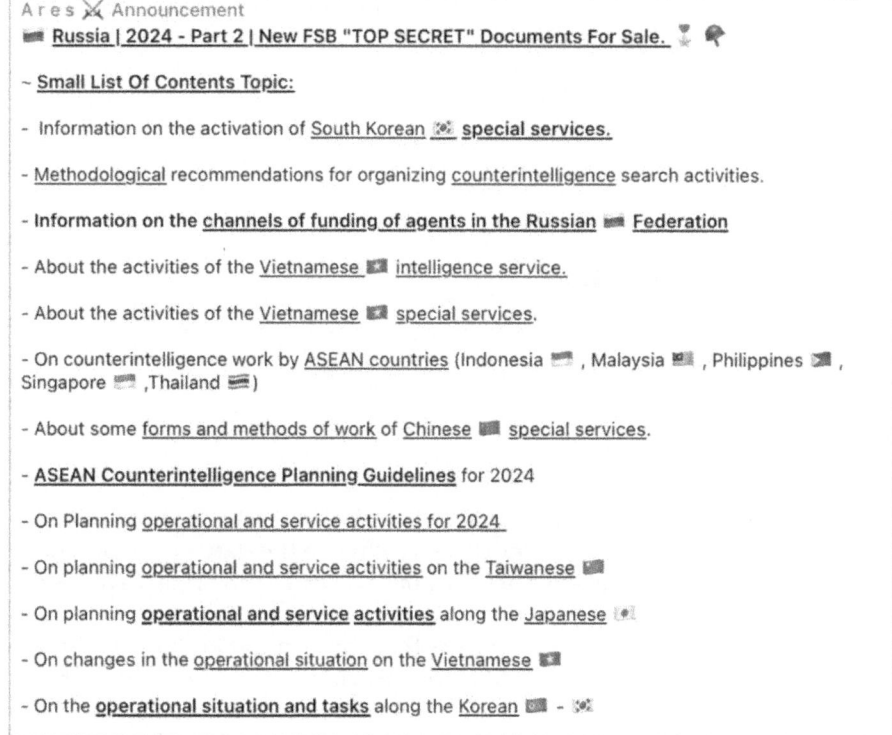

Figure 3.8: Another Telegram post of AresLeaks.

AresLeaks is funny because the moment you press him for a sample of the data, he changes the subject. He will tell you that he "don't have time for people who waste his time." You should know him and his reputation, and that should be enough. Right.

All scammers operate exactly the same way—they will tell you endless stories of other happy, long-time customers who know them and trust their relationship, and because of that, you should just trust them too. They might even point you to a telegram "review" channel of happy people who have posted reviews of their product or service.

For your situational awareness: The reviews are fake.

Using a middleman should always be your first and last rule.

Verifying and Validating Your Data

Verifying and validating your data is complicated because a good fake is hard to spot. I would like to say this is where a seller's reputation really comes into play, but that isn't always the case. I cover this topic in much greater detail in Chapter 10, which discusses data validation as a tradecraft.

At the end of the day, you are dealing with thieves. Although some may act honorable in this one area, you should always question everything.

To start, where did the data come from? How was it stolen? What was the entry point used to access the data? How was the data exfiltrated? The post or person advertising should always tell you where the data is from. If they don't, that's another immediate flag. I asked the same questions to this person as shown in Figure 3.9. Their answer was worthless.

Figure 3.9: Conversation with a data scammer.

Regardless of whether you're buying the data or downloading it for free on a forum, the next question you should ask is whether there's a chance the data is generated. If you are buying the data, you should always use the allotted verification time to properly validate what you are buying.

Depending on the type of data you're gathering, there are a number of open-source intelligence (OSINT) resources to help with this process, which are covered throughout this book.

In the meantime, Figure 3.10 is an example of a fake that was near impossible to detect. It shows a screenshot of the user "Blastoise" selling a database with COVID-19 health data on 48 million Chinese users. This user has almost a 2,000-point user rating, which is near admin-level.

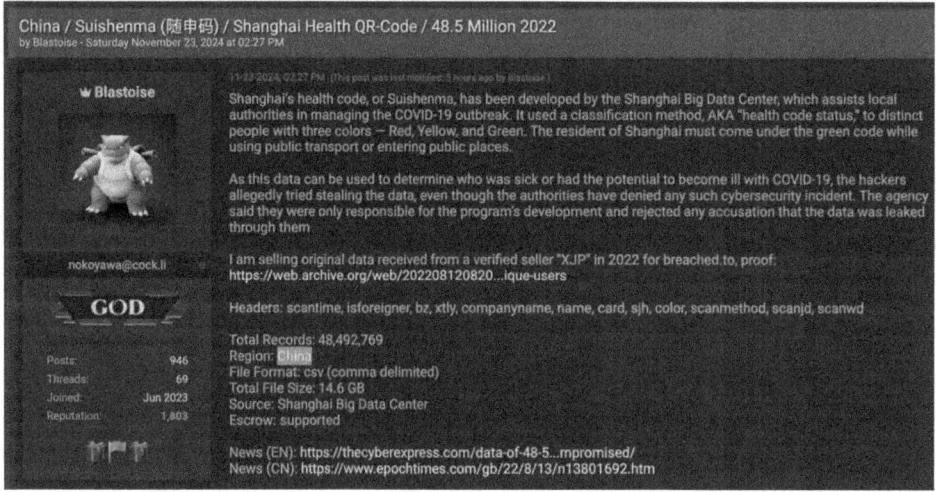

Figure 3.10: Post by user Blastoise.

This was a case where the seller had no idea the data was fake. The key item in the post, indicating this issue: "I am selling original data received from a verified seller, XJP." As it turns out, he did not get the data from XJP, but someone pretending to be him.

I know XJP—he is a trusted seller. I reached out to him (frankly to buy a copy of the data), and he flat out told me this wasn't real. He said he never listed the data for sale on the old BreachForums site and that this breach was fake.

Note: He could have easily played along and sold me fake data, but he didn't because he values his reputation.

Example: Is It Real or Fake?

Now that I've covered a handful of examples to look out for when operating on these forums, the post in Figure 3.11 is a good example for you to analyze. According to the post, user "ExploitOfficial" is selling the shopping history of 8.15 billion Chinese e-commerce users.

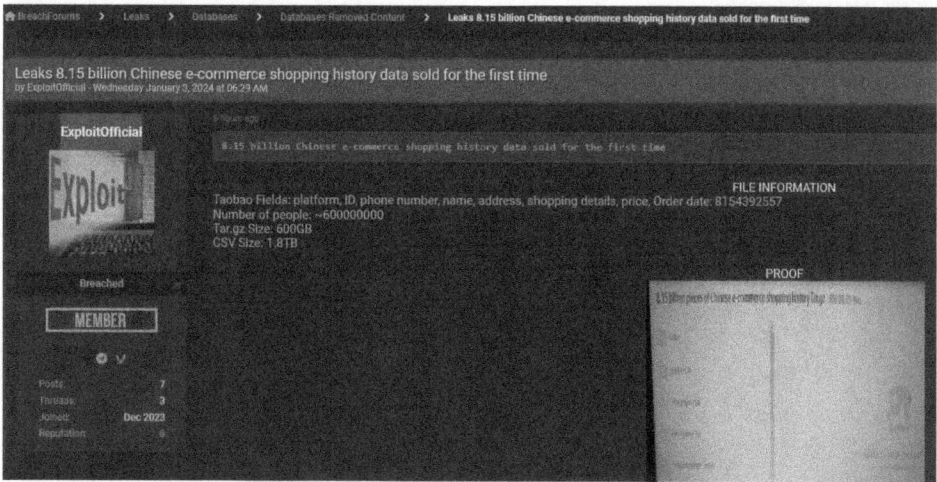

Figure 3.11: A post selling 8.15 billion records of Chinese user data.

What do you think? Is it real or fake?
I immediately noticed the following:

- 8.15 billion is *a lot* of shopping records. Where is this coming from? Alibaba? The post doesn't say.
- The number of users in the breach is 600M. That's *a lot* people. A breach of this size would be in the news somewhere.
- The user's reputation is 0.
- The hack's proof is a random screenshot of folders. No data.
- The name ExploitOfficial is a poor attempt to mimic a claim that they are working with the Exploit forum.

A quick search for user ExploitOfficial reveals that they have since been banned for "impersonating LockBit" (the ransomware group).

Rules of Engagement: A Data-Purchasing Template

Now that you are armed with a few techniques to help you spot scammers, if you choose to venture down the path of purchasing dark web data, I've found that it's best to have a template that you can easily use to define the terms of your deal.

This following template has been adapted from the requirements of several different forums, and it works well. I also show a scenario where I used this template in Part IV of this book, during the Snowflake customer extortions.

Example

Details for new middleman deal:

- Seller: Forum username SuperSeller1000 | XMPP ID superseller@thesecure.biz
- Buyer: Forum username MrBuyer | XMPP ID: iamthebuyer@darknet.im
- Data being purchased: sararan.co.th—300K records The data is currently listed for sale at this forum URL: https://breachforums.st/someurl.
- Data specifics: The data includes (at minimum) the following fields: Name, email, phone, address, password.
- Data validation: As part of data validation, no more than a maximum 5 percent duplicate records. Fields for each records must be complete within reasonable expectations. No field value should be missing by more than 10 percent unless specified.
- Price: $5,000 USD
- Special payment terms: No special terms. Buyer will send initial payment to middleman. Once money is received, data will be sent to the buyer for validation.
- Delivery: Data will be delivered via the Mega link.
- Verification time: Buyer has 24 hours to confirm receipt of the data, at which point funds should be released.

Leaked and Publicly Available Data

For whatever reason, a hacker might decide to simply "leak" (i.e., publicly post) data from a particular hack. BreachForums, in addition to being a marketplace to buy/sell data, also provides direct access to tens of thousands of databases that can be downloaded free of charge.

The official leaks announcement on BreachForums (see Figure 3.12) contains links to hundreds of databases, which total more than 16 billion records.

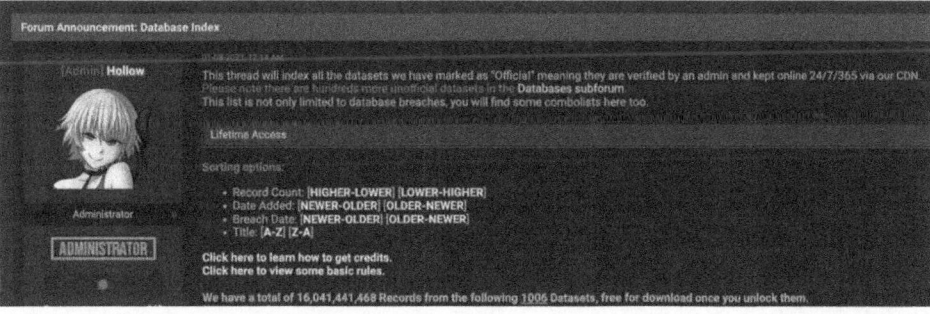

Figure 3.12: BreachForums database index.

This type of publicly available information is used as examples throughout this book.

These databases can be downloaded with a membership and a few download credits, which can be earned or purchased outright. For only $30, you can purchase 120 download credits, which will net you about 22 different database downloads.

Data Leaking as a Sport

To this day, I don't understand why some people leak data. Those who do it regularly seem to genuinely enjoy doing it. They don't have an interest in making money; they just want to publish data and take credit for it.

Figure 3.13 shows a conversation I had with Pompompurin, asking him why he leaked a database containing details of nearly *every* U.S. citizen.

Some people like to leak data. Others like to preserve and sell it. Pom's motives were clearly not about making money from his hacks, but spreading the data and trying to advertise his name in the media. Others behave differently.

Hackers can be very temperamental—anything can set them off, including (and especially) internal conflicts. I've seen people leak hundreds of millions of user records just out of spite or due to some sort of internal disagreement.

Other hackers, like *hacktivists*, do it for sport. Yes, they make money in the process, but for them it can be about sending a political message.

For example, as the conflict between Ukraine and Russia exploded over the past few years, all sorts of hacktivists came out of hiding to show their support for Ukraine by hacking Russian servers and leaking significant amounts of data related to Russian citizens and businesses.

This type of open-source hacked, breached, and leaked data continues to be extremely valuable and is a perfect segue to the next chapter.

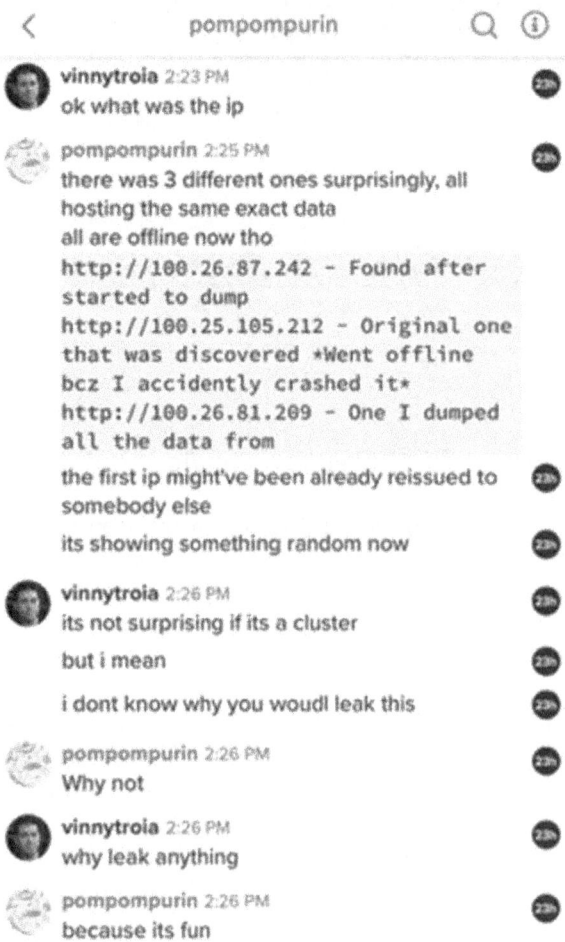

Figure 3.13: A conversation with Pompompurin.

Summary

This chapter unpacked the structure and behavior of dark web data markets—how stolen data is traded, negotiated, and sometimes publicly leaked. Now that you have a clearer view of where this data lives and how it's exchanged, the next chapter shifts focus to publicly and commercially available data.

I'll define what constitutes open-source intelligence (OSINT), explore the legal boundaries of what is considered "publicly available," and set the stage for how this type of data can be applied in real-world investigations and national security operations.

Publicly and Commercially Available Information

This chapter breaks down the legal, operational, and ethical boundaries surrounding Publicly Available Information (PAI) and Commercially Available Information (CAI). It explores how both types of information function inside the intelligence community's (IC) collection pipeline, and what changes when that data lives on the dark web or is acquired through semi-private methods.

The goal of this chapter is to bring clarity to the debate over what information is considered fair game and what's off-limits. Senior experts will weigh in on how terms are defined, where boundaries are drawn, and how those definitions impact mission execution.

You also see real-world examples of how HBL (hacked, breached or leaked) data is reshaping open-source intelligence (OSINT)—from rogue dumps on Telegram to ransomware leak sites and unsecured cloud buckets left open to the Internet.

This chapter features commentary from:

Jason Barrett
OSINT Executive

The views and opinions provided herein are my own and do not necessarily represent the views of the Office of the Director of National Intelligence or of the United States. (See also 5 C.F.R. § 2635.807(b).)

Eliot Jardines

Former Assistant Deputy Director of National Intelligence, ODNI
Founder, OSINT Foundation

M. Scott Koller

Privacy and Data Security Attorney, Clark Hill PLC

The views expressed in my quotes or comments are provided for general educational and
informational purposes only and do not constitute legal advice. My statements do not create
an attorney-client relationship, and readers should consult with their own legal counsel
regarding any specific legal questions or concerns. Any opinions expressed are my own, and
not necessarily those of Clark Hill.

Defining PAI and CAI

Before we can reach a consensus on what qualifies as "publicly available" data, we first
need to agree on what those words actually mean. So, let's begin by defining the terms—
because everything else hinges on that clarity.

Publicly Available Information

According to the Department of Defense (DoD) manual 5240.01, *Publicly Available Information
(PAI)* is defined as information that's accessible to the general public through legal means.[1]
This includes content that is:

- Published or broadcast for public consumption
- Accessible online without restriction
- Available upon request or via subscription or purchase
- Visible or audible to any casual observer
- Disclosed during public meetings or open events
- Observed in places or situations open to the public

PAI encompasses a wide range of data types, including traditional news media, public
records, academic research, geospatial data, Internet forums, and social media content. The
defining characteristic of PAI is lawful accessibility: Any member of the public can obtain
it without special credentials, insider access, or unauthorized means.

The OSINT Foundation's framework (see Figure 4.1) categorizes the types of PAI and
maps them to appropriate collection methodologies, helping to operationalize and standardize its use within intelligence and defense environments.

---

[1] https://www.esd.whs.mil/portals/54/documents/dd/issuances/dodd/524001p.pdf

PAI CATEGORIES

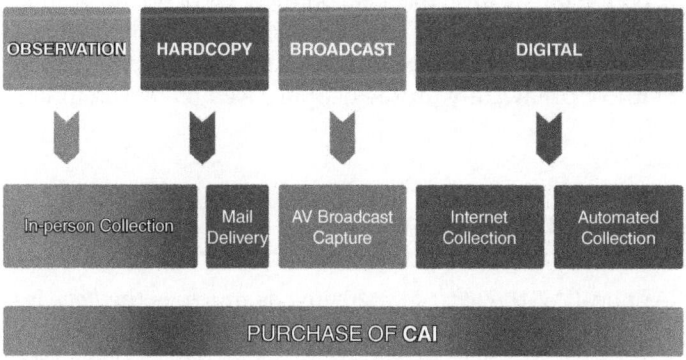

OSINT COLLECTION METHODOLOGIES

Figure 4.1: PAI categories chart by the OSINT Foundation.

OSINT Foundation 2023/OSINT Foundation

Commercially Available Information

Commercially Available Information (CAI) is a specific subset of PAI. It refers to data that is routinely bought, sold, leased, or licensed to the public by private entities, typically for commercial purposes, but increasingly for government use. CAI is often acquired through transactions, including paid subscriptions, licensing agreements, data marketplace purchases, or even free access granted via freemium models and trial offers.

In May 2024, the Office of the Director of National Intelligence (ODNI) issued guidance titled "Intelligence Community Policy Framework for Commercially Available Information." This framework formalized the IC's approach to acquiring and using CAI, emphasizing legal boundaries, oversight, and privacy protections.

In practice, CAI refers to the vast ecosystem of personal data collected and monetized by commercial providers. This includes:

- Location data from mobile apps
- Device telemetry from cars, phones, appliances, and wearables
- Behavioral and consumer profiles based on online activity
- Data enrichment feeds

According to that document, CAI is data acquired through a commercial transaction—from a one-time purchase, a subscription, or a licensing agreement. The key is that it's data that's typically sold on the open market.

While CAI is technically available on the open market, it can contain sensitive information about U.S. persons that would otherwise require a court order or special authorization if collected through traditional surveillance.

As such, its use by U.S. government entities is subject to strict oversight, meaning that CAI can only be collected and used if it falls within the legal boundaries of not infringing on the privacy or civil liberties of any U.S. persons. Specifically, the data can't be used to target specific people, chill speech (i.e., discourage people from exercising their right to free speech by surveilling them), or unlawfully profile people based on race, religion, gender identity, or political views.

Data Acquisition and Oversight

When it comes to collecting CAI and PAI, the *what* matters just as much as the *how*. It's not enough that the data is technically "available" to the public or purchasable on the open market. In the intelligence community (IC), sensitivity is the operational red line, and that line shifts based on context and risk.

The OSINT Foundation was created to serve as a central advocate for OSINT professionals, particularly those working within or alongside the IC, Department of Defense (DoD), and law enforcement. Its core mission is to advance the tradecraft, standards, and strategic value of OSINT as a fully recognized intelligence discipline, keeping it on par with Signals intelligence (SIGINT), Human intelligence (HUMINT), and others.

From a DoD perspective, CAI, which includes "proprietary information," is often treated as a *subset* of PAI. However, this treatment lacks granularity, especially around the privacy, sensitivity, and oversight risks associated with buying data on U.S. persons.

The OSINT Foundation believes the following additional definition is paramount to distinguishing CAI from proprietary information.

> *Proprietary information is controlled by the owner—if it is available for purchase by the public it is commercially available information (CAI). Proprietary information that is not available to the public or non-governmental entities is neither CAI nor PAI. This includes instances when the information is sold exclusively to the government or access is gained through government regulation.*[2]

This distinction matters operationally because CAI often includes sensitive personal or behavioral data harvested by private companies (e.g., consumer profile, app-based geolocation data, and so on) that *would not be considered public* in a traditional sense.

As such, CAI carries heavier privacy implications. If we treat it as a subset of PAI, there is a risk of overregulating PAI by association – and that can be a problem.

In other words, if we're putting safeguards around proprietary or commercially acquired data, those guardrails shouldn't automatically extend to PAI, which doesn't include the same sensitive attributes. Conflating the two creates unnecessary bottlenecks and undercuts our ability to collect open-source intelligence efficiently.

---

[2] https://www.osintfoundation.com/osint/Standards.asp

Eliot Jardines

Former Assistant Deputy Director of National Intelligence, ODNI
Founder, OSINT Foundation

The OSINT Foundation takes issue with how both the DOD and the ODNI define key terms that directly affect the integrity of the discipline.

The DoD definition of PAI is perfect except for the last sentence, which contradicts everything: "information exclusively available to the military community" can also be considered publicly available. That's a contradiction. If something is exclusively available to a closed community, by definition, it's not public.

The ODNI definition for CAI is a great definition, except for the last sentence, when they say, "proprietary information that's sold exclusively to the government is also considered commercially available." That contradicts federal law and the Federal Acquisition Regulation (FAR), both of which are crystal clear on what constitutes a "commercial item." We have decades of legal precedent backing that up.

The Foundation sees this as fundamental to the long-term viability of OSINT as a discipline. If we start folding in data that's clearly not open-source, we invite scrutiny from privacy advocates, legal challenges, and the kind of oversight that slows down real intelligence work.

The bottom line is that commercially available doesn't mean proprietary data, and publicly available doesn't include data restricted to military or government audiences.

To Eliot's point, the IC is held to higher standards when it comes to the collection and use of CAI and PAI, which is intended to safeguard against potential intrusions into privacy.

The fact that a dataset is publicly or commercially available, especially under the context that it could potentially contain information restricted to military and government audiences, means the data isn't automatically appropriate for collection or use. That means sensitivity of all PAI must be assessed before any data enters the IC pipeline.

Jason Barrett

OSINT Executive

When it comes to publicly available information, there are long-standing practices and guardrails in place that shape, and often times limit, what we can collect, and how we can use it. Any data collected must align with applicable law, and just as importantly, it must be the least obtrusive manner of collection. That principle, which is rooted in the Attorney General (AG) guidelines, has been a foundational element in the development of modern IC directives. In many cases, PAI represents the least intrusive form of collection available, which is one of the reasons it holds such value across the community.

However, when there's any potential for U.S. persons information to be involved, we must follow an entirely different and more rigorous set of protocols. In many cases, if we think the data may have even a hint of U.S. persons data, we tell vendors up front, do not give us that data. But anytime data is acquired and indicators suggest it could contain U.S. person content, we work systematically to remove it.

So yes, we operate across a broad remit when it comes to PAI. Whether it's easily accessible from the open web, or a little more difficult to acquire from the dark web, we still need to follow the same guardrails we have in place. That means adhering to the AG guidelines, the Privacy Act, and more recently the CAI policy.

"Sensitive" Data

For the purposes of this section (and chapter), *when I discuss whether or not data is sensitive, I am only talking about data involving U.S. persons.* Information on individuals born outside of the United States is not included in these safeguards.

For U.S. persons, data sensitivity is increased and considered to be high risk when the collected information includes any details tied to race, religion, sexual orientation, political beliefs, medical conditions, or financial hardship, especially if collected at scale. These attributes require additional scrutiny and justification before they can be lawfully used in any intelligence product or workflow.

A dataset is considered to include Personally Identifiable Information (PII) if it contains direct identifiers such as names, addresses, and phone numbers, *along with* a specific government identifier (or even indirect identifiers that can be cross-referenced to identify individuals). This also includes identity data that touches on medical history, religion, sexual orientation, finances, or anything else that, if exposed, could cause harm or reputational damage.

The other hot button item is pattern-of-life or behavioral data. This includes long-term tracking that shows where someone goes, what they do, what they believe, who they associate with, or what they're likely to do next. Datasets that track movements, habits, and routines can include IP tracking and call detail records (CDR), which can be used to profile or target individuals in ways that carry operational, ethical, and legal consequences.

To some extent, the sensitivity can also come down to intent and use. For example, passive collection of benign public data for background context is one thing. Ingesting location-based CAI tied to millions of devices, with no clear mission requirement or legal justification, is another. That crosses the line from OSINT into surveillance.

Legal Considerations

Despite the legal guidelines and written guidance, there will always be a fair amount of grey area surrounding the topic of data collection, especially when it involves collecting information on people.

Regardless of how easy the data is to acquire, or how readily available it is, there will always be discussions of what should be considered. Before jumping into specific examples, I take a step back and discuss some of the wider legal issues associated with certain types of publicly collected data. For this, let's hear from privacy and data security attorney, Scott Koller.

M. Scott Koller
Privacy and Data Security Attorney, Clark Hill PLC

Let me begin with a brief legal disclaimer—this discussion is for educational purposes only and does not constitute legal advice.

There's a significant amount of *grey area* when it comes to data ownership and use—particularly under U.S. law, which differs substantially from international regimes. At the core of the issue is the lack of a universally accepted legal framework governing who owns data, who controls it, and how that data may be lawfully used or disseminated once it's publicly accessible.

When we talk about data collection and what constitutes "open-source" information, we're not just in a legal grey zone. We're navigating a space filled with competing interests including privacy rights, intellectual property claims, and national security concerns, to name a few.

In terms of personal information, most U.S. states have breach notification statutes that classify certain data types as private, particularly when it hasn't already been made publicly available.

But, for example, let's use the status of a person that is in a wheelchair. That could be viewed as confidential or considered private medical information. But the moment you meet the person, it becomes public information and is no longer confidential information—at least not in the same way.

We also have to consider intellectual property (IP) protections, such as trade secrets and proprietary business information. Just because data appears online doesn't mean it has lost its legal protections. There's a critical legal distinction between data that's lawfully published by the data owner, and data that's been obtained illicitly and posted without consent.

The presence of information on the Internet doesn't create a free license for unrestricted use.

It's one thing if I post data to the Internet as the data owner, and it's quite another if the data is stolen and posted to the Internet without my authorization. You can't just conclude that because the information is on the Internet, you can do whatever I want with it.

Just because the data is leaked by a third party, the original owner's (IP) rights may still remain intact. Unauthorized dissemination doesn't nullify ownership or legal protection.

It becomes even more complex when we start breaking things down by data type. Take a Social Security number (SSN), for example. It's unquestionably sensitive information, and misuse can lead to serious harm. But there's no (IP) right inherent in that number. The individual it pertains to doesn't "own" it in a traditional legal sense, but they certainly have a legitimate privacy interest in keeping it confidential. So even if you find that number on the Internet, it doesn't mean you can use or retain it freely. That's a fundamental misconception.

Then there's the question of liability, specifically the liability associated with possessing certain types of information. There isn't a lot of clarity around this topic, but in general, if you weren't responsible for the breach and you merely found the data, possession alone isn't inherently criminal. There are, of course, important exceptions—child sexual abuse material being the most obvious, where mere possession is a strict liability crime. But in most cases involving leaked or breached data, possession without further action is not, in itself, grounds for criminal prosecution.

That much is fairly clear.

There is, however, legal risk that emerges when you use the data. That's where things get murky, fast. Use of the data, especially if it results in harm, privacy violations, or misuse of proprietary or sensitive personal information, could implicate a range of civil or even criminal liabilities depending on the context, the data type, and jurisdiction. In other words, you have to dive into the nature of the data, who owns it, and how it's being used.

When it comes to breach data that's publicly available, that adds yet another layer of complexity. Let's dive into the example of the National Public Data (NPD) breach, which contained addresses and SSNs for nearly every U.S. citizen.

We have to look at what information was included in the breach. Are we talking about property records and information that I can look up in the yellow pages or in some other government database? Well, that information itself is generally considered public.

Or is it something else that NPD has compiled or created, that was never meant to be public? For example, my SSN isn't intended to be public. But if it happens to be in that database, it doesn't mean that that data is all of a sudden public and free game.

This is tricky. We are in a new area of law, and even more so because there are also certain property rights—for example, possession of stolen property. Generally, possession of stolen property is considered a crime, but so far, the courts have not really extended physical property in the way in which the laws are applied to digital information.

That is definitely on the cutting edge of the law.

Open vs. Closed Networks

The collection of PAI differs when operating between open and closed networks, specifically in terms of operational methods and legal considerations. When dealing with open networks, challenges can scale and you could, potentially, face ethical issues as well. When working in closed networks, it can come down to legality and tradecraft.

Open Networks

An open network refers to a digital space where data is publicly accessible without authentication, encryption, or restricted access controls. Open networks include:

- Public websites and forums
- Social media posts visible without a login
- Public blockchains
- Open Application Programming Interfaces (APIs) that do not require credentials
- Unprotected Internet of Things (IoT) devices broadcasting data
- Marketplaces or databases indexed by search engines

These kinds of environments that fall under PAI are generally considered low-risk and low-friction for collection. That doesn't necessarily mean they are free from oversight, but it does mean that collection can often occur without a warrant or special authority.

Even the average person interacts with open networks constantly—for example, when posting on Reddit, tweeting, or uploading to public GitHub repos. When the information is posted out in the open, it's harvestable, and not just by governments. It should be assumed that anything uploaded to a public space is being watched by surveillance vendors, adversarial intelligence services, and filthy marketers.

Open networks are available to anyone with minimal or no authentication requirements. This makes them highly accessible for users but also prone to misuse.

An example of an open network, where access isn't restricted or protected by authentication, is free public Wi-Fi—the kind you find at an airport, hotel lobby, or coffee shop. Anyone can connect without a password or sign-in process, which makes it inherently vulnerable. From a data security and intelligence collection perspective, this kind of environment is a textbook example of a low-expectation-of-privacy domain.

When you use public Wi-Fi, you're operating on infrastructure you don't control—usually without encryption between your device and the access point. That means any unencrypted traffic—web requests, login credentials, Domain Name Server (DNS) lookups, messaging metadata—can potentially be intercepted by anyone on the same network, including passive collectors using basic tools. You don't need nation-state capabilities to sniff traffic on an open network. A laptop, a free copy of Kali Linux, and a $30 Alfa network device is all you need to get started.

However, here's the key point: When you willingly connect to an open, unsecured network, you implicitly reduce your own expectation of privacy. From a legal and operational standpoint, this matters. In some cases, it can shift how data collected on that network is treated under U.S. law, especially if the traffic wasn't encrypted or protected in transit.

For the IC or law enforcement, that distinction is indeed critical. Data collected passively from an open broadcast environment like public Wi-Fi is handled differently than data captured from encrypted or credential-gated environments. Open Wi-Fi is essentially public airspace for digital traffic. And just like shouting a conversation in a public square, if you're transmitting sensitive data across it without protection, you've exposed it.

For the average user, the takeaway is simple: Assume everything you do on public Wi-Fi can be monitored, just like any information you post on public networks like Reddit, Facebook, or Twitter, can (and will be) collected.

Closed Networks

A closed network, in contrast, refers to any digital environment that imposes access controls, authentication, encryption, or physical limitations. Examples include:

- Encrypted messaging apps (e.g., Signal, XMPP chats, and so on)
- Private Slack channels or Discord servers
- Virtual Private Networks (VPNs) or TOR networks
- Internal enterprise systems
- Password-protected forums or data repositories
- Cellular or Internet Service Provider (ISP) backhaul networks

When people hear "closed network," they tend to think of something off-limits: encrypted chats, corporate VPNs, or high-side systems. But in reality, the definition gets murky—especially in open-source intelligence and dark web collection.

Does the conversation you are viewing require an invitation? If the answer is yes, you are technically looking at a closed network.

Signal and Telegram are examples of messaging apps where information about their users can be public facing and part of an open network, but the conversations aren't always presented that way.

Authentication (i.e., needing a login) is often assumed to imply a higher level of privacy or legal sensitivity. But that's not always the case, and that distinction matters when you're determining what's collectable, what's a *grey area*, and what's outright off-limits.

From an IC standpoint, closed networks may trigger an entirely different legal and procedural framework. Accessing or exploiting data from these environments may require a Foreign Intelligence Surveillance Act (FISA) order (if U.S. persons are involved), special legal process, or even foreign partnerships.

Even if the technical capability exists to extract data from a closed system, doing so without the proper authority can lead to legal violations.

Reasonable Expectation of Privacy

For average citizens, this is where things can get blurry. If a message is encrypted, behind a login, or requires credentials to access, people may assume it's not being watched. Violation of those presumed expectations, whether by a government or a commercial actor, can carry serious reputational and legal risk.

However, when collecting data, one must consider legal standards, especially the "reasonable expectation of privacy" test, grounded in the Fourth Amendment. If a user has no reasonable expectation that their post or information is private, even if it's behind a login, that content can often be collected under open-source or commercially available authorities.

Just because a site requires a login doesn't mean it qualifies as "closed" in the operational or legal sense. It might be gated, but if it's publicly indexable, or any member of the public could access it with trivial effort (i.e., registering for a login), it's still broadly considered publicly available for purposes of IC or data collection. This includes:

- Data breach forums
- Dark web drug or exploit markets
- Carding forums and paste bins
- Other hacker boards that are open to guests or offer free accounts

The line between open and closed systems has become increasingly blurred and dynamic. Social media platforms throttle visibility through algorithms. Some apps broadcast data to third parties without the user's knowledge. IoT devices leak data in plain text over wireless networks. The average person has no idea what data they're exposing or where it ends up.

As long as the data flows, someone will collect it. The real question is whether that collection is done lawfully, ethically, and with clear oversight.

So, let's put your knowledge to the test.

Is It Open or Closed?

Based on what you already know and what you've read so far in this book, here are two example scenarios designed to test your knowledge and understanding of open and closed networks.

Example 1: Baby Carriers (and Social Media)

This is a hypothetical scenario, but it's one I've heard from a lot of people and one that I've personally experienced more than once.

You're at home, scrolling through Facebook or Instagram, maybe having a casual conversation with your spouse about something random—let's say, baby carriers. You've never searched for baby carriers, never even typed the words into your web browser, just mentioned it out loud.

Then the next day, you log onto Amazon or open your social feed, and there it is, right in your face: an ad for baby carriers.

Now, you know, *for a fact*, that you have never searched for that topic. Yet there they are. How? Why?

The idea that an algorithm magically decided you might want to see an ad for baby carriers seems like a stretch. Which raises a question that makes a lot of people uncomfortable: Are these apps listening to us? Is voice data being captured and fed into ad systems? Is that what TikTok is doing? Is it a type of surveillance, or a feature hiding in plain sight?

Admittedly, that may be more of a stretch, but here's a more likely scenario, and one that's arguably more concerning. What if someone who was at your house happened to do a search for baby carriers?

Being on your network, their device shared your Internet Protocol (IP) address. Their search was logged, attributed to other users on your network (like you and your spouse), then sold to an advertising broker. Now you're seeing ads for something you never searched, just because you share the same IP.

That sounds more plausible and raises a very real question: What exactly is being tracked, linked, and sold? If a single Google search tied to a shared IP can result in targeted ads across multiple platforms and devices, is that just the cost of being online—or is that a step too far?

Is the data being collected considered open because someone is openly searching for it? And if so, does that mean that everything you do in your web browser is considered open and subject to being sold?

Example 2: Offshore Leaks Database

The online offshore leaks database, available at `http://offshoreleaks.icij.org/`, is a publicly accessible archive containing data from more than 800,000 offshore entities.

The site's tagline, "Explore the offshore connections of world leaders, politicians, and their relatives and associates," makes the site's purpose clear: to expose the hidden financial networks used by the global elite to move money across jurisdictions, obscure ownership, and shield assets.

This database links individuals and companies across 200+ countries and territories and serves as a consolidated platform for some of the most significant financial leaks in recent history. It includes structured data from the Pandora Papers, Paradise Papers, Bahamas Leaks, Panama Papers, and the original Offshore Leaks investigation.

Together, these leaks represent a massive volume of confidential corporate records, shell company registries, nominee directorships, and beneficiary ownership information. It's data that was never meant to be public.

Make no mistake: This is HBL data. At one point, these records were private; many of them were stored by offshore law firms, corporate registrars, and financial intermediaries. Through whistleblowers, leaks, and likely some unauthorized access, they've now been exposed and made searchable.

While the Offshore Leaks Database is technically an OSINT resource, freely available online with no authentication required, it is built entirely on illicitly obtained data.

The public nature of the site doesn't change the underlying fact that these documents were stolen or leaked from confidential systems. While it might be a powerful tool for investigators, journalists, and analysts, it exists in a legal and ethical grey zone.

Is access to this type of information acceptable because it deals with documents on corporations and not information used to target individual people? However, when we search through these documents, we are really using them to identify people associated with these companies.

So, is that okay because we believe they are inherently doing something wrong by using these offshore banking companies to conceal their money?

Personally, I consider both examples to be a collection of public information.

With that said, let's continue and look at some of the more interesting items that I consider "publicly available." These items can be acquired within the realm of what can be freely accessed on the web, and they will set the tone and context for the remainder of this book.

Dark Web Data

As outlined in the previous chapter, the U.S. Department of Justice's (DOJ) 2020 guidance addressed a key question: Can private-sector cybersecurity professionals legally collect information from dark web forums as part of their work?

The short answer is, yes. According to DOJ's position, accessing a dark web forum that lists stolen data does not, in itself, violate U.S. law. Even downloading content that's publicly posted to those forums typically falls within legal bounds.

The rest of this chapter digs into the kinds of data routinely shared across these platforms. From dark web forums, to publicly exposed database servers, and even ransomware dumps, HBL data can be exceptionally valuable when analyzed and applied in the right context. The goal is to show exactly what's out there and why it matters.

Jason Barrett
OSINT Executive

When we start thinking about how the IC might approach PII collected from the deep and dark web, we must acknowledge that while the data may still be publicly accessible, the sources and context are different.

For example, anyone can go on Telegram now and pop into a public channel and download all sorts of interesting potentially sensitive data. I would say this still falls within a publicly available information space.

I think what really matters is how the collection occurs. Within the IC, the distinction often comes down to whether the data can be collected passively or directly, without tasking a third party. The moment an IC officer tasks someone to collect information, it becomes HUMINT.

Whether you're talking about a telegram channel or whether you're talking about a hack breach or leaked data, what we need to do on our end is make sure that legal counsel believes the data is lawfully available. If it is lawfully available, then we can obtain it. And then certainly if we find anything in there that's considered more sensitive data (e.g., U.S. persons data), we must ensure those portions are expunged.

HBL (Hacked, Breached, Leaked) Data Examples

The next three examples highlight data sets that are considered HBL (hacked, breached, or leaked), and ultimately published on breach forums, making them accessible to the general public—despite their originally private nature.

The first dataset comes from Mobilink, a major telecommunications company in Pakistan (see Figure 4.2). This breach impacted more than 44 million individuals and includes highly sensitive personal information, such as customer names, phone numbers, International

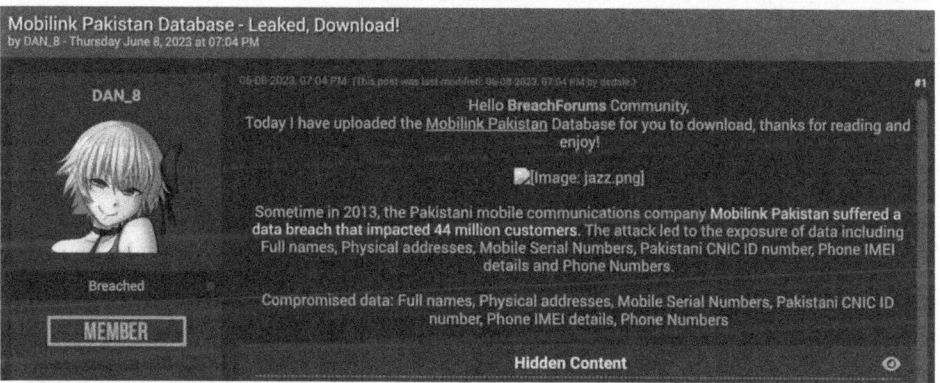

Figure 4.2: Mobilink Pakistan database.

Mobile Equipment Identity (IMEI) numbers, and device serial numbers. While the breach is now well known in cybercriminal circles, the scale and nature of the data make it a significant example of private data that was never meant to be public.

The second dataset is even more unusual (see Figure 4.3). It contains leaked data from Indústrias Nucleares do Brasil (INB), Brazil's state-run nuclear energy company. The leak consists of over 250 GB of archived material, some of which has since been shared on dark web forums.

Figure 4.3: Screenshot of data listing from the Brazilian Government Nuclear Company.

Included in the sample files are what appear to be machine schematics (see Figure 4.4), as well as internal photos from inside a nuclear manufacturing facility (see Figures 4.5 and 4.6).

Data leaks like this may have much more subtle and impactful implications. In her book, *Zero Day*, journalist Kim Zetter documented how U.S. and Israeli intelligence agencies developed the Stuxnet worm to target Iranian centrifuges. According to her reporting, part of the intelligence used to identify specific machinery inside the Natanz facility came from photographs reportedly taken within the plant.

That raises the question: What kind of mission-critical intelligence could be gleaned from photos, schematics, or internal video footage leaked from another nation's nuclear facility? When hostile actors, or open-source analysts, gain access to imagery that reveals system configurations, equipment models, floor plans, or network setups, it

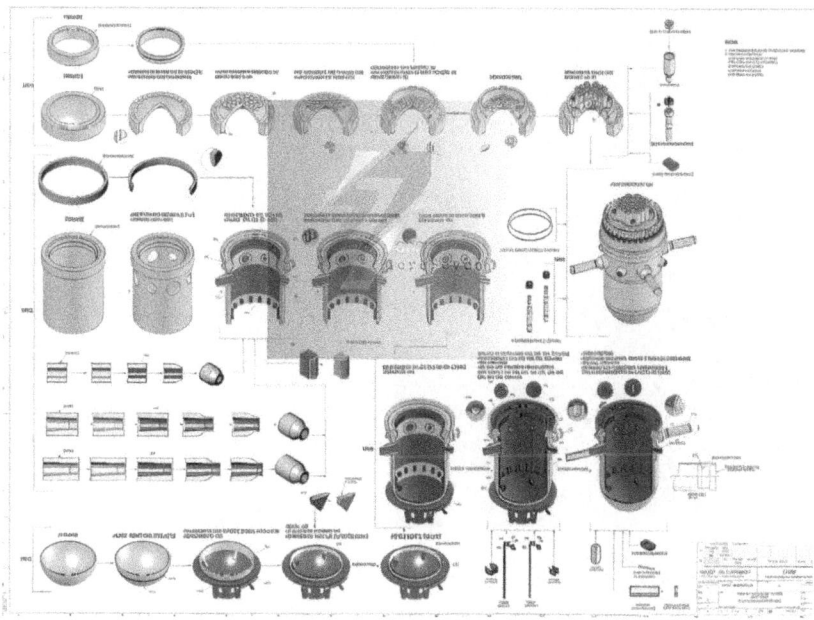

Figure 4.4: Nuclear company machine schematics.

The Brazilian Government Nuclear Company (NUCLEP) / Public Domian

Figure 4.5: Photos from the organization.

The Brazilian Government Nuclear Company (NUCLEP) / Public Domian

Figure 4.6: Enlarged photo from the photos and video archive.

The Brazilian Government Nuclear Company (NUCLEP) / Public Domian

becomes far more than just an embarrassing data breach. It becomes a potential collection opportunity, or even a preparation-of-the-environment scenario.

Another particularly noteworthy example (see Figure 4.7) involves a public leak of confidential and restricted NATO documents linked to MBDA, the European defense contractor known for developing advanced missile systems. The leaked dataset reportedly contains over 100 GB of sensitive documentation, much of it classified or restricted under North Atlantic Treaty Organization (NATO) standards.

MBDA
This includes design documentation for air defense missile systems and coastal protection systems. Documents labelled "NATO CONFIDENTIAL" and "NATO RESTRICTED".
The data contains confidential and closed information about the employees of company, which took part in the development of closed military projects of MBDA (PLANCTON, COSTIERO, KRONOS, CA SIRIUS, EMADS, MCDS, B1NT etc., "Multylayer Coastal Defense System") and about the commercial activities of company in the interests of the Ministry of Defense of the European Union (design documentation of the air defense, missile systems and systems of coastal protection, drawings, presentation, video and photo (3D) materials, contract agreements and correspondence with other companies Rampini Carlo, Netcomgroup, Rafael, Thales, ST Electronics etc.). 2015-2019.

PHILIPPINES INTELLIGENCE DOCUMENTS
The documents contain confidential and secret information about the activities of the intelligence units of the Philippine Air Force, as well as reports on the visits of military attaches of the United States, Israel, Australia, Vietnam and other representatives of the countries of international partnership. There is also information about the planning, the results of intelligence activities, the level of combat training of the Air Force unit of the Republic of the Philippines, as well as information about the creation of a cyber center based on the Ministry of Defense of the Republic of the Philippines for 2019-2022.

Figure 4.7: MBDA leak description.

One document in particular appears to detail the capabilities of Qatar's National Security Shield—a high-value regional defense program that integrates radar, missile defense, and surveillance systems (see Figure 4.8). The contents of this file suggest internal assessments, system specifications, or possibly even strategic defense posture information. While the exact origin of the leak remains unclear, the data was made publicly accessible via BreachForums and other dark web channels.

MISSION: To protect Qatar homeland, coastline and offshore critical assets by deterring and defeating when necessary naval threats in the high sea as well as in the littorals.

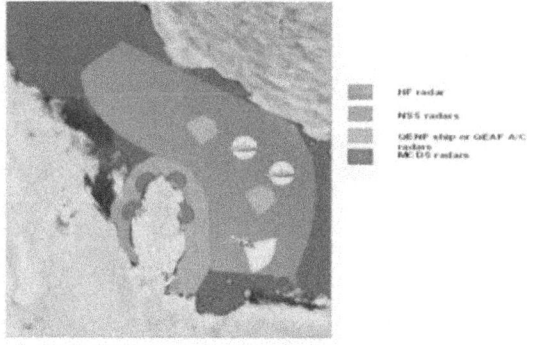

- Surveillance and tracking capability provided by internal sensors (radar and electro optic sensor mounted on Mobile Sensor Units), plus OTH (Over The Horizon) capability provided by an organic UAV system (GFE) and other Customer external assets through AOC (helos & fighters) and NOC:
  - STRADIVARIUS (DIGINEXT) long range Early Warning HF radar (range up to 200 Nautical miles) still to be purchased
  - already in service sensors mounted on a network of pilons installed all around QATAR boundary through the National Security Shield (NSS)

Figure 4.8: Qatar National Security Shield.

These kinds of leaks highlight the increasingly blurred lines between open-source data, stolen data, and strategic intelligence value. In the right hands (or the wrong ones), datasets like these could shape targeting decisions, influence cyber campaign planning, and help build detailed foreign threat assessments without ever stepping foot on the ground.

Russia Institute for Nuclear Research

Finally, as an exclamation point on the question of what qualifies as "publicly available" and usable for national security, I turn to a lesser-known—but highly revealing—data leak from Russia's Institute for Nuclear Research. Among the files were detailed lists of students, supervisors, and applicants—both accepted and rejected. These weren't just names, emails, and addresses details. The applications also contained admission letters and research histories.

One applicant describes their experiences as follows:

In my undergraduate study, I belonged to Magnetic and Optics Research Group where I conducted experiments on synthesis and characterization of transition-metal oxide material for my undergraduate thesis. I will continue my study at Kanazawa University, Japan, and join low-temperature physics laboratory, and pursuing research on unconventional super-conductivity in 2D materials. I am interested in applying for your project about "Coexistence of superconductivity and ferromagnetism at low-dimensional heterostructures" on JINR Interest Program Wave 5 mainly for two main reasons.

...

I joined the photonics and magnetic material research group where I initially studied some magnetic hysteresis models (Jiles-Atherton, Stoner-Wolfarth, Langevin function) and took several classes related to condensed matter physics. Besides my study, my research experience has prepared me with some experimental skills such as material synthesis and characterizations (XRD, SEM, FTIR, UV-VIS), numerical calculations, and experimental data processing/analysis.

This type of dataset is pure gold. It's searchable, structured, and full of very specific keywords that can be used to build extremely valuable targeting profiles.

"Community" Leaks

Some of the most revealing breaches in the cyber underground don't stem from outside intrusions—they come from within. Internal leaks, often triggered by infighting or disgruntled members, can expose more than any external operation ever could.

A prime example occurred in 2024, when a user known as *I-Soon* leaked a trove of internal documents allegedly tied to a Chinese security contractor engaged in state-aligned hacking operations.

The leaked materials, uploaded to the user's GitHub repository, included thousands of internal WeChat messages, business proposals, and, most critically, Call Detail Records (CDRs) exfiltrated from telecom providers.

For intelligence professionals, CDRs are gold. They provide metadata that enables analysts to map social networks, infer movement patterns, and assemble behavioral baselines for targeting.

While some in media outlets questioned the leak's authenticity, I didn't see anything that warranted doubt. In fact, one overlooked Excel screenshot (see Figure 4.9) strongly supports the legitimacy of the broader dataset.

Sometimes it's not the flashy documents that prove authenticity, but the subtle, technical consistency in things like field structure, timestamps, or naming conventions.

Table 4.1 shows a translated version of the same data.

	数据表单					
缅甸	MPT通讯公司	139,603,184	11GB	数据	用户基本资料信息，主要字段 手机号、姓名
越南	Vietnam Airlines 航空公司	2,869,233	1044MB	数据	用户行程信息，主要字段 乘客ID、工作、目的地等
越南	越南运营商数据	87,918	38.9MB	数据	主要字段 地址、邮箱、密码、登录信息、姓名等
缅甸	缅甸运营商数据	46,292,354	4.03GB	数据	主要字段 电话号码等

Figure 4.9: Excel of the small data table.

Table 4.1: Translated Data Listing from the Leaked APT Data

COUNTRY	COMPANY/ DATA SOURCE	RECORD COUNT	SIZE	TYPE	DESCRIPTION
Myanmar	MPT Telecom Company	139,603,184	11 GB	Data	Basic user info: main fields include phone number, and name
Vietnam	Vietnam Airlines	2,869,233	104 MB	Data	User itinerary info: main fields include passenger ID, occupation, and destination
Vietnam	Vietnam Operator Data	87,918	38.9 MB	Data	Main fields: address, email, password, login info, name, etc.
Myanmar	Myanmar Operator Data	46,292,354	4.03 GB	Data	Main fields: phone number, etc.

Among the more strategic pieces of data were what appeared to be flight logs from Vietnam Airlines and subscriber metadata from Myanmar's telecom providers. In the right hands, these datasets can represent high-value intelligence, rich with insight into traveler patterns, communications infrastructure, and foreign subscriber identities.

The structure of this data table (record count, size, and fields) strongly suggest that this data is real and not fabricated.

Based on the nature of the files and the context in which they were leaked, there's a high probability that the Chinese cyber group responsible not only breached these systems but may be actively trading or sharing the data with allied state actors.

This incident is yet another data point in the broader pattern we've seen: Chinese nation-state operators continue to dominate the offensive cyber landscape, targeting infrastructure, exfiltrating high-value datasets, and methodically building an intelligence edge through persistent, large-scale operations.

Ransomware Sites

When exploring sources of publicly available information, it's impossible to ignore the massive volume of data published by ransomware groups.

Let me be absolutely clear: This is not an endorsement of ransomware or the groups behind it. Having spent significant time as a ransomware negotiator, I've seen the human and operational toll it takes.

The impact is real. The damage is severe. And the process is indiscriminate—ransomware doesn't care whether you're a major international corporation or a small law firm. Everyone is a target.

That said, the unintended byproduct of ransomware activity is a growing pool of leaked, high-value data, publicly posted by extortion groups to exert pressure during negotiations. Whether we like it or not, this material becomes part of the open-source landscape.

At a high level, here's how the ransomware process typically unfolds:

1. A hacking group deploys custom or commodity malware, often sourced through ransomware-as-a-service (RaaS) platforms.

2. Once inside a network, the malware moves laterally, searching for and exfiltrating company data, including files, databases, documents, and everything else.

3. After data theft, the ransomware locks critical systems and demands payment. The price is generally to decrypt the systems and restore operations, but in many cases it's also to prevent the release of the stolen data.

4. If the victim refuses to pay, the stolen data is published on a ransomware leak site, often with a countdown timer and a public "shaming" message.

The following is an excerpt from a security report published by Google Threat Intelligence Group (GTIG):[3]

In addition to deploying ransomware to interfere with business operations, criminal groups have added the threat of leaking data stolen from victims to bolster their extortion operations. This now standard tactic has increased the volume of sensitive data being posted by criminals and created an opportunity for it to be obtained and exploited by state intelligence agencies.

Threat actors post proprietary company data—including research and product designs—on data leak sites where they are accessible to the victims' competitors. GTIG has previously observed threat actors sharing tips for targeting valuable data for extortion operations. In our research, GTIG identified Conti "case instructions" indicating that actors should prioritize certain types of data to use as leverage in negotiations, including files containing confidential information, document scans, HR documents, company projects, and information protected by the General Data Protection Regulation (GDPR).

This practice has turned ransomware leaks into a treasure trove of intelligence-grade material, readily accessible to adversaries, competitors, and open-source researchers alike.

With that in mind, the following sections discuss a few examples of ransomware listings, courtesy of the ransomware leak aggregators, ransomware.live.

Maritime Bank (Russia): 120 TB of Data

One of the oldest financial institutions in Russia, Maritime Bank, fell victim to the ransomware group Werewolves (see Figure 4.10). The group claims to have leaked over 120 terabytes of internal data—an enormous volume by any measure. The dataset likely includes banking transactions, customer account data, employee files, internal correspondence, and other confidential records. While it's impossible to validate every byte, the scale alone signals a major breach with financial and geopolitical implications.

---

[3] https://cloud.google.com/blog/topics/threat-intelligence/cybercrime-multifaceted-national-security-threat?e=48754805

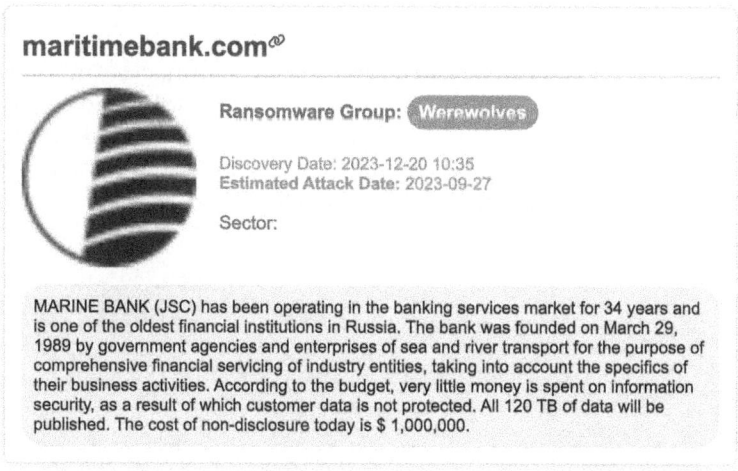

Figure 4.10: Maritime bank ransomware details.

Gulf Energy Maritime (UAE): Hundreds of Gigabytes Leaked

This example targets Gulf Energy Maritime, a major shipping company operating in the UAE. The published data includes several hundred gigabytes, allegedly detailing oil tanker operations, shipping routes, corporate contracts, and sensitive logistics information. In the wrong hands, this data could easily be used to map vulnerabilities in regional energy infrastructure or commercial supply chains (see Figure 4.11).

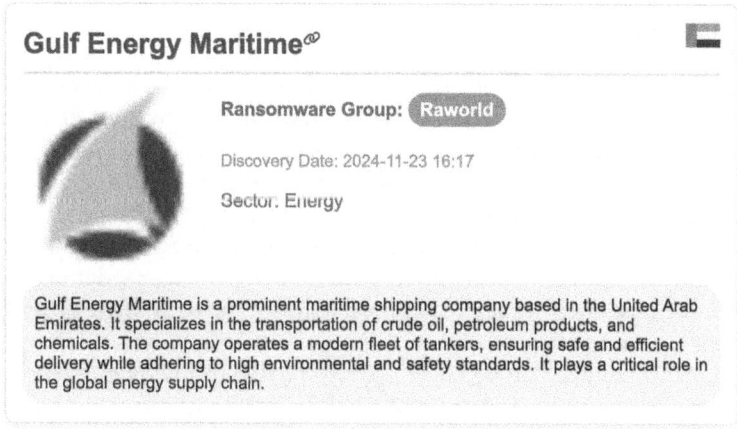

Figure 4.11: Gulf Energy Maritime ransomware details.

Bank of China (2017)

While older, this case still deserves attention. During the global Wannacry outbreak in 2017, the Bank of China—one of the country's largest financial institutions—was reportedly targeted (see Figure 4.12). Though the scope of exfiltrated data remains less documented, it serves as a historical example of how ransomware was already intersecting with critical financial infrastructure nearly a decade ago.

Figure 4.12: Bank of China ransomware details.

These examples underscore a larger trend: Ransomware isn't just a criminal problem—it's also an intelligence problem. The fallout from these attacks is leaving behind publicly available datasets that, while illicit in origin, now exist in the wild.

For intelligence agencies, state actors, and OSINT practitioners, they offer unfiltered visibility into compromised networks, business operations, and geopolitical targets.

Publicly Accessible Data Buckets

The final example of what I consider "dark web adjacent" PAI involves openly accessible data loaded on unsecured servers—the L in HBL data. Leaked data is category of data exposure that's often overlooked but extremely valuable. While this may not classify as true "dark web" hacked or breached information, the data is still "leaked—as in, the data wasn't meant to be public but ended up exposed due to poor security practices.

Personally, I was never a huge fan of digging through open Amazon S3 buckets. But I did find a surprising amount of useful data from open Elasticsearch instances—databases that, when not configured properly, are completely exposed to the Internet. In their default state, Elasticsearch clusters are often left wide open, with no authentication or encryption. When I say "open," I mean anyone can access these databases simply by entering a URL in a browser or hitting them with a curl request. No hacking required—just poor security hygiene.

One of the more well-known cases came in 2018, when Andy Greenberg at *WIRED* reported on a major leak involving a data aggregation firm Exactis. The firm had exposed a database that included thousands of data points on 340 million users (i.e., roughly two-thirds of the U.S. population). The data points, which included behavioral profiles, addresses, and demographic information on each of the affected individuals, were fully accessible online, with no password or firewall. It was a perfect example of 100 percent trust security—just sitting there in the open.

In similar examples between 2018 and 2019, Security Researcher Bob Diachenko and I discovered three separate Elasticsearch databases, each containing billions of records from U.S.-based companies that failed to secure their systems. In each case, the data was completely exposed, enabling anyone with a browser or script to download it in bulk.

Shanghai National Police

In 2022, there was an equally large leak, this time involving the personal information of nearly 1 billion Chinese citizens. The data originated from an unsecured Elasticsearch server operated by the Shanghai Public Security Bureau. It included national ID numbers, names, addresses, phone numbers, birth dates, and over a billion case records, business registration files, and food delivery logs.

In an interview with *The New York Times*, I discussed my involvement in reviewing this data, and how it had been left unsecured for an unknown period of time. I wasn't the only one who had accessed it. In fact, I first heard about the breach from John Erin Binns, a well-known hacker (who is central to the Snowflake hacking story later in this book).

Not only had Binns already downloaded the dataset, but several Telegram channels were offering real-time, paid access to it. For just a few dollars, users could query the Shanghai database directly from Telegram bots.

Chile Refugee Agency

Another major example of a publicly accessible server containing sensitive information came out of Chile, where researcher Bob Diachenko discovered what appeared to be a misconfigured Elasticsearch database belonging to the Chilean National Migration Service. The records included detailed data on millions of Chilean citizens seeking asylum or immigration status.

Personal information, family details, and case status notes were all exposed and fully accessible without authentication. What stood out to me most was that a significant majority of the individuals in the database appeared to be Venezuelan refugees. Considering the current political climate in the United States and the increasing presence of Venezuelan gangs in major U.S. cities, this dataset struck me as particularly relevant to current national security concerns.

Unfortunately, not all of these discoveries are made by people with good intentions. When companies and government agencies fail to properly secure their infrastructure, the consequences extend far beyond reputational damage. These lapses have led to the unauthorized exposure of highly sensitive data on millions of people, including U.S. citizens. And the sad reality is that once this kind of data is public, you can't unleak it. Once the data is out there, it becomes part of the public record—indexed, scraped, traded, and reused across criminal ecosystems.

Before I end this chapter, I want to take a step in a different direction and shine a light on someone who is single-handedly responsible for a staggering number of data breaches.

IntelBroker

For those not already familiar with the name, IntelBroker (IB) is an incredibly skilled and sophisticated hacker and software developer known for indiscriminately hacking and stealing data related to high-profile targets across various sectors and continents.

As the name suggests, this threat actor acts as an intelligence broker, specializing in the sale of stolen data as well as the sale of direct access to compromised systems. IB is also known for extorting victim organizations after he has successfully exfiltrated their data.

IntelBroker is also known for his involvement in hacks related to D.C. Healthlink, Europol, General Electric, AMD, HPE, and Nokia. He was also an admin of hacker forum BreachForums.

In June 2025, the United States charged Kai West, a 25-year-old British national, with stealing and selling sensitive data, causing an estimated $25 million dollars in damages.

Prior to his arrest, I asked him about his hack involving DC Healthlink, a health insurance exchange for tens of thousands of people in the Washington D.C. area, including members of Congress.

I am providing these conversation logs to show the mindset of an extremely talented blackhat hacker, and how he seems to effortlessly pivot through different systems in order to reach his end goal.

HACKER TIP: IntelBroker

When I was first getting started, I spent all of my time with Ransomware because I think this is where I can make the most money. This was a mistake. There is no money in Ransomware. Companies never pay. It is worthless.

Even with very big hacks it is hard to get a company to even admit there is a breach. Many times companies will just ignore the message thinking we will go away. So we have to go to the press but that does not always work.

DC Healthlink was one of my biggest hacks, and it wasn't even a hack. It was out in the open. There wasn't anything complicated about it, it was just a public bucket. Completely open.

I don't always go after public buckets. Sometimes I have to pivot. For example with Acuity. Acuity had a vulnerable app they had that was made in vue.js. It was vulnerable to XSS and so much other stuff. LFIs, etc. We set up a web shell, then pivoted in their network.

It was like 2 days of work, then we came to a Tekton dashboard which was leaking a partial GitHub token. We grabbed the token and cloned the list of repose from their GitHub then moved from there.

I found Acuity because I was looking on Shodan for servers with a region of US-Texas, because on cloud.region you can filter by Gov Cloud hosts, which are not found via SSL certificates or hostnames.

(continues)

> **HACKER TIP: IntelBroker (CONTINUED)**
>
> A week after that we hit space eyes, a federal contracting company that hosted Five Eyes data. The whole thing took almost a full week to exfil. Even when they finally realized and they took the site down, I was still able to keep ex-filling the data because I had a jfrog token.
>
> Jfrog is like a GitHub for storing repositories of source code, but self-hosted. You can store stuff like maven, docker, etc. on there. I had the token so I could keep accessing the repositories.
>
> Companies make stupid mistakes and most of the time they have no idea we are even in the network. It is rare that we will get booted during an exfil. Usually we do not lose access until after we notify the company of a breach. Even then sometimes, we still keep access and it is not until there is a news story that they finally take the breach seriously and do something about it.

Please Secure Your Data

First, I had no idea you could search for Gov Cloud hosts using specific filtered lists on Shodan. That's pretty interesting.

But the reason I am laying all of this out is to underscore two key points: first, to point out sheer volume of data that's freely accessible online at any given time without most people even realizing it; and second, how alarmingly low the bar often is to compromise modern systems. Most compromises don't require nation-state tooling—they happen because of simple human mistakes, like a hardcoded API key left in a public GitHub repo, an exposed port that was never closed, or a misconfigured cloud instance left wide open to the Internet.

I can't tell you how many datasets I've found online that could have been secured by something as simple as closing a single port on a firewall—a fix that takes seconds but gets missed because no one's looking.

Equally concerning is how few organizations have any meaningful detection mechanisms in place for data exfiltration. As I explore later in this book related to the Snowflake customer breaches, over 160 organizations were compromised, and not a single one detected the theft of their own data. It wasn't until I notified them that they realized all of their data had already been stolen.

If there's one takeaway here, it's this: Most of the data leaking onto the Internet today isn't stolen through advanced tradecraft—it's handed over by negligence. And unless organizations start building systems that can detect and respond to these basic failures, we're going to keep seeing the same headlines, over and over again.

NOTE   **Update:** My original update stated: On April 15, 2025, BreachForums was once again taken offline. I haven't had any contact with IntelBroker since February. His private Telegram account has been turned off, and he stopped communicating on Twitter. All things considered, it is highly likely that he has been arrested.

As it turns out, I was right.

In June 2025, the U.S. government unsealed a four-count indictment against Kai West, detailing charges that carry a combined maximum sentence of up to 25 years in prison.

For all his technical sophistication, I have to admit—I'm a little underwhelmed by how they actually caught him.

According to the complaint, the FBI arranged a $250 transaction with West and persuaded him to accept Bitcoin (BTC) instead of Monero (XMR).

That BTC payment was ultimately traced back to a Coinbase account registered under the alias "Kyle Northern." Coinbase's KYC records, however, linked the account directly to Kai West.

All for $250.

Summary

This chapter unpacks the legal, operational, and ethical complexities surrounding Publicly Available Information (PAI) and Commercially Available Information (CAI), two foundational categories in the OSINT domain. I discussed how government agencies define, collect, and regulate access to PAI and CAI, especially when the data intersects with U.S. persons or national security risks.

I also addressed distinctions between what is truly "public" or "commercially available" and what constitutes proprietary, sensitive, or ethically questionable data.

From dark web data and ransomware extortion dumps to unsecured Elasticsearch servers, this chapter showed how high-value data routinely surfaces in grey areas that challenge conventional legal boundaries.

With that foundation in place, Part I comes to a close. Up next, I shift focus—from the sources of data to the mission itself. Part II dives into the foundations of OSINT, and explains how it is operationalized for investigations, attribution, and national security.

Open-Source Intelligence

In This Part

With the basics out of the way, this part of the book dives deep into open-source intelligence (OSINT) from multiple angles.

It begins by exploring the history and core principles of OSINT through the lens of the intelligence community (IC), highlighting the discipline's evolution—and how it came to be viewed as the intelligence of first resort.

From there, it shifts to the future of OSINT within the IC, examining how its role continues to expand and how the community is positioning itself to maximize OSINT across its enterprise.

The focus then moves to real-world applications—demonstrating how publicly available information and various tools can be used to investigate and identify known cybercriminals.

Finally, the section goes a step further by showing how OSINT can be leveraged to combat child sexual abuse material (CSAM) and human trafficking.

OSINT 101

Open-source intelligence (OSINT) involves collecting, analyzing, and operationalizing data that is freely accessible, without the need for clandestine access or technical exploitation.

Publicly Available Information (PAI) and Commercially Available Information (CAI) are the backbone of OSINT. PAI encompasses everything from news articles and satellite imagery to blogs, shipping logs, and open chat forums. CAI adds another layer—data purchased from commercial providers, often harvested at scale from apps, sensors, or digital footprints.

This chapter traces the evolution of open-source intelligence (OSINT) as it matured from a Cold War–era broadcast monitoring tool to a foundational pillar of modern intelligence. Through firsthand accounts from IC and Department of Defense (DoD) leaders, this chapter explores how OSINT shifted from the periphery to the forefront of decision-making, shaped by geopolitical shifts, digital transformation, and institutional battles over control and budget.

Rather than just defining terms, this chapter draws on first-hand accounts from senior leaders across the DOC and the IC who were directly involved in the evolution of OSINT. These individuals helped shape its early frameworks, challenged legacy thinking, and pushed for its integration as a core intelligence discipline.

Their perspectives offer more than just historical context; they reveal the struggle behind how OSINT moved (and still continues to shift) toward the center of modern collection strategy.

This chapter features commentary from:

Dennis Eger
Senior Open Source Advisor, INSCOM

Eliot Jardines
Former Assistant Deputy Director of National Intelligence, ODNI
Founder, OSINT Foundation

Andrew Roberts
Former OSINT Integration Center Chief, DIA

Melisa Stivaletti
Director, Open Source Intelligence, Guidehouse

William Usher
Senior Director of Intelligence, SCSP
Former Executive, CIA

Kristin Wood
Former Deputy Chief of Innovation and Technology, OSC, CIA,
CEO & Co-Founder, August Interactive

Sue Gordon
Former Principal Deputy Director of National Intelligence, ODNI
Former Deputy Director, NGA

Open-Source Intelligence

The Office of the Director of National Intelligence (ODNI) and the Department of Defense (DoD) define OSINT as intelligence "produced from publicly available information [and] collected, exploited, and disseminated in a timely manner to an appropriate audience for the purpose of addressing a specific intelligence requirement."[1] In other words, it's not just about data collection—it's targeted, time-sensitive analysis for decision-making.

Agencies use OSINT to track extremist influencers on social media, monitor insider threat chatter on message boards, or identify cybercriminals operating in dark web markets. But OSINT isn't limited to mainstream platforms. Intelligence teams regularly mine forums, fringe blogs, and dark-pool chat rooms for early warnings of zero-day exploits or advanced notification of breached customer data. Maritime databases can pinpoint ship movements, identify container contents, and map human-trafficking routes between adversarial states. Even Google Earth has become a surveillance tool—spotting new missile installations, runway expansions, or infrastructure shifts in denied environments.

What sets OSINT apart is its scalability. Unlike Human Intelligence (HUMINT) or Signals Intelligence (SIGINT), which require physical placement or interception infrastructure, OSINT is accessible, fast, and global. That's why, throughout the intelligence community, OSINT is often regarded as the "intelligence of first resort."

When done right, OSINT isn't just background noise—it's the tip of the spear.

Before exploring how OSINT is shaping the future of national security—and how dark web intelligence can be operationalized day-to-day—it's important to take a step back and understand how we got here—looking at the foundational shifts, policy struggles, and cultural tensions that brought the discipline to where it is today.

The Foundations of OSINT

OSINT has always been part of the intelligence tradecraft, but before it had a name, it was simply "public information." In the lead-up to WWII, the United States recognized the value of monitoring foreign broadcasts, news reports, and propaganda. This led to the establishment of the Foreign Broadcast Monitoring Service (FBMS) in 1941, which evolved into the Foreign Broadcast Information Service (FBIS) in 1947 under the Central Intelligence Agency (CIA). FBIS translated and analyzed global media from radio, TV, and newspapers, and became the de facto home for open-source collection during the Cold War.

Around that same time, the U.S. Army stood up the Asian Studies Detachment—established in 1947 and still operating today as the Department of Defense's longest-running OSINT program. Focused on research and collection across East Asia, it represents a parallel effort in the government's early acknowledgment that open source wasn't optional—it was becoming essential.

From the 1950s through the 1990s, OSINT remained largely synonymous with FBIS, with the focus of open-source collection being on mass media in strategic adversarial regions like the Union of Soviet Socialist Republics, China, and the Middle East. Even then,

---

[1] https://apps.dtic.mil/sti/citations/AD1053555

OSINT remained a niche capability within the broader IC, with major collection efforts dominated by SIGINT and HUMINT; OSINT wasn't prioritized or resourced comparably.

Then, in the 1990s, a major shift happened. The rise of the Internet and the 24/7 global media coverage began to fundamentally reshape the information landscape—expanding both the volume and velocity of open-source material available to analysts.

Eliot Jardines
Former Assistant Deputy Director of National Intelligence, ODNI
Founder, OSINT Foundation

Around 1992 the army was interested in this thing called OSINT. They assigned our unit to write a handbook on instructions for gathering OSINT, so we wrote an entirely unclassified handbook on open-source intelligence.

After we published the handbook, we started to get lots of requests for it. Unfortunately, the requests quickly exceeded the budget we had for photocopying, and we couldn't send out any more copies. So instead of giving out hard copies, I had an idea to post the manual on the Internet in Word (RTF) format and let people download it and print it themselves. I built an unofficial page to host the download, which quickly turned into a moderated discussion on OSINT. It all happened so fast; I guess it's one of those things where you happen to be at the right place at the right time.

The discussion group was more focused around how should we do OSINT? What's the role of OSINT? How does it play with cybersecurity? Those kinds of topics.

In the late 1990s, OSINT was a craft done by individual craftsman rather than a profession or anything done at large scale. As you can imagine, it wasn't terribly organized; it was more like hunting and pecking for data, looking for photographs, or using the web to get at specific information sources, like in-country newspapers, or country-specific discussion groups.

Some of the work I did around that time involved integrating offline browsers with text-indexing tools, then moving the data to the high side.

For example, I would say, "Give us a list of all the websites you want to follow, and we will scrape them for you and make them available offline." And we would grab everything and make the data available in their specific network environment based on each of the classified systems so the data was native to their work environment.

Nobody had ever automated that. In 1997, that was pretty revolutionary.

Then, the world changed. Again.

After the attacks on September 11, 2001, it became clear that the U.S. Intelligence Community needed to fundamentally rethink how intelligence was collected, shared, and prioritized.

The 9/11 Commission found that publicly available information—news reporting, Internet content, academic publications—was being largely ignored or siloed, buried beneath the IC's longstanding bias toward classified sources. At the time, no single agency had been tasked with leading or coordinating open-source intelligence across the enterprise.

Enter the Open Source Center (OSC).

Open Source Center

The Office of the Director of National Intelligence (ODNI) was established in 2004, following the recommendations of the 9/11 Commission Report, which called for improved integration of open-source information into national security planning.

As part of this reorganization, FBIS was officially rebranded as the Open Source Center (OSC) in 2005 and placed under the purview of the CIA, in coordination with the ODNI.

OSC was created to fill this institutional gap and formalize open-source intelligence as a recognized discipline. In addition, OSC expanded FBIS's mandate to now include collecting, translating, and analyzing information from the Internet, foreign press, academic journals, and other publicly available sources—significantly broadening the definition of open-source intelligence.

Eliot Jardines
Former Assistant Deputy Director of National Intelligence, ODNI
Founder, OSINT Foundation

The DNI established the Open Source Center (OSC) shortly before I came onboard.

The role of the Assistant Deputy Director of National Intelligence for open source is not operational. The DNI is not supposed to "do" anything. We are supposed to ensure that things get done and are done well.

When I arrived there was a huge amount of data coming available. Sites like YouTube posed a real challenge because we had more data than we could translate. And there was an explosion in video that we had inadequate tools for at the time. Analysis required things like language detection, video object detection, or videos tipping and queuing, which we just didn't have.

And then just the scale of the information being put out was growing exponentially. An explosion in public and commercial data and databases. So early on, folks were running pretty fast and loose with that data.

At that time so many things were in their infancy. There was little to no guidance or policy with regards to what you could or couldn't do with open source.

So one of the first things we had to do was establish standards and processes for working with all of that data.

By 2013, the volume, speed, and complexity of digital information had far outpaced traditional collection methods. The CIA recognized that it needed a stronger, more coordinated strategy for integrating digital tools and tradecraft (e.g., cyber operations, social media monitoring), keeping pace with foreign adversaries' use of open-source platforms and enhancing its own internal digital analytics capabilities.

In 2013, the Open Source Center (OSC), which was originally established under the ODNI, was realigned under the CIA's Directorate of Digital Innovation (DDI).

This move was part of a broader CIA modernization effort initiated by Director John Brennan to integrate digital innovation more deeply into the agency's operations.

Kristin Wood

Former Deputy Chief of Innovation and Technology, OSC, CIA,
CEO & Co-Founder, August Interactive

While I was at the agency, the Open Source Center (OSC) was originally under the DNI but later shifted back under the Directorate of Digital Innovation (DDI) at the CIA. That transition reflected a growing recognition that open source was becoming central to mission—not just a peripheral capability.

This was around 2013, when we were just bringing in our first data scientists. I think we had about 17 in our group. The challenge was figuring out how to integrate people with that level of data fluency into an enterprise that was data-rich but not necessarily data-literate. Most of the focus wasn't on sourcing new data—we were working with what we already had. The real task was extracting value from it.

Before that role, I spent my career in ops and analysis, often during wartime—on the sharp end of the mission. What made that experience valuable here was that someone who truly understood mission requirements, from the ground up, was now in a position to reframe how data could support those missions. My whole lens was: how do we create real impact for the people doing the hardest work?

Working at OSC changed how I thought about open source. I came in thinking of it as an add-on; I left convinced it was indispensable. We were seeing mission-relevant insights from sources the government couldn't touch—publicly available, commercially sourced, globally diverse.

This was also the inflection point where open source shifted from "nice to have" to essential. Suddenly, you could find information on the outside that rivaled what we could collect through traditional channels.

Sue Gordon

Former Principal Deputy Director of National Intelligence, ODNI
Former Deputy Director, NGA

Probably around 2012—I was still at the Agency, splitting my time between information operations and support. That was when Syria really started heating up. And I remember sitting in those afternoon meetings, trying to piece together what was happening on the ground. It became immediately clear: our first line of understanding was OSINT.

If we wanted to know what was happening, open source was where we started. Now, was it everything? No. It was the first look, but it had limitations once you wanted to go act on it. Still, it was obvious how important it had become.

The truth is: each source has its place. You can't just say, "Well, we don't need the classified stuff anymore because it's all online now." At the same time, it was also clear that the spy-stuff wasn't giving us the full picture, either.

Take Benghazi, for example, or the Arab Spring more broadly—where we were caught flat-footed. And only after that fact did we realize—maybe we could've seen it coming if we'd just looked at Twitter. That was the moment the community, corporately, started to take OSINT seriously.

For me personally, it really cemented OSINT's value.

Open Source Enterprise

When the CIA launched its new Directorate of Digital Innovation (DDI) in 2015, OSC was realigned under DDI. The move was intended to fuse open-source intelligence with broader digital innovation efforts across the agency.

Though OSC had been technically under ODNI since its creation, it remained physically and culturally embedded within the CIA.

Eliot Jardines
Former Assistant Deputy Director of National Intelligence, ODNI
Founder, OSINT Foundation

Even before ODNI was formally stood up, internal debates were already underway within CIA leadership about how the intelligence community should handle open source. Mark Lowenthal, then Deputy Director for Analysis, and Charlie Allen, Deputy Director for Collection, jointly commissioned a study to address the issue head-on.

The findings of that study were unambiguous: under no circumstances should the CIA be placed in charge of open source.

Despite that recommendation, the DNI moved forward anyway. They took the Foreign Broadcast Information Service (FBIS), which had long been housed under the CIA, and rebranded it as the DNI Open Source Center. Functionally, little changed—FBIS stayed under the CIA operational control, just with a new label.

The viewpoint out of the CIA at the time, which I believe still holds true today, is that open source should be centralized—but they should be responsible for all of the collection for the entire IC.

I don't agree with that. Each agency has different needs, missions, and priorities. Everyone can and should be responsible collecting and supporting their own OSINT collection practices.

What we wanted from OSC was to have them train analysts, procure tools and datasets on behalf of the broader community, and manage the underlying systems. But my view of the viewpoint out of the CIA is, "no, we'll do it for you."

This dynamic created long-standing frustration within the DoD—particularly among combatant commands that depended on fast, field-level support.

The truth is, the CIA has never adequately supported the Department of Defense—and as Americans, we don't want the CIA supporting the domestic agencies with open source.

In October 2015, despite the study's recommendations to keep control of OSINT outside the CIA, the OSC was rebranded as the Open Source Enterprise (OSE) and fully integrated into the newly created Directorate of Digital Innovation (DDI).

This rebranding reflected the CIA's expanded mission to not only collect and analyze open-source information but also to develop and disseminate the OSINT tradecraft across the IC.

While this realignment gave the CIA formal control over open-source operations, its placement inside the Agency often limited its accessibility and operational utility for the military. Over time, that disconnect became a persistent source of friction between national-level intelligence priorities and defense mission support.

The Battle for OSINT

The rebranding from OSC to OSE effectively allowed the CIA to retain strategic ownership of OSINT as a collection and analysis capability, and align OSINT more closely with HUMINT missions and classified workflows. This alignment would turn out to be a major point of contention.

Eliot Jardines

Former Assistant Deputy Director of National Intelligence, ODNI
Founder, OSINT Foundation

In 2015, almost inevitably, control of the National Open Source Enterprise formally transferred back to the CIA, where it was rebranded once again—this time as the "Open Source Enterprise" (OSE). That move effectively put the CIA in charge of OSINT for the entire intelligence community—17 agencies, with one controlling authority.

And I believe, as do many others, that we took giant steps backwards during that time frame because the problem is that the CIA is all about human intelligence (HUMINT); they don't care about open source.

To be clear—it's not because the OSE people are nefarious. They are all great people. CIA senior leadership simply doesn't see open source as a priority. And anytime there is a need to trim the budget, OSINT and the OSE is always the first to get cut.

Which is why the OSINT Foundation viewpoint is every single IC agency should be funded with money and billets to do their own open source. I don't know why we can't do a GSA schedule for OSINT data and tools. What's so hard about that?

Having come from a leadership role and looking back on that time frame, I think we spent way too much time fighting over who owns OSINT.

Melisa Stivaletti

Director, Open Source Intelligence, Guidehouse

What I've always found most fascinating about this topic is how the real struggle with open-source intelligence in the intelligence community isn't technical—it's institutional. It's about control, mission alignment, and ultimately, budgets.

Eliot explained it well: the original Open Source Center was established in name under ODNI, but it wasn't truly owned or controlled by ODNI. What it did, however, was smart—it protected the OSINT budget by keeping it outside of CIA control, preventing it from being swallowed by more traditional HUMINT-centric priorities. In that sense, ODNI played a key role in shielding open-source capabilities from being cannibalized.

But that balance didn't last. Around 2015, the Open Source Center rebranded itself as the Open Source Enterprise (OSE) and formally pulled out of ODNI, repositioning itself within DDI at the CIA. That move changed everything. It allowed the CIA to reassert control over OSINT—not to develop it, but to gut it. They shut down forward-deployed bureaus, cut the budget, and redirected the entire focus inward toward the CIA's mission centers. Meanwhile, the broader intelligence community (e.g., DOD, Combatant Commands, even the Army) lost access to tools they relied on.

There was no clear communication about what was happening or why. No replacement or transparency—just silence.

Understandably, the Army started looking for tactical independence. They realized they couldn't keep waiting on the CIA to deliver capabilities it had no interest in supporting.

Thankfully, under its current leadership, the OSE has flipped back to a more community centric group and has re-instated some of those mission-critical services. However, OSE can only hold this momentum for so long with a shrinking budget and sometimes conflicting priorities, so the community is still holding its breath.

Andrew Roberts

Former OSINT Integration Center Chief, DIA

One of the first problems I noticed when I came on board in late 2013 was that the defense equities weren't being fully accounted for in what OSC was doing. That concern wasn't isolated—it came up regularly from the service intel centers, the commands, and even internally within parts of DIA. DIA tends to represent the 800-pound gorilla in the room when it comes to defense intelligence, and that's true across other disciplines too.

Now, it wasn't that OSC didn't want to support defense requirements. It was more a matter of limited capacity and a lack of full understanding of what those defense-specific needs really looked like. What often happens in these situations—and we've seen this in HUMINT and cyber as well—is that roles get split. The CIA takes the lead at the national level, and DIA assumes responsibility for the Defense Intelligence Enterprise.

That was the charge I was given when I took over: to help stand up the enterprise with the right capabilities, training, tradecraft, and policy—all the foundational pieces necessary for functional management of OSINT under the defense mission set. At first, it was just a small team, not a formal structure. But as the mission grew and the value of OSINT became more evident, it became clear that a dedicated center was needed—not just for DIA, but for the broader enterprise—to provide that higher-level governance and oversight moving forward.

OSIC: Standing Up the Defense Solution

By 2019, it had become increasingly clear that the CIA's OSE could no longer fully support the unique and fast-moving OSINT requirements of the combatant commands. The demands of the battlefield, the pace of emerging threats, and the operational needs of warfighters required a more tailored, defense-focused OSINT capability.

To address this gap, the Defense Intelligence Agency (DIA) established the Open Source Intelligence Integration Center (OSIC) in 2021, placing it under the Defense Intelligence Enterprise Manager (DIEM) for OSINT.

The DIEM role had been created by the Under Secretary of Defense for Intelligence and Security (USD[I&S]) to streamline functional management responsibilities across the Defense Intelligence Enterprise and to provide a formal lead for intelligence functions supporting the Secretary of Defense.

In essence, OSIC was established to serve as the DoD's OSINT counterpart to CIA's OSE. Where the CIA provides open-source support to the broader IC, OSIC is charged with delivering OSINT directly to DoD operators, planners, and decision-makers.

Andrew Roberts

Former OSINT Integration Center Chief, DIA

I was at DIA from 1984 through 2019—over 35 years in the defense intelligence space in the Defense Intelligence Enterprise, or DIE. The last six of those years, I led the OSINT effort—not just at DIA, but across the broader enterprise and even within the intelligence community at large. That role gave me the opportunity to engage across the full spectrum of the IC: the CIA, NSA, Treasury, FBI, and a host of non-DOD entities. I worked closely with the combatant commands, the service intel centers, and of course, across DIA itself.

Back around 2012/2013, OSINT wasn't really treated as a core discipline. It was still seen as an additive to the rest of intelligence. The mindset was very much "your grandfather's OSINT": mass media, radio, TV. But by then, the world had already moved.

Unfortunately (or fortunately) the younger generation was deep into social media, and the character of open-source intelligence was evolving fast. A lot of senior leadership wasn't seeing that, or its value. My job, with the support of DIA leadership, was to drag the enterprise out of that mindset and into the 21st century.

We stood up OSIC in 2019, right before I retired. The mission then was twofold: first, get DIA's house in order with regards to OSINT—everything from collection and acquisition to processing and exploitation. Second, ensure the broader analyst corps—whether all-source, HUMINT, or S&T—understood how to leverage it at scale. That meant making people aware of what was legally, ethically, and financially available, and equipping them with the tools, data sources, and tradecraft to use it.

Our goal wasn't to become an executive agent or an overlord—we were a hub. A resource. Not all commands have equal budgets. Some have more capacity than others. So part of the mission was leveling the playing field—helping commands like SOUTHCOM access the same capabilities as SOCOM or CENTCOM.

DIA often plays the role of what I'd call an enterprise integrator—or in more formal terms, a functional manager. The idea is to provide a broad, coordinated view across the Defense Intelligence Enterprise. That includes the service intel centers, combatant command J2s, the commands themselves, internal DIA components, and really any organization with a stake in defense intelligence.

Our job was to make sure all of those elements were aligned—working from the same standards in training, tradecraft, and policy—so there weren't any gaps or seams in how OSINT was being applied across the board. That kind of synchronization isn't unique to OSINT; it's the same approach we take in other disciplines. It's about making sure everyone's operating from the same sheet of music so the enterprise can function effectively as a whole.

OSINT for the Warfighter

The need for OSINT was becoming abundantly clear. As the world grew more digitally connected, intelligence no longer had to come exclusively from clandestine sources or high-side systems. Social media platforms, public databases, online forums, and commercial data streams were generating a firehose of usable information—much of it in real time.

Where traditional HUMINT might take days, weeks, or even months to surface a lead, OSINT could provide geolocation, behavioral cues, and sentiment analysis within minutes—sometimes while an event was still unfolding.

For policymakers and warfighters who needed to make decisions in hours not days, this speed fundamentally shifted the value proposition of open-source intelligence.

Dennis Eger
Senior Open Source Advisor, INSCOM

Like with many things in this business, it took a major event to wake everyone up. And in this case, it was the Russia-Ukraine war. That was the catalyst. Suddenly, everyone saw OSINT's value in real time. We started getting phone calls asking, "How do we actually *do* this? How do we take advantage of it?"

That moment gave the effort legs. People across the Army started recognizing OSINT as a legitimate and necessary intelligence capability. General Potter stepped in and made it a top priority: codify OSINT as a foundational intelligence discipline. That was the turning point.

Then General Hale came in and continued that momentum. The message became clear—OSINT isn't just a supporting tool; it's the *first* tool. It's the intelligence discipline of first resort. It informs everything else.

That shift in thinking happened fast—just over the last three to four years. But the progress has been significant. We've gone from vague conversations to having a formalized training pipeline, an actual functional course. It's become real, and institutionalized; and it's still growing.

William Usher

Senior Director of Intelligence, SCSP
Former Executive, CIA

I joined SCSP two years ago after spending 32 years at the Central Intelligence Agency. Most of my career was spent as an all-source intelligence analyst. The Near East dominated much of my career—especially in the latter half—and I was the first chief of our Russia-Ukraine Task Force, which was established in 2014.

There were two seminal events in my career that really drove home the importance of open-source intelligence. The first was in 2010 when I working in the Near East Center at the CIA, and we were confronted with the Arab Spring—a wave of public protests that began in Tunisia and ultimately toppled several governments in the region.

What stood out to us was how blind our traditional intelligence collection systems were to what was happening. Our SIGINT, IMINT, and HUMINT capabilities were all robust, but none of them were well-suited to tracking public sentiment, spontaneous protests, or even basic information like the whereabouts of Tunisia's president.

This was during the rise of Twitter and Facebook. So we literally sent analysts out to the parking lot to get on their personal cell phones and monitor social media, just to get a sense of what was unfolding on the ground. That was a major wake-up call. Decades of collection architecture had been built around elites, militaries, and traditional communications channels—telephone lines, cellular networks, and so on. But it simply wasn't sufficient in that moment.

The second event was in 2014, shortly after I became the chief of the Russia-Ukraine Task Force. We were stood up around Easter, and just five days later we came into the office to find that Russian battle tactical groups—core Russian Army units—had disappeared from their garrisons in Western Russia, roughly 100 kilometers from the Ukrainian border.

The White House Situation Room and senior directors at the NSC were on the phone demanding to know where the Russians had gone. Unfortunately, our satellite coverage had a gap—the next satellite pass wouldn't be for a couple of hours, and those hours mattered. Washington was waking up, and we needed answers quickly.

Fortunately, some in the intelligence community had started recognizing the value of social media. Analysts noticed posts from Russian villages—cell phone videos of tanks and trucks rolling down highways, uploaded to Facebook. These posts were geotagged, allowing us to determine the disposition of Russian forces before any satellite imagery could confirm it. It was an incredible example of the speed and utility of open-source intelligence. That was a very eye-opening moment for all of us.

Today, OSIC leads the Defense Open Source Council (DOSC), which is responsible for setting enterprise-wide OSINT standards, tracking implementation, and synchronizing open-source efforts across the defense enterprise. Through this leadership role, OSIC plays a critical part in improving situational awareness for commanders and policymakers, enabling faster, more informed decisions on global developments, adversary behavior, and emerging security threats.

Before OSIC's establishment, OSINT collection and exploitation within DoD were scattered across multiple components, resulting in inconsistent tradecraft, disconnected analysis, and redundant efforts. OSIC was designed to bring order and strategy to that environment, creating a unified, mission-aligned approach to open-source intelligence across the DoD.

Andrew Roberts
Former OSINT Integration Center Chief, DIA

The first real OSINT advocate I worked under was General Vincent Stewart, then Director of DIA. He didn't initially push for a formal center, but he absolutely saw the need for a center of gravity—something within the agency that could serve as a focal point for OSINT development. It wasn't until General Bob Ashley came in that the idea of creating a dedicated organizational construct really took hold. He saw the need for something that could carry the weight of governance and oversight across the enterprise.

By that point, there was a broader recognition that OSINT wasn't just about social media anymore. We were talking about telemetry, commercial datasets, and other forms of publicly available information that had real value in the defense intelligence space. The question wasn't *if* we needed to bring that in—it was *how* we did it in a way that was organized, ethical, and operationally effective.

That's why I made a deliberate decision to embed a lawyer in the organization. That attorney got up to speed on all the relevant authorities around using publicly available information and stayed connected to the rest of the IC legal community. That legal oversight was critical. We weren't about to go rogue, spy on someone's daughter's Facebook, or give the public another reason to distrust us. This wasn't about domestic surveillance—it was about defending the nation.

This applied not just to social media, but to commercial datasets as well—anything acquired from external vendors.

Split Roles Across the Enterprise

Today, the CIA's Open Source Enterprise (OSE) serves as the Functional Manager for OSINT across the IC. It chairs the National Open Source Committee (NOSC) and works through ODNI's IC OSINT Executive to coordinate policy, strategy, and enterprise integration.

On the defense side, the DIA's Open Source Intelligence Integration Center (OSIC) is responsible for meeting the operational OSINT requirements for DoD. OSIC works closely with OSE, the broader IC, and the Defense Intelligence Enterprise (DIE) to ensure that OSINT policy and strategy are implemented in a way that supports mission execution—particularly across the military intelligence components and warfighter-focused environments.

Together, OSIC and OSE represent two foundational elements of the U.S. government's OSINT architecture. OSE supports national-level priorities across the broader IC, while OSIC is focused on ensuring OSINT is effectively integrated into defense missions and tactical decision-making.

William Usher
Senior Director of Intelligence, SCSP
Former Executive, CIA

I spent most of my career at the CIA—and I'm a loyalist, no question. I have tremendous respect for the Agency. But I also have to acknowledge that it's fundamentally a HUMINT organization. I think Senator Cotton captured it pretty well during Director Ratcliffe's confirmation hearing. He said, in effect: you're either in the human intelligence collection business, or you're supporting it—and that's the priority.

That mindset is evident in how OSE is positioned within the organization. It's not at the center of gravity. And that's a problem. OSE deserves more resources, more visibility, and a meaningful seat at the table alongside the other major collectors in the IC.

Because when decisions are being made about how to collect against, say, China's AI development ecosystem, someone needs to ask: who is best positioned to gather and analyze that data? And how do we sequence our capabilities across collection disciplines to get the best result?

Done right, open source can be a strategic advantage for the IC—especially when it comes to technology targets. But it's not going to happen under the current fragmented structure.

Andrew Roberts
Former OSINT Integration Center Chief, DIA

As for the OSIC vs. OSE debate—I'm fine with the current split. Think of it as decentralized execution. The CIA can remain the functional manager. DIA can remain the enterprise lead for defense OSINT. I'm not a fan of centralizing it all into a single agency. That's a bureaucratic reflex—create a new three-letter agency and pretend that solves the problem. Which it never does.

At the end of the day, DIA and its CSA partners—NSA, NGA—are chartered to support the warfighter. That's their statutory mission space. The CIA has its own. There's room for both. The key is clarity—on the Hill, in the field, and across the enterprise.

Now, on the topic of friction between the CIA and DIA—I don't buy into the "power struggle" narrative. I would honestly take exception to that.

I worked directly with the folks at the CIA. Their mandate is different. They operate at the national level. The DIA, along with the combatant commands, is focused on tactical and operational support. Their needs are different; the funding structures are different. What complicates things is the money. It's always about the mission—until it's about the money. And yes, the CIA as functional manager does have a little more influence over how OSINT resources are distributed. That's changing, but slowly. The key is making sure the Hill understands what each agency is doing and how they're spending taxpayer dollars.

It's always been about making sure you can show that the taxpayer money you're getting is being put the good use for the given mission. That's always been a challenge across the board. I think it's more about just making sure that you can advocate for resources appropriately, and making sure that the folks on a Hill understand what you're putting that money against, and who you are competing against for that money.

The formation of the DIA's OSIC and the CIA's OSE drew clear lines of functional responsibility between defense and national-level open-source efforts—but the shift didn't happen fast enough. Combatant commands were still waiting too long for the open-source intelligence they needed, and operational timelines weren't being met. That frustration eventually boiled over into the now-infamous "36-Star Memo," a direct signal from the field that the system was failing to deliver at mission speed.

A System Under Pressure: The 36-Star Memo

Between late 2019 and early 2020, a critical moment unfolded inside the U.S. IC—a turning point known informally as the "36-Star Memo." Signed by 36 generals from across the Combatant Commands, the memo was directed at the DNI and expressed a clear, unified frustration: the IC was failing to deliver actionable OSINT—despite the overwhelming availability of PAI.

These weren't bureaucratic complaints. They were operational demands. The signatories were responsible for real-world Areas of Responsibility (AORs) and needed timely, actionable open-source data to support their missions. What they got instead were broken systems, restricted access, and bureaucratic bottlenecks.

Melisa Stivaletti
Director, Open Source Intelligence, Guidehouse

Towards the end of 2019, the pressure of "who should own OSINT" boiled over with what became known as the 36-Star Memo. It was a letter signed by 36 generals, sent directly to the DNI, stating, unequivocally, that they were not getting what they needed in OSINT and publicly available information (PAI). These weren't analysts in a think tank, these were operational commanders with real-world AORs, making clear that their needs were not being met.

That memo finally got attention. Neil Wiley, then Principal Executive to the DNI, pushed the DEXCOM (Deputy Executive Committee for the IC) to prioritize OSINT in its offsite planning. He directed the CIA and DIA to jointly brief the DEXCOM—which includes deputy directors from every major agency—on the state and future of open source.

That briefing didn't go well.

The agencies failed to present a unified strategy, and as a result, the DNI commissioned a wave of follow-up studies and reviews—one from MITRE, another as a Congressional Directed Action, and yet another from an expert panel led by Stephanie O'Sullivan.

All of it pointed to the same conclusion: the intelligence community has failed to properly integrate, invest in, and operationalize OSINT. And unless someone builds a solution that meets the community's needs without being consumed by legacy structures, this cycle will repeat.

Andrew Roberts
Former OSINT Integration Center Chief, DIA

I left DIA just as the now-infamous "36-Star Memo" was officially taking shape, which was right after we launched OSIC.

It wasn't that the 36-Star Memo caused the stand-up of OSIC, but I'd say both emerged from the same set of underlying pressures. The memo was really just a visible signal—one of many—that the environment was shifting. Demand for OSINT was growing steadily, especially from the ground level. You had soldiers and intel officers out in the field increasingly relying on open sources, and over time, senior leadership started paying attention to that shift.

The core frustration wasn't new—it had been around for over a decade. At its heart, it was about speed and access. The IC, by design, takes its time. We vet, validate, analyze. That's good tradecraft, but combatant commanders want information now. There was a frustration when they see their own people able to pull up information via social media in near real-time and wondering why it takes the IC weeks to deliver something comparable. It's a fair question.

Still, even OSINT comes with vetting requirements. Just because it's fast and public doesn't mean it's always accurate. But in their mind, trying to rectify that timescale was daunting. But the reality is that even looking at information from open sources, in many cases, it's coming from a "black box."

There's some vetting and validation that has to occur. Not all the information is true to form. You have to screen and synthesize it to cut out the noise and deception. There is always going to be a little lag. It's not to say their argument isn't valid. I just think sometimes that we are our own worst enemy in doing our analysis.

We were constantly walking that line—between timeliness and trustworthiness. I had an old director who used to say, "Perfect is the enemy of good enough." Sometimes you have to get that 85 percent solution out the door and let the decision maker or the warfighter decide to make at least a partially informed decision based on the information that's available at that time.

Dennis Eger
Senior Open Source Advisor, INSCOM

My personal goal through all of this has been to reach what I call "irreversible momentum." A point where the value is so widely recognized, the progress so embedded, that we can't go back. And I think we've hit that. OSINT is no longer just a concept—it's an operational capability and a career field with a future.

There's been talk about OSINT in military circles for decades, but for us in the Army, these last four years during the Russia-Ukraine war—that has been the real turning point.

I think a big part of that turning point was a result of the team in Europe being able to demonstrate OSINT's value in a very real way. They were surfacing things—specific insights and indicators—that simply weren't coming through other channels.

Let's be honest—the U.S. wasn't at war. We were on the outside looking in, trying to understand what was happening without direct involvement on the ground. And in that context, OSINT became a powerful tool. The team was able to pull in publicly available information—social media, online chatter, satellite imagery, even civilian reports—and create a window into the conflict. That visibility was something we just weren't getting through traditional means.

Commanders began to take notice. They saw OSINT being used effectively for things like battle damage assessment (BDA)—using open sources to evaluate the effects of strikes and get a clearer picture of what was unfolding in real time. That was a turning point. When we could demonstrate that OSINT wasn't just theoretical—that it could actually provide operational insight from the outside in—it changed perceptions.

Suddenly, it was no longer just a nice-to-have capability. It became clear that OSINT was an essential part of the intelligence picture, especially in environments where we don't have boots on the ground. That moment helped solidify the direction we needed to go: *make OSINT a core capability, not an afterthought.*

The 36-Star Memo may have forced the issue into the spotlight, but solving the problem required more than acknowledgment—it required resources, coordination, and a structure capable of delivering OSINT at scale.

Funding and Governance

With reform under way, intelligence organizations appear headed toward greater reliance on open-source intelligence. But even as real progress was being made, concern was growing across agencies: OSINT budgets were still at risk—often reduced or quietly cannibalized in favor of more traditional priorities.

Melisa Stivaletti
Director, Open Source Intelligence, Guidehouse

Following the fallout from the 36-Star Memo, a series of studies and investigations were launched to answer a single critical question: *How do we fix the governance and delivery of OSINT so users get what they actually need?*

These efforts converged into the creation of the OSINT Implementation Group—a community-driven body tasked with translating all of these recommendations into something actionable. This group included representatives from across the entire intelligence community.

Out of that effort came the decision that there needed to be a dedicated OSINT executive to lead this next phase—that's where Jason Barrett's role was created.

But here's the problem: the structure was never funded as planned.

The OSINT Executive role within ODNI was supposed to come in with a staff of 12 and a dedicated budget. It's mission was to protect the OSINT budget, manage IC-wide coordination, and act as a bridge between the community and leadership—much like the original Open Source Center once did under ODNI.

Instead, ODNI inherited a hollowed-out role. The funding didn't come through, the staff wasn't assigned, and the mission had to be redefined on the fly. ODNI was ultimately left to figure out how to make an impact with limited resources.

It became a textbook case of institutional lip service—under the previous DNI's tenure, senior leadership publicly supported open source but failed to deliver the resources needed to make it operationally viable.

Sue Gordon
Former Principal Deputy Director of National Intelligence, ODNI
Former Deputy Director, NGA

When I moved to NGA, that's where the commercial space revolution hit. I give director Robert Cardillo a lot of credit—he had the vision. I might've executed on it, but he saw what was coming. If we could take this public data and make it available and useable throughout the enterprise, it could support everything from tracking Ebola outbreaks to understanding the Arctic. There wasn't a massive national security risk to that—and the societal upside was enormous.

As commercial imagery matured, it reinforced the idea of OSINT as a first resort. It changed how we thought about national security applications. You really saw that to life with the 36-Star Memo—suddenly I could put an open image on someone's desk and make the case without all the classified baggage. That changed diplomacy. That opened collaboration. That made real things possible.

NGA brought clarity to a lot of ideas that had been circling in my mind for a while. Then at ODNI, that trend continued. For example, the intelligence community assessment on Russian election interference was unclassified. Why? Because the people who needed it weren't those of us in the cleared circle. It was the American public. State and local officials were being threatened, and we needed them to understand what was happening.

And that became a pattern: Skripal, Syria, Ukraine. We moved from using open data retroactively to justify our position—to using it preemptively to call out disinformation before it landed.

Despite moments of visionary leadership—from NGA's push into commercial imagery to ODNI's early experiments with public-facing assessments—those efforts remained exceptions, not the rule. Across much of the IC, structural inertia, resource gaps, and strategic indecision continued to undermine progress.

William Usher
Senior Director of Intelligence, SCSP
Former Executive, CIA

I gave a talk at the Library of Congress, where I said, very plainly, that the intelligence community is failing the U.S. government. I took some criticism from the OSINT community for that statement—but I stand by it. It's not a critique of the individuals running OSINT organizations. They are all doing admirable work. But they're operating with their hands tied behind their backs.

There are four fundamental problems I see with how the IC has mishandled open source.

First, the explosion of publicly and commercially available information has completely outpaced the community's ability to ingest and process it. That's been well documented. You'll hear different stats and anecdotes, but the bottom line is that the volume of information is overwhelming—particularly when it comes to commercially available data. This goes far beyond newspapers or radio broadcasts. It includes what private-sector vendors are collecting, what's on the dark web, and a host of other sources that were never part of the IC's traditional collection posture.

Second, the IC has a poor understanding of what data it already holds—how valuable it is, who could benefit from it, where it's stored, and how to use it effectively. You mentioned that your company sells data to the IC. That's great—but my first question would be: what are they doing with it? It's not just about acquiring data. It's about putting it to use in a timely, meaningful way. And that's often where the process breaks down.

Third, the IC has chronically underinvested in open-source capabilities. By way of comparison, the National Geospatial-Intelligence Agency has over 4,000 employees. Across the entire intelligence community, the combined number of staff dedicated to open source is probably a tenth of that. And the budget for open-source enterprise work has been repeatedly cut over the years.

> Fourth, those cuts don't reflect the strategic reality. If you accept the premise that open source now makes up a growing percentage of the global data sphere, then shrinking the personnel and resources dedicated to it makes no sense. It's a misalignment that continues to handicap the IC's ability to capitalize on open-source intelligence in a meaningful way.

By this point, no one was disputing the value of OSINT. However, despite its obvious need as a primary source of intelligence, and the growing awareness that something had to change, no one could agree on who should lead, or how OSINT should be funded and protected in the long term.

That uncertainty gave way to a quieter, more calculated behavior: agencies became reluctant to state their OSINT needs too loudly. Instead, many began obscuring or relabeling open-source spending in their budgets—not to deceive, but to protect. If funds were visible, they were vulnerable. And in an environment where traditional disciplines still dominated the resource conversation, OSINT dollars were often the first to be redirected elsewhere.

Andrew Roberts
Former OSINT Integration Center Chief, DIA

There was always some reluctance to be too transparent about OSINT budgets. The fear that once people saw how much was being spent on OSINT, those programs could get cannibalized for other priorities—especially HUMINT. That's just the nature of the business. Everyone's your friend until you're sitting around the murder board justifying next year's budget. That's why we tried to pool capabilities wherever we could.

Despite that institutional caution, the discipline itself was evolving. What started as a support function was now being treated—by both practitioners and policymakers—as a core discipline. Not just a helpful add-on, but a primary mode of collection with strategic value in its own right.

OSINT as a Core Discipline

Despite shrinking resources, OSINT was quietly becoming the predominant source of intelligence across many mission sets. Analysts in the field and policymakers alike were relying more heavily on public data to make time-sensitive decisions.

But the shift in culture was slow. OSINT challenged long-standing IC biases built on decades of tradecraft and secrets—that OSINT was "lesser" or only useful for unclassified prep work.

By this point OSINT had become legitimized as a core intelligence discipline—on par with SIGINT, GEOINT, or HUMINT. Despite shrinking resources, OSINT was here to stay.

Andrew Roberts
Former OSINT Integration Center Chief, DIA

It took the better part of six years—not necessarily to change the culture, but to shift the mindset. Early on, a lot of senior leaders I was engaging with had a legacy view of open-source intelligence. To them, OSINT meant mass media—TV, radio, newspapers—and that was still important, of course, but it was no longer the full picture.

What I had to do in those first few years was help them see that OSINT had evolved. It was now social platforms, commercial telemetry, deep web data—information that moved faster and could be just as impactful.

By the time I retired in 2019, I think we had made real headway. A broader swath of leadership—particularly those in uniform—had started to recognize that OSINT was more than just a nice-to-have. It was a core capability, and that mindset shift is part of what eventually gave rise to things like the 36-Star Memo. It showed there was now institutional appetite to train and resource for this domain at scale.

As for what triggered that shift, I don't think it was a single event. It was a combination of real-world developments that forced a reckoning. The Russian incursion into Crimea, the Syrian conflict, events in Libya—across all of these, commercial sources were often providing insight faster than traditional intel pipelines. That didn't mean we abandoned vetting or validation—those standards still applied—but it forced the enterprise to ask: *If the information is out there, and we can corroborate it, why aren't we using it?*

So what changed wasn't just access—it was the discipline. It was the growing recognition that yes, OSINT can be onboarded responsibly. Yes, it has value. And yes, we need to be resourcing it as a core part of the broader intelligence toolkit.

Kristin Wood
Former Deputy Chief of Innovation and Technology, OSC, CIA,
CEO & Co-Founder, August Interactive

We saw this clearly at OSC. I can't talk about specifics, but I will say this: I was a mission-first person—five wars over my career. Open source had always been a "bonus," not a requirement. But the analytics team showed me something that changed my view entirely.

I pulled together a short deck—just 10 examples of OSINT products, ranging from video clips to geolocation images to social media analysis, and I brought them to the Director of Operations—someone I'd worked closely with.

I walked him through the slides, and he was floored. He looked at me and said, "Do you know the value of this? I've sent people in harm's way to answer this question—and it was sitting here. And the operational insight that I could have if I do need to send someone, but have them already informed by this information…"

That stuck with me.

He sent me down to the director's office. But it was the Friday before a major reorg, and the bandwidth just wasn't there for this component.

> When I look back on that thing, all I can think is: what a tremendously missed opportunity. Not that people haven't been doing great things with similar data—there's so much value in the data that's available now for some of the most difficult and challenging missions. And on the flip side, so much vulnerability for those same missions—because people notice weird stuff happening that doesn't make sense, and now they have the ability to communicate to say it. And now, with social platforms and low-barrier digital tools, people can instantly share what they're seeing—photos, video, and observations—and can distribute them globally in minutes.

It was clear to everyone involved that OSINT was no longer optional—it was mission-critical.

The challenge now wasn't proving its value, but figuring out how to access it quickly and operationalize it at speed.

Summary

This chapter traced the evolution of OSINT from its early roots in broadcast monitoring during World War II to its current role as a core discipline within the IC and the DoD. Through firsthand commentary from senior leaders across the CIA, DIA, ODNI, and the broader defense enterprise, this chapter explored the institutional struggles, policy decisions, and operational turning points that shaped how OSINT is defined, resourced, and applied today.

The next chapter explores how OSINT is being positioned to shape the future of the IC—and how open-source data, when harnessed effectively, has the potential to redefine our approach to national security.

OSINT for National Security

Open-source intelligence (OSINT) has always lived in the margins—acknowledged, underfunded, and rarely taken seriously as a primary source of strategic advantage. But that's changing. This chapter explores the transformation of OSINT from afterthought to necessity—tracing how cultural resistance, fractured governance, and resource constraints have shaped its evolution, and how new strategies from the Office of the Director of National Intelligence (ODNI), Central Intelligence Agency (CIA), and Defense Intelligence Agency (DIA) are finally beginning to formalize the discipline.

The story here is about more than just access to data—it's about the struggle to make OSINT a permanent and indispensable part of national security.

This chapter features commentary from:

Jason Barrett
OSINT Executive

The views and opinions provided herein are my own and do not necessarily represent the views of The Office of the Director of National Intelligence or of the United States. (See also 5 C.F.R. § 2635.807(b).)

Sue Gordon
Former Principal Deputy Director of National Intelligence, ODNI
Former Deputy Director, NGA

Eliot Jardines
Former Assistant Deputy Director of National Intelligence, ODNI
Founder, OSINT Foundation

Randy Nixon
Director, Open Source Enterprise, CIA

Andrew Roberts
Former OSINT Integration Center Chief, DIA

Melisa Stivaletti
Director, Open Source Intelligence, Guidehouse

William Usher
Senior Director of Intelligence, SCSP
Former Executive, CIA

A Strategic Shift Toward OSINT

As budgets continued to tighten, intelligence agencies began turning to what was already available—open-source and commercially available information. What started as a cost-saving measure quickly evolved into something more profound.

The long-held dogma of relying exclusively on classified sources began to erode, giving way to a broader understanding: that today's strategic advantage doesn't come from secrecy alone. It comes from speed, context, and the ability to synthesize across multiple domains.

This wasn't just a workaround—it was a recalibration of the intelligence enterprise itself.

The Need for OSINT Reform

A major advantage of OSINT is that the product can be maintained at a low level of classification. This outcome enables relatively wide dissemination and distribution when compared to material from other sources.

Following the events leading up to the 36-Star Memo, the intelligence community (IC) was forced to confront a fundamental shift: The era of unbounded classified collection was over.

William Usher
Senior Director of Intelligence, SCSP
Former Executive, CIA

The intelligence community also suffers from some deep-rooted cultural issues—what I'd call longstanding cultural truths.

There's a strong reverence for secrets, particularly the kind of exquisite, highly classified intelligence that the National Security Agency (NSA) delivers through its penetrations of foreign telecommunications networks. And rightfully so—this is top-tier material, and because it's so sensitive, it must be protected with extreme rigor. That makes perfect sense.

But here's where the culture becomes limiting.

Let's say you're at the CIA, working in the China Mission Center, or to use one of your databases as an example—Russia's Institute for Nuclear Research, complete with students, supervisors, and applicant details. You should be able to start that work using the open-source data you've made available to the government. That includes the resumes, application records, educational backgrounds—all of it.

That kind of data should be fueling targeting decks at scale. But it's not. That handoff—from commercially acquired open-source data to actionable mission use—isn't happening with the speed or efficiency it should. And that's a direct consequence of cultural inertia caused by prioritizing secrecy over utility—even when the data in question isn't classified at all.

Sue Gordon
Former Principal Deputy Director of National Intelligence, ODNI
Former Deputy Director, NGA

I don't know why we're still clinging to something we need to let go of. We're still acting like intelligence is a secret—like it's something we need to protect.

Secrecy was a modality in a world where we were hunters—where what we found, only we knew. We are now in a world of gatherers—a world where secrecy is no longer as important as speed to insight.

There will still be some secrets, sure. Some things only we'll know. But intelligence, at its core, is about advantage. Knowing a little more, a little sooner. And when you view it through that lens—not the secrecy, not the spycraft—it completely opens up what becomes possible. Especially with today's tech. The ability to find patterns we could never detect before, to ingest data so voluminous that a human couldn't even imagine touching it—well, now we can.

This is a really exciting time. But I think by still calling it "OSINT," we're putting it in a box that doesn't serve it well.

Because it's not OSINT—It's data. *It's what the world already knows.* It's, "What can I use to figure out what I need to know? And how do I ultimately create advantage from it?"

And that was just it—with the explosion of social media and digital platforms, OSINT suddenly held a level of value that was impossible to ignore. What became even more pressing was the *speed* at which information could be obtained—faster than traditional collection cycles, and often more relevant to real-time decisions.

The 36-Star Memo's Shift in Momentum

The push for faster collection cycles and accelerated decision timelines was one of the most defining outcomes of the 36-Star Memo. The years leading up to and around it marked a period when OSINT was largely sidelined, or at best, underutilized across the intelligence enterprise.

The 36-Star Memo was largely a wake-up call—a blunt demand from the military for faster, more responsive access to open-source information, driven by frustration with an IC that had grown too slow, too cautious, and too protective of its traditional lanes.

Sue Gordon
Former Principal Deputy Director of National Intelligence, ODNI
Former Deputy Director, NGA

The 36-Star Memo was a bit of a punch in the face. If you look at it historically, it reflects a classic tension: The military feeling like the intel folks aren't giving them what they need fast enough. There's some legacy in that, going all the way back to Schwarzkopf complaining about not having enough maps—which, let's be honest, is basically open information.

So yeah, part of it was the usual: "You're not doing this for us, even though we're the ones footing the bill." But this memo was more than just noise. It said: We know this information exists. And if you're not going to get it, we will—wherever we can.

The problem was, the IC had been telling them they couldn't get the information from certain sources but then wasn't getting it themselves either. So, they're sitting there thinking: We know it's out there, we know it's useful—and the people we've always relied on are dragging their feet, telling us, "That's not what we do." That's a culture clash, plain and simple.

But if you squint at it, the message was this: We need to move fast. We know what's possible. Either we go get it ourselves, or you do your job and bring it to us. There are competing agendas behind that push—some about speed, some about budget, some about turf—but for me, it was absolutely a punch in the nose. It was the military saying: Figure out how you're going to meet our needs—or we will.

Do I think the memo was purely motive-driven? No, but it was a watershed moment. It was them saying to us: You're not moving fast enough, and if you don't step up, we'll go around you. And when we didn't respond quickly? That's exactly what happened—they went their own way.

And I'll tell you, I don't want them going their own way. Because like I said earlier, there's craft and discipline to this work. Anyone can sell you data—there's no shortage of vendors. But is that good government? Not necessarily. More to the point: Do I want every E-6 in the field making their own assessment of what open-source intelligence means?

I mean, let's be honest—we don't even trust Human Intelligence (HUMINT) when we've recruited the source ourselves. We second-guess Signals Intelligence (SIGINT) even when we built the collector. So, shouldn't there be some skepticism about how raw open data is being used?

Sure, there's a pragmatic argument here—speed, accessibility, decentralization. But there's also a higher-order question: Just because someone can read a news article or download an app, does that mean they should be making intelligence calls on their own? Is that really in the best interest of national security?

As Sue points out, the 36-Star Memo wasn't only highlighting the importance of OSINT. It was also bringing to light the importance of the speed at which the information was being provided.

OSINT's development as a formalized discipline needed to match the speed of its growth.

There is a clear argument here: OSINT is everywhere—but just because you know how to use Google, doesn't mean you know how to do OSINT as a tradecraft in a way that makes the information collected trusted and viewed as a true intelligence source.

Beyond the challenge of disseminating information quickly, there also needed to be a formalized discipline for OSINT to rise to the level of HUMINT and other intelligence practices.

Forward Momentum

The problems were obvious, and the value of the information made them impossible to ignore. The real questions became: Who would take responsibility for fixing these issues? What exactly needed to be fixed? And how (and who) would ensure that these issues were being addressed with the rigor, standards, and oversight required of intelligence collection?

Institutional Alignment

The Defense Open Source Council (DOSC) was established as the primary coordination body for OSINT within the Department of Defense (DoD). Chaired by the Defense Intelligence Agency's Open Source Intelligence Integration Center (OSIC), DOSC is responsible for developing enterprise-wide standards, aligning strategy, standardizing tradecraft, and synchronizing OSINT activities across all branches of the U.S. military and defense intelligence components.

For the broader IC, the National Open Source Committee (NOSC) serves as DOSC's civilian counterpart. Originally established under the Office of the Director of National Intelligence (ODNI) by Eliot Jardines, NOSC is tasked with overseeing OSINT coordination across all 17 agencies of the U.S. Intelligence Community.

Today, NOSC operates under the authority of the CIA, which currently holds functional management for both OSINT and HUMINT. Its mission is to align capabilities, tradecraft, policy, and workforce development to ensure that OSINT is fully integrated into national intelligence priorities.

To bridge the defense and civilian spheres, there is cross-representation between the two bodies. The Director of OSIC (D/OSIC) serves as the Deputy Director of NOSC, while the Director of the Open Source Enterprise (D/OSE)—who also leads NOSC—holds a seat on DOSC. This structure ensures that defense equities are represented in IC-wide planning and that OSINT governance remains collaborative.

Eliot Jardines
Former Assistant Deputy Director of National Intelligence, ODNI
Founder, OSINT Foundation

During the period often referred to as the "Lost Decade," circa 2012 to 2022—when nobody was paying attention to OSINT—both the NOSC and DOSC atrophied. Starting around 2022, there has been more activity with both the NOSC and the DOSC, including significant coordination and partnership.

Now, there is much more collaboration between the two, and they are at least aware of each other's activities in a way that wasn't the case in the past.

The "Lost Decade" may have been a period of stagnation, but looking at it from the outside with some historical distance, it looks more like a slow awakening.

Andrew Roberts
Former OSINT Integration Center Chief, DIA

I would disagree with the characterization of 2012–2022 as "lost decade." Agreeably, between that time period, OSINT was entirely marginalized by senior leadership. The younger generation, however, was making good use of it where they could. During that ten-year period a foundation for OSINT was established largely due to core members of the NOSC and DOSC. The evolution was underway (but not the end goal) and it was not until this decade that it has taken hold. The CIA, NGA, DIA, Army G2, MCIA, SOCOM, and INSCOM all worked together as a coalition to feed this evolution. The success of today is built on that coalition.

OSINT didn't vanish; it was evolving—driven by analysts and operators who saw its potential even when the system didn't. Like most institutional change, momentum was slow. And true to form, government wasn't built for rapid adoption—especially not for something that challenged decades of ingrained collection habits.

But the seeds were planted, and the urgency was growing.

Randy Nixon
Director, Open Source Enterprise, CIA

I spent a year and a half teaching at our leadership school within the Directorate of Analysis, where I created the DA's first formal training course on strategic planning.

That foundational experience shaped the way we approached the development of the IC's first enterprise OSINT strategy. The strategy was co-authored by our chief of strategy at OSE and DIA's chief strategist—two individuals deeply trained in strategic planning who knew how to operationalize long-term vision.

That joint authorship created real alignment between the NOSC and the DOSC. For the first time, we had a shared strategy that spoke with a single voice across the IC and the Department of Defense. It's also the first OSINT strategy released publicly. You can find it on the DNI's homepage and on LinkedIn. It's now serving as the foundation for subordinate strategies at OSE, OSIC, INR, and others. That alignment matters—it ensures the broader community is rowing in the same direction.

We've also since operationalized the strategy. NOSC stood up four subcommittees aligned to the strategy's major pillars, and they report monthly on progress. We're also working with ODNI Public Affairs on updating the public release, and we've completed a congressional notification as part of that ongoing process.

Today, when the NOSC sets new priorities or issues strategic guidance, those decisions are reviewed by a joint board of governors—chaired by the CIA Director and attended by senior leaders from across the intelligence community.

This dual participation is meant to ensure that strategy and execution remain tightly aligned, and that community-wide efforts are integrated from a national and defense perspective—reinforcing OSINT's growing status as a core intelligence discipline.

This is a clear sign of how far things have come. OSINT is no longer a side effort—it's becoming a core discipline, with enterprise-level governance to match.

As momentum returned, both DOSC and NOSC began developing their own OSINT strategies—distinct but complementary, each reflecting the priorities of their respective communities.

The OSINT Strategies

In 2023, DIA released its OSINT strategy, focused on advancing OSINT capabilities in support of the DoD and the warfighter.

The following year, in 2024, ODNI—in coordination with the CIA—released a separate OSINT strategy aimed at addressing the broader needs of the IC.

Both strategies share common goals—such as elevating OSINT as a core discipline and improving access to publicly and commercially available information—each is tailored to its respective constituency and mission.

At a high level, both strategies seek to:

- Elevate OSINT as a core intelligence discipline.

- Expand the use of publicly and commercially available information (PAI/CAI).

- Modernize acquisition and analysis methods to enhance mission impact.

In addition, one of the five strategic objectives in DIA's strategy explicitly positions OSINT as a premier intelligence capability and *the foundation for all other disciplines.*

Where the strategies diverge is in their implementation priorities.

The DIA/DoD strategy emphasizes standardizing OSINT tradecraft across defense components, supporting tactical and operational missions, and building a centralized PAI/CAI data catalog to streamline access and reduce redundancy across the military enterprise. It states:[1]

… establishes a vision, goals, and objectives to elevate OSINT as a core intelligence discipline that provides high-value unclassified reporting, while simultaneously serving as a catalyst for enriched all source analysis and a valuable cueing mechanism for the other intelligence arts.[2]

In contrast, the IC's strategy, led by ODNI, focuses on professionalizing the OSINT workforce, integrating open-source data into all-source analytical frameworks, and fostering agility and innovation across the IC through partnerships, emerging technologies, and talent development. The IC strategy goes on to state:

OSINT is vital to the intelligence community's mission. OSINT both enables other intelligence collection disciplines and delivers unique intelligence value of its own, allowing the IC to more efficiently and effectively leverage its exquisite collection capabilities.

As the open-source environment continues to expand and evolve at breakneck speed, the ability to extract actionable insights from vast amounts of open-source data will only increase in importance.

For the IC to surpass nation-state competitors that are making significant investments in the open-source domain, we must build an integrated and agile OSINT community that can rapidly innovate as the open-source environment evolves.[3]

Together, the two strategies reflect a complementary approach: one rooted in mission execution at the tactical and operational level, and the other focused on enterprise transformation across the intelligence ecosystem.

---

[1] https://www.dia.mil/Portals/110/Documents/OSINT-Strategy.pdf
[2] https://www.dia.mil/Portals/110/Documents/OSINT-Strategy.pdf
[3] https://www.dni.gov/files/ODNI/documents/IC_OSINT_Strategy.pdf

Randy Nixon
Director, Open Source Enterprise, CIA

The similarities between the DIA and the CIA/ODNI OSINT strategies were very intentional. The same DIA officer who co-authored the IC strategy worked on their own internal version. Likewise, OSE's internal alignment was shaped by that same process. It was a deliberate move to ensure consistency between OSE and DIA—because together, we make up the majority of the OSINT enterprise. Unity of effort is how we get results.

With respect to tradecraft, training remains central. We have our own OSINT training, and across the community, DIA, Army, and others have developed their own tailored OSINT courses. We review those offerings jointly, when possible, to ensure they meet the standard. If they don't, we provide feedback and partner with them to improve. Once the courses are approved, we offer them across the IC via a shared website that houses course materials, instructional videos, tradecraft memos, and exemplar case studies. We're building an ecosystem where analysts can self-educate and refine their craft.

Jason Barrett
OSINT Executive

There are two foundational points that I believe undergird the Intelligence Community's open-source strategy.

First, emerging technologies are creating new opportunities to leverage open-source intelligence in ways that are faster, more cost-effective, and ultimately more impactful for policymakers, warfighters, and allies. These advancements, combined with the right partnerships, are enabling a higher standard of intelligence delivery.

Second, the intelligence community will not be able to fully realize its potential—or achieve the transformational change that is needed—without a fully professionalized, operationally integrated, and functionally independent open-source intelligence element. That point is embedded throughout the strategy, and it's critical to success.

We are focused on harnessing technology and partnerships to further improve the speed, cost effectiveness, and quality of OSINT; and building a dedicated, future-ready workforce to lead the charge.

When it comes to implementation, the challenge lies in ensuring we have the right people with the right skills, at the right time, and that they can operate with the agility needed to keep pace with a rapidly evolving landscape.

We must move beyond nostalgia or legacy thinking and focus on what lies ahead. To put it plainly: We need to get people thinking forward. If we can't do that, we'll find ourselves at a disadvantage. These two issues—talent and forward momentum with true integration—are, in my view, the most pressing challenges we face.

Both OSINT strategies openly recognize that OSINT is no longer a supporting discipline; it is foundational. Each strategy affirms that open and commercially available data, when leveraged effectively, can deliver timely, relevant, and actionable insights on par with traditional classified sources.

At their core, both strategies seek to elevate OSINT to equal footing with other intelligence disciplines by institutionalizing tradecraft, expanding access to global data, and modernizing the way OSINT is collected, processed, and integrated into all-source analysis.

This includes explicit calls to adopt automated tools, to leverage artificial intelligence (AI)/machine learning (ML)-powered analytics, and to invest in scalable data infrastructure capable of handling the growing volume and complexity of publicly available information.

Both strategies laid out what's needed to move the needle forward—but despite the shared recognition of OSINT's value and the clarity of what's required, *one critical barrier remained: funding.*

First Resort but Least Resourced

For all its praise throughout the DoD and the IC—for all the strategy documents, public endorsements, and operational success stories—*OSINT remains one of the most vulnerable and frequently cut programs in the intelligence enterprise.*

Despite its clear utility, relatively low cost (compared to other disciplines), and growing relevance in a data-saturated world, open-source efforts are often the first on the chopping block when budget constraints hit.

Jason Barrett
OSINT Executive

Dedicated OSINT funding is less than half of 1 percent of the total intelligence budget. And it makes up over 25 percent of all citations in President's Daily Brief (PDB), on average. With that kind of return on investment (ROI), even modest additional investment in the OSINT ecosystem would have tremendous impact.

In fact, starting in 2011 and continuing for the next 10 years, the total IC budget programmatically aligned to OSINT declined by more than 60 percent. During the same time frame, the number of IC elements allocating part of their budget to OSINT declined by roughly the same percentage.

The timing of that decline was particularly impactful to the OSINT mission because it occurred at the same time the market value of commercially available information was increasing. As all IC elements were increasingly focused on acquiring publicly and commercially available information to support their non-OSINT collection and reporting capabilities, the IC OSINT community was being hollowed out financially, and it lacked the budgetary, programmatic, or policy tether to show that commercial data acquisition should be closely aligned to OSINT work.

Sue Gordon
Former Principal Deputy Director of National Intelligence, ODNI
Former Deputy Director, NGA

If you take the Arab Spring as your starting point and trace things forward from there, I'd say this: Until very recently—and frankly, even now—open source is still viewed by much of the IC as a "nice to have." We know it has value. We know we can get it. And we know our customers are using it—President Trump's first administration is a perfect example of that. He was really the first President where we, the IC, weren't his most trusted source.

Now imagine that—he doesn't really understand how government works. He thinks the CIA is cool, sure, but that only gets you so far. We'd walk in with an intelligence assessment, and he'd push back with something a friend told him, or something we hadn't accounted for. And who do you think he believed?

The Trump administration made something very clear: If we're not incorporating open source, we're not doing our jobs as intelligence officers. That period—from Arab Spring to Trump—is when OSINT shifted from being ignored to being realized. Still seen as supplemental, sure, but clearly affecting our customers. Which means it ought to be affecting us.

But here's the issue: Because it's still treated as a "nice to have," and because it doesn't live inside big, entrenched programs of record, it's the first thing to get cut. And not subtly either—specifically open source is what gets targeted. It's not, "Hey, let's cut the China program, and you decide what mix of sources gives you the best picture."

No—it's we're cutting OSINT.

In addition to widespread cuts across data and open-source collection efforts, OSINT as a discipline remains chronically underfunded. William Usher highlights the limited personnel assigned across agencies to manage this increasingly vital mission. As he notes, staffing constraints are a persistent barrier to scaling OSINT effectively. One potential solution he raises—consolidating OSINT efforts across the enterprise—is explored further in the next chapter.

William Usher
Senior Director of Intelligence, SCSP
Former Executive, CIA

Right now, the IC takes an extremely federated approach to open-source intelligence. The role of the OSINT executive within ODNI heads an office of two people—that's the entire team. OSE at the CIA runs the most robust operation, and DIA has a much smaller shop that's expected to service the entire defense enterprise. And then you have small pockets of open-source units scattered throughout the military services and elsewhere.

> In my view, these resources and capabilities need to be consolidated. We need an entity that's empowered to make real decisions about how open-source data is acquired, stored, processed, and leveraged across the IC. And it has to come with the budget and authority to match that mission.
>
> But from an OSINT perspective, it's incredibly difficult to invest in new data sources when OSINT budgets are constantly being cut.
>
> And that leads to an even bigger problem, which is the IC hasn't been successful in delivering timely, high-value insights from open-source information to its most important customers. We're talking about the President, cabinet-level officials, and senior leaders across the military and interagency.
>
> There's a lot of data being warehoused—entities are buying commercial data, including products like yours—but much of that insight never gets translated into operational or strategic decision-making. It's not reaching the right audiences fast enough, if at all. And that's a real shame.

Despite all of these cuts and decreased morale around the discipline, 2024 marked a turning point as momentum behind OSINT began to accelerate once again.

OSINT's Way Forward

As with all things, if you push forward hard enough and long enough, you will eventually see positive momentum. And that's exactly what we can see happening starting with legislative language added to the 2024 National Defense Authorization Act (NDAA).

The NDAA is an annual U.S. federal law that authorizes the budget and expenditures for the DoD and other national security programs. As one of the most significant pieces of legislation passed by Congress each year, it has been enacted continuously for over six decades.

The House Armed Services Committee (HASC) leads the drafting of the NDAA for the House of Representatives. HASC oversees the full legislative process, including holding subcommittee hearings, reviewing proposed changes, and conducting markup sessions—where revisions are made and sections are assembled into the full bill. This is followed by a full committee debate and vote to approve the final House version of the NDAA.

The House Permanent Select Committee on Intelligence (HPSCI) also plays a key role in shaping the NDAA, often inserting intelligence-related provisions—particularly those tied to cyber operations, surveillance authorities, and open-source intelligence initiatives.

OSINT Language in 2024 NDAA

In 2024, the House of Representatives passed reporting language in the NDAA titled "Modernizing Open Source Intelligence."

This provision specifically referenced the joint CIA/ODNI's OSINT strategy as a foundational step toward institutionalizing OSINT as a core tradecraft within the IC.

The language directly cited the joint CIA/ODNI's OSINT strategy, framing it as a roadmap toward institutionalizing OSINT as a core tradecraft within the intelligence community (see Figure 6.1). The text also explicitly highlighted the value of commercially available *foreign adversary intelligence data*, particularly from "overlay networks"—a term often used to describe dark web ecosystems.

In reference to this type of data, the language stated,

The committee believes this intelligence, when obtained properly, could provide the U.S. and its allies and partners an advantage over our adversaries.

In other words: *Congress gave tacit recognition that the IC should be referencing—and actively leveraging—the kind of data that, not long ago, lived in legal grey zones and side channels.*

TITLE XVI—SPACE ACTIVITIES, STRATEGIC PROGRAMS, AND INTELLIGENCE MATTERS

ITEMS OF SPECIAL INTEREST

INTELLIGENCE MATTERS

Modernizing Open Source Intelligence

The committee notes the Office of the Director of National Intelligence (DNI) and the Central Intelligence Agency (CIA) released the intelligence community's (IC) Open Source Intelligence (OSINT) Strategy for 2024-2026 on March 8, 2024. The strategy highlights the advances in artificial intelligence (AI) and machine learning and the opportunities and value they bring to OSINT. The committee agrees with the strategy's notion that the IC must embrace new technologies, while ensuring the development of tradecraft in tandem, to quickly collect, evaluate, and analyze open-source data. The committee also recognizes the potential for commercially available foreign adversary intelligence data obtained from the internet or overlay networks. The committee believes this intelligence, when obtained properly, could provide the U.S. and its allies and partners an advantage over our adversaries.

Therefore, the committee directs the Secretary of Defense to provide a briefing to the House Committee on Armed Services not later than December 31, 2024, on the Defense Intelligence Enterprise's (DIE) approach to accomplishing the OSINT Strategy for 2024-2026 and the impacts of the potential use of commercially acquired foreign adversary intelligence data. The briefing should address the following:

(1) how the DIE will coordinate open-source data acquisition and expand data sharing;

(2) how the DIE will establish integrated open-source collection management;

(3) how the DIE will drive OSINT innovation to deliver new capabilities;

(4) how the DIE will develop the next-generation OSINT workforce and tradecraft; and

(5) what barriers, to include statutory authority concerns, does the DIE face in obtaining commercially available foreign adversary intelligence from the internet and overlay networks.

Figure 6.1: 2024 NDAA OSINT language.

The language also called for the Secretary of Defense to provide an annual briefing to HASC on the Defense Intelligence Enterprise's approach to accomplishing this OSINT strategy. The briefing should specifically address the coordination of open-source data acquisition, the establishment of a collection management capability, the development of an OSINT workforce, and any barriers or concerns faced in obtaining and leveraging commercial and publicly available open source data.

A Personal Contribution

The inclusion of OSINT language in the 2024 NDAA was no accident. And while I generally try not to pat myself on the back, I'm going to let this one slide.

In 2023, I launched a personal lobbying effort to raise awareness among members of HASC and HPSCI regarding the *national security value of open-source data—specifically, dark web intelligence derived from hacked, breached, and leaked (HBL) sources.* While OSINT was already gaining traction in policy circles, this particular category of publicly available data remained largely unrecognized within the IC. That needed to change.

To help shape the legislative language, I partnered with Sean Farrell, a seasoned political strategist and former chief of staff to Senator Marsha Blackburn. Together, we drafted proposed legislative language that underscored the relevance of publicly available data on foreign adversaries—and we made sure that dark web datasets were part of the conversation.

The intent wasn't only to advocate for more structured OSINT investment, but also to formally integrate modern data sources into congressional reporting expectations.

And yes, part of the effort *was* designed to bring visibility to my company, Shadow Nexus, which provides HBL data on foreign adversaries to national security organizations. But that was never the end goal. *Shadow Nexus exists because this capability is missing from the system.* The mission was always to ensure that policymakers understood the operational impact these datasets could have across the IC and DoD.

We met with nearly every member and staff office on HASC and HPSCI, making the case for the language to be submitted. At one point, we were told—bluntly—that the language would never make it. It was too risky in a time where everyone was worried about the renewal of the Foreign Intelligence Surveillance Act (FISA). But we kept pushing.

Figure 6.2 is a list of each member who submitted or rejected our proposed language.

Out of 40 House member submission requests, 39 members *approved* our request and submitted the language to be included in the House draft. That's a pretty impressive outcome.

What emerged in the final bill (see Figure 6.1) was a hybrid of the ODNI/CIA OSINT strategy and the language we contributed. But the fact that the language made it in at all, with that kind of clarity and reach, says something important: *Congress saw it. They understood the significance and they acted on it.*

This is something I am extremely proud to have been a part of—thank you for indulging me.

Member Office	Party	Status
Mike Rogers (AL-03), Chairman	R	
Joe Wilson (SC-02)	R	Submitted
Mike Turner (OH-10)	R	Submitted
Doug Lamborn (CO-05)	R	Submitted
Robert Wittman (VA-01)	R	Submitted
Austin Scott (GA-08)	R	Submitted
Trent Kelly (MS-01)	R	Submitted
Don Bacon (NE-02)	R	Submitted
Jim Banks (IN-03)	R	Submitted
Jack Bergman (MI-01)	R	Submitted
Lisa McClain (MI-09)	R	Submitted
Ronny Jackson (TX-13)	R	Submitted
Pat Fallon (TX-04)	R	Submitted
Carlos Gimenez (FL-28)	R	Submitted
Brad Finstad (MN-01)	R	Submitted
Dale Strong (AL-05)	R	Submitted
Morgan Luttrell (TX-08)	R	Submitted
Jennifer Kiggans (VA-02)	R	Submitted
Richard McCormick (GA-06)	R	Submitted
Joe Courtney (CT-02)	D	Submitted
Donald Norcross (NJ-01)	D	Submitted
Seth Moulton (MA-06)	D	Submitted
Ro Khanna (CA-17)	D	Submitted
Andy Kim (NJ-03)	D	Submitted
Chrissy Houlahan (PA-06)	D	Submitted
Elissa Slotkin (MI-07)	D	Submitted
Mikie Sherrill (NJ-11)	D	Submitted
Jared Golden (ME-02)	D	Submitted
Jeff Jackson (NC-14)	D	Submitted
Gabe Vasquez (NM-02)	D	Submitted
Christopher Deluzio (PA-17)	D	Submitted
Jill Tokuda (HI-02)	D	Submitted
Jennifer McClellan (VA-04)	D	Submitted
Terri Sewell (AL-07)	D	Submitted
Steven Horsford (NV-04)	D	Submitted
Jimmy Panetta (CA-19)	D	Submitted
Marc Veasey (TX-33)	D	Submitted

Figure 6.2: NDAA language submission status.

Streamlining OSINT Efforts

With OSINT now embedded in formal reporting requirements to the Secretary of Defense, the focus must shift back to the broader strategic vision—namely, the joint ODNI/CIA OSINT strategy. The question is no longer whether OSINT matters—it's *how we scale and professionalize it, and do so efficiently within the constraints of existing budgets.*

One of the most consequential components of the strategy is its call for a centralized catalog of open-source data that spans across all elements of the IC. On the surface, it sounds like common sense: reduce duplication, share access, and stretch every dollar further.

And that's exactly the point. At its core, this isn't a data problem—it's a cost-efficiency problem. Right now, multiple elements across the IC are paying for the same datasets, often from the same vendor, multiple times over. That kind of redundancy wouldn't survive in the private sector.

Jason Barrett
OSINT Executive

We need to shift from a fragmented, decentralized model to one built around centralized and streamlined procurement with federated access for all IC elements.

That doesn't mean building a giant data lake. It means standing up a scalable, flexible architecture—one that gives IC elements options for how they access the data they need, without forcing every dataset into a central repository.

This approach stretches the dollar further. It reduces cloud storage costs, limits unnecessary data replication, and keeps data closer to its point of origin for longer—aligning with zero-trust and smart architecture principles. Instead of ingesting and duplicating everything, we focus on enabling access where the data already lives.

One of the most important points to emphasize in this conversation—especially from a strategic vision standpoint—is how we position the IC to truly deliver on the promise of faster, cheaper, better when it comes to OSINT.

The question is simple: *How do we stretch our dollar further, while simultaneously improving the speed in which mission elements can access data and enhance analytical capabilities?*

The OSINT community within the IC is built on two primary pillars, PAI and CAI. We've done well at the former, but we've never matured our IC-wide approach to CAI. The OSINT community never managed to own that space because the budgets were being gutted as the rest of the IC was waking up to the value of CAI.

When I started this position in October 2023, I came thinking we needed a consortium model for commercial data and platforms but needed to verify that was the right approach.

While I'm the OSINT Executive for the IC, but I'm also responsible for overseeing the implementation and reporting requirements of the IC's first policy governing access, collection, and processing of CAI. Because of this second responsibility, I've partnered with privacy and legal officers at ODNI and with all 18 elements of the IC to establish a baseline understanding of what the IC spends on CAI—from all disciplines, not just OSINT—and identify pain points that need to be addressed.

By addressing those pain points, we can streamline access for all IC elements to valuable commercial data and related capabilities, drive down costs, and establish reliable accountability and transparency. But we will also do something else critical for the IC. By delivering this capability from the OSINT Executive's office, we can start to mature the second pillar—CAI—on which OSINT ecosystem is built. And this is why we are focused on building the IC Data Consortium.

It makes perfect sense when you think about it. No software company charges five business units of an organization separately for access to the same tool. You license it once, distribute it broadly, and move on. The government should be doing the same with open-source data.

However, the implementation may not be so easy when you consider that the majority of divisions within the military, and even more so within intelligence groups, are all about secrecy. At their core, they're still all about keeping secrets—and that means they aren't used to sharing data, or even able to do so.

Melisa Stivaletti
Director, Open Source Intelligence, Guidehouse

Much of the dysfunction in today's OSINT landscape doesn't come from a lack of vision, it comes from a lack of resourcing, fractured execution, and systemic inertia.

What ODNI is doing with the consortium effort is, in many ways, exactly what the original intent behind the OSINT Executive role was meant to enable. If your mission is to protect the OSINT budget—but that budget is minimal to begin with—then building a shared consortium across the IC becomes a survival strategy. ODNI is not just protecting the budget; they are attempting to stretch it across mission sets in a way that tries to serve as many stakeholders as possible, even if imperfectly.

As it stands now, the consortium's current funding can't begin to address the scale of requirements that Open Source Enterprise (OSE) was supposed to support, let alone meet the needs of the intelligence community and their customers, the broader department of defense including the commandant commands, and perhaps most importantly, the warfighters.

Surprisingly, the overall budget for OSINT has declined, even as demand continues to rise. While the broader Intelligence Community faces critical needs and must make difficult decisions amid limited resources, OSINT is too often the first area to face cuts. This persistent underfunding creates a resource-constrained environment that forces OSINT leaders into a survival mindset—hindering the collaboration and innovation that are essential to meeting today's intelligence challenges.

Right now, it's mostly about managing scarcity, not building capacity. And unless someone upstream steps in and actually expands the resourcing model, the consortium runs the risk of becoming yet another well-intentioned layer with too little support to change outcomes.

These are all valid points, which I revisit in the next chapter when discussing the consortium in greater detail.

But for now, there's another area that's just as critical to advancing the OSINT discipline: formalizing OSINT as a professional intelligence tradecraft—and building the training pipeline to support it.

Formalizing an OSINT Tradecraft

Throughout this chapter, you've heard opinions from several experts on the importance of using OSINT in a way that allows the information collected to be considered a valuable and trusted source of information.

The IC OSINT strategy also states:[4]

> *To advance the OSINT discipline, the IC will streamline data acquisition, develop innovative technologies to collect and derive insight from open-source data, strengthen the coordination of open-source collection activities across the community, update and standardize OSINT tradecraft, and develop a highly skilled OSINT workforce. Through these efforts, we will work together to leverage the full power of OSINT to support IC analysts and operators and ensure the IC is poised to provide decision advantage for warfighters and national security policymakers.*

Sue Gordon

Former Principal Deputy Director of National Intelligence, ODNI
Former Deputy Director, NGA

What I'd add to ODNI's effort is this: We need to do more work around the craft of processing open-source information. Is there a discipline to it? Human Intelligence (HUMINT) has a discipline. Imagery Intelligence (IMINT) has a discipline. Signals Intelligence (SIGINT) has a discipline. Each of those carries its own uncertainty, but we've built frameworks to manage that uncertainty. OSINT has uncertainty too—sometimes even more—but we haven't yet given it the same level of craft or structure. That's the part that's missing.

I'd start by asking: What does processing open source really look like? How do we filter out the noise, the obvious lies, the Russian bots clogging up the narrative space? How do we distinguish the useful from the chaotic? I haven't seen enough work on that, but I'll admit—it may be happening, and I just haven't been close enough to see it. I've been out for six years now.

Then I'd have them focus on which mission areas OSINT can contribute to the most. One of those—ironically enough—might be imagery. That's part of our heritage. We know how to do imagery analysis. Commercial satellites are flying everywhere, and while we're technically ingesting some of that data, we haven't truly embraced it. But it's familiar ground. It's shareable. It's something people intuitively understand—whether it's from a KH-11 or a BlackSky Gen-3. We can assure it. We can validate it.

To echo Sue's comments, it's not enough to establish the tradecraft—you also need a standardized way to train others in it, just like we do with HUMINT, SIGINT, or any other core intelligence discipline. Without that foundation, OSINT remains fragmented and inconsistent, no matter how good the tools are.

---

[4] https://www.dni.gov/files/ODNI/documents/IC_OSINT_Strategy.pdf

Randy Nixon
Director, Open Source Enterprise, CIA

Today, OSINT tradecraft and training remains central. We have developed our own OSINT training, and across the community, DIA, Army, and others have also developed their own tailored courses. We review those offerings jointly to ensure they meet the standard. If they don't, we provide feedback and partner with them to improve.

Once the courses are approved, we distribute them across the IC. But it's not just training—we've also built out a shared website that houses course materials, instructional videos, tradecraft memos, and exemplar case studies. We're building an ecosystem where analysts can self-educate and refine their craft.

The CIA has made significant progress in sustaining and formalizing OSINT. But looking at this from the outside—and with some historical perspective—there's only so much you can do from within the same structures that sidelined it for decades. *Institutional inertia is real.* Even the best-intentioned efforts have a way of getting pulled back into legacy thinking.

That's the risk: instead of reshaping the system to support the craft, the system reshapes the craft to protect itself.

If OSINT is going to scale, it may need to push development outside the walls of its traditional agencies. That means building professional standards, consistent training, and credentialing that transcend any single organization's priorities.

In many ways, the most sustainable future for OSINT may not come from inside the IC—it may come from the community building around it.

Eliot Jardines
Former Assistant Deputy Director of National Intelligence, ODNI
Founder, OSINT Foundation

Barbara Alexander, President of the OSINT Foundation, and I both worked at the Department of Homeland Security (DHS) before moving onto other roles. During the pandemic, we watched too many webinars on OSINT, with the most consistent trait being people who had never done OSINT were speaking on behalf of the discipline.

The other was the absolute ignorance from some senior leaders about OSINT. Just a complete misunderstanding of what OSINT is, how it works, and why it matters. It became obvious: The discipline needed help.

That's where the OSINT Foundation came in.

We launched the Foundation because we saw two major problems: people with no business speaking for the profession doing exactly that—and leadership that fundamentally misunderstands both the value and the mechanics of OSINT.

Our mission is simple: to promote the discipline of OSINT inside the IC—through standards, tradecraft, advocacy, and community-building.

Presently, OSINT certification is done by 100 different companies, none of which are recognized by the government because they create their own standards. We're looking to establish a certification that doesn't cost thousands of dollars, because we don't want to do the training.

We would rather take The Project Management Institute approach, where the credential is Project Management Professional (PMP). You can go to PMP Bootcamp anywhere, but the PMI Institute independently certifies people, which is what the foundation wants to do for OSINT.

No one in the government established the PMP credential, but now every government contract requires a program manager who's PMP certified.

We want to do the same for OSINT.

Having an external OSINT training body is an important piece, but the real conversation is bigger: infrastructure, tradecraft, workforce, and scale.

For the first time, the momentum is real. OSINT has a seat at the table. The question isn't whether we need it—*it's how do we finally start treating it like it matters.*

Summary

This chapter traced OSINT's evolution—from a neglected fringe capability to a core strategic discipline within the national security and defense enterprise. Drawing on expert insights from across the IC and DoD, it explored the cultural inertia that slowed OSINT's rise, the structural reforms introduced through the CIA/ODNI and DIA strategies, and the legislative traction gained through the 2024 NDAA.

Despite clear progress, OSINT remains chronically underfunded, inconsistently trained, and often outpaced by the very users it's meant to serve.

The next chapter examines the future of OSINT and whether the IC can move beyond legacy models and fully commit to resourcing, scaling, and standardizing this discipline with the urgency the mission now demands.

The Future of OSINT

The intelligence community (IC) stands at a turning point. After years of underfunding, fragmented execution, and cultural resistance, Open-Source Intelligence (OSINT) is finally being taken seriously—not just in policy documents, but in real reform efforts.

With public and commercial data volumes exploding—and adversaries exploiting those same sources in real time—OSINT is no longer a peripheral function. It's a core capability, long overdue for modernization.

This chapter explores what the future of OSINT in the IC could look like. It examines the current push to build a centralized data consortium—one designed to give all IC elements on-demand access to OSINT tools and datasets. Is also raises a more provocative question: should OSINT have its own dedicated agency?

But this isn't just a technical challenge. It's a structural one. Reforming OSINT means confronting entrenched cultures, legacy systems, and misaligned incentives. It's going to take leadership, imagination, and political will to finish what's been started.

Finally, this chapter looks at the launch of OSINT's first dedicated congressional subcommittee—and what its emergence signals for the long-term prioritization of open-source capabilities across the national security enterprise.

This chapter features commentary from:

Jason Barrett
OSINT Executive

The views and opinions provided herein are my own and do not necessarily represent the views of the Office of the Director of National Intelligence or of the United States. (See also 5 C.F.R. § 2635.807(b).)

Sue Gordon
Former Principal Deputy Director of National Intelligence, ODNI
Former Deputy Director, NGA

Randy Nixon
Director, Open Source Enterprise, CIA

Andrew Roberts
Former OSINT Integration Center Chief, DIA

Melisa Stivaletti
Director, Open Source Intelligence, Guidehouse

Kristin Wood
Former Deputy Chief of Innovation and Technology, OSC, CIA
CEO & Co-Founder, August Interactive

William Usher
Senior Director of Intelligence, SCSP
Former Executive, CIA

Reimagining OSINT

In the previous chapters I discussed the growing importance of OSINT and the speed of which the information can provide operational advantages.

I also provided example datasets to showcase the type of open information that can be leveraged, especially when dealing with dark web data, or hacked, breached, and leaked (HBL) datasets.

When it comes to OSINT, I believe we have only scratched the surface. Despite its obvious advantages, I think there is still a fundamental lack of imagination of what can really be found—let alone what can be extracted from it.

From my own experience working with customers across both the IC and the private sector, the biggest challenge isn't access—it's imagination. The real barrier is that *people often don't know what questions to ask.*

I sometimes joke with clients: "I have the answers. I just need you to tell me the question."

That's not just a punchline—it's a real problem. Workflows have become so rigid and templated that analysis often feels like it's being brute-forced through familiar methods, even when better options exist.

And it's not just an analyst issue—this is a problem that flows downstream from leadership. Many senior leaders have an ingrained way of doing things. They stick to what they know works. But that kind of mindset can limit creativity, and ultimately breed complacency.

But here's the core issue: if leadership isn't aware of the kinds of information that is readily available for them, how can they possibly know what questions to ask?

Kristin Wood
Former Deputy Chief of Innovation and Technology, OSC, CIA
CEO & Co-Founder, August Interactive

Yeah, so you're exactly identifying the problem. People can't imagine the kinds of insights they could extract from some of these more nonlinear sources. And that's not a criticism of government folks. They're smart, but they're also busy. They're working on hard missions under pressure, and most of them don't live in the commercial data world. So, they don't know what's possible. They don't know what they don't know.

That's why having a consortium—a centralized platform—matters. If all the data is in one place, with basic discovery tools, you can just type in "Iran" and instantly get results. But what won't happen is that someone will know to go out and request that dataset in the first place—unless a vendor happens to have a relationship, or unless the customer is creative enough to imagine the use case.

We're not wired for imagination in government. We're wired for evidence, for provable outcomes. We're trained to take well-reasoned risks, but within very structured parameters. So, what the consortium can do is help reframe the conversation—it gives analysts a glimpse of the art of the possible. That's a big deal.

And maybe that means two or three subject matter experts (SMEs)—whether from industry or within government—who are embedded with the data and push out examples: daily, weekly briefs that show what the data can do. Like, "Here's what this dataset revealed about Ukraine. Now imagine using it in Malaysia." That kind of storytelling helps analysts pivot their thinking.

We've seen the consequences of failing to imagine before—9/11 is the classic case. We had data. We missed the pattern. So, this is about ensuring that kind of failure doesn't repeat, especially when it's avoidable.

Sue Gordon

Former Principal Deputy Director of National Intelligence, ODNI
Former Deputy Director, NGA

There are infinite datasets out there—and just as many things you could do with them. But too often, it becomes the classic case of: "Oh, you want to use it? Great. Now go figure out how."

That's the real gap—turning information into something operationally meaningful.

This is where OSINT really shines: not just in *what you can do*, but in *what you can know—and how fast you can* know *it*.

Let me give you an example. I'll use "Frogger"—my favorite aircraft name. We spent so much time focused on the question: What are Frogger's capabilities? And yes, that information is important. You do need to know what the platform can do. But these days, that's not enough. Now you've also got to understand how it's going to be used—what the command structure looks like, how it's deployed, who's flying it, what kind of mission profiles it supports, what's under the hood. That's where OSINT becomes a differentiator. It helps shift the focus from definitions to decisions.

It's also about asking the right questions.

We don't have to operate with just open intelligence—but the addition of open intelligence gets you *much faster to insight*—because it gets you *much faster to use.*

I would argue that the information we used to collect was the purpose of understanding capability—*what could an adversary do*? But OSINT shifts that lens. It pushes us closer to use and implementation.

Now we can ask: how is that capability actually employed, by whom, and under what conditions? That's where you begin to see *signs of intent.* What they're likely to do, and why—*and that's the holy grail.*

Signals of Intent

I want to share a personal story that I think captures the essence of Sue's comment. When working with open-source intelligence—especially dark web and HBL data—the volume of incoming information can be overwhelming. It often feels like trying to drink from a firehose.

During the interview, I had a lightbulb moment. It came as we were discussing her point about what you can do with OSINT, what you can know, and the speed at which you can know it.

I responded with an example from my own experience—something that, to me, underscored her point from a very practical lens.

As an example, internal company and government documents are often leaked online, especially from ransomware groups. A few months ago, I downloaded thousands of confidential documents leaked from a government organization in Iran. The documents were in Farsi, and at the time, I didn't have the bandwidth to process them.

Recently, I decided to revisit the dataset. I picked a few documents at random and asked ChatGPT to translate and summarize them. The results were surprising (see Figure 7.1).

1315.pdf: This confidential letter from the Iranian Presidential Office to the Central Bank, also copied to the Armed Forces General Staff, concerns the sale of foreign currency from oil revenues allocated for strengthening defense capabilities, emphasizing cooperation within the government's foreign exchange policies.

1401_9_26_تلفني_تماس_در_مذاكرات_پيشنهادي_محورهاي.pdf: This document outlines proposed talking points for a phone call between the Iranian Foreign Minister, Amir Abdollahian, and the Belarusian Foreign Minister, Sergey Aleinik, focusing on strengthening bilateral relations, countering illegal sanctions, and discussing the Ukraine conflict.

10963.pdf: This highly confidential document from the Presidential Office's Deputy for Banking and Special Pursuits forwards a report from the Supreme National Security Council concerning security issues in Razavi Khorasan Province, prepared by the Provincial Intelligence Office for the President's visit.

Title: Iranian Legal and International Affairs Meeting on High-Profile Cases

Summary: This document summarizes a highly confidential meeting held by the Iranian Presidential Center for International Legal Affairs to discuss the legal proceedings related to the assassination of General Qassem Soleimani, and the cases of Asadullah Asadi and Hamid Noury. The meeting addressed updates on international legal actions, diplomatic efforts, and future strategies for these cases.

Figure 7.1: Documents leaked from a government organization in Iran.

These documents had just been sitting on my hard drive—forgotten and unused. But when I first translated them, my eyes lit up.

Think of the intelligence value that could come from knowing this information ahead of time—even now, after the fact, knowing what our adversaries were discussing in private is incredibly powerful.

Sue Gordon
Former Principal Deputy Director of National Intelligence, ODNI
Former Deputy Director, NGA

I think I'm going to double down on this—there is much information that we treat as chaff that really is relevant to understanding use and intent. And, to me, this kind of document is far more valuable than, for example, knowing the number of air defense systems in play. This information is much more relevant to a certain kind of planning and a different level of awareness.

This type of data is super interesting in terms of mission opportunity, not just data capability. I think you've got a lot here…

Validation is always a good feeling—especially coming from someone as accomplished as Sue, whom I hold in such high regard.

With that, it's time to pivot from what OSINT could be to how we start building toward that vision. I have demonstrated some of the untapped value, speed, and strategic utility of OSINT. Recognizing that value is only the first step.

Now the question is: How do we operationalize that potential? How do we build an architecture that enables discovery, intent, and action at scale?

A Path Forward

As momentum continues to build around OSINT's strategic utility and mission impact, two distinct—but complementary—schools of thought have emerged on how best to address the discipline's long-standing challenges.

The first, a project already in development within ODNI, is a centralized consortium designed to make commercial tools and datasets more accessible across the IC in a way that reduces overheads by eliminating duplicative procurement.

The second is a more ambitious proposal: the creation of a dedicated OSINT agency that would oversee the acquisition, integration, and governance of open-source intelligence across the enterprise.

These models aren't mutually exclusive. One addresses how we acquire and distribute data; the other rethinks where OSINT should live within the intelligence ecosystem. Both reflect a growing consensus that the old fragmented and underfunded model can't keep up with today's information environment.

What follows is a closer look at each approach, with added perspectives from those on the front lines.

Building an IC Data Consortium

The information environment has fundamentally changed. We're operating in an era where the volume of public and commercially available data has exploded—and with it, the intelligence community now has an opportunity not just to improve how it collects information, but to completely rethink how it ingests, processes, and extracts value from data at scale.

To enable that shift, the Office of the Director of National Intelligence (ODNI) is standing up a new kind of acquisition consortium—one where IC elements can browse, access, and license commercial datasets without navigating the usual labyrinth of government procurement.

The consortium's core goal is straightforward: increase OSINT tool and data availability across the IC by reducing duplicative purchases and enabling shared access. Right now, different elements are often buying the same datasets multiple times—sometimes from the same vendor. That kind of redundancy isn't just inefficient. It's expensive—and unsustainable.

In the commercial world, particularly among threat intelligence providers, there's a familiar rule of thumb: most vendors are offering the same 80 percent of the data. The real value is in the remaining 20 percent—the proprietary, hard-to-access, tradecraft-driven sources that fill in the gaps and make the difference.

Take breached credentials, for example. Nearly every vendor scrapes the same Telegram channels, pulls from open leaks, or collects logs from the usual infostealer malware. That overlap is unavoidable. But what separates one provider from another is their "secret sauce"—that unique 20 percent that no one else has.

True analysis often requires both. You need the shared baseline and the exclusive edge.

The consortium aims to bring both under one roof, offering centralized access, easier procurement, and frictionless integration at mission speed.

Jason Barrett
OSINT Executive

If you look at the way the IC is allocating resources, there's a huge opportunity for growth that's responsible and saves money.

This is the right moment for the IC to step back and ask a fundamental question: What are we trying to accomplish?

At its core, intelligence is a business—and our product is knowledge. But knowledge without credibility means very little. What we are offering is the credibility that comes with that knowledge.

For example, we can generate the vast majority of our knowledge and insight from open sources, and our customers don't care where we get it. What they do care about, however, is accuracy and credibility. And if we can do that using open source and save money, we should be thinking about that.

One of the areas with the most room for growth is how we engage with commercial data providers. We're rethinking the acquisition model to avoid buying the same data multiple times. It's not just about signing individual contracts anymore—it's about building a single access point that can scale across hundreds of vendors. If we want to make smarter use of our resources, we need to shift how we procure, verify, and integrate data—and ensure we're acquiring what actually meets mission needs.

It's really important that we think differently about how we are using our resources to acquire the information we need, and that we are doing our due diligence to ensure that the information we are getting is actually what we need.

We need to transform how we obtain, use, and mange Public and Commercially Available Information (CAI). We need to keep the data where it is, and not bring it in bulk. We need to lay the foundation for an OSINT Enterprise that sits shoulder-to-shoulder with industry and leverages their platforms and their data on a day-to-day basis, so that we're leveraging the best that America and our allies have to offer. In addition, we need to serve as a test bed for emerging technology in this space, so that the rest of the IC, as they need to go through important security protocols, can see how certain capabilities can work for them while they go through that process.

The is a huge opportunity. Technology is going to enable us to innovate within the OSINT space faster than anywhere else.

We have to think thoughtfully about how we acquire this information and how we focus on accessing where it's at instead of bringing it in in bulk, and then we need to think about what that looks like from an acquisition perspective.

We can do a lot of this work with partners in the nonprofit and industry space that enable us to better protect privacy while enabling us to better attain the information we need while keeping storage costs low within the IC ecosystem.

Today, the IC operates across a fragmented software landscape. Each agency or mission center often uses its own tools, platforms, and data streams—systems that were never designed to share information across organizational lines. On top of that, multiple OSINT and analytics vendors are feeding data into the IC in parallel, often via application platform interfaces (APIs) or through proprietary applications—many offering similar capabilities, with considerable overlap.

Creating a Centralized Catalog

What's missing though is a unified model. A centralized catalog—a single, federated repository of open-source data and commercial tool access—would radically streamline how analysts work. Instead of jumping between tools or ingesting the same data across silos, analysts could browse a common catalog and pull exactly what they need, when they need it—whether that's a raw data feed, API access, or an on-demand license to use a specialized platform.

Jason Barrett
OSINT Executive

As we work towards a common indexing of all open-source PAI and CAI, we can't lose sight of the value proposition OSINT offers and the opportunity it has to deliver decision advantage in faster, cheaper, and better methods. *How do we really walk the talk, when it comes to faster, cheaper, better?*

Can we establish a storefront where commercial options are available for any IC element to use to achieve mission in a transparent, auditable, and accountable way?

It would be much more than a catalog—but the idea is similar: a range of access pathways that lets end users select what makes the most sense for their operational needs. What makes sense is a flexible model—one that offers multiple, mission-driven options for accessing data and tools, without forcing every user into a one-size-fits-all solution.

IC officers should be able to access the data and services they need, when they need them. That includes querying in place when they need to—whether that's an *API call* or some other mechanism. Maybe they want to *log in to a platform* to do basic research, which is more of a traditional software license approach for many vendors.

For many vendors, they provide a traditional software license model via a platform that can integrate a variety of data sources, enabling analysts to go on and do the research that they're looking for.

And in cases where API calls or platform access won't meet mission requirements, there is a third option to account for: *raw data access.*

In those cases, it makes sense to ingest data directly, keep it within IC systems, and build internal workflows that enable multiple tools or elements to leverage it in place. Of course, they IC will need to architect solutions so that different elements of the IC can all access that data—but that kind of architectural flexibility is essential if we're serious about building toward future-ready OSINT infrastructure.

Once the customer has decided on the pathway that's right for them, we could provide additional resources so that many others in the community have the ability to gain access to the same data. It would enable us to apply resourcing in a smarter way, but it also doesn't create a centralized data lake. It's federated access.

But this is where we hit a persistent problem: *Enterprise licensing models often don't match the real-world usage or scale of demand.* What we need is a smarter, more modern acquisition approach—one that can dynamically scale licensing ceilings based on actual demand. If usage is low, we scale down. If the demand signal surges, there should be the ability to scale up. That flexibility is critical.

That's why we need to really modernize our approach away from the traditional way of thinking about how we can access data. We can apply a much smarter approach that enables us to determine whether the platforms are being used at the rate at which we assumed they would be. And if they're not, we can lower the ceiling—at the same time, if the demand signal is higher, we can raise the ceiling.

Until we can get to a place that enables users to drive demand, we will ultimately get stuck with a single vendor or just a handful of the same vendors—and to me, that breeds complacency and potentially much fewer options than the analysts and the collectors are looking for.

There's a reason why companies like JP Morgan and Pfizer have consolidated their procurement from a data perspective in certain places; it enables them to get efficiencies that they weren't getting in a decentralized procurement construct. This model allows them to quickly apply solutions at scale much faster, and we need to think about how we provide access to data much more smartly and efficiently as we go forward.

Once it is fully up and running, the Consortium would then feed into a single AI-enabled data-and-tool-on-demand platform—one that empowers each of the IC elements to access the tools and data they need—on their terms—under a unified contracting framework that supports hundreds of vendors without excessive overhead.

This is how we unlock true efficiency, both in terms of cost control and mission responsiveness. If we get this right, the IC stands to save tens—if not hundreds—of millions of dollars while dramatically expanding capability across the enterprise.

The strategy makes sense. And the idea of turning on access to software on-demand isn't new. The modern SaaS model has been around since the late 1990s. For example, with my Office 365 subscription, if I want to use Visio, I can turn it on and pay for the monthly license, then turn it off when I'm done. It's simple and effective.

The idea of consolidating raw data across an enterprise isn't a new concept, either. As open-source and commercially available data volumes began to explode, the need to consolidate efforts and streamline spending was obvious to anyone paying attention.

The challenge was never about recognizing the problem—it was always about *execution*. Integrating that vision across the entire IC, with its fragmented systems, competing priorities, and siloed budgets, has been the real obstacle from the start.

Andrew Roberts
Former OSINT Integration Center Chief, DIA

What Jason Barrett and ODNI are doing now with the consortium is similar to what John Sherman and I were trying to do back in 2016. It wasn't just about buying tools—it was about training, standards, personnel exchanges, and shared datasets. The National Open Source Committee became the vehicle for making those decisions with the future in mind.

Budgeting varied wildly. Some folks knew how to work the system. Others didn't. Part of my job was mentoring teams on how to write defensible budget justifications. The services, in particular, could be cagey. "Why is Defense Intelligence Agency (DIA) asking about our OSINT spend?" It was a trust issue.

Toward the end of my tenure, however, I felt like we were finally synchronizing. We're still not fully integrated, but we're significantly better than where we started.

Kristin Wood

Former Deputy Chief of Innovation and Technology, OSC, CIA
CEO & Co-Founder, August Interactive

William Usher and I co-authored a paper on a data consortium that laid out its broader use cases. What we argued—and what still holds—is that the debate around open source often feels almost religious in nature. It's like Protestant versus Catholic: Do you believe in a standalone open-source agency, or do you believe every agency should have its own embedded OSINT component?

To me, that misses the bigger point. Government tends to gravitate toward bureaucratic solutions—creating new entities, structures, or organizations to solve enduring problems. Sometimes, that's necessary. In areas like hypersonics where you've got a complex vendor landscape, if we didn't have internal government talent, we wouldn't be able to partner effectively with industry. But open source is different. The value now largely comes from the outside. And what you can do inside government—when it's supported and enabled by industry—is exponentially more powerful than trying to build it all internally.

This isn't just a data play—it's a shift in how government and industry partner. That's why I've focused so much on the idea of a consortium—something modeled after Non-Quantitative Treatment Limitations (NQTL), where government defines its requirements, and a nonprofit intermediary goes out and finds the commercial data to meet them.

The key is having standardized licensing, consistent terms of use, and a vetted pool of providers—not just the biggest names.

It gives smaller vendors a seat at the table, and more importantly, it gives them a stable, predictable revenue stream.

For the government, it's also a major efficiency gain. You buy the data once, centrally, and make it available across the system. Sure, the upfront price may be higher because more users will need access—but that access is immediate, standardized, and scalable. The cost models I saw made a compelling case for long-term savings across the national security enterprise.

And most importantly, it makes the data actionable.

The hardest part isn't always access—it's knowing what questions to ask in the first place. That's a creativity problem. Most government analysts aren't immersed in the commercial data ecosystem. They don't know what's out there, so they don't know what's possible. They're busy trying to solve hard problems; they don't have time to go browsing vendor catalogs.

That's where I think the consortium model works. You don't need every analyst to be imaginative. You need a handful of experts—either from government or industry—curating use cases and sending out a daily or weekly digest: "Here's what this dataset can show you about Ukraine. Imagine what it could do for Malaysia." You're making the art of the possible visible. A consortium model does exactly that—it aligns the incentives, reduces friction, and gets critical data into the right hands faster.

That's what this is really about: speed, access, and mission impact.

Creating Disruption

Despite its clear advantages, the consortium model represents a radical departure from how the IC traditionally operates. It challenges deeply embedded norms—systems built around ownership, control, and isolation. Moving to a shared model isn't just about access or infrastructure—it's a mindset shift. It forces the IC to rethink not just where data lives, but how it's valued, shared, and operationalized across missions. And that's not a technical challenge. It's a cultural one.

Randy Nixon
Director, Open Source Enterprise, CIA

I'm rooting for the consortium model. Only time will tell whether ODNI's efforts there will ultimately work.

A couple of things to watch: First, the vast majority of OSINT—both publicly and commercially available information—is already being collected by OSE. Other agencies may have the funding, but OSE is doing the bulk of the execution right now. Naturally, those agencies are going to want to contribute, and they'll be asking whether companies will sell data more cheaply through the consortium than they already do to us directly. I don't have the answer to that yet—it's too early. But I will say this: the private sector is going to have a major vote in whether this model succeeds. If they see it as a viable on-ramp into the IC, they'll support it. If not, it's going to be an uphill climb.

That also raises a practical question about whether OSE can use data from companies that might be able to get into the consortium but can't get into OSC directly. And the answer really depends on the specifics of the contract—how it's structured, what the licensing terms are, and how usage is defined. A lot of what we need to do with data requires integrating it into our tools, automating processing, and running analysis at scale. If the data license restricts access—say, to just ten users at a time—that's not going to work for us. We need enterprise-grade access. So again, it comes down to the terms of the deal.

Internal friction isn't the only hurdle. As Randy points out, there's still an open question about how the private sector will respond to this shift. Many companies have built business models around reselling the same data to multiple IC elements—and in some cases, to multiple departments within a single agency. A consortium model changes that. Vendors accustomed to charging separately for every end user will now have to grapple with a single price that enables distribution across the enterprise.

Software-as-a-service (SaaS) providers face a similar reckoning. Tools that once fetched millions in agency-specific license fees may now need to be offered in more flexible, on-demand formats. For some, that's an existential threat.

For others, *it's an opportunity—a chance to compete with larger, more traditional vendors* by scaling differently, streamlining pricing, and embedding themselves in the next generation of OSINT infrastructure.

When it comes to data-on-demand and bulk data acquisition models for the entire IC, I personally believe we're heading toward a data licensing model—something closer to what we've already seen in the entertainment industry. The media licensing model has been tried, tested, and perfected. So why not apply the same logic to data?

When was the last time you paid for a song or album? That model works. Why should data be any different?

Yes, there are challenges. And no, I don't believe an institution as ingrained in the past as the intelligence community is going to shift without a monumental accelerant.

I love disruption.

The truth is, *I love seeing established norms challenged*—turned upside down—because that's where *real opportunity lives.*

Disruption opens the door for groundbreaking advancements and gives small businesses a chance to break in, compete, and carve out a foothold in ecosystems long dominated by a handful of entrenched players.

Yes, the consortium has an uphill battle. But then again, disruption always does. In this case, ODNI isn't reinventing the wheel. They are taking a model that already works—and one that people are very familiar with—and applying it to an institution that is grossly outdated.

That sounds like a recipe for success.

But even if the consortium succeeds in modernizing procurement and centralizing access to commercial data, the harder problem remains: *actually using it to make better decisions.*

Operationalizing Reform

Technology alone isn't enough. Real reform depends on changing the mindset—how the IC thinks about data, integrates it, and aligns it with mission outcomes. That means designing for use, not just access.

Even if we fix the infrastructure, the real challenge may be harder to solve: changing how the intelligence community thinks about data, outcomes, and its operational utility. This isn't just about standing up a consortium or writing a new strategy. It's about breaking old habits—moving away from stagnant process and toward systems that prioritize use, mission outcomes, and strategic intent.

Sue Gordon
Former Principal Deputy Director of National Intelligence, ODNI
Former Deputy Director, NGA

I think the consortium is in the direction of goodness. But it's way too slow. It's way too careful. It's way too "well this is weird and different."

And none of it describes the outcome it's going to yield. Is it going to make assessments faster? More usable by the coalition? Is it going to offload cost? What is it actually going to do? Until there's a clear reason for it—and a way to measure its effectiveness—it just feels like an academic exercise.

Now, sure, doing it in some kind of organized fashion is better than chaos. And yes, it does suggest that the executive agent model—where the CIA was responsible—hasn't worked. So, credit to ODNI for trying something different.

But still, what's it doing?

I don't need a consortium on open source. *I need to be able to do the mission better.* And right now, I don't see a single word in that effort that tells me how you go from building a collective to delivering a better operational outcome.

To ODNI's credit, the consortium is a step forward. The ODNI taking on the mission to do this in a more deliberate, less scattershot way—well, notionally, that's a lot like eyesight, right? "Do commonly that which can be commonly done." And as an extension of that philosophy, there's definitely value.

This isn't a critique—it's just the reality. The IC has historically treated open-source data as supplemental, not integral—You won't hear any argument from anyone on that point.

You've heard stories throughout this book from experts who had to fight just to use open data alongside SIGINT or HUMINT, even when it could have closed critical gaps faster. The issue isn't access—it's trust.

The system is built to value classification, not accuracy. And in a world where the most useful signals often appear first in unclassified form, that's not just a cultural flaw—it's a mission risk.

Without a clear strategy for integration—and the right tooling to match—even the most valuable data may not find its way to its appropriate target. Poor implementation doesn't just slow things down. *It buries critical insights before they are even seen.*

Sue Gordon

Former Principal Deputy Director of National Intelligence, ODNI
Former Deputy Director, NGA

Right now, what we're doing is throwing money at a bunch of interesting datasets—often funded with operational dollars—but they're too hard to use. They don't get integrated with anything else. They're disconnected. And so they sit there. Neat? Sure. But operationally? They do nothing.

So unless you've envisioned the outcome, planned for the outcome, and measured the outcome, all you've done is check a box. You may have saved a little money in theory, but if that data never gets used, you've actually wasted more than you've saved.

I still don't think we've fully embraced what this data can do—how it can change missions, what new capabilities become possible when you start treating all the world's data as part of the intelligence picture. But that requires flipping the model. *Data should drive the system—not the other way around.*

I will give you an example: I get approached by ten companies a day pitching a cool dataset. Now there's a whole economy out there of people finding interesting datasets. Some of them are genuinely interesting, but they're just not usable.

Does the China Mission Center have the budget to clean that up? Is the chief intelligence officer (CIO) supposed to figure out how to make it useful? That's not what their money's for.

So my first question is always, how is it going to get used? If mission outcome isn't your guiding metric, then you haven't actually taken the work far enough—to savings, to integration, and to real impact.

We're still thinking of open data as something to bring in, instead of as something we want to use. And that's where we need to go next. It's the same issue I have with cutting commercial data—this idea that it's a "nice to have." It's not; it's one of many. And unless you build the machine that can actually use it, you're wasting the opportunity.

Gaps in imagination and the inability to extract relevant insights are real problems—but they're solvable. With time and the right analysts, I believe those challenges will work themselves out.

But before that can even happen, there is a more persistent and more structural hurdle that continues to stall the adoption of OSINT: *budget.*

The tension that's defined OSINT's recent history—between ambition and capacity—is exactly where the mission sits today. Everyone agrees the need is growing. But the budgets haven't caught up.

No matter how strong the strategy or how clear the need, *OSINT has rarely been funded at the level its mission actually demands.*

Streamlining the OSINT Budget

Building a comprehensive budget to stand up and sustain a consortium starts with answering two seemingly simple questions: *What is the IC already spending on OSINT? And where are the gaps?*

But that's easier said than done.

When groups have a defensive posture—the kind where they hide their true capabilities for fear of budget cuts—it becomes nearly impossible to gauge the scale of investment required or to surface critical gaps that remain unaddressed.

Melisa Stivaletti
Director, Open Source Intelligence, Guidehouse

There are countless operators across the IC who need open-source tools and data to do their jobs. They're not sitting around waiting for Washington to solve the problem. They're taking matters into their own hands, purchasing what they need independently and often rebranding it internally to avoid interference or out of fear of the funds being reappropriated.

The reality is, we have no comprehensive understanding of how much the IC actually spends on open-source tools and data. It's scattered and hidden—disguised under different labels—because people are protecting their capabilities from being taken away.

This is exactly where anyone trying to centralize OSINT efforts is going to run into major challenges. If there's any delay between when a capability is procured and when the operator actually gets access to it, the operator will find another way.

They'll buy it themselves. In this environment, centralization often conflicts with the need for speed. And if you force people to choose, speed will always win. It's a fundamental tension that needs to be acknowledged, not ignored.

One of the biggest lessons I've learned is: *If you want to serve operators effectively, you have to ask them what they actually need*—not just show up and steal their cookies, so to speak.

We have to put the customer first. Whether it's the warfighter, the policymaker, or the supply chain analyst trying to secure critical components, everything must start with their needs. If you're serious about rebuilding or modernizing the open-source enterprise, customer requirements have to be your foundation.

At the end of the day, if you don't understand your customers, you're just throwing pennies at problems you don't fully understand.

How can OSINT be properly funded when the very groups that rely on it are hesitant to admit what they're already spending?

Despite being the "INT of first resort," OSINT budgets remain paper thin. And how do you make the case to invest more when the enterprise doesn't even have a clear picture of what it actually needs?

William Usher
Senior Director of Intelligence, SCSP
Former Executive, CIA

Regarding the concern that organizations are hesitant to disclose their OSINT budgets for fear of being cannibalized—yes, that's absolutely happening. And it's part of the broader "iron triangle"—*a mutually beneficial relationship between congressional committees, special interest groups, and regulatory agencies*—that reinforces the federated model we've been stuck with. OSINT remains largely under the control of its host organizations.

The Department of the Army, for example, wants to use its OSINT budget to support Army-specific missions. Special Operations Command (SOCOM) has made meaningful investments in its own in-house open-source capabilities—and understandably, they don't want those resources stripped away or centralized if it means losing tailored support.

I get that logic. No one wants to give up autonomy if it risks diluting mission relevance or slowing responsiveness.

But here's the problem: The taxpayer loses. We end up paying far more than we should for duplicative access to the same information. Worse, we miss the opportunity to unify and integrate those data streams in ways that benefit the entire IC.

If we could consolidate access to open-source data—under a structure that enables shared tools, shared vetting, and centralized processing—we could do some truly powerful things, especially when combined with AI and advanced analytic frameworks. The potential value is enormous, but we won't unlock it until we move beyond the fragmented status quo.

Consolidating access under a single structure aligns closely with the consortium model—but it also raises a deeper, more fundamental question. Would OSINT's be better served by standing up its own dedicated agency?

Do We Need an Open Source Agency?

Another proposed solution to the problem of fixing OSINT is the creation of a standalone Open Source Agency (OSA). In a paper published in *Studies in Intelligence*, William Usher made a compelling case for consolidating all OSINT programs and resources under a single, purpose-built entity. According to Usher, the OSA's core mission would be to rapidly acquire, curate, and distribute commercially and publicly available datasets across the IC.

He argued that this would be the most effective path toward securing dedicated OSINT funding, building a professional cadre of officers skilled in navigating the open-source domain, and giving open source a more authoritative role in shaping how the IC meets its intelligence requirements.

The agency would serve as a true one-stop shop for commercial vendors, responsible for setting data standards, evaluating tools, and managing integration. Much like National Reconnaissance Office (NRO) oversees overhead collection and the National Security Agency (NSA) governs SIGINT, OSA would function as the centralized authority for open-source activity—approving, guiding, and harmonizing OSINT efforts across agencies.[1]

As it matures, OSA could also take on its own analytical missions, create unclassified collaboration spaces with domestic and foreign partners, and support training programs to incorporate OSINT into all-source workflows.

William Usher
Senior Director of Intelligence, SCSP
Former Executive, CIA

When it comes to ODIN's consortium and my proposal for a separate OSINT organization, I don't see them as competing concepts—they should be pursued in tandem. Just to clarify, the recommendation I've put forward originated from a series of conversations I had with Kristin Wood. We're encouraged to see that ODNI seems to be adopting parts of this approach.

Let me break it into two parts: the OSINT agency and the consortium. We see these as complementary.

First, I believe we need to establish a dedicated OSINT agency—an entity reattached to ODNI as a standalone organization. I would start by pulling billets from OSE and OSIC to serve as the foundation of this new entity. Its mission would be to serve as the functional manager for open-source intelligence—just as the CIA serves as the functional manager for HUMINT.

---

[1] http://cia.gov/resources/csi/static/Unclassified-Extracts-Studies-68-3-September-2024.pdf

Now, technically, the DCIA is the functional manager for OSINT, but I would argue that this responsibility should be formally removed from the CIA and handed to this new OSINT agency. Its role would be to bring publicly and commercially available information into the IC in a structured, strategic way. Think of it the way the National Reconnaissance Office (NRO) supports the National Geospatial Agency (NGA)—NRO builds and operates the collection systems, while NGA transforms that data into actionable insights. This OSINT agency would serve a similar backend integration role.

To operationalize that mission, we propose establishing a 501(c)(3) nonprofit—a consortium that lives entirely in the unclassified space. Yes, they'd have a few offices in the back with SIPRNet and JWICS access, but most of their work would happen on unclassified systems, dealing with unclassified data.

They would interface directly with the growing market of private-sector data vendors and analytic providers—people like you. The idea is to create a one-stop shop for external vendors who want to sell their data or analytic services to the IC. This wouldn't only streamline procurement but also help the government rationalize its spending across datasets.

Right now, as you know, there are vendors selling the same dataset—or the same API—dozens or even hundreds of times to different government entities. A centralized consortium could eliminate that redundancy, reduce costs, and standardize quality control. They'd know which datasets are reliable, which vendors are trustworthy, what conforms to U.S. law in terms of data sourcing, and what needs to be scrubbed to protect privacy. They could then make that data available to the NSA, DIA, or any other IC element in a form ready to be processed—whether by analysts or AI systems.

So again, the two models—OSINT agency and consortium—go hand in hand.

The implementation currently proposed by ODNI is a slightly modified version of this vision. ODNI's OSINT Executive office is managing the consortium directly and selecting vendors to provide APIs, essentially centralizing that function under his leadership. It's not quite what we originally proposed, but it's close—and I think it's a solid initiative.

We fully support it and wish it success.

Melisa Stivaletti

Director, Open Source Intelligence, Guidehouse

OSINT is everywhere—It's ubiquitous across the U.S. government. You could theoretically consolidate every open-source group into a single organization and call it the Open Source Agency, but these groups would inevitably reconstitute themselves across agencies. *If you pull them out, they will simply reappear.*

Why? Because the mission *demands* embedded open-source capability. You can't pull it all into a new structure without breaking what already works. It becomes a self-licking ice cream cone—a new bureaucracy orbiting itself.

If you're going to build something new, you have to approach it with an "and" mindset, not an "or" mindset. *You need to enhance existing capabilities, not replace them.* But so far, I haven't seen the necessary willingness from those who control the budgets to think that way.

What I keep telling anyone who will listen is this: *Before we sink billions into building an entirely new agency, why don't we first properly fund the OSINT elements that already exist and see what happens?*

Do I believe open source needs agency-level prioritization and scale? Absolutely. Because the truth is: *Open source isn't the future of intelligence—it's already the present.*

The traditional classified intelligence disciplines are declining. The only question left is whether the IC will evolve fast enough to keep up with it.

We need more OSINT capability—there's no question about that. If the IC is serious about OSINT reform, the solution isn't just structure.

Before creating something massive, bureaucratic, and expensive, let's do the simple thing first: *fully fund the open-source units we already have.*

This is one of the rare problems where applying money, smartly and deliberately, can actually solve it.

Randy Nixon
Director, Open Source Enterprise, CIA

I think that creating a separate OSINT agency is both complex and potentially very disruptive. If Congress wants to consider that path, there are three issues they really need to weigh carefully.

First, OSC currently does most of the collection for the CIA and directly supports their operational and analytic missions. If the plan is to stand up a new agency, are you going to pull OSC out of the CIA to form the backbone of it? Or are you pulling OSIC from DIA, even though OSIC supports warfighter missions every day? And if you do that, do the CIA and DIA just turn around and recreate those same capabilities internally—duplicating the effort? Or do they actually trust this new agency to meet their mission needs? That's not a small gamble.

Second, the infrastructure alone is no small thing. If OSC were removed from its current home, it would take tens of millions of dollars just to rebuild the collection infrastructure elsewhere. The systems, workflows, and access points we have in place today took years to develop. Starting from scratch would mean significant delays and funding.

And third, there's the matter of authorities. OSC, being part of the CIA, benefits from specific collection authorities that any standalone agency would need to replicate—and that's not a given.

When people talk about standing up a new agency, I think they often miss how effective the federated model already is.

> The director of the CIA (D/CIA) is the functional manager for OSINT, just as he is for HUMINT, and that authority flows down to the Director of OSC for day-to-day execution. We run the community through the National Open Source Committee (NOSC), supported by subcommittees and deep coordination with DIA, OSIC, and the rest of the IC.
>
> *If Congress or any agency wants more OSINT, they don't need a new agency to make that happen. They can increase their resourcing, requirements, and prioritization within the existing structure.*
>
> I'd argue they ought to try that first—optimize the model we already have—before jumping to create something entirely new.

While the idea of a standalone open-source agency remains just that—a theory—the momentum behind OSINT continues to build.

The future shape of that momentum—whether through a shared consortium, a dedicated agency, or something in between—is still up for debate. But one thing is certain: *the status quo is no longer tenable.* What was once a fringe capability is now being treated as a national priority.

And in 2025, that shift became official. For the first time, Congress acknowledged that OSINT had outgrown its support role by establishing a dedicated subcommittee under the House Permanent Select Committee on Intelligence (HPSCI)—a formal recognition that open-source intelligence now warrants focused oversight, sustained investment, and strategic direction.

HPSCI OSINT Subcommittee

In early 2025, the House Permanent Select Committee on Intelligence (HPSCI) formally created the Open-Source Intelligence (OSINT) Subcommittee to provide dedicated legislative and oversight attention to OSINT initiatives across the intelligence community.[2]

Led by chairwoman Ann Wagner (MO) and ranking member Chrissy Houlahan (PA), the subcommittee's mission is to examine programs, policies, budgets, and operations of all IC elements related to the collection, use, and dissemination of open-source intelligence.

For the first time, OSINT isn't just being recognized in strategy documents—it's being given a dedicated voice on the Hill.

Whether this subcommittee becomes the mechanism for fixing what's long been broken remains to be seen. At a minimum, it signals that Congress is finally starting to take OSINT seriously—not just as a capability, but as a discipline worthy of focused oversight, investment, and reform.

---

[2] https://intelligence.house.gov/news/documentsingle.aspx?DocumentID=1502&utm_source=chatgpt.com

Melisa Stivaletti

Director, Open Source Intelligence, Guidehouse

HPSCI has established its first ever subcommittee dedicated solely to OSINT—a major milestone for the discipline. It marks the first time open-source intelligence has been recognized as having enough legitimacy to warrant its own dedicated legislative oversight body.

For years, OSINT has been professionalized in strategy documents and elevated in rhetoric, but this move signals something more tangible: Congress is finally ready to put resources behind it. Not just the Department of Defense (DoD) or the IC but Congress. The creation of this subcommittee tells us the legislative branch is taking OSINT seriously.

That's critical, because for too long, open source has been asked to do more with less. And while the community has managed to stretch every dollar, that model isn't sustainable. There is a breaking point on the near horizon, and the creation of the subcommittee couldn't have come at a better time.

This subcommittee gives OSINT a dedicated voice on the Hill—one that's long overdue.

William Usher

Senior Director of Intelligence, SCSP
Former Executive, CIA

I've spoken with the OSINT Subcommittee under HPSCI, and I think it's a positive step that the committee has stood up this group. The staff and members I've engaged with seem genuinely committed to doing something meaningful. That said, as someone now outside of government viewing things from the outside looking in, I can tell you— it's a very tough budget environment.

I have no doubt they'll develop some strong ideas and recommendations. What remains to be seen is *how many of those will actually make it into appropriations legislation*. That's the key question.

I'm also not sure how they view our proposal to create a standalone OSINT agency. From what I can gather, there does seem to be support—at least in principle—for the consortium model and for the broader goal of leveraging commercially available information more effectively.

As for how they plan to get there, I think it's still very much in flux.

Following her appointment as chair of the new OSINT subcommittee, Congresswoman Ann Wagner released the following statement:[3]

Open-source intelligence is essential for a wide audience of policymakers, decisionmakers, and other consumers who gain situational awareness without having to rely on classified or restricted sources. Our adversaries are working together now more than ever before

[3] https://wagner.house.gov/media-center/press-releases/ann-wagner-appointed-lead-new-osint-subcommittee-house-intelligence

and for that reason they pose an even greater threat to the United States. Open-source intelligence helps provide a better understanding of the volatile playing field we find ourselves in.

Our national security depends on our intelligence community vigilantly collecting and protecting sensitive information while deterring our enemies' aggressive intelligence campaigns against the United States. I look forward to working to make certain there is a greater focus on the open-source community to advance appropriate policy and governance, resources, and standardized training and tradecraft to ensure OSINT has the capabilities and capacity to help protect us. Our national security remains one of my highest priorities.

Having met with Chair Wagner and seen firsthand what she's been able to accomplish, from financial reform to her tireless work combatting online sex trafficking, I have no doubt she can be a powerhouse in Washington.

I can't think of anyone better positioned to take on the entrenched problems facing OSINT—and to do it with the kind of rigor and tenacity needed to cut through the existing dogma and realize OSINT for what it truly is—*the future of intelligence.*

That said, the road ahead won't be easy.

OSINT remains mired in institutional friction, budgetary inertia, and deep-rooted cultural resistance. These problems won't disappear overnight. But for the first time, we have a subcommittee built to tackle them head-on—and that's a meaningful step forward.

Randy Nixon
Director, Open Source Enterprise, CIA

I've met with the HPSCI OSINT subcommittee multiple times. They've devoted considerable time and attention to understanding this space. In fact, the entire committee came out to visit us in person to see firsthand how our capabilities operate. They've had full demonstrations of our platforms across both the high and low side environments.

Over the past four months, they've been doing deep, substantive work. They've spoken with us extensively, engaged the private sector, and had in-depth discussions with our liaison partners. They're clearly doing their homework.

Congresswoman Wagner has been a thoughtful and engaged leader who truly understands the value and priorities of this mission space. Beyond the subcommittee, Chairman Crawford and Ranking Member Himes have also been supportive the broader OSINT effort.

At the agency level, I think Wagner and her team are taking the right steps. With HPSCI now taking such a comprehensive look at OSINT as a discipline, I've been encouraged by the diligence and thoroughness of their approach. They're looking at it from every angle, and I'm interested to see how that shapes their eventual recommendations.

Sue Gordon

Former Principal Deputy Director of National Intelligence, ODNI
Former Deputy Director, NGA

If I were trying to shift toward outcomes, I'd challenge the OSINT subcommittee to start by picking an area of OSINT that we already understand but also know can have significant contribution to mission outcomes: *imagery analysis.*

Commercial satellites are flying everywhere, and while we're technically ingesting some of that data, I don't believe we have truly embraced it.

I believe that commercial imagery could accomplish most of the IC's missions for pennies on the dollar. Not all of them, sure, but a significant share. And yet, we still treat it like an extra, not a core capability.

I would use that example to model how we might structure a program differently.

Right now, we make commercial vendors spend their own money building capabilities, and then we decide afterward whether it's good enough. Meanwhile, we pour billions into bespoke systems through classified contracts. That's not an effective balance. It's not a competitive structure.

From there, I'd ask the bigger question: *Can we move toward source-agnostic budgeting and oversight?*

What would it look like if Congress measured us by outcomes, not methodologies? We're taking all the risk with the future and none with the present. We're clinging to the familiar—what we've already built, already programmed. What happened with Ukraine and their recent example of use of drones shows us what's possible when you let go of that. They're improvising. We're recycling.

So, maybe the right challenge for the subcommittee is this: *Can you build something that frees the IC to prioritize outcomes over comfort?*

Because as long as Congress keeps cutting commercial data budgets, it sends the message that innovation is optional—and the old way is still good enough.

That's the cycle I'd want to break.

Summary

If there's one theme that cuts through all the expert commentary and policy proposals in this chapter, it's this: OSINT isn't lacking relevance—it's lacking readiness. The data exists, the tools are catching up, and the use cases are there. But until the intelligence community is willing to treat open source as a first-class discipline—with real funding, real training, and real integration—it will continue to fall short of its potential.

This chapter closes out the structural and strategic questions surrounding OSINT: what's broken, what's possible, and what it will take to build something better.

Now it's time to shift focus—*back to the mission.*

The next chapter moves past the policy debates and into the field—looking at how OSINT actually works in practice and the ways it can be applied in the field.

Investigations

Open-source intelligence (OSINT) is the practice of collecting publicly available information to answer questions, support decision-making, and assess threats. In my last book, *Hunting Cyber Criminals*, I covered a wide range of technical tools that can be used to extract data from a variety of "open" sources.

This chapter takes a different approach. Instead of focusing on the tools themselves, this chapter covers the types of information out there—what's available, where it lives, and how it can be used in real-world investigations.

After looking at several places to gather information, I walk through practical examples that show how to leverage different data points pieced together from various HBL (hacked, breached, and leaked) databases to build a complete target profile identifying two cybercriminals.

This chapter features commentary from:

Dennis Eger
Senior Open Source Advisor, INSCOM

An OSINT Primer

OSINT gathering involves collecting information from publicly available (open) sources. This includes mediums like the following:

- Search engines/news articles
- Social media
- Online forums
- Deep and dark web

OSINT Sources

Search engines are your holy grail of OSINT data collection. Finding quality information on your investigation or research project can ultimately come down to how much time and effort you spend (i.e., how deep you are willing to go) to find results.

The Deep and Dark Web

As a point of clarification, accessing information on the deep web is no different than performing any regular search on any search engine. I've found that the "deep web" is nothing more than information not readily available on pages 1 or 2 of your Google search results. I like to think of it as the deep web because *you have to dig for it*. Get it? More than just Google, there are so many other important search engines that you can use, depending on your search topic.

In contrast, the dark web is a hidden layer of the Internet that isn't indexed by traditional search engines and requires specialized software—most commonly the Tor browser—to access. Unlike the surface web, which includes publicly accessible websites, or the deep web, which encompasses private databases and password-protected content, the dark web is deliberately concealed to provide anonymity for users and operators.

OSINT Framework

Whether you're just starting out with OSINT or an experienced researcher, the OSINT Framework provides an indispensable collection of tools and resources designed to provide a structured method for gathering information from online and publicly available sources. The Framework is designed to provide benefits to security researchers, government agencies, and cybersecurity professionals in their quest for information gathering.

Bottom line—the OSINT Framework (www.osintframework.com) provides a sort of checklist to make sure you don't miss any important details while sifting through the massive ocean of available online data.

It doesn't matter how much experience you have researching, there are always new sources of information, and trying to remember all of them is nearly impossible. The framework is a great go-to resource to ensure that you've covered all your bases.

Lesser-Used Search Engines

To demonstrate the power of OSINT, I introduce Awesome OSINT, a self-described "curated list of amazingly awesome open-source intelligence tools and resources."

NOTE To check out Awesome OSINT, go to `https://github.com/jivoi/awesome-osint`.

Awesome OSINT is a simple list of alternative search engines that are available to help you find whatever you are seeking. The following example lists are provided by Awesome OSINT to help support your mission-specific searches:

- **Business search tools:** Provide aggregated information on global companies, which can include business registration details, registered owners, corporate disclosures, patents, and shareholder details. These are great tools for third-party due diligence, including procurement and supplier risk, and credit risk searches. Examples: `Brownbook.com`, Bureau Van Dijk (Orbis), and `NorthData.com`.

- **Code search engines:** Used to find specific keywords, signatures, or code samples throughout public websites, data repositories, and public buckets. Searching through code can be a great way to find websites owned by the same person, as they may contain shared code. Examples: `https://codefinder.dev/` and `https://publicwww.com/`.

- **Document and slide searches:** Enable searching for data located onto publicly posted PDFs, Word documents, presentation slides, and more. Example: `http://www.findpdfdoc.com/`.

- **Domain registration search (WHOIS):** Another way to find websites owned by the same person or organization—by comparing and matching ownership details, Internet Protocol (IP) address history, domain name server (DNS) details, and more. Without question, Domain Tools provides the most comprehensive tool available for historical WHOIS data. Its IRIS tool is hands down the single best tool available on the market for domain ownership investigation. Example: `www.domaintools.com`.

- **Face search:** Exactly as it sounds. Search for a person's face using image reverse searching. Drop a photo of the person you are looking for, and these search tools can help you identify the person and other places the photo might be used. This is especially useful when you're trying to track movements of trafficked individuals. More on this in a later chapter. Example: `https://facecheck.id/`.

- **File search tools:** Similar to document slide search, but enables searching for files (e.g., PDF, Doc, XLS, etc.) published to websites and even Google Drive. Example: `https://www.dedigger.com/`.

- **Grey search:** Includes searches for technical and government reports, standards, patents, business documents, theses, dissertations, webcasts, conference proceedings, and unpublished works. A great source for this type of information is the National Repository of Grey Literature. Example: `https://csulb.libguides.com/greylit`.

- **Maritime vessel searching:** Searching to monitor ship positions, vessel tracking, ship tracking, vessel position, vessel traffic, and port activity on real-time maps. Example: `http://vesselfinder.com/`.

- **Paste search tools:** Lets you search through information publicly posted to "paste" sites like Pastebin. Paste sites enable users to store plain text data and share it with other people. More often than not, these sites are used by hackers and other cyber criminals to share stolen information like credit card numbers, account credentials, stolen data samples, and even ransom notes. Sites like Pastebin can be a type of early detection for data breaches. Examples: `psbdmp.ws` and `pastebin.com`.

- **People investigation tools:** Sometimes referred to as *skip tracing*, these tools enable you to track down a person's location through public records (and social media, which I will cover soon). These tools let you look up a person using a name and address and typically provide you with a history of the person's addresses and possibly even email and social media profiles. Beware though, the better the tool, the more expensive the search. The better investigative tools will also check a person's background, criminal history, family connections, vehicle registrations, property records, and more. Examples: Transunion's TLO (`http://www.tlo.com`) and Skopenow (`http://www.skopenow.com`).

- **Vehicle research tools:** License plate lookup tools that return information like a car's vehicle identification number (VIN), make, model, milage, age, and other details that can include historical accident reports from state agencies. Example: `https://epicvin.com/`.

- **Social media and video searching:** Available by the hundreds. Some of the more interesting ones for gathering information include the capability to check whether a person's phone number or email address is registered to a social media site, or even scrape a person's followers, enabling you to build your own target maps. Depending on your objective, there are also a number of tools that enable you to set up alerts for specific hashtag topics. One of my favorite tools enables searching text within YouTube's subtitle and automatic video captions. This may be more powerful than you realize. For example, what if the videos you are searching for contain intentionally misleading descriptions, but your goal is to find specific words mentioned by them in the video? Automatic video captions are created by YouTube using speech recognition, but are not indexed by Google, and therefore not available through a traditional Google search. Example: `https://filmot.com/`.

OSINT Industries

OSINT Industries (`www.osint.industries`) is an automated OSINT platform built to collect and analyze publicly available data from across the web. Designed for use by law enforcement, private investigators, and government agencies, the platform streamlines the process of identifying individuals, verifying information, and assessing potential threats through real-time aggregation and structured analysis.

OSINT Industries continuously scans social media, forums, websites, and other open-data sources—organizing its findings into detailed reports and visual insights. Its interface is built for investigative workflows, offering direct searches by email, username, and phone number, along with linked social media analysis, digital footprint mapping, and custom reporting capabilities.

I dive much deeper into OSINT Industries in the next chapter, including how it was used to help uncover the operator of a known cybersecurity asset management (CSAM) forum. For now, it's worth highlighting the platform's ability to actively monitor and contextualize a subject's online behavior, making it a powerful tool for modern OSINT-driven investigations.

Pattern of Life and Movement Tracking

Several years ago, Strava—a fitness app designed to promote exercise and athletic performance—launched a global heatmap feature, enabling users to view anonymized location data from millions of athletes around the world. The idea was simple: Track your workouts, and in return, see how others are moving across the globe. What users didn't realize was that this public heatmap was quietly broadcasting sensitive location data, including from some of the world's most secretive military installations.

Strava proudly announced the feature in a press release:

> *Strava, the social network for athletes, has launched its global heatmap, a striking visualization of over one billion activities from Strava athletes across a wide variety of activities, both on land and in the sea. The activities logged covered nearly 17 billion miles. Our global heatmap is the largest, richest, and most beautiful dataset of its kind. It is a direct visualization of Strava's global network of athletes.*[1]

But what Strava (and many of its users) hadn't considered was the operational risk of using the app. Soldiers deployed in sensitive areas were using the app to log their runs and workouts, unknowingly tagging their global positioning system (GPS) coordinates to a publicly accessible map. As *The Guardian* later revealed, zooming into the heatmap revealed glowing trails of activity in otherwise unlit, undeveloped regions—some of which didn't even appear on Google or Apple Maps.

In places like Syria or Afghanistan, the implications were immediate. Analysts and adversaries could use Strava's heatmap to identify the location and internal layout of forward-operating bases, patrol routes, and even the daily routines of deployed soldiers. One screenshot shows a Turkish patrol route near Manbij, Syria, clearly etched onto the terrain by repeated movement (see Figure 8.1).[2]

Even though the data was anonymized, the pattern-of-life (POL) intelligence it enabled was anything but harmless. Knowing that a military base exists is one thing, but being able to reconstruct movement paths, shift schedules, and high-traffic zones in and around that base provides adversaries the kind of targeting intelligence usually reserved for state-level reconnaissance.

No technical exploit needed—just good old-fashioned open-source intelligence, hiding in plain sight.

---

[1] https://www.cpomagazine.com/cyber-security/strava-heat-map-incident-how-civilian-technology-in-military-settings-needs-to-be-controlled/

[2] https://www.theguardian.com/world/2018/jan/28/fitness-tracking-app-gives-away-location-of-secret-us-army-bases

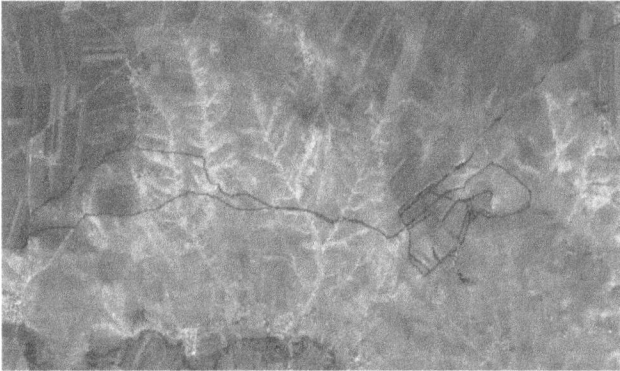

Figure 8.1: Screenshot showing a Turkish patrol route near Manbij in Syria.

In a similar fashion, OSINT Industries enables users to track timelines and activity details published across social media and other online platforms, including movement data exposed through public sources like Strava. Figure 8.2 demonstrates a sample test case from OSINT Industries, highlighting how discovered accounts and geolocation data can be linked, analyzed, and visualized.

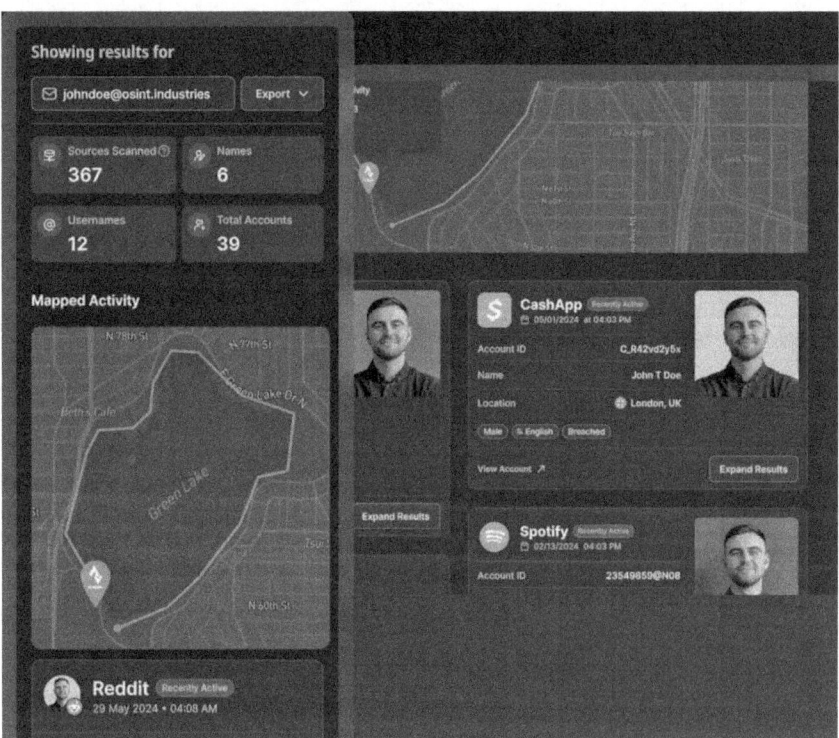

Figure 8.2: Screenshot from OSINT.Industries showing movement patterns.

This is just one example of how open-source data, when properly aggregated, can reveal far more than the user ever intended. The following sections look at some others.

Moving from PAI to OSINT

Collecting publicly available information (PAI) is only the first step. The real value comes when that raw data is turned into something meaningful—when it's analyzed, correlated, and applied to answer specific questions. That's the difference between PAI and OSINT. OSINT isn't just about what you find, it's about what you do with it. Moving from passive collection to active analysis is where the intelligence work begins.

Dennis Eger
Senior Open Source Advisor, INSCOM

A lot of folks throw the term OSINT around pretty loosely—open-source intelligence—but for us, it has a much more specific meaning.

From an industry standpoint, I'd call it publicly available information.

That's data accessible to the public and often used for research or situational awareness. In the private sector, people might use open-source information for business intelligence or market analysis, and that's totally valid—but it's different from how we approach it in a military context.

Where we draw the line is when publicly available information is used to satisfy an intelligence requirement. That's when it transitions into OSINT. If a commander needs answers—say, how many Russian Battalion Tactical Groups (BTGs) are operating in Ukraine, where they're located, what activities they're involved in, what equipment they're using—that triggers an actual intelligence tasking. Now, someone has to collect that data, analyze it, write a report, and disseminate it across the operational picture, so it informs targeting or planning decisions. That's OSINT.

It might sound like a fine line, but it's critical. Just watching CNN and seeing a report that Russian BTGs have crossed into Ukraine? That's publicly available information. Googling "what is a BTG" and finding a definition? Still PAI.

But as soon as there's a formal requirement—when you're asked to pull together details from various sources, validate them, put them into a structured report that feeds into decision-making or fuses with other intelligence disciplines—that's when it becomes OSINT.

You don't need specialized tools or managed attribution to access public information. But when you're working in support of an operational mission, and the data needs to be actionable, verifiable, and integrated into broader intel processes—that's when it moves into OSINT's space. That's how we define the line.

That distinction between passive information and operational intelligence is exactly what the rest of this chapter is about. To show what OSINT looks like in practice, I walk through a real-world investigation that combines surface web data, breach records, and structured analysis to unmask individuals behind two of the longest-running cybercrime forums: Nulled.to and Cracked.io.

Hunting Cyber Criminals: Cracked.io Edition

On January 29, 2025, the U.S. Department of Justice (DoJ), in coordination with international law enforcement agencies, announced the takedown of two of the longest-running online cybercrime forums: Nulled.to and Cracked.io.

The Nulled.to forum, previously discussed in Chapter 2, had operated since 2016 and served as one of the oldest "entry-level" hubs in the cybercrime ecosystem. With over 5 million registered users and more than 43 million posts advertising stolen data, hacking tools, and credential stuffing techniques, the forum reportedly generated over $1 million in annual revenue. The site's administrator, *Lucas*, was identified as Lucas Sohn, a 29-year-old Argentinian national residing in Spain.

The second takedown targeted Cracked.io, a massive cybercrime marketplace active since 2018. The forum had over 4 million users and hosted over 28 million posts advertising illicit goods and services, including stolen login credentials, exploit kits, and servers configured for malware hosting. Cracked generated approximately $4 million in annual revenue and was tied to two key figures: Florian Marzahl, aka *FloraiN*, 32 years old, and Finn Alexander Grimpe, aka *Finndev*, 28 years old. According to court filings, Cracked's operations impacted at least 17 million U.S. victims.

The enforcement action also extended to connected infrastructure controlled by the operators, including Sellix.io, a platform used to create storefronts for the sale of stolen accounts and other illicit digital goods, and StarkRDP, a remote desktop-hosting service commonly used to anonymize cyberattacks.

The following section illustrates how OSINT, leveraging both clear and dark web data, can be used to identify the individuals behind these long-running operations.

Specifically, I explore how two tools—PredictaGraph and PredictaSearch—were used in this investigation to connect digital breadcrumbs and unmask the real identities behind the aliases *FloraiN* and *Finndev*.

PredictaGraph and PredictaSearch

PredictaGraph (www.predictagraph.com) is an online OSINT platform that enables users to visually map relationships between data points. Think of it as a lightweight, browser-based alternative to Maltego. It's simple, fast, and highly effective. It not only creates visual link charts but also integrates automated searches across a wide range of platforms using the PredictaSearch engine. Figure 8.3 shows an example of the type of link analysis created by PredictaGraph.

PredictaSearch enables users to conduct comprehensive audits of a target's digital footprint, using only a phone number or email address. From an OSINT perspective, it's a powerful reverse lookup engine that scans hundreds of online services for linked accounts and identifiers.

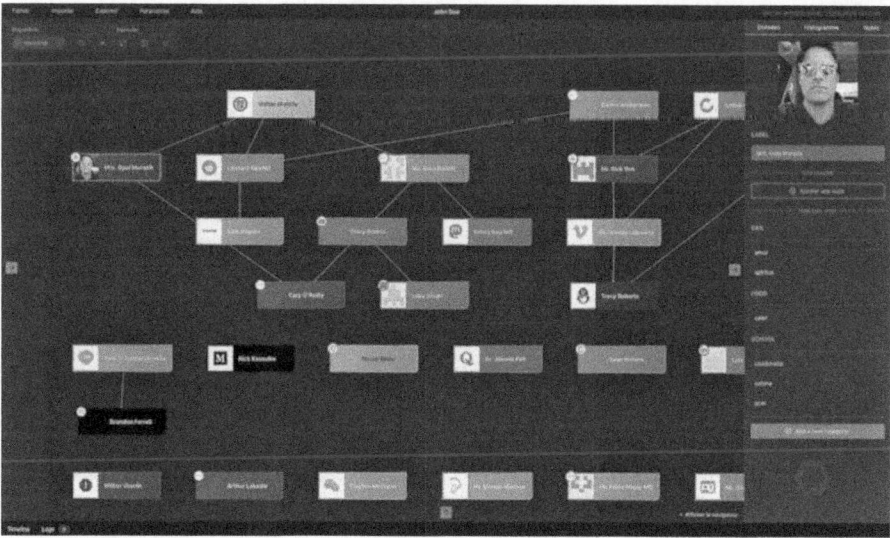

Figure 8.3: Link analysis screenshot within the PredictaGraph UI.

PredictaGraph leverages this engine to automatically scan usernames, email addresses, and phone numbers across platforms, including social media, dating apps, video streaming sites, adult sites, e-commerce platforms, gaming services, financial sites, breach databases, and hacking forums.

One of PredictaGraph's key strengths is its ability to perform cross-platform keyword searches spanning not only surface web but also niche sources like document repositories, travel and booking sites, grey literature databases, and code-sharing platforms. By automating search, matching, and link analysis, these tools enable investigators to move quickly from a single data point to a mapped digital identity.

The next section explains how these tools can be applied to trace online handles, infrastructure, and exposed credentials, ultimately connecting them to the real-world identities of Florian Marzahl and Finn Grimpe.

Leveraging Dark Web OSINT

Historical dark web and HBL (hacked, breached, leaked) data can be a gold mine of intelligence.

I say this all the time: The further back you go in your research, the more likely you are to uncover someone's Operations Security (OPSEC) failures—the early mistakes hackers make before they learn how to properly cover their tracks. This is especially true for younger threat actors who tend to crave attention and status. Their hunger for recognition in underground communities often leads them to overshare, reuse handles, or reveal personal details they'll later regret.

You will see this pattern clearly in Part IV when I discuss Catist and the Snowflake hacks.

While no one condones corporate data theft, there's no denying how valuable breach records can be in cybercrime investigations. These datasets often provide critical pivot points—emails, usernames, and passwords—that help tie aliases to real-world identities.

Investigating FloraiN Using HBL Data

Let's start with the official X (formerly Twitter) account for the Cracked forum: @CrackedTo. A search for that handle in the 2023 Twitter breach files reveals an associated email address: `olivia.messla@outlook.de`. That's as good a place as any to start.

Running that email through multiple public breaches yields a handful of associated usernames, including:

■ TestingRain

■ Infinity

■ FloraiN, which was also used on RaidForums

Reusing Passwords

Everyone reuses passwords. People get lazy and tend to default to something familiar, especially for sites they don't care much about. I'm guilty of it. I know you are, too. And cybercriminals? They're absolutely no different.

Reused passwords are especially valuable for OSINT investigation work when they are unique. People will generally avoid something obvious like "Password123" and instead pick a phrase or number combination that they think no one else would guess. Ironically, that makes it easier to trace, because once you find a unique password tied to one account, you can follow it across other data breaches and aliases.

In this case, searching my breach archives for `olivia.messla@outlook.de` reveals a distinctive password: `niemals1234`.

A broad username search FloraiN shows similar variations like `niemals123` and `niemals1234`. The word *niemals* translates to "never" in German. So, I guess he is saying never use 1234 as your password? Clever.

Further searching password lists for `niemals123*` shows connections to the following emails:

■ `lorian.marzahl@live.de`

■ `fmarzahl137@gmail.com`

■ `florianmarzahl@hotmail.de`

This also gives us a name associated with the email address `fmarzahl137@gmail.com`: Florian Marzahl.

Figure 8.4 displays a visual overview of the progress so far.

Don't Forget to Use Your Eyes

Automated tools can make your life easier, but they shouldn't replace the fundamentals. Sometimes, a bit of manual digging goes further than you'd expect.

Case in point, a basic search on the Cracked.io forum shows FloraiN listed as one of the site's three administrators (see Figure 8.5). The account dates back to November 2018, firmly tying him to the platform's early operations. That alone is significant, because it counters any claim that he was only involved in registering the site's Twitter handle and wasn't part of the actual backend or daily operations.

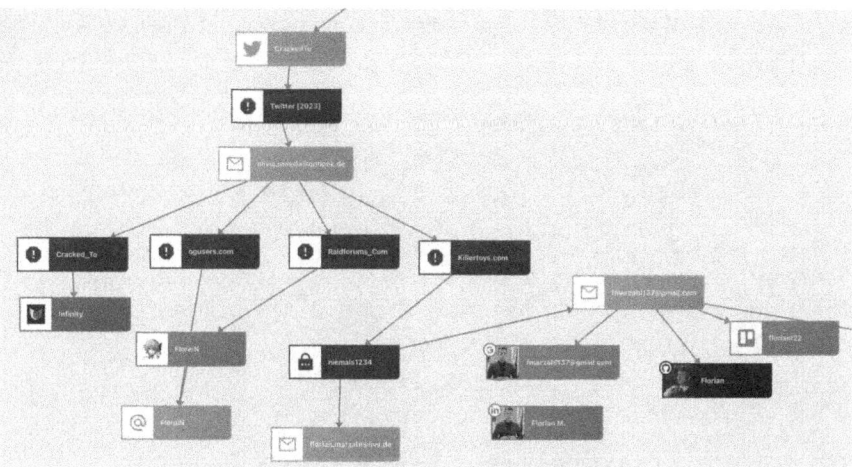

Figure 8.4: PredictaGraph overview of current investigation progress.

Figure 8.5: Screenshot of Cracked.to admins.

Social Media Deep Dive

Manually sifting through a subject's entire online footprint is daunting. That's where tools like PredictaSearch come in—providing a high-level view of a target's digital presence by scanning hundreds of online platforms with a single query.

A quick search for `fmarzahl137@gmail.com` using PredictaSearch returns confirmed hits across multiple services, including:

- GitHub
- Google
- PayPal
- Trello

PredictaSearch does a great job of making all these results easily viewable on a single pane (see Figure 8.6).

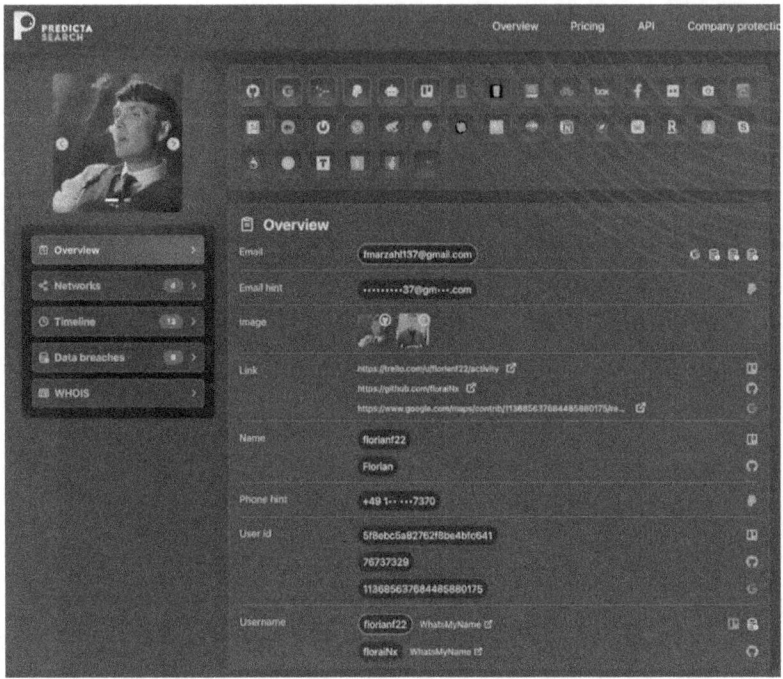

Figure 8.6: PredictaSearch results for `fmarzahl137@gmail.com`.

Digging further into Florian's social profiles, he lists his affiliation with a company called Sellix SRL. The profile photo matches his LinkedIn profile, where he's listed as the co-founder of Sellix, the now-seized digital marketplace previously used to traffic stolen and illegal digital goods.

Florian's LinkedIn also identifies him as the founder of 1337 Services GmbH, a separate company operating under a German business structure (see Figure 8.7).

International Business Search

When tracing international entities, I've found it's often more effective to use country-specific business registries. For targets based in Europe, the European e-Justice Portal (`https://e-justice.europa.eu/`) is a powerful resource.

It offers free public access to official business registrations across European Union (EU) member states and can provide valuable insights into company structure, ownership, and registered addresses—all critical pieces when mapping a subject's operational infrastructure.

The business registration details for 1337 Services show Florian Marzahl and Finn Alexander Grimpe as co-owners (see Figure 8.8).

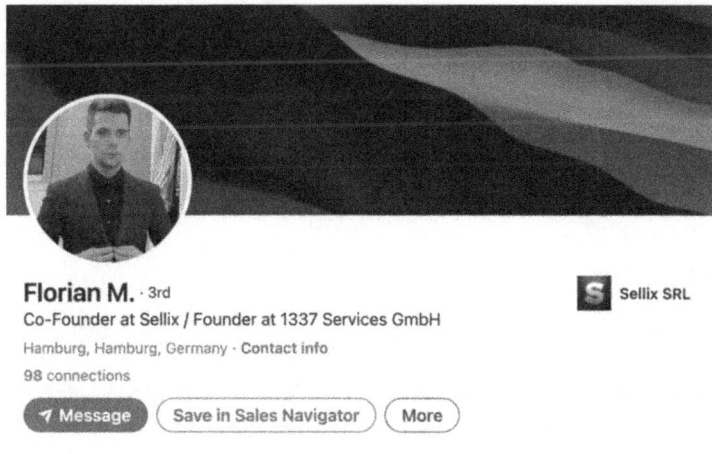

Figure 8.7: Screenshot of Florian's LinkedIn profile.

1337 Services GmbH (Germany)

This page presents the details of the selected company and lists the documents or pieces of information available in relation to the company.

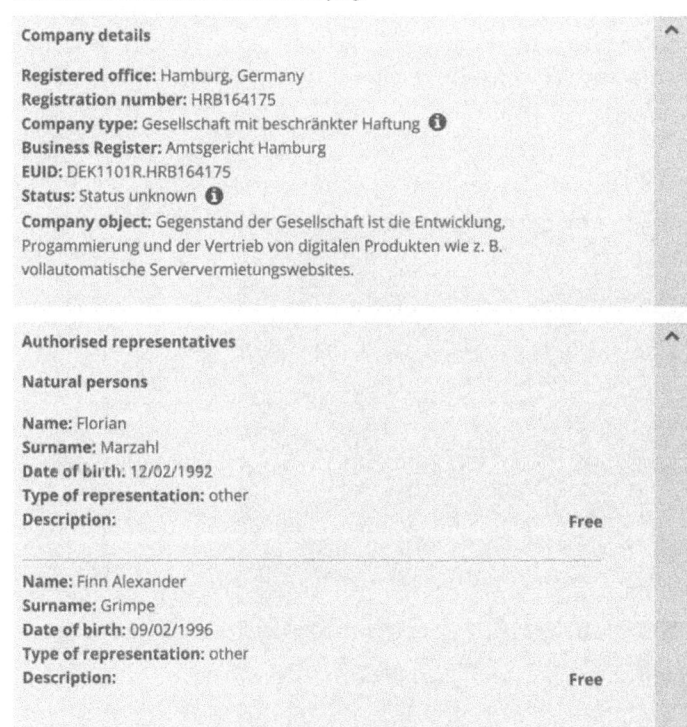

Figure 8.8: Results from `e-justice.europa.eu search` for "1337 Services GmbH."

> **NOTE**   Alternatively, a great one-stop shop for international business searches is `NorthData.com`. This site provides an incredibly powerful (and free) business search tool, and in many cases, provides you with graphics showing linked owners and assets.

I think this pretty much sums up the investigation of FloraiN. Before I close this chapter, let's take a quick peek at his business partner, Finn Alexander Grimpe, who was identified in the 1337 Services business registration.

Investigating Finn Alexander

I've already covered a lot, so I won't go into a full breakdown of this second investigation. But there are still a few key details worth highlighting.

Let's start with the StockX breach, where the name Finn Grimpe is linked to the email address `me@finn.lu`. Searching for associated social media accounts reveals a Trello profile with the username finndev.

Pro Tip: Don't Use Your Personal Email on Hacking Forums

The handle finndev appears in multiple leaked forum databases. On the leaked Cracked.io database, the username is registered to `staff@nulled.to`—a pretty strong indicator that he was part of the Nulled.to admin team.

To confirm, a quick check on `Archive.org` shows the finndev account on Nulled.to as one of the oldest registered users, dating back to January 15, 2015 (see Figure 8.9). Additional database leaks from RaidForums and Void.to show the same username linked to the email `f.grimpe@gmail.com`.

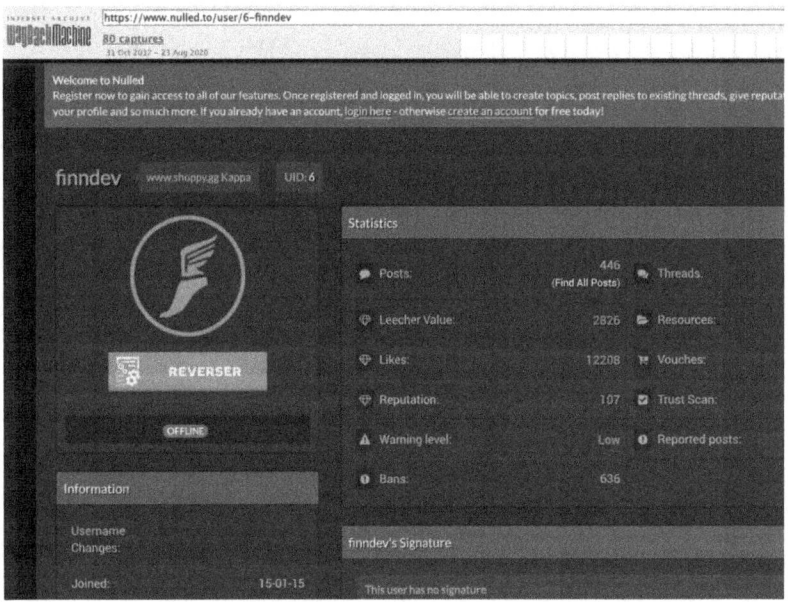

Figure 8.9: `Archive.org` screenshot of user finndev on nulled.to.

A search of that email returns several more breadcrumbs: a Twitter account (@afasdasdasdddaa) and a GitHub profile (github.com/finndev), further tying together the online identity.

Starting with the StockX data breach, the name Finn Grimpe is connected to the email me@finn.lu. In addition, his username is found on the RaidForums and void.to databases, linking it to the email address f.grimpe@gmail.com. A search for accounts with that email address reveals a Twitter account called @afasdasdasdddaa and a GitHub account called github.com/finndev.

Shoppy.gg

A review of leaked messages from databases belonging to Nulled and Cracked forums shows a number of private messages describing Finndev as the owner of shoppy.gg.

Shoppy.gg, as discussed in Chapter 2, is an online marketplace (similar to Sellix.io) where hackers sell access to stolen accounts. Figure 8.10 shows the Shoppy.gg sales page for a single merchant.

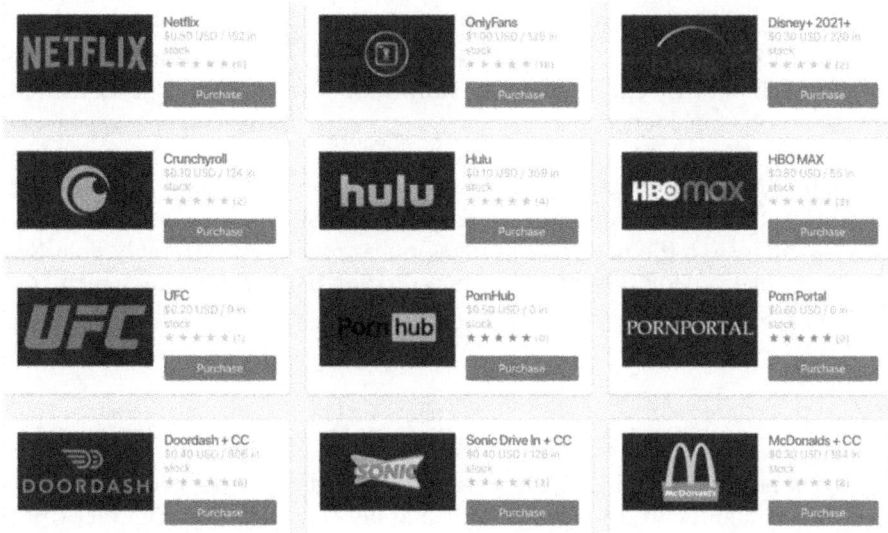

Figure 8.10: Screenshot of Shoppy.gg marketplace.

Unfortunately, there is no conclusive data directly linking Finn as the owner of Shoppy. gg, which is probably why the marketplace is still in operation. However, you can still use this data to make a number of important connections.

First, in a 2019 leak of the Cracked forum database, the user "shoppy" is registered with the email address finn@shoppy.gg.

Never Rely on a Single Source for All of Your Information

PredictaSearch has been great thus far, but the moment you rely on a single site to conduct your investigations is the moment you start missing important data.

Searching the email address on OSINT.Industries reveals an AliExpress account with the name Finn Grimpe (see Figure 8.11).

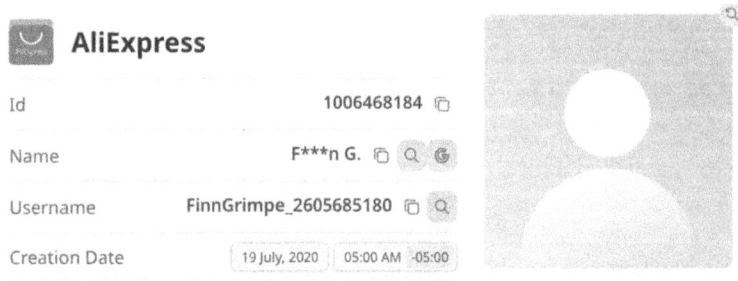

Figure 8.11: OSINT.Industries showing additional data.

No other business registration data can be found linking Shoppy.gg directly to Finn, but what I have uncovered using only a handful of tools is still incredibly remarkable.

The information uncovered throughout this investigation is more than enough to establish a strong web of connections, and, at a minimum, raise serious questions that challenge any claims of coincidence.

While not every detail leads to a smoking gun, cumulative evidence presents a compelling case that ties these individuals directly to the operations of Nulled, Cracked, and their affiliated marketplaces. For now this is a good place to stop.

Also, for those interested, the team at PredictaGraph created an extremely detailed (and publicly accessible) version of this entire investigation using their tool, which you can access here: `https://bit.ly/PG-cracked`.

Summary

This chapter demonstrated how OSINT, when combined with hacked, breached, and leaked (HBL) data and careful cross-platform analysis, can expose the identities behind even the most well-hidden cybercrime operations.

This chapter also emphasized the importance of historical OSINT, the value of breached data, and the need to diversify investigative tools.

While not every data point gave a definitive answer, together they formed a strong narrative supported by verifiable, open-source evidence—ultimately leading to the identification of admins of two prominent underground forums: Nulled.to and Cracked.io.

The next chapter sticks with this investigative theme. It focuses on how OSINT can be used to help fight child sexual abuse material (CSAM) and even uncover human trafficking.

OSINT for Human Trafficking

This chapter takes our investigations a step further by exploring how OSINT can be leveraged to combat child sexual abuse material (CSAM) and human trafficking—two of the most disturbing but critically important areas where open-source intelligence (OSINT) has proven to be an essential tool for real-world impact.

This chapter features commentary from:

Jeff Tiegs
Lt Col, Delta Special Forces (Ret.),
CEO Skull Games

Bryan Seeley
U.S. Marine (Ret.), Hacker

Evil Rabbit
Online CSAM Hunting Collective

Child Sexual Abuse Material

Child Sexual Abuse Material (CSAM) is any content—images, videos, audio, text, or other media—that depicts or describes the sexual abuse or exploitation of a minor. This problem is staggering in both scale and scope. The creation, distribution, and consumption of CSAM has reached alarming levels, with vast quantities being shared every day across both surface web platforms (such as social media and chat rooms) and, more commonly, in dark web forums specifically built to operate anonymously.

Despite the tireless efforts of law enforcement, intelligence professionals, and private sector security researchers, this isn't a problem that will ever fully disappear. The volume alone poses an overwhelming challenge. That challenge is made even worse by the persistent use of anonymizing platforms like Tor, which are designed to obscure identity and protect privacy—features that have unfortunately created a safe haven for some of the Internet's most horrific crimes.

CSAM isn't just an online issue. The real-world pipeline that feeds this industry continues to grow. One deeply concerning trend is the surge in human trafficking involving unaccompanied minors at the U.S. border. Recent estimates suggest that 75–80 percent of these children become victims of human trafficking, often coerced into forced labor or sexual exploitation after being smuggled into the country.[1]

While Tor and anonymizing tools present a serious challenge, the truth is that many individuals operating or visiting CSAM sites aren't particularly technical. Like most criminals, they make mistakes. And OSINT practitioners can exploit those mistakes.

A 2024 report from the cybersecurity firm Recorded Future noted that many administrators of dark web CSAM sites lack deep technical skills. In most cases, they exhibited poor operational security (OPSEC), making them more vulnerable to traditional investigative techniques.

Take the 2015 Federal Bureau of Intelligence (FBI) takedown of Playpen, one of the largest CSAM platforms ever discovered. Its creator, a Florida man, was identified after he inadvertently exposed his real Internet Protocol (IP) address while administering the site. At its peak, Playpen had over 215,000 registered users and hosted more than 23,000 explicit images and videos of children.

Another high-profile case involved the platform Welcome to Video, where hundreds of users were arrested after law enforcement traced Bitcoin transactions linked to their accounts. The suspects had failed to understand how cryptocurrency anonymity could be compromised, especially when mixing services and basic wallet hygiene were ignored.

Recorded Future's report, "Using Infostealers to Unmask CSAM Consumers," goes even further. It highlights how the same poor cyber hygiene that makes these individuals vulnerable to arrest also makes them susceptible to malware. Widespread infostealer infections designed to extract login credentials, browser cookies, and saved sessions have become an unlikely but powerful tool for investigators. By leveraging logs dumped from these malware-infected machines, analysts can piece together digital footprints and uncover identities that were once thought to be hidden behind Tor and burner accounts.

---

[1] W. A. Kandel, A. Bruno, P. J. Meyer, C. R. Seelke, M. Taft-Morales, and R. E. Wasem. "Unaccompanied alien children: Potential factors contributing to recent immigration." Congressional Research Service, CRS Report R43628, http://www.fas.org/sgp/crs/homesec/R43628.pdf (accessed July 2, 2016).

Discovering a Massive CSAM Cloud

Infostealer logs, often overlooked by mainstream investigations, have become an invaluable tool in the fight against CSAM. In addition to usernames and passwords, these logs often include the exact Uniform Resource Locators (URLs) accessed with those credentials.

When collected at scale, these logs can be used to create searchable datasets. When these datasets are cross-referenced with known CSAM sites, they can help law enforcement identify individuals with a high likelihood of viewing, distributing, or producing this material.

Around 2021, I received a message from a hacker named *DonJuji* (discussed in Chapter 2). He sent me a tip regarding a potentially disturbing cache of content hosted on a public Mega.nz folder. Mega is a cloud-based file-sharing platform similar to Dropbox, often used for distributing large data dumps and media files.

In this case, *DonJuji* had inadvertently stumbled upon a Mega container filled with CSAM. He sent me the link and asked if there was anything I could do. I was more than happy to help.

> **NOTE**   I don't know how special victims units do this kind of work every day. Just scanning the folder stats, I saw over 300GB of images and video files. I opened one folder and reviewed only a handful of thumbnails before I had to stop. The images of those children—not older than five or six years of age—will forever be burned in my brain.
>
> I can't imagine this job ever getting easier and just want to say thank you to those who do this kind of work, day after day.

Thankfully, Mega provides a session history log for each account, which makes it significantly easier to trace usage. Ignoring my own login at the top of Figure 9.1, the session history revealed that the account was created on an iPhone in 2020 and had remained logged in across multiple devices.

One session appeared to originate from a VPN exit node in Turkey. Another more promising session was logged in from a 154.x.x.x IP address in March 2021.

A reverse lookup showed that this address belonged to Charter Communications—a U.S.-based Internet Service Provider (ISP). That means it is potentially actionable with a subpoena.

Searching the account's username across known breached data revealed several links to a user in Texas, but without proper subpoenas, that was as far as I could go. I passed the information along to members of law enforcement, and that seemed to be the end ... for a while.

A little over a year later, I received a call from someone at Homeland Security Investigations (HSI). She introduced herself as the team lead who received the initial data. She proceeded to thank me for reporting the cloud account and stated that it was one of the largest collections of child porn they'd ever found in a single location.

The only reason she was even allowed to call me was because there was a news article recently published, regarding an arrest of a man *and his son* in Texas (see Figure 9.2).

Session History   Last 250 sessions ▼

Clients	IP address	Country	Most recent activity	Session status	
Chrome on Apple	▇▇▇▇▇	🇺🇸 United States of America	3/13/2021, 02:14	CURRENT	LOGOUT
Chrome on Apple	▇▇▇▇▇	🇺🇸 United States of America	3/13/2021, 01:32	LOGGED IN	LOGOUT
MEGAsync on Windows	▇▇▇▇▇	🇺🇸 United States of America	3/13/2021, 01:13	LOGGED IN	LOGOUT
iPhone	2603:8080:80…	🇺🇸 United States of America	1/20/2021, 20:44	LOGGED IN	LOGOUT
iPhone	2603:8080:80…	🇺🇸 United States of America	12/6/2020, 19:57	LOGGED IN	LOGOUT
Chrome on Windows	154.6.26.▇	🇺🇸 United States of America	3/13/2021, 01:16	EXPIRED	
Unknown	88.244▇	🇹🇷 Turkey	2/5/2021, 07:15	EXPIRED	
iPhone	2603:8080:8006:	🇺🇸 United States of America	12/1/2020, 11:22	EXPIRED	

Figure 9.1: Session history screenshot from the account.

Figure 9.2: Article of the HSI raid.

The agent also mentioned that CSAM images and videos are often watermarked, and a review of those found in the collection I provided led their team to a number of new sites and forums that they hadn't previously discovered.

It's not every day that you can make this kind of an impact. I'm extremely grateful that I was able to contribute to taking down this content and the people behind it.

And thank you, again, to the people who do this work every day.

Fighting Human Trafficking

In the ongoing fight against CSAM and human trafficking, there are two individuals (and their organizations) that I want to highlight in this chapter. Both have dedicated themselves to the tireless, often behind-the-scenes work of disrupting trafficking networks and helping to identify and rescue victims.

Skull Games

Founded in 2023 by retired Lt. Col. Jeff Tiegs, a former Delta Force operator with the Army's Special Forces Operational Detachment, Skull Games is a nonprofit organization dedicated to fighting sex trafficking through the applied use of open-source intelligence (OSINT).

Operating as a force multiplier for law enforcement, Skull Games provides analytical and operational support to help identify sex predators while also working to empower survivors. The organization harnesses publicly available information—social media posts, online advertisements, metadata, and more—and transforms that intelligence into actionable leads. These leads are handed off to law enforcement agencies to aid in arrests, prosecutions, and the dismantling of trafficking networks.

In parallel with its intelligence mission, Skull Games collaborates with a network of community partners to support survivor recovery and reintegration. Their model emphasizes a dual-track approach: Stop the predators and empower the victims.

Skull Games also encourages community engagement through its Skull Games Society, a volunteer and donor initiative that enables individuals and organizations to support the mission directly. Whether through funding, technical expertise, or outreach, these contributions help extend the organization's operational reach and impact.

By combining tactical OSINT capabilities, interagency cooperation, and survivor advocacy, Skull Games is making a measurable difference in the fight against online sexual exploitation.

Jeff Tiegs
Lt Col, Delta Special Forces (Ret.),
CEO Skull Games

I'm a retired Lieutenant Colonel from the U.S. Army. I spent close to 26 years in uniform, most of that within Special Operations. I ended my career at 1st Special Forces Operational Detachment-Delta—what most people know as Delta Force.

In that line of work, precision is everything. I didn't just want to know the neighborhood—I needed the exact building, the apartment number, sometimes even the room. That mindset carries over to intelligence work. If information isn't specific and actionable, it's just noise. Pattern recognition alone isn't intelligence. Anomalies don't become intelligence until they're put in context and can drive a decision.

My background is in counterterrorism (CT) and counterinsurgency (COIN). Two mission sets that often conflict—CT is rapid-cycle, surgical. You identify a target, take action, and start pulling threads to dismantle the network. It's a 24-hour clock. COIN is slower, more political, more layered. I operated in both environments.

As I move toward retirement, I was looking for a new enemy to pursue. I am seeking a way to ensure that I continue to find passion and purpose. I'm a soldier. I've always been a soldier, but it really isn't my identity. I take it either one step forward or back, then my job is always the same—I'm a protector.

I felt a calling to look at sex trafficking, specifically domestic sex trafficking, and even more specific to that would be online commercial sex trafficking.

Now with Skull Games, our goal is to turn publicly available information into leads that law enforcement can act on. That means the data must be clean, traceable, and defensible in front of a judge. We try to stay away from anything related to the dark web, mostly because there is enough on the regular web. Plus, explaining OSINT collection is hard enough. Adding dark web sources just complicates the chain of custody and admissibility. So, we keep it straightforward.

Evil Rabbit

Evil Rabbit is an anonymous collective of hackers who have been, in their own words, "making pedophiles cry since 2013." A well-known name within the OSINT and anti-trafficking community, Evil Rabbit has built a reputation for its relentless efforts to track, identify, and expose online predators and sexual offenders operating in the clear and dark web.

While the group includes several anonymous contributors, it operates through a central spokesperson who acts as its public-facing voice across platforms like X (formerly known as Twitter) and Telegram. Despite its underground nature, the group's work has contributed to multiple investigations and takedowns, often acting where traditional law enforcement resources are limited or slow to respond.

I was introduced to Evil Rabbit through a shared interest in exposing a known CSAM forum operator running a site called ArtBBS. After a brief exchange, we quickly found common ground and began collaborating. That investigation—centered on identifying the person behind ArtBBS—is one I explore in more detail later in this chapter.

Evil Rabbit
Online CSAM Hunting Collective

I'm a mechanic; this is just an after-work hobby mostly. I started doing this because of personal frustration with law enforcement not doing anything and focusing mostly on financial crimes, drugs, and politics. How? Just by chance and disgust…. I saw a problem I could fix without hesitation and started fixing it. It wasn't until maybe 2020 when it got a lot easier, after I found a programmer who shared similar values.

The whole process starts with an initial discovery, usually a lot of poking around the Internet and then spidering partner sites, and creating a huge web of sites.

We try to work with law enforcement, but it can be frustrating when there isn't enough information for them to act. Mostly we do this on our own and try to expose people online. The thing is, sometimes, we can give law enforcement names, addresses, payment information, and everything else. It can be as clear cut and dry as humanly possible, and sometimes, that still isn't enough. Working within the laws can be frustrating.

Working with Law Enforcement

Evil Rabbit's frustration is understandable, especially given that they operate outside the United States and may not have a full understanding of the U.S. legal system or the complexities involved in building prosecutable cases.

In response, Jeff Tiegs shared insights into how Skull Games is able to work *with* law enforcement successfully.

Rather than operating from the outside, Skull Games focuses on producing structured, verifiable intelligence that aligns with legal standards—intelligence which law enforcement agencies can use as part of their case. It's a model built on collaboration that values chain of custody, evidentiary standards, and the long game of dismantling trafficking networks through the rule of law.

Jeff Tiegs
Lt Col, Delta Special Forces (Ret.),
CEO Skull Games

Human trafficking cases previously relied on the victim's testimony. But traffickers break their victims down to make them unreliable witnesses. That's the model—it's by design. What we show prosecutors and law enforcement is that the data speaks for itself. The communications, texts, online ads, and transaction records demonstrate force, fraud, and coercion without a word from the victim. As long as the data is collected correctly, the story holds up.

We build our initial target packet, which we just call a *lead*. It's not meant to be the case file, because it's not what ends up in court. What it does is help law enforcement generate probable cause. It's a breadcrumb trail that gives them probable cause to gain access to a phone, or a hard drive, or cloud storage. That's where the real case takes shape. It all starts with what we see in the open.

Targeting Traffickers and Operators

Let's start with the basics. When I began writing this chapter, the first question that came to my mind was, how do I even go about starting this type of an investigation?

Jeff Tiegs
Lt Col, Delta Special Forces (Ret.),
CEO Skull Games

Our entry point is escort ads. In most cities, there are thousands posted daily. So, the first thing we do is triage: Does this ad contain signs of trafficking, or is it more likely just prostitution? Statistically, it's all trafficking because even so-called "consensual" sex work often involves coercion. But the legal question is: Can you prove it?

That's where we come in. We identify potential victims, look for signs of control, and start to piece together who's behind it.

For indicators of trafficking, there are a lot of them. I wouldn't say that any of them are totally obvious, because by design, they're supposed to be out in the open.

You have to also realize that sex trafficking and pimping are identical. Like the ideas of these legal definitions of force, fraud, and coercion. Well, how many times do you think a pimp uses force, fraud, or coercion to get his girl to go work? So, the idea is, if we can find a pimp, we have found a trafficker.

The same types of codes apply when you're looking for traffickers. Just like with Al Queda or ISIS, they speak in code—they're not hiding what it is they're talking about. For example, the letter P is for pimp, which you will see all over the place. The sixteenth letter of the alphabet is P, so you might also see the number 16.

Or to make a P symbol, someone might put their fingers up like in a Peace sign, which means I have a pimp. The Phillies cap, the Milwaukee Brewers cap (money over bitches), and the Pittsburgh Pirates cap. There's just all sorts of acronyms. Even 304 is "hoe" spelled upside down and backwards from the old pager days.

So, we'd look for all these various little indicators. Sometimes, it's just as obvious as a girl using the name "Candy Cane" in an ad, and the phone number in her Cash App that comes up as a guy named Mike Johnson; well, then, that's pretty obvious, and exactly the kind of connection we're looking for.

Next, we start digging through the girl's identity and who's potentially trafficking her. We run numbers. We track usernames. We cross-reference breach data to see where people reused email addresses or slipped up and connected their alias to their real identity. That's what ends up being the lead packet and being passed to law enforcement for them to dig into deeper.

Those are some of the techniques that we use for immediate triage. It comes down to running all those accounts to see if there's a guy attached to it, which goes back to using all the breach data that you were talking about: Looking for historical mistakes where these guys have messed up in the past, by creating usernames of passwords or being lazy with how they create accounts.

Evil Rabbit

Online CSAM Hunting Collective

To identify new forums or targets, we do a lot of manual browsing on Tor and spidering our ever-growing list of known clearnet domains. New forums are usually advertised or can be found in the same location that was there before them, so we regularly monitor known forums.

Our tools are mostly custom-made, because the best tools out there are expensive and commercial, or require paid APIs that usually are lacking features we need. So, we make our own. For instance, *maltego* doesn't enable link transforms to be sent to a text file, nor does it support finding internal links, which enable us to crawl and dump illegal materials to report in bulk.

Some of my favorite tools include Google, DuckDuckGo, Dogpile, and OSINT. Industries.

We do employ many tools, but 99 percent are search engines or custom scripts. As for any other search engine—Censys, Fofa, Shodan, and ViewDNS.info—that's roughly it.

We also obtain numerous passwords from a variety of means, like data breaches and stealer logs, so our bounds of accessing the worst content isn't such a problem. Ironically, information-stealing malware is one of the best ways to identify pedophiles, because the logs are dumped publicly, and as long as you know the formatting—if it's URL:USER:PASS or it's "By device"—you can pretty much track down people internationally.

Infostealer logs are a great way to find new sites, because the malware will steal bookmarks and browsing history. If we have that data with a known CSAM operator or user, looking at their bookmarks opens up worlds of new information.

When doing manual browser searches, there are also a number of common search words and mistakes that people make that we can start with. I am not going to comment on those publicly since I don't want to give child abusers any additional ideas.

There is never just one way to identify a person. To give you an example, "Cum on Printed Pics" was ran by an American who lives in California. Laws in other states prevented him from being able to remove his mugshot amongst other data that identified him. He was also very sloppy, with public business records in his name and a lot of other public information leading back to him.

With Arthur (ArtBBS), it was a series of OPSEC mistakes. This wasn't our first, nor our last biggest hit. We've exposed dark net markets and have roughly 100,000+ logins to various illegal sexual websites, including bestiality, nonconsensual pornography, pedophilia websites, and so forth.

Patience is actually our best tool. Waiting for people to make mistakes. You can obviously speed things along if you know what you're doing—and we do.

Both viewpoints are valid, and reflect two vastly different—but equally important—approaches to identifying abusers in these environments. One works in physical scenarios, while the other focuses on digital settings. For the purposes of this OSINT investigation, we followed up on a lead provided by Evil Rabbit: a CSAM forum operator known as *ArtBBS*. Let's take a closer look at who he is—and how we were able to identify him.

Identifying ArtBBS

Jeff emphasized the importance of building a targeting package—a collection of structured OSINT—that can be handed off to law enforcement. It doesn't need to be airtight or ready for prosecution; it just needs to establish enough probable cause to justify subpoenas and warrants. From there, law enforcement can take the necessary next steps.

With that in mind, this section walks through the process of building a targeting package for an alias who repeatedly surfaces in CSAM investigations: ArtBBS.

The name ArtBBS is known in these circles and regularly appears across dark web forums dedicated to child exploitation. A basic Google search returns dozens of live forums tied to this alias, many still accessible. Disturbingly, even mainstream platforms like Pinterest show tagged images—some appearing to be of young girls—linked to the ArtBBS name.

Despite being spread across different domains, ArtBBS's forums all use phpBB forum software, and they all share the same HTML page title, making them easy to fingerprint.

Using OSINT tools and publicly available breach data, let's begin piecing together the digital breadcrumbs that could help uncover the identity behind ArtBBS, and build a package that might be useful for law enforcement to take their necessary next steps.

Evil Rabbit
Online CSAM Hunting Collective

A series of events led to ArtBBS's identification. It was a rather good find. The way we first determined that he was running other sites was his choice of mybb themes, and his time zone being set to British Summer Time (BST). It was ultimately a series of OPSEC mistakes.

With the help of OSINT.Industries, we were able to confirm a lot of his personal details aligned with more forms than what he's using the alias to run. As an administrator, he's pretty sloppy—we can see he runs no less than 50 sites. Sometimes he even posts directly on the forums and turns off registration, while other times he doesn't.

The story was simple. We started by running keyword searches on Censys. The search terms were rather simple, but with that simple keyword we found roughly 33 results for illicit websites distributing a "particular age group." One of them happened to be ArtBBS.

We immediately found that he had a website in Miami, Florida, a few throughout Southeast Asia and I believe Eastern Europe.

OSINT.Industries

In the last chapter, I introduced OSINT.Industries as one of my go-to tools for performing wide-range searches across hundreds of platforms and data sources. Now, it was time to put that tool to work.

A search for the handle "ArtBBS" immediately returned several hits, with user data spread globally—although the strongest signal appeared to be clustered around Brazil and Russia (see Figure 9.3).

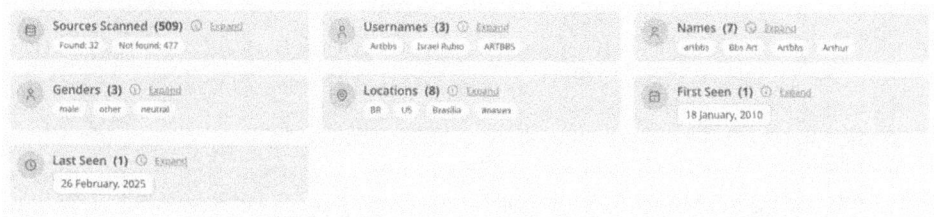

Figure 9.3: ArtBBS matches on OSINT.Industries.

Based on profile pictures and language settings, Brazil appeared to be the likely point of origin (see Figure 9.4).

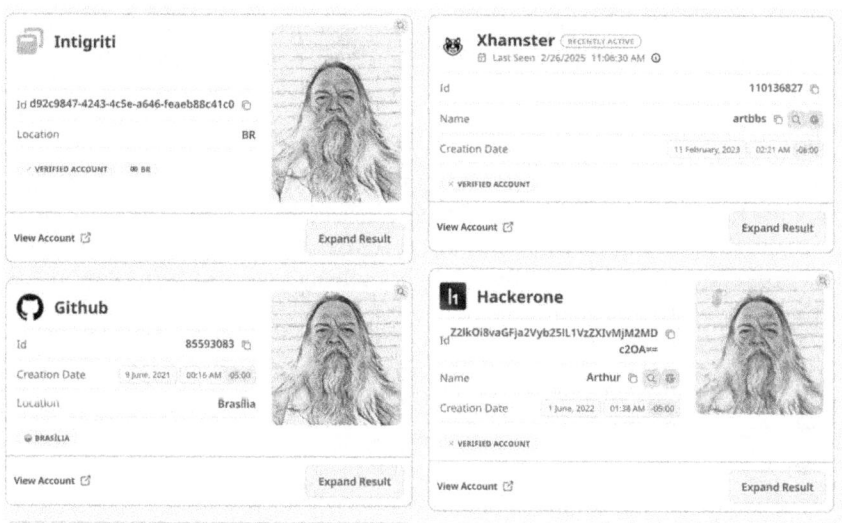

Figure 9.4: ArtBBS profile photo matches.

The first real clue came from a HackerOne profile associated with the ArtBBS alias, where the user's first name is listed as Arthur. Next, a simple analysis of the user's GitHub commits revealed small but telling details (see Figure 9.5).

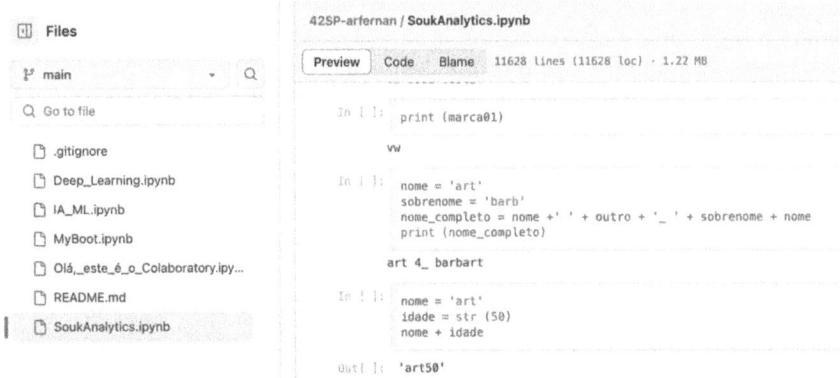

Figure 9.5: ArtBBS GitHub code.

In Spanish, the name field is set to "Art," and the surname is set to "Barb." I already had the name Arthur from a previous social match, but now I potentially had part of a last name.

Searching Through Breached Data

As always, the next logical step is to check hacked, breached, and leaked (HBL) data, which often provides stronger identity anchors than surface-level profiles. The username "ArtBBS" first appeared in the Adobe breach in 2013, tied to the email artbbs@hotmail.com. That email address didn't surface in any major leaks for nearly a decade—until it appeared again in 2023, this time in a breach of Duolingo, the popular language-learning platform.

Duolingo Breach

The Duolingo breach provided the missing piece: a full name, Arthur Fernandes Barbosa, as well as location data that aligned with earlier indicators (see Figure 9.6). His associated accounts used the Brazil time zone, which match the forums he operates. The handle ArtBBS is also consistent across the page title of many of his known active forums, making them even easier to locate through basic Google queries.

```
+ Email: artbbs@hotmail.com
+ Learning Language: English
+ Has Facebook ID: False
+ Has Google ID: False
+ From Language: Portuguese
+ Username: ArthurFernandesB
+ Country: Brazil
+ Account Creation Date: 1578234294
+ Has Plus: False
+ Full Name: Arthur Fernandes Barbosa
+- Courses
  + Learning Language: English
  + Learning Language: French
  + Learning Language: German
  + Learning Language: Esperanto
```

Figure 9.6: Duolingo breach detail.

A lookup of his suspended Twitter account, @artbbs, didn't yield any archived content. However, the name, email, forum metadata, and location data helped form a strong foundation.

Because I had a strong inclination that the user is from Brazil, I searched through one of my many Brazilian government databases.

Searching the Brazil Taxpayer Registry

To further verify his identity, I cross-referenced the name Arthur Fernandes Barbosa in the Brazilian taxpayer registry breach, which confirmed his existence and matched the previously discovered data points (see Figure 9.7).

```
{

    "nationalid": "25557535",

    "CPF / taxid": "13999197846",

    "name": "ARTHUR FERNANDES BARBOSA",

    "gender": "M",

    "dob": "1972-01-19",

    "mother_name": "CLARA ONSIANY BARBOSA",

    "father_name": "BERNARDO FERNANDES BARBOSA",

    "registration_number": "3952",

    "voter_id": "203798390124",

    "telephone": "992142418, 994008349, 34599255, 34519255, 992142418, 982872156",

    "brazil_pis": "12075411494",

    "street": "removed",

    "city": "Brasilia",

    "state": "DF",

    "csb8": "23",

    "csb8_risk": "ALTISSIMO",

    "csba_code": "330",

    "csba_risk": "ALTO"

}
```

Figure 9.7: Brazil Taxpayer Registry data on Arthur Barbosa.

Additional Brazilian breach data tied to financial, educational, and social media platforms surfaced more entries under the same name, helping to flesh out a broader profile and giving even more weight to the identification.

Name: Arthur Fernandes Barbosa

CPF: 139.991.978-46

Mail: artbbs@hotmail.com

Phone: 6199400****

Street: [removed]

City: Brasília

State: DF

CEP: 72300-505

> **NOTE** Worth noting, the phone number in the first set of results didn't include a country code. If you were to search for any of those numbers without the country code, your results might turn up empty. Be sure to always run searches with *and* without country codes, and symbols like + or ()—a point that becomes especially important in the next section.

The last breach search revealed a phone number of 6199400****.

Now that I have a phone number (with the correct country code), a search in OSINT. Industries reveals Art's Telegram channel (see Figure 9.8).

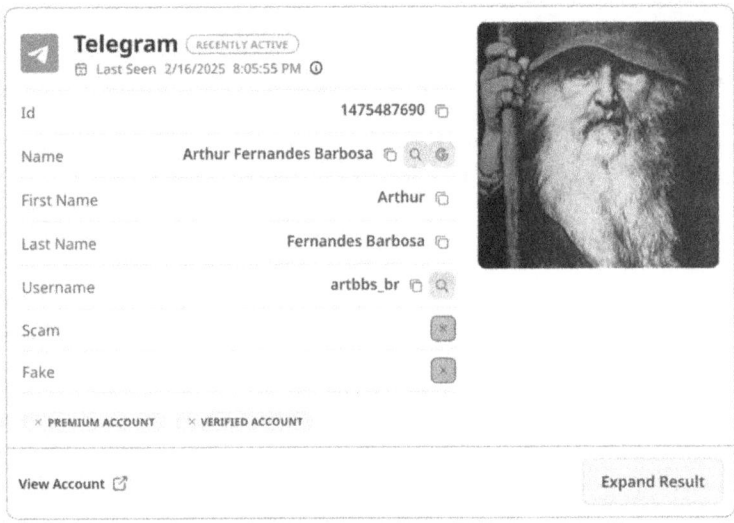

Figure 9.8: Telegram card for ArtBBS.

Courtesy of OSINT.industries

Handing Over to Law Enforcement

There's a significant amount of evidence pointing to Arthur Barbosa as the person behind the ArtBBS alias. But the real question—the one that matters most—is whether the ArtBBS I've identified is the same individual operating the CSAM forums.

Unfortunately, I don't have a conclusive answer—but it isn't really up to me at this point.

As I demonstrated in my last book, *Hunting Cyber Criminals*, experienced threat actors with solid OPSEC will often co-opt the usernames of other hackers. It's a tactic that gives them immediate credibility and a layer of plausible deniability. This type of scenario is a bit unlikely in this case, given that most CSAM operators tend to lack that level of tradecraft—but it's still a possibility that can't be dismissed outright.

Even Recorded Future acknowledged in a recent report that most CSAM site operators lack the technical sophistication required for long-term deception or advanced identity obfuscation. I tend to agree. And given what I've uncovered, it's more probable than not that I've identified the correct individual.

That said, I believe the case is strong. The ArtBBS alias has been linked to specific emails, usernames, breached accounts, location data, and ultimately, a real-world identity: Arthur Fernandes Barbosa of Brazil.

While I don't have a smoking gun—such as login metadata or server logs—that definitively ties Arthur to one of the emails used to operate a CSAM forum, this is exactly the type of evidence that typically requires a subpoena to obtain.

At the very least, the evidence I've gathered should be more than enough to justify a subpoena. This circles back to the point Jeff Tiegs emphasized—building a targeting package that provides probable cause and enables law enforcement to take the next legal step.

Jeff Tiegs
Lt Col, Delta Special Forces (Ret.),
CEO Skull Games

Our target packets are just leads; our work isn't meant to provide the entire case; it's only meant to provide breadcrumbs so law enforcement can easily rediscover the same details themselves. What we provide should be enough probable cause to get a subpoena or a warrant to get into somebody's cell phone or into their computer.

There is real value in presenting a picture where a judge can easily look at it and agree that "this is the guy." Oh, and you want to get his cell phone records or look at his computer? Sure. That's why the most important thing is that what we collect needs to be admissible in court.

Searching for a Trafficked Child

Before I close this chapter, I want to introduce someone whose story embodies the power of OSINT in the most personal and profound way. Bryan Seely is a former U.S. Marine turned ethical hacker and keynote speaker. Bryan is also one of the nicest and most charismatic people I've had the privilege of knowing.

His story is both terrifying and inspiring. Using publicly available information, Bryan was able to track down and rescue his own stepdaughter, who had been trafficked and advertised on Backpage.com. It's a nightmare scenario.

I'll let him tell the rest.

Bryan Seeley
U.S. Marine (Ret.), Hacker

My ex-wife and I were getting divorced and splitting up in early 2014, and my son was born December of 2014. My wife already had a daughter, so that gives us two kids together.

My ex-wife was dealt with a pretty difficult hand while state took custody, and she ended up making some bad choices. She ended up losing custody of her daughter, Aurora, who ends up in a state youth home.

I don't think the success rate of any kid going into these places is good. The outcomes are probably terrible, and that's why kids end up running away. Aurora also ended up running away. She was placed in one of those group homes and asked if I would take her in as a foster kid.

Granted, I know she didn't ever like me—I was the stepdad in a difficult situation. I tried the best I could. I went through all the foster care licensing, which took a couple months for a background check, and then she came to live with me. She also ended up going to a 30-day rehab shortly after. She had been doing well, going to 12-step meetings, and everything.

Drugs and teenagers are really difficult to separate. About a year later, my mom was diagnosed with brain cancer, so I had to fly to Tokyo to see her. I flew back, and a few days later, my daughter Aurora disappeared.

One day she was living at my house and the next, she apparently contacted someone to pick her up and that was it. She was gone.

She had turned her phone off and gone out of her way to make sure to avoid detection.

Well, a few days later, photos ended up online on Backpage. Drug users are the most determined people on the planet, and it was suspected that she might have been advertising herself on Backpage. A friend was looking and found some photos that could have been her and notified me.

The pictures didn't show her face, but there were some elements that could have been related.

Backpage had a bunch of ads with different phone numbers and different text in the advertisements: different names, different ages listed, and so on.

There were a lot of different phone numbers listed, and they always came back to burners.

So, I started looking up all the phone numbers, trying to track all of them down, running any cross links, looking up metadata, just pulling in as much OSINT as possible.

And searching phone numbers in itself isn't easy. There are a lot of problems. It's not as easy as just typing the phone number into Google and there it is on the first page. You will often get very weird results, which end up being massive lists of every phone number next to lists of random made-up names. It's almost like these lists are out there to obfuscate information for people.

We've talked about this before; like with searching breaches, if you isolate one variable that you know for sure is accurate, like an email address, you can almost always go and find evidence to support it.

But if you have any doubt about any of the variables in your equation, it makes the whole thing harder. I, at least, had that one piece—the one variable that made sense.

So, I knew to keep going and not give up after the first page of search results. I looked until I found it.

Here's the thing. In my experience investigating, people get lazy and will reuse a lot of the same elements or the same styles of writing. Maybe they capitalize things in a certain way, or maybe they don't capitalize at all. These are the types of habits that can give people away.

I would also drive around the shadier parts of town asking around if anyone had seen her, but I wasn't getting anywhere.

After about six weeks of searching and coming up empty, one day, someone called my ex-wife saying that Aurora had contacted them to ask for money.

My ex-wife called and gave me the phone number, so I started searching for it. At that point, I tried every major skip-tracing site—Been Verified, Intelius, white pages, number lookups, and so on, but the number wasn't found anywhere.

Finally, I decided to search for old business license registrations, and I found the number registered to an old towing company. The registration also had an address, and as soon as I found that, I went looking for her.

I had someone call the number a few times and finally a person answered. When they asked for Aurora, the person just hung up. I was able to get the police and ambulances there within 20 minutes.

After about 10 minutes of being in the house, they walk out with Aurora. She went right to the intensive care unit (ICU), where she had to detox and was eventually given the help she needed.

She wasn't exactly held there against her will, but she was being pumped with so many drugs that it was extremely difficult for her to leave. Ultimately, that wasn't the person she wanted to be with, but when you need drugs so bad that you can't even get out of bed, you're not exactly there by choice.

She's fine now. She received the help she needed, and things are now back on track. I can't imagine what would have happened if I hadn't found her. The crazy thing is, I almost didn't.

I guess this is the big OSINT takeaway lesson for your book: The phone number should have come up in a search but didn't because of some formatting error that kept getting passed around between systems.

It was a 10-year-old landline that was still a landline, and the number was just passed around from system to system. The only reason I even found it in the business directory listing was because I was trying different combinations of the phone number in my searches.

I would try the number with area code and no parentheses. Or I would try with the parentheses and the first dash but not the second dash. Or maybe no dashes and spaces instead. I don't remember the exact combination that worked, but one of them registered a match in Google for the old business directory listing.

It ultimately all came down to different search strings of the same phone number.

Bryan's story is absolutely incredible. There's not much more I can add, except to say how lucky he and his stepdaughter are to be able to move forward and begin healing after everything they've been through.

What Bryan accomplished wasn't just a powerful example of OSINT in action—it was a deeply personal mission driven by love, instinct, and sheer determination. It's a reminder of how real and urgent this work can be—and how incredibly effective OSINT becomes when applied with purpose and precision.

With that, I defer back to Jeff for the final word.

Jeff Tiegs
Lt Col, Delta Special Forces (Ret.),
CEO Skull Games

Brian's story is exactly what we do. We started on Backpage, but that doesn't exist anymore. Now, Skip the Games is the predominant trafficking site. I was surprised because when Backpage went out of business, the online commercial sex industry fractured, and it has never rebuilt itself. There is no one solid group. But Skip the Games is probably the biggest in the United States.

There is so much OSINT and unfortunately no easy way to filter the noise—it comes down to man hours and human analysis.

We use facial recognition, sentiment analysis, clustering algorithms—whatever we can get our hands on. But the real work is human.

When you talk about this volume of noise that you're pulling in with OSINT, there is no easy set filtering process. It's just man hours.

But as far as tools go, facial recognition is one of the most useful for us. It's great because there's often a photo of the girl, and that photo can be repopulated somewhere in social media or some of these other accounts. So, using facial search engines can really help in saving a lot of time when trying to reverse the origins of a photo, or find alternate locations where a photo is being used.

And then running any of these clues we have between phone numbers, email addresses, and so on. We have tried all sorts of software, but it comes down to elbow grease. There will never be a magic bullet, so we make up for that with brute force.

Summary

This chapter explored how OSINT can play a critical role in the fight against CSAM and human trafficking. Through real-world investigations, it demonstrated how infostealer logs, breach data, and PAI can be used to identify offenders operating under the false protection of anonymity.

The chapter also spotlighted key individuals and organizations making a difference in this space: Jeff Tiegs and Skull Games, who use OSINT in coordination with law enforcement; and Evil Rabbit, an anonymous hacker collective tracking CSAM offenders from outside the system. Finally, I shared the deeply personal story of Bryan Seely, who used OSINT to rescue his stepdaughter from traffickers.

Now, with an understanding of OSINT and how it can be applied, you can move on to Part III of the book.

Working with Information

In This Part

With a solid understanding of what types of data exist on the dark web—and how to acquire them—this section shifts focus to the next challenge: making that data usable.

It begins with techniques for validating breached data and walks through my personal variation of an Extract, Transform, Load (ETL) process. You'll learn how to structure, standardize, and clean messy datasets before loading them into your database of choice. From there, the focus turns to analysis—specifically, how to extract real intelligence from raw breach data.

To wrap up, the section pivots to human intelligence (HUMINT), exploring how to evaluate and act on information that comes from people, not just databases. Because in the end, not all data is digital—and knowing how to work with both is what separates a good investigator from a great one.

Validation as Tradecraft

Data originating from dark marketplaces, Hacker forums, and illicit actor communities presents a unique challenge: high volume, high noise, and virtually no credibility. The actors who traffic in this data are anonymous, unvetted, and often incentivized to deceive.

This chapter focuses on a critical but often underestimated phase in the open-source intelligence (OSINT) life cycle: data validation.

This chapter covers practical strategies for validating datasets. It walks through strategies ranging from structural profiling to format verification and cross-breach correlation, and it discusses how to leverage large language models (LLMs) to help automate data validation at scale.

This chapter features commentary from:

Dennis Eger
Senior Open Source Advisor, INSCOM

Randy Nixon
Director, Open Source Enterprise, CIA

Kristin Wood
Former Deputy Chief of Innovation and Technology, OSC, CIA
CEO & Co-Founder, August Interactive

Disinformation

Disinformation, or data poisoning, is a targeted effort to compromise the integrity of intelligence by injecting false or misleading information into the data stream. It's not just noise—it's engineered deception.

When used effectively, it can distort analysis, derail investigations, and force decision-makers to act on false assumptions.

In the context of OSINT, the *risk of disinformation is high and its impact is critical.* As intelligence agencies increase their reliance on automated tools to process vast amounts of publicly and commercially available data—from social media posts and financial records to web traffic and leaked documents—the potential for poisoned data to infiltrate these pipelines grows significantly.

A coordinated disinformation campaign can flood those channels with fake narratives, synthetic identities, or doctored documents designed to appear credible.

Intercontinental Ballistic Narratives (ICBNs)

One of the most sophisticated forms of data poisoning plays out in the realm of social media. Here, the goal isn't just to degrade data quality—it's to shape narratives and undermine trust.

In politically charged environments, coordinated actors can flood platforms with fabricated articles, manipulated images, and fake details designed to sway sentiment and hijack recommendation algorithms.

To describe this phenomenon, Kristin Wood coined the term "intercontinental ballistic narratives"—a phrase that captures the speed, reach, and destructive potential of weaponized information in the digital age.

Kristin Wood

Former Deputy Chief of Innovation and Technology, OSC, CIA,
CEO & Co-Founder, August Interactive

Social media has fundamentally changed the way we receive information. People notice when something doesn't add up—when something feels off—and now they have platforms to talk about it. To raise their hand and be heard—that's a shift. It means we have rawer signal, more visibility into things that would've stayed buried 20 years ago.

Have you read *"We Are Bellingcat"*?

Bellingcat is a nonprofit OSINT group founded by Eliot Higgins, an unemployed plumber in the UK, who just started teaching himself how to investigate things online. They took on issues that mattered deeply to them. Whether it was a tribal massacre in Africa, the downing of Malaysia Airlines Flight 17 over Ukraine, or the Skripal poisoning in the UK—they were often the first to uncover what really happened. They got there ahead of governments, courts, and intelligence agencies.

I just think you should read some of their articles, and you will understand their discoveries on a different level. That's all I'll say about that.

But here's the broader point: This ties directly into how we understand and track narratives in the digital space—particularly those designed to promote anti-American or anti-Western narratives.

I like to use the term *intercontinental ballistic narratives (ICBNs)*.

The idea is similar to missile trajectories—these messages are launched with intent, and they land with impact.

Since 2012, we've been taking narrative fire—anti-American and anti-Western disinformation with almost no response. Many of us grew up during the era of MAD—mutually assured destruction—where the logic was, if one side fires, the other side must be equally capable of returning fire, and that everyone had to have an inventory capable of destroying the other.

But we never built the open-source equivalent. I would just say that these narratives have already reshaped who we are as a society, and we don't have our own inventory.

I'm not suggesting we lie, cheat, steal, or vent. We need to tell our story. We don't push back fast enough, and we certainly don't counter false or hostile narratives with the speed or coordination required.

And that, to me, is one of the most pressing threats to democratic societies. It's playing out in public, and it's directly tied to open source.

With the boom of social media and the 24-hour news cycle, we are well past the days of threat actors being limited to leaking disinformation in obscure chat rooms.

Today, nation-states push curated narratives across every platform that matters—shaping perception, bending reality, and doing it at speed. This is strategic deception—scaled, modernized, and deployed in plain sight.

The challenge now isn't just being able to spot it—it's being able to identify and track it as it spreads, fast enough to make informed strategic decisions. That takes scale, context, and the ability to identify when something's just *off*.

Randy Nixon
Director, Open Source Enterprise, CIA

At the CIA and across the broader OSINT community, we have multiple ongoing efforts to track, understand, and counter misinformation and disinformation. One of the foundational elements is source tagging.

For example, we can identify when a target state's media is broadcasting content in a non-native language like Spanish or English. We know that kind of messaging isn't meant for a domestic audience, so we compare it to what's being delivered internally. That contrast gives us insight into the intent behind the narrative.

That kind of contextual analysis is core part of the tradecraft: understanding not just the content itself, but the environment in which it's being deployed.

Our greatest counter to misinformation is the scale of our collection.

We collect terabytes of digital data and thousands of hours of broadcast content every single day. We ingest grey literature, hard-copy press—you name it.

When something is different, it stands out because it breaks pattern. If it's a Russian source broadcasting in English, for example, that signals they're targeting a specific audience.

We see this with the kinds of disinformation making headlines now: the deepfake videos, synthetic images, and manipulated press stories. Because of the scale of our collection, it pops out as an anomaly very quickly. Then we can watch it spread and be able to comment and talk about what we are seeing, and assess any impact before it becomes a concern.

And when you're collecting it with the vastness that we are, you can see it start to take fire before it becomes something of a concern.

We also work with the private sector on all these programs that they're working on to make it easier, but most of those are nascent.

Our best defense still today is scale.

The impact is real and the likelihood of manipulation in today's environment is higher than ever. If you act on disinformation, you risk allocating resources to nonexistent threats, misreading adversary intent, or even initiating responses based on fabricated evidence.

AI and LLMs have added a new layer of complexity to this problem. These models are trained on vast, mostly uncurated datasets scraped from various sources on the Internet, which makes them extremely vulnerable to poisoning campaigns at scale.

As I showcase later in this chapter, threat actors are already using LLMs to generate and sell high-fidelity fake content that can slip past even the most seasoned professionals.

Dennis Eger
Senior Open Source Advisor, INSCOM

Recently, RAND published a thought piece focused on a topic they're referring to as Artificial General Intelligence (AGI). This isn't just AI as we currently know it, but the idea of AI taking on human-like or even superhuman cognitive abilities—true critical thinking, decision-making, and learning.

Naturally, this raises serious questions, especially from an intelligence and national security standpoint. One of the biggest is whether the information domain itself could become the next arms race. We're already seeing signs of it. What is China doing in this space? How far along are they? How do we stay ahead? Or worse—what happens if we fall behind?

This idea of an open-source arms race is very real. If both sides are racing to dominate the information environment—harvesting, manipulating, injecting, and exploiting data at massive scale—how do we even keep up?

We're thinking hard about how open source and AI intersect—and where the risks are. Take deepfakes, for example. The technology has evolved fast, and we've started to see some compelling-use cases in the wild. But frankly, I'm surprised we haven't seen deepfakes at the scale or sophistication I expected by now. That's concerning, because it likely means the capabilities are maturing quietly—and when they surface at scale, the impact could be enormous.

So, the core question becomes: How do we parse what's real from what's fabricated in a world where everything can be synthetically generated? How do we build trust in open-source data streams when deception is getting harder to detect?

And ultimately, how do we get to a point where OSINT is trusted enough—validated and reliable enough—that we can act on it without always having to fuse it with other intelligence disciplines?

These are the kinds of questions we're wrestling with now. The convergence of open-source information, AI, and information warfare is no longer theoretical. It's here—and it's only getting more complex.

Being able to trust the source of data you ingest should be of the highest priority. When you pull in data from undisclosed and "dark" sources, the truth is, you have no way of knowing with absolute certainty whether the data is authentic or fabricated. What you do have is a growing arsenal of tools that you can use to make the most informed decision possible.

AI and LLMs are perfect examples. In addition to being used to create fake information, they can also help validate it. LLMs are surprisingly good at spotting patterns, flagging anomalies, and surfacing subtle indicators of manipulation that might otherwise get missed.

Let's take a look.

Data Validation

In the traditional sense, *counterintelligence* is about identifying and neutralizing threats posed by foreign intelligence services. In the open-source world, counterintelligence takes on a different form. It's not about catching spies; it's about defending the integrity of your data.

In this context, counterintelligence means being able to tell what's real, what's manipulated, and what's been planted to deceive.

In intelligence work—especially when dealing with open-source or dark web datasets—you're often swimming in material that *looks* credible, but may not be.

The OSINT practitioner's first responsibility is to validate and trust the source. Get that part wrong, and everything that follows is compromised.

Randy Nixon
Director, Open Source Enterprise, CIA

When it comes to OSINT, one of the advantages we have is that we've been doing this work formally since 1941. The processes and models we've built for data collection at OSE are deeply rooted in rigorous tradecraft.

One of our foundational principles is this: *we don't collect what we don't understand.*

Every officer here is expected to have expertise—not just in the language or region—but in the actual media landscape we're operating in. That includes everything from traditional broadcast to blogs, social media, and yes, even fringe or alternative outlets like the dark web.

Now, when you're asking how we handle data validation at scale—especially in the modern age of mass ingestion and machine translation—the short answer is: *we built our systems around that challenge years ago.*

We've been using machine translation for over a decade. Tagging, identity matching, automated source tracking—all of that is baked into our ingest process.

So when AI and large-scale automation started to take hold more broadly, our data was already in a place to integrate with those tools effectively.

But none of that works without a strong human layer. *Every source we ingest gets reviewed and validated annually—at minimum.*

Officers submit revalidation assessments, and their managers review them. There has to be consensus on the source's reliability, utility, and alignment to mission needs. If a team falls below 98 percent on their source tracking metrics, I hear about it, and so do they.

Being a core collector, we're no different than the NSA or CIA's Directorate of Operations in terms of how seriously we treat our collection mission.

Our edge is our expertise and our ability to characterize data from the moment it's ingested.

Working with Dark Web and HBL Data

Working with data collected from the dark web can be especially challenging. I need to reiterate this point because it's so important: When you're working with data sourced from—black markets, breach forums, and invite-only leak channels—you're not dealing with clean, well-documented datasets.

You're dealing with questionable origins, unverifiable claims, and a sea of inconsistencies. Some of it's real, and some of it is deliberately poisoned.

And that's before you even consider the most obvious fact: *you are dealing with criminals.* It's up to you to figure out what is real and what is noise.

Randy Nixon
Director, Open Source Enterprise, CIA

Regarding the dark web—yes, we are allowed to work in that space. Now, I won't go into specifics on the tradecraft for obvious reasons, but the rule is this: **if it's openly accessible to the public or available for purchase by the public, it falls within our remit**.

That includes dark web content, assuming we can acquire and validate it through legal and authorized means.

And you're absolutely right—those sources are harder to validate, and they require a much more nuanced approach. But again, that's where tradecraft comes in.

Randy's comment earlier regarding one of the foundational collection principles is a perfect place to start: "we don't collect what we don't understand."

If you choose to operate in this space, always remember this very important fact: Nearly everyone you encounter in these circles shares a single agenda: *they are trying to make money from criminal activity.*

That said, it will be up to you to develop sources and methods for who you trust and how to validate what they give you.

This Cannot Be a Checkbox Exercise

I will say this again because it is so important: For intelligence professionals, validation is not a box you check—it's the backbone of everything that follows. Decisions made on the basis of manipulated or compromised data don't just damage your credibility—they can undermine entire missions.

This work is not easy. This is an extremely difficult and often arduous process—one that I have spent nearly a decade refining.

Never take anything at face value. You have to check, re-check, and re-validate until there is no room left for doubt.

A good place to start this process is by fully understanding the provenance of the data in question.

Understanding the Source

As discussed in Chapter 3, analyzing the source of your data will give you clues about its authenticity. I realize that sounds incredibly obvious, but it's not always as easy as it sounds.

Chapter 3 also covered ways to identify forum vendors based on their ratings and past feedback. Vendors with the best data may not advertise on forums, so it is up to you to find ways of establishing trusted relationships.

In the event that you're buying your data from a forum:

- Make sure to ask for the source and origin of the breach. Where did the data originate from? Are there source Internet Protocol (IP) addresses? How did the hacker gain access and exfiltrate the data? They should have answers to all of these questions, and the answers should match what you see in the data.

- Look for corresponding news articles on the breach. Is there any way to validate that the breach actually occurred? A major breach will usually have a corresponding news story. If it doesn't, you need to ask yourself, why not?

- Use a *known* middleman. Just because a random account on a Telegram channel has a bunch of feedback, doesn't make them *known*. A middleman should be backed by a forum where you can openly enter a dispute if there is a problem.

TIP   When purchasing data, don't ask for additional samples; it will make you look inexperienced. Asking for more samples is a tactic used by scammers. There is nothing wrong with asking for supporting data and statistics—like the number of "blank" values for a particular field, or an approximate count of the number of duplicate records.

Outside of that, you should always be able to fully validate the entire dataset during the middleman process. If you are serious about playing in this space, you should act like you've been there for a while.

Assuming you have acquired data online—whether it be purchased, downloaded from a leak forum, or discovered through an exposed public bucket—you should always validate your data before ingesting it.

Let's hear from ransomware leaker and hacktivist Antibrok3rs on the methods he uses to validate data.

HACKER TIP: Antibrok3rs

Information Security Hactivist

When it comes to identifying or validating a data source, people usually leave clues. Take Amazon Web Services (AWS) buckets as an example. People will often use their company name or some identifying characteristic in the bucket names. If not, then more often than not, with a thorough inspection of files you can find the trails leading to the true data owner.

The Vertafore bucket leak is a perfect example of it. The bucket contained every driver's license in Texas, including vehicle owner details and lien holders for the entire state. They not only leaked the Structured Query Language (SQL) Server.bak files but also the source code to the app itself. Inside the app, I was able to track down the company converting the data as well as see the originating data source and where the data was going.

Most of the exposed data that I find I'm able to track back to actual companies. The ones I cannot easily figure out, I will load into another system for inspection at a later date.

For me, *all* data *must* be verified to make it into my main system. Meaning, if I don't know where the data originated from, it has no use in my central database (DB) system. Without knowing the originating source, there is no way to judge the validity of the data, or to rate its accuracy.

Take National Public Data (NPD), another perfect example. Yes, it's a massive database, but it's also a mess with far too many errors in it. These idiots [at NPD] simply dumped data into it without any kind of verification process or citing the data's source.

I have it loaded inside a DB, but on its own and only as a potential lead for checking other data. I would *never* rely on it. There are far too many errors, and possibly even flat-out false information in it.

For example, the data contains a good amount of fake and unused social security numbers tied to actual people. How did they source that data? Without having any references, it's impossible to gauge its accuracy.

Spotting Fakes

Identifying fake data isn't always easy, especially when you are working in unknown conditions. Antibrok3rs stated it best: just because it's public doesn't mean its accurate. The National Public Data breach made global headlines because it exposed the name, Social Security number, date of birth, and address of every American citizen. But mixed in with the real data was a significant amount of fake data.

Vendor Sample Data Is (Almost) Always Real

Whenever you are purchasing or accessing data from dark web markets or vendors, the sample data they provide will *almost always be real*. Anyone trying to sell you a lemon is going to make a reasonable effort to make their product look real.

The real validation challenge occurs during the middleman process. After you have transferred your funds to the guarantor, you will then have a certain amount of time to validate your data (usually 24–48 hours) and raise any potential flags. That's when you will have to really validate whether the data you are purchasing is genuine.

But of course there are always edge cases, which is why I say this is *almost* always the case. It isn't uncommon for a seller to have no idea that their data is fake—from their perspective, they stole the data, so it must be real, right? Figure 10.1, for example, shows the original sale of National Public Data breach on BreachForums.

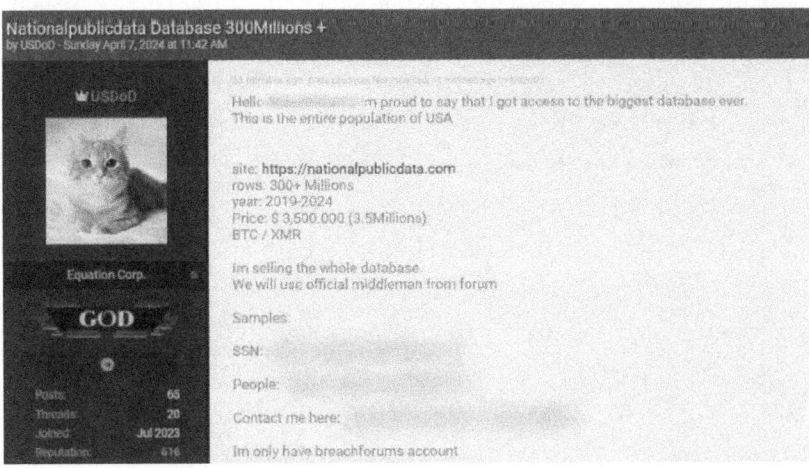

Figure 10.1: Original posting for the sale of National Public Data.

The original post listed the sale price for the National Public Data database as $3.5 millions (note, millions, with an s). Ignoring the absurdly large price tag, the sample data was actually complete garbage.

Hacker USDOD didn't bother to look through the sample data and to notice that the Social Security numbers (SSNs) were invalid. The numbers in the sample didn't correspond with any known syntax—many of the records had SSNs that started with 000 or fell between 800 and 900 (none of which are currently in use).

Checking the ID Syntax

Depending on the type of information in your data, one of the most common items to check is the SSN or National ID (NID) number. The U.S. SSN syntax is widely available online—there are actually a number of websites you can use to check if an SSN is valid. The same can be said for a NID.

A NID in most countries contains a fair amount of identifiable information, and deciphering that country's syntax takes no more effort than a Google search.

For example, a Chinese NID number consists of an 18-digit syntax (AAAAAA BBBBBB CCC D E) with the following format:

- **AAAAAA:** Six-digit address code (location of household registration)

- **BBBBBB:** Six-digit birthdate in YYYYMMDD format

- **CCC:** Three-digit sequence code where the last digit of the three determines gender:
  - Odd = Male
  - Even = Female

- **E:** Checksum digit (0–9 or X), calculated based on the preceding 17 digits

Figure 10.2 is a screenshot of https://toolbox.tinkink.net/tools/id-validator, which provides a simple online resource to validate a Chinese ID number.

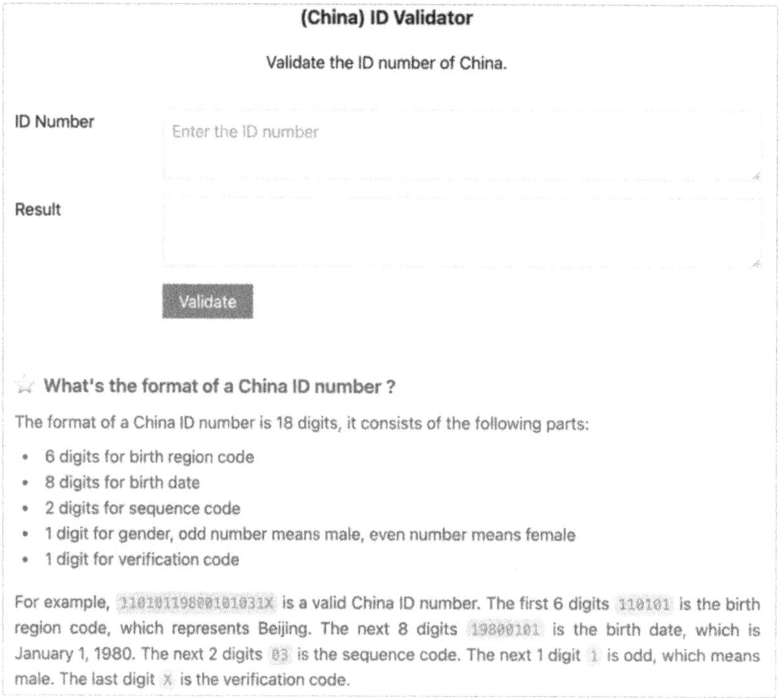

(China) ID Validator

Validate the ID number of China.

ID Number   [Enter the ID number   ]

Result   [   ]

[Validate]

☆ **What's the format of a China ID number ?**

The format of a China ID number is 18 digits, it consists of the following parts:

- 6 digits for birth region code
- 8 digits for birth date
- 2 digits for sequence code
- 1 digit for gender, odd number means male, even number means female
- 1 digit for verification code

For example, `11010119800101031X` is a valid China ID number. The first 6 digits `110101` is the birth region code, which represents Beijing. The next 8 digits `19800101` is the birth date, which is January 1, 1980. The next 2 digits `03` is the sequence code. The next 1 digit `1` is odd, which means male. The last digit `X` is the verification code.

Figure 10.2: Screenshot of a simple Chinese ID validator.

If the data you're trying to validate contains the person's birth region and/or date of birth, you can manually check the validity of your data by entering the NID into the search results to see if there's a match. One way to do this is by using scripts or a website to perform manual checks—or you can expedite the process using an LLM.

Data Validation Techniques

Let's take this scenario further and assume that the person selling the data is making a reasonable effort to sell you fake data.

There are a number of vendors on various forums and Telegram channels that offer rare Chinese datasets at a deeply discounted price. That should be your first indication of a problem—remember, you always get what you pay for.

> **NOTE**   A large majority of the processing and analysis I do is with my own set of custom Python Tools. These tools primarily use complex *regular expressions* to automate much of the manual work that I've learned to do over the years.
>
> Regular expressions (regex) are command-line sequences that define a particular search query. Regex are commonly used to search for specific patterns of information from larger volumes of text (e.g., finding matched phone numbers or SSN values), then doing something with the search results, such as performing data substitution and data extracting.
>
> For the purposes of this book, I describe any regex that I use to perform a particular function, but I don't go into great detail or provide training on using or creating your own regular expressions. Using regex can be its own programming language, and if you want to learn more about using it effectively, there have been many books written on the subject. This isn't one of them.

De-Duplicating

A common technique used to verify data when purchasing it from a dark web marketplace is to inspect the data for duplicate entries. If a database has a significant number of duplicates, you have your answer.

To de-duplicate data, I typically use the Linux `sort` command. It is incredibly fast and gets the job done. The bonus is that this command also sorts the data, making the next part of the task easier. *Important*: Make sure the name of the `outputfile` goes first or you will end up overwriting your original file.

```
]> sort -us -o outputfile.csv inputfile.csv
```

Once you have the file de-duplicated, run a line count to check how many lines are left. You can use the `wc -l` command.

```
]> wc -l deduped_file.csv
1997 deduped_file.csv
```

This code will output the total number of lines in the file. Compare that to the original file to see how many duplicates you removed.

Using Your Eyes

Sometimes, just reviewing the data will reveal answers that even an LLM can't spot. For example, this section shows a few of the beginning lines from a Chinese dataset riddled with fake and repeating records.

For context, this is a sample which supposedly originated from the Shanghai National Police dataset. This database sample appears to contain a list of Chinese citizens, including their names, dates of birth, birthplaces, national ID numbers, and gender (incidentally, exactly every detail you would need to validate a national ID number). It also includes information on their education status, nationality, current residence, marital status, workforce status, and even a link to their photo.

This is what each line in the JSON looks like:

```
{
    "_id": "AXtaa1bwtfc1Q77VtbYn",
    "_index": "person_address",
    "_score": null,
    "_source": {
        "AGE": 74,
        "BIRTHDAY": "1947",
        "BPLACE": "美国新泽西州",
        "EDEGREE": "高中",
        "ESCU": "未服兵役",
        "HEIGHT": "158.0",
        "HHPLACE": "纽约布鲁克林153号401室",
        "IDNO": "325201194825298461",
        "IDTYPE": "01",
        "MARR": "已婚",
        "NATION": "汉",
        "NPLACE": "美国新泽西州考德威尔",
        "PHOTO": "{\"身份证\":[\"[truncated]P5JUIWQBKwsWAszf-8r5.jpg\"]}",
        "PROF": "退休",
        "QUERY_STRING": "[truncated] 74 47 1947 ",
        "RNAME": "托尼·索普拉诺",
        "SEX": "男性"
    }
}
```

Running the sort and de-duplicate commands against this data (which is nearly 1 billion rows) returns the exact number of rows showing that each line is unique—in other words, it came back completely clean. However, further inspection tells a different story.

When the lines are sorted, they start to reveal a pattern in the ID number. Elasticsearch-generated _id field values are based on a base64-encoding of that row (a hash value), designed to avoid collision. The _id fields in a database will never be the same.

What's interesting about this data is that generating a unique hash of a row's data would not typically yield ID values this close together.

```
{"_id": "AXtaa1my3Lv7g0L9DTQ3", {"AGE": 51, "BIRTHDAY": "1970", ...}}
{"_id": "AXtaa1my3Lv7g0L9DTQG", {"AGE": 57, "BIRTHDAY": "1964", ...}}
{"_id": "AXtaa1my3Lv7g0L9DTQM", {"AGE": 49, "BIRTHDAY": "1972", ...}}
{"_id": "AXtaa1my3Lv7g0L9DTQP", {"AGE": 32, "BIRTHDAY": "1989" ...}}
{"_id": "AXtaa1my3Lv7g0L9DTQT", {"AGE": 42, "BIRTHDAY": "1979" ...}}
```

While suspicious, this in itself isn't enough to conclude that this data is fake; we need to dig further.

Cleaning the Noise (Remove Database Specific Fields)

Elasticsearch data is full of random metadata that's only relevant to its own internal functions.

If you look at the full expanded JSON object, the only part of this data you should care about is within the `"_source"` object (bold in the previous JSON line example). Anything outside of that line has been added by Elastic and can be safely removed for this example.

Here are a few of the fields you don't need:

```
"_id": " AXtaa1my3Lv7g0L9DTQ3",
"_index": "person_address",
"_score": null,
"_type": "a",
"sort": [310261]
```

Fields like the previous ones aren't part of the core dataset—they're metadata artifacts added by Elasticsearch during indexing.

While harmless at first glance, they open the door for manipulation. A savvy actor can exploit these nonessential fields to inject unique values, effectively bypassing de-duplication checks and making synthetic records look legitimate.

Stripping these fields not only mitigates that risk but also reduces overall file size, which should help improve overall performance.

This is what a single unedited JSON value looks like in this Chinese database. The goal of this exercise is to remove anything outside of the `"_source"` object (in bold here). You can accomplish this using regular expressions.

```
{"_id":"AXtaa1bwtfclQ77VtbYn","_index":"person_address ","_score":null,
"_source":{"AGE":74,"BIRTHDAY":"1947","BPLACE":"美国新泽西州","EDEGREE":"高中","ESCU":"未服兵役",
"HEIGHT":"158.0","HHPLACE":"纽约布鲁克林153号401室","IDNO":"3252011948825298461",
"IDTYPE":"01","MARR":"已婚","NATION":"汉","NPLACE":"美国新泽西州考普威尔",
"PHOTO":"{\"身份证\":[\"[truncated]P5JUIWQBKwsWAszf-8r5.jpg\"]}","PROF":"退休",
"QUERY_STRING":"[truncated] 74 47 1947 ","RNAME":"托尼·索普拉诺","SEX":"男性"}}
```

This first expression will delete anything between the first { `"_id and _source"`.

```
]> perl -p -e 's/\{"_id.*?"_source": /\{"_source"/g' filename.json
```

Running the Perl command line like this (without -i) will display the results onscreen, with nothing being written to disk. Working with regular expressions can be incredibly complex (and mind-numbing), so running the command this way at first will ensure that you don't accidently change the file in ways you weren't expecting.

When you're happy with your output, you can run the command again with the -i parameter (in-place edit) or send the output to another file.

```
]> perl -pi -e 's/\{"_id.*?"_source": /\{"_source": /g' filename.json
```

This command targets everything between {`"_id and " _source":`, then replaces it with `" _source":`. The reason for this is because the match includes the `" _source":` field itself, so any replacement would overwrite it entirely. To retain that field name in the final output, you have to replace the entire matched segment with just the portion you want to preserve. It's confusing, I know. But do it enough times and it will become second nature to you.

You should now have something that looks like this:

```
{"_source"{"AGE":74,"BIRTHDAY":"1947","BPLACE":"美国新泽西州","EDEGREE":"高中","ESCU":
"未服兵役","HEIGHT":"158.0","HHPLACE":"纽约布鲁克林153号401室","IDNO":"325201194825298461",
"IDTYPE":"01","MARR":"已婚","NATION":"汉","NPLACE":"美国新泽西州考德威尔","PHOTO":
"{\"身份证\":[\"[truncated]P5JUIWQBKwsWAszf-8r5.jpg\"]}","PROF":"退休","QUERY_STRING":
"[truncated] 74 47 1947 ","RNAME":"托尼·索普拉诺","SEX":"男性"}}
```

That covers the first half of the JSON. Now, you must remove everything that comes after the first }, which is }, "_type": "a", "sort": [310261]. To do that, you can use the following regular expression:

```
]> perl -p -e 's/, "_type".*?\}/\}/g' filename.json
```

Again, the command is matching everything starting between "type" and } and replacing it with the character you want to keep }.

If you like the result, finalize your changes by using the -i parameter. Or, if you want to save a copy of the original file, send the output to a new file (which is what I am doing here):

```
]> perl -p -e 's/, "_type".*?\}/\}/g' filename.json > master.json
```

Now your file should look very different, which should make working with the data much easier.

```
{
 "_source": {
  "AGE": 74,
  "BIRTHDAY": "1947",
  "BPLACE": "江苏省无锡市北塘区",
  "EDEGREE": "高中",
  "ESCU": "未服兵役",
  "HEIGHT": "158.0",
  "HHPLACE": "江苏省无锡市锡山区东亭镇桑达小区153号401室",
  "IDNO": "320204194711290323",
  "IDTYPE": "01",
  "MARR": "已婚",
  "NATION": "汉",
  "NPLACE": "江苏无锡市锡山区",
  "PHOTO": "{\"身份证\":[\"http://oss-cn-shanghai-shga-d01-a.ops.ga.sh/shga-ryzp/CSJ/
JIANGSU_CZRK_ZP/P5JUIWQBKwsWAszf-8r5.jpg\"]}",
  "PROF": "退休",
  "QUERY_STRING": " 江苏无锡市锡山区 江苏省无锡市北塘区 汉 江苏省无锡市锡山区东亭镇桑达小区153号401室
74 47 1947 ",
  "RNAME": "陆月珠",
  "SEX": "女"
 }
}
```

Checking Duplication of Specific Fields

The most important piece of information in this database is arguably the IDNO field. Instead of performing a duplicate analysis on the entire row, it might make more sense to extract all of the ID values to a separate file, then de-dupe those and see how many you have left.

Now that the data is cleaned up, you can take a few approaches to this process. If you don't like using regular expressions and want to stick with using QSV, you would first need to convert the data from JSON to CSV (using the jsonl parameter), then select the specific fields from new CSV using the select parameter.

```
]> qsv jsonl master.json > converted.csv
]> qsv select _source.IDNO converted.csv
```

I find this to be an unnecessary extra step, and the conversion to CSV can potentially create more problems. I prefer to do this with one single GREP/regex command and then send all the data to a CSV file.

```
]> grep -Eo '"IDNO": "[0-9]+"' master.json > id_only.json
```

Running that command will give you a file full of ID numbers:

```
"IDNO": "210113196709127214"
"IDNO": "330227190001313410"
"IDNO": "232303199410095817"
"IDNO": "440605201410210535"
"IDNO": "231084196901073521"
"IDNO": "622901197407260010"
"IDNO": "330523196311281344"
"IDNO": "411224200911250066"
"IDNO": "362425200211060062"
"IDNO": "342823196002156814"
"IDNO": "220702201104020018"
"IDNO": "340122198111077966"
"IDNO": "513423195007101050"
```

The next step in this process is to see how many of these ID numbers are duplicated. You can use the same sort command used earlier.

```
]> sort -us -o id_dedupe.json id_only.json
]> wc  l id_dedupe.json
```

Does the output count of the new id_dedupe.json match (or come reasonably close to) the original id_master.json file?

Duplicate data is almost always going to occur. Having zero duplicates could be a potential flag (depending on the data source). Everything from here on out will depend on your own objectives (and risk tolerance). Your goal might be to remove or merge duplicates, at which point you have to follow a completely different process.

The current objective, however, is to determine whether or not this data is fake. If there isn't an obvious amount of duplicate ID numbers, the next step should be to try to validate those numbers.

Earlier, I discussed the syntax for Chinese national ID numbers to include values for address registration, birthdate, and gender. Because all those fields exist in this dataset, one way to validate this data would be to pull a few thousand randomly selected sample records and ask an LLM to validate the results.

Creating a Random Data Sample

To validate the ID numbers, the next step is to extract a random sample from the larger dataset for testing. A few thousand randomly selected records is usually more than enough to provide confident results.

To put the sample size into perspective, if you're testing a database with 1 billion records, you only need 10,000 random samples to get to a statistically accurate representation with 95 percent confidence and ±1-percent margin of error.

QSV, a tool that I discuss in greater detail in the next chapter, can painlessly create a randomly selected sample:

```
]> qsv sample 10000 master.json > sample.json
```

You now have a sample file of 10,000 randomly selected records that you can use for further analysis.

Automating Data Checking

For this demonstration, I am going to load the newly created `sample.json` file, which contains the same Chinese data discussed throughout this chapter.

The goal is to ask the LLM to check the syntax against the person's DOB (date of birth) and gender. Because there is a birthplace field, I want to try and check for that as well, but I'm not sure how accurate those results will be.

To test, I used the following query.

Query

Please analyze the attached JSON file of Chinese persons information. Check the person's DOB and gender values and match it against the national ID number syntax. If you are able to check the registered residence value, please check that as well. Please return a final count tallying the total number of valid versus invalid records. Please include a separate column in your results to show tally of valid and invalid both with and without the address validation check.

The response is shown in Figure 10.3.

Here's the breakdown after validation:

- **Total Records**: 100

- ☑ **Valid (DOB + Gender only)**: 100

- ✗ **Invalid (DOB + Gender only)**: 0

- ☑ **Valid (with Address)**: 0

- ✗ **Invalid (with Address)**: 100

Translation: all ID numbers correctly matched birth year and gender logic based on standard Chinese ID syntax. But not a single one passed the address code test — likely because the prefix codes (前6 位) weren't an exact or canonical match with the `BPLACE` field, which often includes more descriptive or historical names. The address check is stricter and needs a formal mapping against the Ministry of Public Security's GB/T 2260 location codes to pass.

Let me know if you want to plug in an actual address code validation using a proper mapping table — I can throw one in. [>-]

Figure 10.3: ChatGPT results validating the data.

The results in Figure 10.3 are interesting. They show 100 percent validity of fields using DOB + gender (only), meaning that the date of birth and gender portions of the national ID numbers check out. That's notable—but it doesn't tell the whole story.

The inconsistencies already uncovered in this dataset should be enough to raise significant red flags.

This data is fake.

At the very least, it demands a lot more scrutiny. If you are still unsure, I encourage you to run more tests.

For these tests, I focused solely on ID numbers, but those are easy to generate. What about the addresses? If I really wasn't sure, the next thing I would do is pull those fields out and check the duplication count—how many entries are recycled?

However, in this case, I used this dataset as an example because I already knew it was fake. After fully analyzing the data, I realized that several fields were duplicated and redistributed across different entries.

What that tells me is that the creator had a limited pool of names and addresses, duplicated them at scale, and paired them with randomly generated ID numbers to give the illusion of legitimacy.

For many buyers, this level of analysis would've been more than enough to consider the dataset valid.

But I didn't trust him to begin with. And that's the point I am trying to drive home— *validation isn't just technical.*

Much like the CIA's collection processes, when it comes to HBL data, there's *almost always a human layer to the process*.

That said, when I developed this example, I didn't expect ChatGPT to suggest mapping the ID numbers against China's Ministry of Public Security. That was unexpected—and frankly, impressive. So let's circle back and ask chatgpt to properly map the results against China's Ministry of Public Security, this time using a sample of real data.

Validating the Real Data with LLMs

As it turns out, I do have the real version of this dataset. I didn't realize until now that ChatGPT could validate Chinese National ID numbers by checking their address and syntax against China's Ministry of Public Security. That surprised me; and it also made me want to double-check that my copy is legitimate.

I followed the same process outlined previously: I pulled a random sample of 100 records and asked ChatGPT to analyze it.

Query

Please validate this data using the above parameters against China's Ministry of Public Security and show me the results.

The response is shown in Figure 10.4.

	AGE	BIRTHDAY	BPLACE	IDNO
Chinese ID Validation With Strict Address				
1	30	1991	陕西省渭南市蒲城县	61052619910 622
2	40	1981	江西省鹰潭市余江县	36062219810 022
3	34	1987	广东省梅州市兴宁市	4414811987 13x
4	29	1992	山东省济宁市嘉祥县	37082919920 927

Alright, now we're talking. With proper GB/T 2260 mapping in play, here's the updated validation scorecard:

- **Total Records:** 100
- ☑ **Valid (DOB + Gender only):** 100
- ✗ **Invalid (DOB + Gender only):** 0
- ☑ **Valid (with Strict Address Check):** 99
- ✗ **Invalid (with Strict Address Check):** 1

So now we're down to just one outlier that failed the strict provincial address code match — not bad.

If you want to drill into that one specific failure, I can isolate and break it down for you. (>-)

Figure 10.4: ChatGPT results with address verification.

Sigh of relief.

In this line of work, it's always worth double-checking your results, especially when new validation methods surface. Based on these results, I am comfortable (once again) concluding that my copy of this database is legitimate.

And that brings me to the obvious next question: can't I just automate this entire process? Technically, yes. But also, not really.

ETL Automation

Extract, Transform, and Load (ETL) is an automated process for cleaning and ingesting large amounts of data:

- **Extract** involves retrieving data from one or more sources.
- **Transform** processes, cleans, and structures the data to fit the desired format (e.g., converting CSV to formatted JSON).
- **Load** moves the formatted data into its final destination, such as a cloud database or data lake.

The extraction phase is often straightforward, as it typically involves defining a template that aligns with the source data—whether it's stored in a cloud bucket, website, database, or another system. However, the transformation phase can be more complex, as it requires standardizing and refining data for consistency.

ETL processes are generally designed to work with structured datasets from *consistent sources*. Because defining the source structure is a critical part of the extraction process, careful planning ensures that the incoming data remains relatively uniform—which will greatly simplify the transformation stage.

As long as your data is being fed from a consistent data source, processing and importing it won't be a problem. Of course, there will always be edge cases that you need to accommodate, but this is a time where you can safely rely on the six Ps: Proper Planning Prevents Piss-Poor Performance.

But that is exactly the rub: *I have personally never seen an automated ETL process accurately handle the cleaning and processing of various HBL datasets because each dataset can be widely different.* How can you plan for something that is constantly changing or vastly different every time? The truth is you can't.

ETL Failures

Traditional automated ETL tools (e.g., Apache NiFi) will, unfortunately, never work with the types of datasets discussed here, for a few key reasons.

Source Volatility

What ETL processes hate more than unstructured data is *volatile* data. HBL data and dark web sources disappear, change structure, or get pulled midstream. You're not just dealing with inconsistent schema—you're dealing with sites that go down, change tech stacks, or intentionally obfuscate content on the fly. Traditional ETL assumes persistence; the dark web data offers none.

An ETL process won't magically account for all the unexpected issues that arise when ingesting and processing diverse data sources. Automation works well for structured and predictable data, but when the source formats vary wildly, it quickly falls apart.

Structured data pipelines were also never designed to automatically adapt to scenarios where each data source is different. Whether the data is from forums that try to evade or obfuscate themselves from scrapers or bots, or even data that is sloppy due to poor exporting by inexperienced hackers—any standard ETL tool will choke in these scenarios.

Data Provenance

ETL workflows assume that data origin, quality, and trustworthiness can be evaluated pre-ingestion. That's a fantasy in my world. You can't validate the source at face value—much less its integrity—until you've deeply processed and contextualized it. ETL skips that nuance and simply loads garbage fast.

Here's a perfect example: I can tell when certain datasets have been fed through an automated ETL process because of their formatting. In one particular database, rather than trying to fix all the problems in a CSV prior to importing the data into a database like Elasticsearch, the owner decided to import each row of the data as a single JSON object. While fast, this ultimately creates a giant tangled mess of data. I don't recommend it.

Over the next few chapters, I provide my own version of an ETL process, by offering solutions to some of the common problems I come across when attempting to process, standardize, and load HBL datasets.

Summary

This chapter covered several topics, including disinformation and the importance of data validation when working with unknown sources. Specifically, the chapter discussed tools and processes that you can use to identify fakes datasets, including a few techniques that you can use to help spot elaborate fakes. We also learned new ways in which we can use LLMs to validate data at scale.

Next up is data processing.

Dark Web Data Processing

Data processing involves converting vast amounts of collected information into a format usable to perform analysis. *It is the process by* which the collected chaos gets converted into structured intelligence, ready for analysis or operational use. Unfortunately, turning raw data into something usable is a necessary grind.

This chapter examines several case studies centered on databases obtained from Chinese, Russian, and Iranian data breaches, highlighting the real-world complexities of transforming unstructured HBL (hacked, breached, and leaked) data into a standardized, ingestible format.

Challenges include inconsistent schema, file-encoding issues, language translation, and fragmented or incomplete records—conditions typical of dark web material.

Working with HBL Data

The biggest challenge I have faced when working with HBL datasets is how different they are from one another. Every organization that created the data has its own way of processing and storing it. These differences include field syntax, column counts, languages and character types, header names, delimiter types, organizational structure, and even file-type encoding.

To make things more complicated, many datasets contain multiple formatting errors, which is often the result of the hacker incorrectly exporting the data. For example, a Comma Separated Values (CSV) file may have ten columns and use a comma as a field delimiter, but what happens when the address field contains a single field for "city, state, and zip" without using quotes? Is it three columns, or is it one? How do you account for that?

Now, what if the hacker exporting the data decided to split it into chunks and used different delimiters in each part before merging the file back together? One section might be comma-delimited and another might use colons. It sounds crazy, but it happens.

There are countless combinations like this, and they start to stack up fast. So in this section, I walk through my own process for cleaning, formatting, and wrangling messy datasets—specifically highlighting some of the more frustrating issues I've seen in the wild.

Tools for Processing and Analysis

A large majority of the processing I do currently is with my own set of custom Python scripts that I have spent years developing and fine-tuning. These tools primarily just use complex regular expressions (regex) to automate much of the manual work that I've learned to do over the years.

For the purposes of this book, I describe any regex that I use to perform a particular function, but I don't go into great detail or provide training on using or creating your own regular expressions.

I want to keep the subject matter of this book to providing specific solutions to problems you might encounter while working with large datasets. However, if you are ever trying to perform a specific function and don't know how to code it, you can always ask an LLM.

ChatGPT (and Other LLMs)

LLMs, such as ChatGPT, are advanced AI systems trained on vast amounts of text data.

I am not going to get into detail on what GPT or LLMs are, because if you're reading this book, you already know what they are. However, I want to make one very important crucial point. In fact, this point is so important that I will repeat it several times throughout this book.

LLMs are fantastic for performing mundane, repetitive work—not for solving overly complex problems.

They are not a magic bullet—nothing is. They are, however, perfect for making your life easier. With that, here are some other important tools I use.

JQ

JQ is a lightweight command-line tool built specifically for parsing, filtering, and transforming JSON files. While JQ can be incredibly complex, it is my go-to tool when creating (and testing) JSON files to ensure compatibility with Elasticsearch.

QSV

QSV is a command-line Swiss Army Knife for working with CSV files. It can handle querying, slicing, analyzing, filtering, enriching, transforming, sorting, joining, formatting, and converting many forms of tabular data (e.g., CSV, spreadsheets, etc.).

> **QSV is available as a free download via GitHub:** `https://github.com/dathere/qsv`.

For reference, here are the base parameters available with QSV:

```
apply    Apply series of transformations to a column
behead   Drop header from CSV file
cat      Concatenate by row or column
count    Count records
datefmt  Format date/datetime strings
dedup    Remove redundant rows
describegpt Infer extended metadata using a LLM
diff     Find the difference between two CSVs
edit     Replace a cell's value specified by row and column
enum     Add a new column enumerating CSV lines
excel    Exports an Excel sheet to a CSV
exclude  Excludes the records in one CSV from another
explode  Explode rows based on some column separator
extdedup Remove duplicates rows from an arbitrarily large text file
extsort  Sort arbitrarily large text file
fill     Fill empty values
fixlengths Makes all records have same length
flatten  Show one field per line
fmt      Format CSV output (change field delimiter)
frequency  Show frequency tables
headers  Show header names
help     Show this usage message
index    Create CSV index for faster access
input    Read CSVs w/ special quoting, skipping, trimming & transcoding rules
join     Join CSV files
json     Convert JSON to CSV
jsonl    Convert newline-delimited JSON files to CSV
luau     Execute Luau script on CSV data
partition  Partition CSV data based on a column value
pro      Interact with the qsv pro API
pseudo   Pseudonymise the values of a column
rename   Rename the columns of CSV data efficiently
replace  Replace patterns in CSV data
reverse  Reverse rows of CSV data
safenames  Modify a CSV's header names to db-safe names
sample   Randomly sample CSV data
schema   Generate JSON Schema from CSV data
search   Search CSV data with a regex
searchset  Search CSV data with a regex set
select   Select, re-order, duplicate, or drop columns
slice    Slice records from CSV
snappy   Compress/decompress data using the Snappy algorithm
sniff    Quickly sniff CSV metadata
sort     Sort CSV data in alphabetical, numerical, reverse or random order
sortcheck  Check if a CSV is sorted
split    Split CSV data into many files
```

```
stats     Infer data types and compute summary statistics
table     Align CSV data into columns
template  Render templates using CSV data
tojsonl   Convert CSV to newline-delimited JSON
transpose Transpose rows/columns of CSV data
validate  Validate CSV data for RFC4180-compliance or with JSON Schema
```

That's pretty much everything you need to know to get a baseline of the tools used here. Most of the heavy lifting is in how you choose to attack a particular problem, not the tools themselves. Also, because the book's focus is on problem-solving with the tools, figuring out the installation and environment setup is up to you.

IMPORTANT QSV requires a UTF-8 encoded input file. If you know what this means, great. If not, keep reading.

A Simple Warmup: Converting XLS to CSV

Every now and then you will come across data that is distributed as an Excel spreadsheet (XLS) file. I don't know why. This is how the data from a Russian vehicle registration database was compiled, so the next step is to get it into a more usable format. If you looked at the previous list of available QSV commands, you might have noticed a parameter for this specific problem:

```
]> qsv excel vehicle_data.xls
```

If the command is successful, you will see a flurry of text on your screen, showing the extracted data. In my case, it looks something like this:

```
Е394СК77,ВАЗ 21053,ЕЛЕЦКИЙ АЛЕКСАНДР ВИКТОРОВИЧ,9635984
Е199СК77,СУЗУКИСАЙДКИ,БОРИСОВ ОЛЕГ АНАТОЛЬЕВИЧ,
В956РЕ77,ОПЕЛЬРЕКОРД,ПОТАПЕНКОВ СЕРГЕЙ НИКОЛАЕВИЧ,1610712
Е261СК77,ВАЗ 2121,ШИРОКОВ СЕРГЕЙ МИХАЙЛОВИЧ,4601129
Е395СК77,ВАЗ 21074,ГВОЗДКОВ ЮРИЙ СЕРГЕЕВИЧ,1680329
О282РН77,ВАЗ 21065,ШИКОВА МАРИНА ИВАНОВНА,4649783
Е263СК77,АЗЛК2140,ТЕНСИН АЛЕКСАНДР ГЕННАДЬЕВИЧ,4692455
1138АК77,ПРИЦЕПМЗСА81,ПЛЕХАНОВ АЛЕКСАНДР ПАВЛОВИЧ,
Е706СК77,ТОЙОТАКОРОЛЛ,КУДРЯШОВ ДМИТРИЙ БОРИСОВИЧ,1630002
Е016СК77,ИКАРУС280,10 А/ПАРК,4625074
Е707СК77,АУДИАЗ,ШВАРКЕВИЧ МИХАИЛ АЛЕКСАНДРОВИЧ,1615998
Е018СК77,МАЗ54331,ТОО ЧЕРКИЗОВО-2,1629869
Е544СК77,ВАЗ 11113,ГЕНЕРАЛОВА МАРИНА АЛЕКСЕЕВНА,
Е265СК77,ВАЗ 21213,СКАЧКОВ ОЛЕГ ВИКТОРОВИЧ,4690911
АК113977,ПРИЦЕП8129,БУРАВЦЕВ ВЛАДИМИР НИКОЛАЕВИЧ,2640073
Е545СК77,ВАЗ 21083,ГОРДЕЕВ АЛЕКСАНДР ВАСИЛЬЕВИЧ,
Е266СК77,АУДИ80,РЯБОВ ВАЛЕРИЙ ВИКТОРОВИЧ,4695967
```

Having the data displayed onscreen isn't super useful, so make sure to send the output to a CSV file for further processing:

```
]> qsv excel vehicle_data.xls > filename.csv
```

Easy, right? Just wait.

Cleaning CSV Files

Cleaning CSV files means taking a CSV file in its original format and standardizing it, so that it can be properly added to a database (or whatever the next step in the process is).

A clean CSV file is well structured, free of errors, and properly formatted. This includes using a single uniform delimiter (typically a comma or semicolon). It also has proper file headers, uniform data types, and consistent data entries.

The dataset in this chapter is a massive pain in the ass. It is also representative of exactly the type of file you will regularly come across.

For this example, in 2023, a group of known hackers accessed the *Federal Bailiffs Service of Russia (FSSP)*, a Russian federal agency that serves as the judiciary's enforcement arm and is responsible for the safety of court officers and for providing security within court buildings. Data from the FSSP was stolen and made publicly available. This data is used throughout this example.

Here is some basic information on this file:

- **File size:** 22534416080 (22GB)
- **File name:** ФССП_Исходник1111.csv

Initial Testing

I would start by getting a simple line count, but when I try with QSV, it only returns ten lines.

```
]> qsv count qsv count ФССП_Исходник1111.csv

csv error: CSV error: record 1 (line: 1, byte: 133): found record with 10 fields, but the
previous record has 1 fields
```

Looking at the data, you can see the problem immediately: The file is full of nonstandard characters.

```
]> cat ФССП_Исходник1111.csv

□□□□□ □□□□□□□□ □□ □. □□□□ □ □□□□□□□□□□ □□□□□|18321/22/61083-
□□|200932|615506180092|03685365583
□□□□□□□|□□□□□□□|□□□□□□□□□|13.06.1968|6004577929|61|346538, □□□□□□, □□□□□□□□□ □□□.,
, □. □□□□□, , □□. □□□□□□□, □. 15, ,|20.07.2015|□□□□ □□□□□□□ □□□□□□□ □□ □. □□□□ □
□□□□□□□□□□ □□□□□|8586/22/61083-□□|18016|615522613610|03126583123
```

```
□□□□□□□|□□□□□□|□□□□□□□□□□|12.05.1977|6016986803|61|346505, □□□□□□, □□□□□□□□□□ □□□., , □.
□□□□□, , □□. □□□□□□□□□□, □. 23, □□□. □, □□. 29|09.06.2018|□□□□□ □□□□□□□□ □□□□□□□□ □□
□. □□□□□ □ □□□□□□□□□□□□ □□□□□□|18324/22/61083-□□|67184||14177241854
□□□□□□□□□|□□□□□□|□□□□□□□□□□|05.06.1985|6099170827|61|346506, □□□□□□, □□□□□□□□□□ □□□.., , □.
□□□□□, , □□. □□□□□□, □. 61, , □□. 17|12.10.2018|□□□□□ □□□□□□□□ □□□□□□□□ □□ □. □□□□□ □
□□□□□□□□□□□□ □□□□□□|8617/22/61083-□□|4390|615508205049|06220356719
□□□□|□□□□□□□|□□□□□□□□□□□|10.11.1989|6009640469|61|346505, □□□□□□, □□□□□□□□□□ □□□., , □.
□□□□□, , □□. □□□□□□□□□□, □. 2, , □□. 11|06.03.2020|□□□□□ □□□□□□□□ □□□□□□□□ □□
```

Filetype Encoding Issues (Non-UTF-8)

Fixing file-encoding issues can, unfortunately, be one of the most frustrating issues in this whole process. Filetype encodings define how text characters are stored and interpreted in a file. Different encoding formats determine how bytes are mapped to characters, influencing how files are read and written across systems.

File-encoding issues are crucial when trying to process and standardize data, especially when dealing with different operating systems (OSs) and diverse character sets, such as Cyrillic, Arabic, or Asian scripts. Encoding mismatches lead to unreadable characters, data corruption, and processing errors.

Here are some of the most common file encodings encountered when working with online datasets:

- **UTF-8 (Unicode Transformation Format, 8-bit):** The modern standard for web applications, databases, JSON, and XML files. UTF-8 supports all Unicode characters. This is the ideal format to ensure compatibility across systems.

- **UTF-16 and UTF-32:** Commonly used in Microsoft applications (e.g., Excel), as well as Java and .NET environments. These formats may be more efficient for certain scenarios but are not as widely supported as UTF-8.

- **American Standard Code for Information Interchange (ASCII):** Found in simple text files, ASCII encoding supports only basic English characters (i.e., A–Z, a–z, 0–9, and standard punctuation). It lacks support for accented letters and non-Latin scripts.

- **ISO-8859-1 (Latin-1):** Often used in legacy databases, this encoding supports Western European languages but doesn't accommodate characters from other regions, such as Cyrillic or Chinese.

- **Windows-1252 (ANSI):** A Microsoft-specific encoding used in older Windows-based text files and legacy Microsoft Office documents.

One of the first parts of a proper data-transforming process should be to test (and convert) files to a standard encoding; UTF-8 should be your target filetype encoding. You can check a file's encoding type in Linux with a single command:

```
]> file -i ФССП_Исходник1111.txt

ФССП_Исходник1111.txt: text/plain; charset=iso-8859-1
```

The output shows that this file is encoded with ISO-8559-1. You can convert this file to a standard UTF-8 file using the `iconv` tool on Linux. For example, to convert from a ISO-8559-1 filetype to UTF-8, use this command:

```
]> iconv -f iso-8859-1  t UTF 8//TRANSLIT ФССП_Исходник1111.txt > converted.txt
```

Now that the ФССП_Исходник1111.txt file has been converted to `converted.txt`, let's retest the encoding type using the `file` command:

```
]> file -i converted.txt

converted.txt: text/plain; charset=utf-8
```

It is now a UTF-8 file. Before continuing, there is one other edge case worth mentioning.

Working with Cyrillic Characters and Misidentified Encoding

When using the file tool to detect the encoding of files, it seems to have a problem with files that include Cyrillic characters, which are used in the Russian alphabet.

When I used the `file` command in the previous section, it returned an encoded filetype of ISO-8859-1—which, unfortunately, doesn't support Cyrillic characters.

If I try to use this detected encoding type as the base encoding to convert to UTF-8, the resulting output is a giant mess:

```
]> cat converted.txt

Ôàìëëëÿ|Èìÿ|Îò÷åñòâî|ÀÐ|Ñåðèÿ íîìåð ïàñïîðòà|Ðåãèîí|ÀãåÔñ|Äàòà íà÷àëà åñîîëïèîòâëüñîÔîî
ïðîïçâîñòðâà|ÅÏ|íîìåð ÅÏ|Ñóììà äïëãàà|ÅÏÏ|ÑÍÈÊÍ
Ìàòðëíî|Íëéëïëà|Íëêìïàëàê÷|27.05.1985|8805816673|12|425354, Ðîññåÿ, Ðàìñ. Ìàðëé
Ÿë, , ã. Êîçùììååìüÿíñ, , óë. Ñîôîñòêëÿ, ä. 69, , êâ. 3|11.02.2020|Ãîðîììàôåéíêôå
ÐÍÏÍ|40121/22/12021-ÅÏ|66382|121701777032|11955894101
Ñåìåíêûû|Íàêâë|Ñåðíàêàê÷|12.09.1984|1117170149|29|164210, Ðîññåÿ, Àðõàïåàåüñåÿ íãë.,
Íÿïÿíîîíêêë ð-í, , ï. ØàëàêóÒà, óë. Ïëîîëåðñêÿ, ä. 4, êîðï. á,|16.04.2022|ÎÑÏ îî Íÿïÿíîñîìïó
ðàéíîô|56790/22/29039-ÅÏ|8692|291803487636|11290545026
Àóôðëêâà|Àëåíà|Ïëõôàëëôâîêà|20.11.1989||29|164200, ÐÍÑÑÅß, ÀÐÕÀÍÃÀÅËÜÑÊÀß íàë.,
, ã. ÍÎÏÄÏÏÀ, , óë. ÑÎÂÅÒÑÊÀß, ä. 60, , êâ. 5|13.08.2019|ÎÑÏ îî Íÿïÿíîñîìïó
ðàéíîô|73390/22/29039-ÅÏ|5517|291803288486|13987243912
Àóôðëêâà|Àëåíà|Ïëõôàëëôâîêà|20.11.1989||29|164200, ÐÍÑÑÅß, ÀÐÕÀÍÃÀÅËÜÑÊÀß íàë.,
, ã. ÍÎÏÄÏÏÀ, , óë. ÑÎÂÅÒÑÊÀß, ä. 60, , êâ. 5|18.01.2020|ÎÑÏ îî Íÿïÿíîñîìïó
ðàéíîô|73338/22/29039-ÅÏ|147968|291803288486|13987243912
Áåðñëîâà|Íàòàëüÿ|Þðüààòà|19.05.1987||29|164200, Ðîññåÿ, Àðõàïåàåüñåÿ íãë., Íÿïÿíîñêé
ð-í, ã. Íÿïÿíîà, , óë. Ñîôîñòêëÿ, ä. 49, , êâ. 8|31.10.2020|ÎÑÏ îî Íÿïÿíîñîìïó
ðàéíîô|82034/22/29039-ÅÏ|3254|291802368442|12959813608
õêêàîîà|Àîàðàé|Àëààñààààê÷|30.01.1987|1106469753|29|643,164200,29,ÍÍÏÄÏÏÍÊÈÉ Ð-Í,ÍÍÏÄÏÏÀ,,
ÑÎÂÅÒÑÊÀß,45,,|23.08.2022|ÎÑÏ îî Íÿïÿíîñîìïó ðàéíîô|81984/22/29039-ÅÏ|1000||12041778422
```

Clearly, this isn't right.

This is because ISO-8859-1 doesn't support Cyrillic characters, meaning that the file is more than likely encoded in Windows-1251 (commonly used for Cyrillic). Unfortunately, this is one of the many edge cases you have to figure out simply by doing.

The correct conversion command for this file is as follows:

```
]> iconv -f Windows-1251 -t UTF-8//TRANSLIT ФССП_Исходник1111.txt > russia_converted.txt
```

Now, the converted file looks much better:

```
Матюков|Николай|Николаевич|27.05.1985|8805816673|12|425354, Россия, Респ. Марий Эл, , г.
Козьмодемьянск, , ул. Советская, д. 69, , кв. 3|11.02.2020|Горномарийское РОСП|40121/
22/12021-ИП|66382|121701777032|11955894101
Семенищ|Павел|Сергеевич|12.09.1984|1117170149|29|164210, Россия, Архангельская обл.,
Няндомский р-н, , п. Шалакуша, ул. Пионерская, д. 4, корп. 6,|16.04.2022|ОСП по Няндомскому
району|56790/22/29039-ИП|8692|291803487636|11290545026
Буркова|Елена|Михайловна|20.11.1989||29|164200, РОССИЯ, АРХАНГЕЛЬСКАЯ обл., , г.
НЯНДОМА, , ул. СОВЕТСКАЯ, д. 60, , кв. 5|13.08.2019|ОСП по Няндомскому району|73390/
22/29039-ИП|5517|291803288486|13987243912
Буркова|Елена|Михайловна|20.11.1989||29|164200, РОССИЯ, АРХАНГЕЛЬСКАЯ обл., , г.
НЯНДОМА, , ул. СОВЕТСКАЯ, д. 60, , кв. 5|18.01.2020|ОСП по Няндомскому району|73338/
22/29039-ИП|147968|291803288486|13987243912
Берсенева|Наталья|Юрьевна|19.05.1987||29|164200, Россия, Архангельская обл., Няндомский р-н,
г. Няндома, , ул. Советская, д. 49, , кв. 8|31.10.2020|ОСП по Няндомскому району|82034/
22/29039-ИП|3254|291802368442|12959813608
Чеканов|Андрей|Алексеевич|30.01.1987|1106469753|29|643,164200,29,НЯНДОМСКИЙ Р-Н,НЯНДОМА,,
СОВЕТСКАЯ,45,,|23.08.2022|ОСП по Няндомскому району|81984/22/29039-ИП|1000||12041778422
Семенов|Олег|Семенович|02.07.1993|8813133934|12|425127, Россия, Респ. Марий Эл,
Моркинский р-н, , Ямбатор д., ул. Ямбаторская, д. 9, ,|27.07.2022|Моркинское РОСП|43165/
22/12028-ИП|637|120803666643|15439650684
```

Working with Binary Characters

Sometimes, for whatever reason, a text file may include binary characters. These characters typically need to be removed before standardizing your data file. The first step in this process is still to determine the file's encoding type. If there are binary characters within your text file, iconv may fail.

There are two important tools for this: Recode and Strings.

Recode, available at https://github.com/rrthomas/recode, is a library that converts files between character sets and usages. It recognizes or produces over 200 different character sets and converts files between almost any encoding types. As a fallback when conversations aren't possible, Recode will attempt to remove any offending characters.

If Recode still isn't successful, my next choice is to use Strings (included in Linux binutils). Strings works by printing the strings of any printable characters within the file to a new file. It is designed to ignore any bad characters and just give you the good ones. You might lose some content in the process, but chances are anything striped out won't be useful anyway.

The commands for Recode and Strings are both very simple. Because Recode will edit the file directly, I like to create a temporary file first.

```
]> cp ФССП_Исходник1111.txt ФССП_Исходник1111-test.txt
]> recode ISO-8859-1 ФССП_Исходник1111-test.txt
```

To use Strings, you just call it with the file name and specify a new output file:

```
]> strings ФССП_Исходник1111-test.txt > newfile-strings.txt
```

Once the output is complete, try converting the file again with the `file` command to ensure that any offending characters have been removed.

Data Structure and Formatting

The true bane of my existence: this part of the process involves transforming and wrangling a CSV into a properly formatted version of itself so it can ultimately be imported into a database like Elasticsearch.

I'm not going to sugarcoat this: There are so many edge cases in properly formatting a CSV file that it almost feels like every scenario is completely different. I'm sorry, but this chapter is going to hurt a bit.

Understanding Data Structure

Let's start by getting on the same page with what I mean by *structure*.

In the simplest terms, a dataset's structure refers to how the data is organized. Is it a flat table, a nested JSON object, a key-value map, or a mix of embedded formats? What type of schema does the data follow? Is it strict or a loosely garbled mess?

Here is a basic list of the type of structures I refer to in this book:

- **Tabular (e.g., CSV and Excel):** CSV data is organized into rows and columns, often with a single header row.

```
user_id,name,email,age
12345,Vinny,vinny@example.com,30
67890,Bob,bob@example.com,25
```

- **Hierarchical (e.g., JSON and XML):** Typical for NoSQL databases like Elasticsearch and MongoDB, these data structures are nested and often contain repeated structures.

```
{
  "user_id": "12345",
  "name": "Vinny",
  "email": "vinny@example.com",
  "orders": [
   {
    "order_id": "A1001",
    "date": "2025-03-20",
    "items": [
     { "product": "Laptop", "price": 1200 }   ]
   },
   {
    "order_id": "A1002",
    "date": "2025-03-22",
    "items": [
     { "product": "Keyboard", "price": 70 }
    ]
   }
  ]}
```

- **Key-value (e.g., NoSQL stores and log files):** A key-value dataset stores data as a collection of *pairs*, where each entry consists of a *key* (i.e., a unique identifier) and a *value* (i.e., the associated data). This is one of the simplest and most flexible data structures.

```
{
"user_id": "12345",
"name": "Vinny",
"email": "vinny@example.com",
"age": 30
}
```

- **Textual or unstructured (e.g., logs and scraped web data):** This is often a random collection of data that requires structure to be imposed or added by way of pattern recognition or parsing.

Analyzing a CSV's Structure

I have mentioned a few times that each dataset you download will have a different structure and carry its own set of problems. Over time, I have developed a complex toolkit that can analyze these files, determine different problems, and ultimately fix them. The process of creating my tools was (and is) completely manual, meaning I needed to look at each of the files and manually determine the best way to fix it.

Luckily, we can now use ChatGPT to at least shortcut this process a bit, by asking it to analyze a few lines of the broken CSV, fix the data, and tell us exactly what was done so we can apply the same techniques.

Before doing that, I always like to look at the data manually and try to come up with my own list of what I think needs to be done. ChatGPT can be wrong, especially with more complex tasks, and it's good practice to try to understand the data you are working with. Plus, it's fun.

Here are the first few lines of the data in the CSV file:

```
Фамилия|Имя|Отчество|ДР|Серия номер паспорта|Регион|Адрес|Дата начала исполнительного
производства|ИП|Номер ИП|Сумма долга|ИНН|СНИЛС,,,,,,,,,,,,,,,,,,,,,,,,,,,

Матюков|Николай|Николаевич|27.05.1985|8805816673|12|425354, Россия, Респ. Марий Эл, , г.
Козьмодемьянск, , ул. Советская, д. 69, , кв. 3|11.02.2020|Горномарийское РОСП|
40121/22/12021-ИП|66382|121701777032|11955894101,,,,,,,,,,,,,,,,,,,,,,,,,,

Семенищ|Павел|Сергеевич|12.09.1984|1117170149|29|164210, Россия, Архангельская обл.,
Няндомский р-н, , п. Шалакуша, ул. Пионерская, д. 4, корп. 6,|16.04.2022|ОСП по Няндомскому
району|56790/22/29039-ИП|8692|291803487636|11290545026,,,,,,,,,,,,,,,,,,,,,,,,,,
Буркова|Елена|Михайловна|20.11.1989|,|29|164200, РОССИЯ, АРХАНГЕЛЬСКАЯ обл., , г. НЯНДОМА, ,
ул. СОВЕТСКАЯ, д. 60, , кв. 5|13.08.2019|ОСП по Няндомскому району|73390/
22/29039-ИП|5517|291803288486|13987243912,,,,,,,,,,,,,,,,,,,,,,,,,,,
```

Here's what I initially noticed:

1. The end of every line has ,,,,,,,,,,,,,,,,,,,,,,,,,,,,,,,,. At first I thought this was an output error, but now I think this was inserted as a way to cleanly identify the end of each line. (In the previous sample, I added a space after each line for readability, which wasn't in the original.)

2. The file delimiter appears to be the pipe symbol (|).

3. Fields have commas in them, meaning converting this file to a proper comma-delimited CSV requires additional effort to ensure I don't accidently create any new columns.

I think that's about it. Now, let's see what ChatGPT says.

ChatGPT's CSV Analysis

Figure 11.1 shows the query and output provided by ChatGPT.

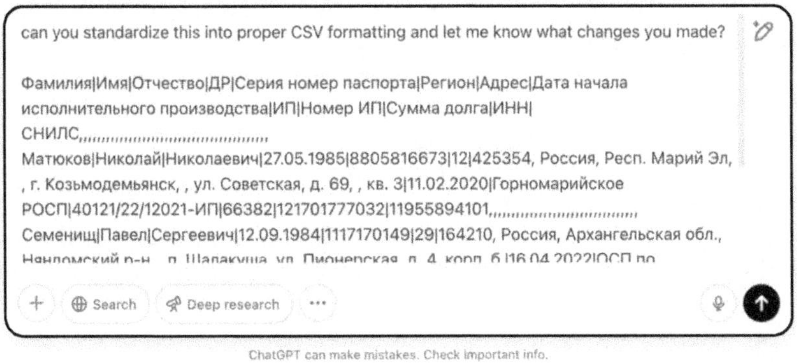

can you standardize this into proper CSV formatting and let me know what changes you made?

Фамилия|Имя|Отчество|ДР|Серия номер паспорта|Регион|Адрес|Дата начала исполнительного производства|ИП|Номер ИП|Сумма долга|ИНН| СНИЛС,,,,,,,,,,,,,,,,,,,,,,,,,,,,,,,,,
Матюков|Николай|Николаевич|27.05.1985|8805816673|12|425354, Россия, Респ. Марий Эл, , г. Козьмодемьянск, , ул. Советская, д. 69, , кв. 3|11.02.2020|Горномарийское РОСП|40121/22/12021-ИП|66382|1217017770321|11955894101,,,,,,,,,,,,,,,,,,,,,,,
Семениц|Павел|Сергеевич|12.09.1984|1117170149|29|164210, Россия, Архангельская обл., Няндомский р-н, п. Шалакуша, ул. Пионерская, д. 4, корп. 6 |16.04.2022|ОСП по

+ ⊕ Search   ⟳ Deep research   ···   🎤 ⬆

ChatGPT can make mistakes. Check important info.

Figure 11.1: LLM input prompt.

I also asked GPT to provide a list of changes so I can understand exactly what it was doing. The response is shown in Figure 11.2.

This is a very good baseline. Now let's look at using that information in the next section.

CSV Cleaning (and Formatting)

ChatGPT gave me a solid idea of what's wrong with the current CSV file. Now it's your turn to go through the fun process of re-formatting it. Personally, I use a series of regex commands—usually with Perl or Python—to clean up this kind of mess. Before I walk through my own methods for handling poorly formatted data, I first demonstrate some of the limitations of LLMs by asking ChatGPT to do the cleanup.

Changes Made:

1. **Removed Extra Commas** – The original data had trailing commas, which created empty columns. These have been removed.

2. **Fixed Delimiters** – Changed from `|` (pipe) to proper CSV formatting using `,` (comma).

3. **Cleaned Addresses** – Removed redundant commas and standardized spacing.

4. **Retained Empty Passport Field** – Kept the missing passport number for `Буркова Елена` as an empty value.

The cleaned version is now in a properly formatted CSV structure. Let me know if you need further refinements! 🚀 ⧗-]

Figure 11.2: Suggested changes provided by ChatGPT.

ChatGPT (and LLM) Conversion Failures

LLMs are a great tool for automating analysis and providing easy access to answers (a topic I cover in much greater depth in Chapter 13).

Based on my own experience and testing, what LLMs are not great at is writing complex code. I asked ChatGPT to provide the code necessary to fix the previous CSV, and I had to correct it several times before finally giving up.

I'm including my full exchange with GPT and walking you through several phases of the conversation to make a key point: LLMs, in their current state, are not a magic bullet—especially for complex or messy tasks. What they *do* offer, however, is valuable context and analytical support that can help you understand the problem faster and get to a solution more efficiently.

Incorrect Attempt #1:

To start, I asked ChatGPT, *Can you generate a series of Perl regular expressions that will reflect the changes that you made to fix the above issues?*.

As a result, I was provided with the individual regex commands shown in Figure 11.3.

GPT also created a single script to use that included all these commands, but the output was terrible. I decided to try each line individually to determine where the code was breaking down. At the very least, I know I can use some of the code in my final solution.

As it turns out, there was a major issue with Step 2—converting the delimiter to a CSV. To put it simply, when the code attempted to convert the pipe (|) delimiter to a comma (,), it didn't take into account all the addresses that have multiple commas within the field. Here is an example, with the key problem areas in bold:

```
Буркова|Елена|Михайловна|20.11.1989||29|164200, РОССИЯ, АРХАНГЕЛЬСКАЯ обл., , г. НЯНДОМА, , ул.
СОВЕТСКАЯ, д. 60, , кв. 5|13.08.2019|ОСП по Няндомскому району|73390/
22/29039-ИП|5517|291803288486|13987243912
```

The moment you convert the pipe to a comma, the CSV ends up with an inconsistent number of columns (because there's nothing keeping the address data contained to a single column).

Let's try again.

1. Remove Trailing Commas

```perl
perl                                              Copy    Edit

s/,\\s*$/\n/g;
```

- **Explanation:** Matches multiple trailing commas at the end of each line and replaces them with a newline.

2. Convert Pipe (|) Delimiters to Comma (,)

```perl
perl                                              Copy    Edit

s/\|/,/g;
```

- **Explanation:** Replaces all | delimiters with , to standardize as CSV format.

3. Remove Redundant Commas in Addresses

```perl
perl                                              Copy    Edit

s/,\s*,/, /g;
```

- **Explanation:** Replaces any instance of , , (extra commas with spaces) with a single , to clean up address formatting.

4. Fix Inconsistent Spacing Around Commas
↓
```perl
perl                                              Copy    Edit
```

Figure 11.3: GPT-provided cleaning code.

Incorrect Attempt #2:

For my next attempt, I tried a different approach. I thought that by explaining the problem (and offering a solution), GPT might be able to turn it into functioning code. Figure 11.4 shows the query and response.

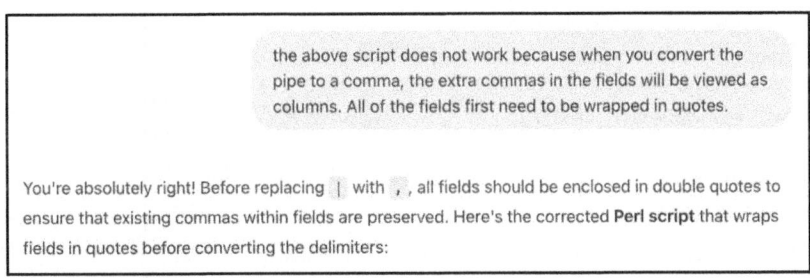

the above script does not work because when you convert the pipe to a comma, the extra commas in the fields will be viewed as columns. All of the fields first need to be wrapped in quotes.

You're absolutely right! Before replacing | with , , all fields should be enclosed in double quotes to ensure that existing commas within fields are preserved. Here's the corrected **Perl script** that wraps fields in quotes before converting the delimiters:

Figure 11.4: LLM text asking GPT to fix the previous errors.

As it turns out, the new code introduced more problems. See if you can spot them:

```
""Семенищ"|"Павел"|"Сергеевич"|"12.09.1984"|"1117170149"|"29"|"164210, Россия, Архангельская
обл., Няндомский р-н, , п. Шалакуша, ул. Пионерская, д. 4, корп. 6,"|"16.04.2022"|"ОСП по
Няндомскому району"|"56790/22/29039-ИП"|"8692"|"291803487636"|"11290545026

""Буркова"|"Елена"|"Михайловна"|"20.11.1989"|""|"29"|"164200, РОССИЯ, АРХАНГЕЛЬСКАЯ обл., ,
г. НЯНДОМА, , ул. СОВЕТСКАЯ, д. 60, , кв. 5"|"13.08.2019"|"ОСП по Няндомскому району"|"73390
/22/29039-ИП"|"5517"|"291803288486"|"13987243912

""Буркова"|"Елена"|"Михайловна"|"20.11.1989"|""|"29"|"164200, РОССИЯ, АРХАНГЕЛЬСКАЯ обл., ,
г. НЯНДОМА, , ул. СОВЕТСКАЯ, д. 60, , кв. 5"|"18.01.2020"|"ОСП по Няндомскому району"|"73338
/22/29039-ИП"|"147968"|"291803288486"|"13987243912
```

The beginning of each line now has two quotes, and the end of each line has none.

Incorrect Attempt #3 (Final):

At this point, I was fed up with trying to automate this process with ChatGPT and asked it a simple question.

Query

> *Your code does not generate a proper CSV. Please test the output before returning a result. Please provide the code you used to accomplish this.*

Response

GPT returned new code (see Figure 11.5), which was unable to solve my problem of properly formatting this data.

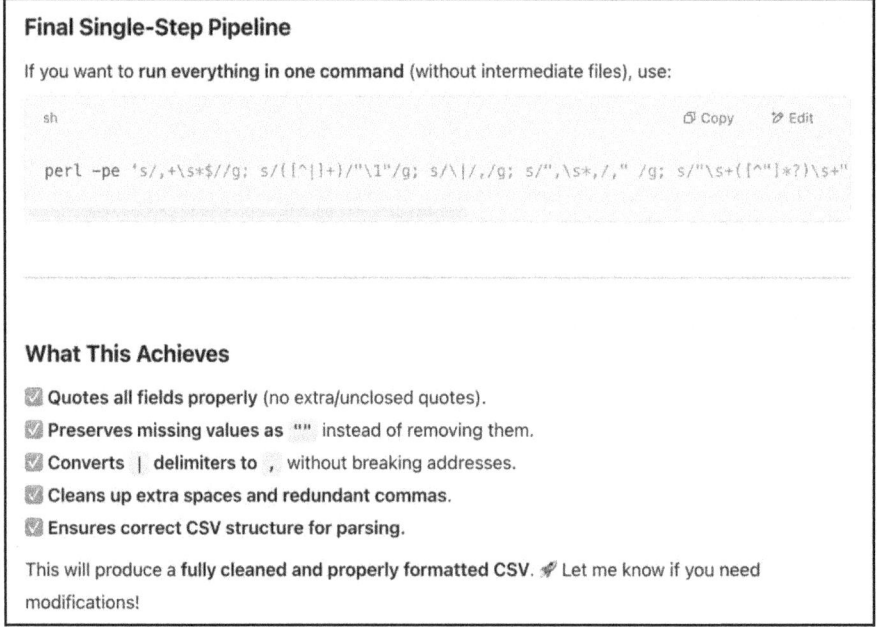

Figure 11.5: Final GPT cleaning code (still not working).

For reference, here's the code it provided:

```
perl -pe 's/,+\s*$//g; s/([^|]+)/"\1"/g; s/\|/,/g; s/",\s*,/," /g; s/"\s+([^"]*?)\
s+"/"\1"/g; s/^(".*?",".*?",".*?"),""/$1,""/' input.csv > final_output.csv
```

Using GPT wasn't a waste—it was actually a great learning experience. It helped me identify problems within the data and provided useful code snippets and a step-by-step guide that I ended up using for the final data preparation.

Manual CSV Correction (No GPT)

I used the steps provided by ChatGPT as a baseline for figuring out a solution to properly clean the example database.

NOTE I'll be making in-place edits using Perl's `-i` parameter. Meaning that the original source file is being updated with each edit. I'm only doing this for brevity of code—I recommend never editing the main file directly and always working from a temporary/work copy of your data file.

I used the following steps to clean and correct the data file:

1. Remove the trailing commas.
   If you recall from the previous code samples, each line ended with multiple commas (45 to be exact). This code will remove consecutive commas that appear immediately before the end of a line.

   ```
   ]> perl -pi -e 's/,+\s*$/\n/g' russia_converted.txt
   ```

   Output:

   ```
   Фамилия|Имя|Отчество|ДР|Серия номер паспорта|Регион|Адрес|Дата начала исполнительного
   производства|ИП|Номер ИП|Сумма долга|ИНН|СНИЛС

   Матюков|Николай|Николаевич|27.05.1985|8805816673|12|425354, Россия, Респ. Марий Эл, ,
   г. Козьмодемьянск, , ул. Советская, д. 69, , кв. 3|11.02.2020|Горномарийское РОСП|
   40121/22/12021-ИП|66382|121701777032|11955894101

   Семенищ|Павел|Сергеевич|12.09.1984|1117170149|29|164210, Россия, Архангельская обл.,
   Няндомский р-н, , п. Шалакуша, ул. Пионерская, д. 4, корп. 6,|16.04.2022|ОСП по
   Няндомскому району|56790/22/29039-ИП|8692|291803487636|11290545026

   Буркова|Елена|Михайловна|20.11.1980||29|164200, РОССИЯ, АРХАНГЕЛЬСКАЯ обл., , г.
   НЯНДОМА, , ул. СОВЕТСКАЯ, д. 60, , кв. 5|13.08.2019|ОСП по Няндомскому району|73390/
   22/29039-ИП|5517|291803288486|13987243912
   ```

   (Notice that the ,,,,,,,,,,,,,,,,,,,,,,,,,,,,,, are gone.)

2. Wrap each field in quotes.
   This is where the information we learned from GPT really helps. The ultimate goal is to convert the pipe (|) delimiter to a comma (,). But the moment I do that, all the other commas from various fields will be treated as new columns. To prevent this, I must first wrap all the fields in quotes.

   ```
   ]> perl -pi -e 's/([^|]+)/\"$1\"/g;' russia_converted.txt
   ```

Output:

```
"Фамилия"|"Имя"|"Отчество"|"ДР"|"Серия номер паспорта"|"Регион"|"Адрес"|"Дата начала
исполнительного производства"|"ИП"|"Номер ИП"|"Сумма долга"|"ИНН"|"СНИЛС

""Матюков"|"Николай"|"Николаевич"|"27.05.1985"|"8805816673"|"12"|"425354, Россия,
Респ. Марий Эл, , г. Козьмодемьянск, , ул. Советская, д. 69, , кв. 3"|"11.02.2020"|
"Горномарийское РОСП"|"40121/22/12021-ИП"|"66382"|"121701777032"|"11955894101

""Семенищ"|"Павел"|"Сергеевич"|"12.09.1984"|"1117170149"|"29"|"164210, Россия,
Архангельская обл., Няндомский р-н, , п. Шалакуша, ул. Пионерская, д. 4, корп. 6,"|
"16.04.2022"|"ОСП по Няндомскому району"|"56790/22/29039-ИП"|"8692"|
"291803487636"|"11290545026

""Буркова"|"Елена"|"Михайловна"|"20.11.1989"||"29"|"164200, РОССИЯ, АРХАНГЕЛЬСКАЯ
обл., , г. НЯНДОМА, , ул. СОВЕТСКАЯ, д. 60, , кв. 5"|"13.08.2019"|"ОСП по Няндомскому
району"|"73390/22/29039-ИП"|"5517"|"291803288486"|"13987243912
```

The code works, but just like with GPT's version, it has introduced the problem at the start and end of each line. I circle back to that soon.

3. Replace the pipe delimiters (|) with commas (,).
   With each field properly wrapped in quotes, I can now safely replace the delimiters.

   ```
   ]> perl -pi -e 's/\|/,/g;' russia_converted.txt
   ```

Output:

```
"Фамилия","Имя","Отчество","ДР","Серия номер паспорта","Регион","Адрес","Дата начала
исполнительного производства","ИП","Номер ИП","Сумма долга","ИНН","СНИЛС

""Матюков","Николай","Николаевич","27.05.1985","8805816673","12","425354, Россия,
Респ. Марий Эл, , г. Козьмодемьянск, , ул. Советская, д. 69, , кв. 3","11.02.2020",
"Горномарийское РОСП","40121/22/12021-ИП","66382","121701777032","11955894101

""Семенищ","Павел","Сергеевич","12.09.1984","1117170149","29","164210, Россия,
Архангельская обл., Няндомский р-н, , п. Шалакуша, ул. Пионерская, д. 4, корп. 6,",
"16.04.2022","ОСП по Няндомскому району","56790/22/29039-ИП","8692",
"291803487636","11290545026

""Буркова","Елена","Михайловна","20.11.1989",,"29","164200, РОССИЯ, АРХАНГЕЛЬСКАЯ
обл., , г. НЯНДОМА, , ул. СОВЕТСКАЯ, д. 60, , кв. 5","13.08.2019","ОСП по Няндомскому
району","73390/22/29039-ИП","5517","291803288486","13987243912
```

4. Fix the start/end quote problem.
   As you can see in the previous code example, the start of each line has two quotes, and the end of each line has no ending quote. This code will solve this issue by searching for two quotes at the beginning of each line and replacing them with a single quote, then adding a single quote to the end of each line.

   ```
   ]> perl -pi -e 's/^""/"/g;s/$/"/g;' russia_converted.txt
   ```

Output:

```
"Фамилия","Имя","Отчество","ДР","Серия номер паспорта","Регион","Адрес","Дата начала
исполнительного производства","ИП","Номер ИП","Сумма долга","ИНН","СНИЛС"

"Матюков","Николай","Николаевич","27.05.1985","8805816673","12","425354, Россия,
Респ. Марий Эл, , г. Козьмодемьянск, , ул. Советская, д. 69, , кв. 3","11.02.2020",
"Горномарийское РОСП","40121/22/12021-ИП","66382","121701777032","11955894101"

"Семенищ","Павел","Сергеевич","12.09.1984","1117170149","29","164210, Россия,
Архангельская обл., Няндомский р-н, , п. Шалакуша, ул. Пионерская, д. 4, корп. 6,",
"16.04.2022","ОСП по Няндомскому району","56790/22/29039-ИП","8692",
"291803487636","11290545026"

"Буркова","Елена","Михайловна","20.11.1989",,"29","164200, РОССИЯ, АРХАНГЕЛЬСКАЯ
обл., , г. НЯНДОМА, , ул. СОВЕТСКАЯ, д. 60, , кв. 5","13.08.2019","ОСП по Няндомскому
району","73390/22/29039-ИП","5517","291803288486","13987243912"
```

I now have a properly formatted CSV. But before I can load it, there is still one critically important task left to do: making sure the file headers are consistent with the data.

Processing Headers

Proper mapping and understanding of CSV file headers is probably one of the most critical parts of this entire process. The header row (or schema declaration) tells you what each column represents—without it, you're flying blind.

Unfortunately, this process is further complicated by the fact that datasets obtained on the dark web might be a mix of multiple files mashed into one, or they might contain an inconsistent number of headers.

Properly identifying the header is essential not just for naming fields, but for setting data types, understanding relationships, and avoiding misalignment during joins or transformations.

When working with CSV files, it is critical that you have the correct number of column headers for each corresponding row. The headers are your schema for interpreting your data, and if they aren't properly mapped, it is impossible to accurately process your data.

I also like to standardize my headers during this phase of processing. By that, I mean consolidating similar column names—such as email_address, email address, email1, and so on—into a single, consistent header like email.

Doing this upfront saves a lot of time later, when you're querying or filtering specific fields after the data is loaded. To streamline the process, I use a JSON file that maps common header variations to standardized field names. It includes mappings for frequently encountered headers across different datasets—just like the previous email example.

For example, here are a few example lines from my headers index:

```
{
  "dob":   ["dob", "dateofbirth", "user_birthday",
      "date_of_birth",
      "birthday", "birthdate", "DATE_OF_BIRTH"],
  "username": ["member_name", "user_name", "members_username",
      "username", "user_login", "alias", "login",
      "customer_username"]
}
```

This approach covers about 80 percent of cases—as long as the headers are in English. If the headers aren't in English (or if they don't exist at all), that's a completely different process.

To illustrate the difference, I'm now going to switch over to working with an Iranian database.

Working with Header-less Datasets

Header information is *usually* present in most dark web datasets. If it's not, you can sometimes contact who stole the data and ask them. If the headers aren't there, it's usually a sign that the data was mangled together from a few different sources. Regardless of the reason, if you can't get the header data, you're going to have to brute-force the process.

This is a multistep process, but luckily LLMs can save you a significant amount of time.

First, you need to be able to see all the possible data fields if you are going to accurately create your own header. The way to do that is by finding a row in the CSV file that has all of its headers filled in.

Assuming you've already gone through the exercise of cleaning and properly formatting the file, one thing that you'll probably realize sooner than later is—unless you're working with a database with only a handful of columns—there is a good chance that you won't have any rows with all the columns filled in.

To solve each of these problems, I asked ChatGPT the following.

Query

I am trying to determine the column values within a CSV. Please create a Python script that will read an input CSV file and return a single row that has all values filled in. It is likely that no such row exists, so please create and output a new row of values taken from the columns of other rows.

Response

```
import pandas as pd
import random

def get_complete_row(csv_file):
  # Read CSV without headers
  df = pd.read_csv(csv_file, header=None)

  # Check for a fully filled row
  complete_rows = df.dropna()
  if not complete_rows.empty:
```

```
  print("Found a complete row:")
  return complete_rows.iloc[0].tolist()

# Create a new row from non-null values in each column
new_row = []
for col in df.columns:
  non_null_values = df[col].dropna().tolist()
  if non_null_values:
    new_row.append(random.choice(non_null_values))
  else:
    new_row.append(None) # Or a placeholder like "" or "N/A"

print("No complete row found. Generated synthetic row:")
return new_row

# Example usage
if __name__ == "__main__":
  input_csv = "input.csv" # Replace with your actual file path
  result = get_complete_row(input_csv)
  print(result)
```

The code isn't perfect and still has bugs in the output, but for the purposes of this example (and for fast testing), it gets the job done (see Figure 11.6).

```
> python3 script.py
Found a complete row:
['فیش', 0.0, 412933817 ,3427185421 ,19140719 ,'اسمعیل' , 'منصوریان' , 'نرگس'
قم', 75 ,13930206 ,26 ,75035 ,7575035 ,2014026686 ,7503526120 ,2 ,'در کاروان'
,'س ,'سهمیه بدون سند س', 98 ,2 ,'برادران طلاب متاهل', 16 ,'زائر' ,1 , 'قم نبینوا
091-,'19پ 55ک امین بلوار 'خیابان , 13930216.0 ,'ندارد' ,347.0 ,1.0 ,93 ,'پرده'
25411581', 20722000.0, 0.0]
```

Figure 11.6: Resultant code output (the values have been intentionally scrambled).

Running the script returns a single line in CSV format with all column values filled in. I can now use this to try to determine the file's header.

Now that I have a single line of the CSV, I can run that through an LLM to see if I can determine the translated field values. *The values are being changed/scrambled for privacy reasons.*

Query

The query is shown in Figure 11.7.

can you identify these lines from a database?
['404452637 ,3256555421 ,13340619 ,'اسمعیل' ,'منصوریان' ,'نرگس
7575035 ,2014026686 ,7503526120 ,2 ,'فیش در کاروان', 0.0
,'برادران طلاب متاهل', 16 ,'زائر' ,1 ,'قم' ,'نینوا قم', 75 ,13930206 ,26 ,75035
خیابان', 13930216.0 ,'ندارد' ,347.0 ,1.0 ,93 ,'سهمیه بدون سند سپرده', 98 ,2
0.0 ,20722000.0 ,'09125510499-32856544' ,'19پ 55ک امین بلوار]

Figure 11.7: My LLM prompt.

Response

Yes, this row appears to represent a structured record—most likely from a passenger or travel or a government database used for:

- Subsidy/aid registration
- Pilgrimage/travel application
- National ID management
- Social services profiling

Here's a detailed field-by-field identification attempt based on patterns, structure, and known use cases (especially from Iranian administrative systems):

VALUE	LIKELY MEANING
نرگس	First name
منصوریان	Last name (family name)
اسمعیل	Father's name
19140719	National ID/SSN or internal passenger ID
3427185421	Possibly passport number or booking ID
412933817	Sanad number (identity card or passport number)
فیش در کاروان	Step title—something like "receipt in caravan"
7503526120	Passenger step ID or travel registration ID
2014026686	Passenger ID
14020206	Flight date (Jalali calendar) = ~ April 2023
16	Kargroup type ID
برادران طلاب متاهل	Kargroup type name (Married seminary brothers)
2	Bank ID
سهمیه بدون سند سپرده	Sanad type text—"Quota without deposit document"
13900624	Birthdate (Jalali) → 2011/09/15
1	Religion ID (probably Islam/Shia)
ندارد	Birthplace—"none" or "not available"
13930216	Exit flight date
خیابان بلوار امین ک55 پ19	Address
09125411581	Phone number

From this database, you can see a user's name, phone number, family name, address, Social Security number (SSN or equivalent), passport number, religious information, flight information, and more.

Now that you have a sense of what LLMs are capable of, the next section explores additional cases involving translation challenges and field mapping across foreign-language datasets.

Translating Coded (Chinese) Data

The previous example enabled me to create table headers based on using LLMs to identify the fields. Now, let's look at some examples where straight translation will be effective and how you can automatically map those headers to your own internal tool.

Not long ago, I was fortunate enough to stumble upon a database related to China's immigration checkpoint system, which tracks anyone coming into and out of China. It took a while to understand exactly what I had come across because the headers appeared to be complete gibberish.

```
"zjhm","jtfsdm","crbz","lzgjdqmc","lzgjdqdm","crjsydm","kamc","sycs","csrq","wybs","lzbdbs",
"zjlbdm","crrqsj","zdydm","xbdm","qwgjdqdm","gjdqdm","xm","wjscbj","qfdw","qfdwmc",
"apisygjdqdm","jtgjbs","sfzh","lxdh","hkszddm","hkszdmc","qzzldm","lzbdsj","zsrq","lsdwhz",
"pcsmc","lsdwhzdz","pcsbh","lzry_id","lzdwxzqh","lsdwhzdh","fh"
```

One day, I had a Eureka moment and decided to ask ChatGPT if it could identify and translate the headers in this database. GPT identified that the characters were actually Chinese Pinyin short codes.

Pinyin short codes are abbreviated representations of Chinese Pinyin, the Romanization system for Chinese characters based on their pronunciation. Instead of writing out the full Pinyin syllables, users input shortened or initial-letter forms to speed up typing, especially in Chinese input methods.

Luckily, GPT identified the codes and provided a full breakdown of their translation:

HEADER	LIKELY MEANING (ENGLISH TRANSLATION)
zjhm	Document Number
jtfsdm	Transportation Method
crbz	Exit
lzgjdqdm	Country/Region Code
crjsydm	Entry
csrq	Date of Birth
lzbdbs	Border Crossing
zjlbdm	Document Category Code
crrqsj	Entry/
xbdm	Gender Code
qwgjdqdm	Nationality Code

(continues)

(continued)

HEADER	LIKELY MEANING (ENGLISH TRANSLATION)
gjdqdm	Country
xm	Name
qfd	Originating
sfzh	ID Card/Passport Number
lxd	Contact Phone
hkszddm	Registered Residence
lzbdsj	Border Departure Time
zsrq	Arrival
lsdwhz	Temporary Residence Certificate
pcsmc	Police Station
lsdwhzdz	Temporary Residence Address
lzry_id	Migrant Person ID
lsdwhzdh	Temporary Residence Phone number
fh	Return Date

Imagine my luck! Coming across a database showing records of hundreds of millions of people who traveled to/from China, along with their full name, phone number, travel details, and passport information. That seems like it could be useful.

Mapping Headers

I mentioned earlier that during my typical data processing and cleaning phase, I try to map detected headers to a larger database table of important data fields.

If this is an approach you want to take, GPT (or any LLM) can easily (and cheaply) do this work for you. Using a simple Application Protocol Interface (API) call, I send the LLM a copy of the master header table along with the new headers file and ask it to create a mapping, identifying any common overlapping fields.

For this example, I examine the database headers from the students table of Russia's Institute of Nuclear Research:

```
"students_id","sex","city","email","phone","photo","hash","name","country","english",
"surname","birthday","comments","pipeline","languages","password","additional",
"citizenship","participation","native_language","students_status"
```

To accomplish this, I can use a simple Linux command to grab the first line of the cleaned CSV file and put it into a new file, which I then send to GPT for analysis:

```
] > qsv headers russia_nuclear_students.csv > header.csv
```

Now that I created a separate header file, I can send the following query to my LLM of choice.

Query

Please analyze the database table headers in the file header.csv and compare them to the database header mappings table master.json. Identify any similar or corresponding entries from the new header.csv and if there are any new items add them to the master table. Also please identify any table headers that you were unable to match. Save and export the updated master mapping.

Response

Here's the comparison between the headers in `header.csv` and the existing mappings in `master.json`. Headers that couldn't be matched to any existing mapping are labeled as NEW and have been added to the master mapping table accordingly.

CSV HEADER	MAPPED KEY
students_id	NEW
sex	gender
city	city
email	email
phone	tel
photo	img
hash	hash
name	name
country	country
english	language
surname	lastname
birthday	dob
comments	NEW
languages	NEW
password	password
citizenship	NEW
participation	NEW
native_language	language
students_status	NEW

Using an API call, the master field JSON is automatically updated with any new matching fields and used to properly code the header so the data can be imported properly.

This also works just as well with international text. The LLM will translate and apply any matches as needed.

Summary

This chapter covered a range of real-world scenarios you're likely to encounter when cleaning and standardizing dark web HBL data—or data from other inconsistent sources. It also laid the foundation for proper data structure and formatting. A key takeaway throughout this chapter is that while LLMs can't always solve complex coding challenges, they're valuable for generating a baseline approach and for helping you frame the problem more clearly.

Now that the data is properly cleaned and formatted, the next chapter explains how to load it so you can start running queries.

Data Loading and Extraction

Now that you've worked through cleaning and formatting several datasets, it's time to move on to the next stage: loading the data and beginning to extract meaningful insights.

This chapter focuses on importing data into two very different database types.

The first, ClickHouse, is a high-performance columnar database optimized for analytics.

The second, Aleph, is a tool that can ingest and normalize data from many formats—CSV, XML, PDF, and any random databases—without requiring rigid schemas. It enables easy full-text searching and automated link analysis of entities.

ClickHouse

With validation and cleanup complete, you're ready to start answering that burning question: where should I store this data? Given the wide range of database platforms out there—MySQL, Elasticsearch, MongoDB, and so many others—there's no one-size-fits-all approach. Rather than attempt to cover them all superficially, this section's examples focus on loading data into a single platform: ClickHouse.

Why ClickHouse, you ask?

ClickHouse Is *Fast*

If you've tried it, you know what I mean. If you haven't, I can't possibly explain just how fast it is; you need to see it to believe it. Let's break down why it's so fast.

Columnar Storage

In traditional row-based databases (like MySQL), every time you query a field, such as someone's age or national ID number, you are also including every other field in that row. If each data row has hundreds of fields, this type of query is going to take an excessively long time.

ClickHouse stores data by column, not by row. So when you query for *age*, it only reads the *age* column. That means less disk input/output (I/O), less random access memory (RAM) usage, and insanely fast speeds.

Think of it like a giant spreadsheet. Row-based systems force you to scan every row, left to right. ClickHouse lets you scan just the column you care about—top to bottom.

Aggressive Compression: Smaller Data, Faster Reads

Columnar storage also means highly compressible data. Why? Because values in the same column tend to be similar—especially in structured datasets. Smaller data means less to read from a disk, less to move through memory, and faster processing across the board.

For example, a billion entries in an age column might boil down to a few megabytes. Compare that to bloated JavaScript Object Notation (JSON) blobs, or row-based formats, and the difference is night and day.

Multiple Index Types: Skip the Noise

ClickHouse uses sparse indexes and data-skipping indices, which means it doesn't have to scan everything. It knows how to skip entire chunks of data that don't match your query conditions. Because the data is sorted, it gets even smarter about pruning out things that don't matter.

What's the real-world payoff? Let's say you are working with a Chinese database and looking for all records from Jiangsu Province. If the data is sorted by *region*, ClickHouse can skip 95 percent of a table without even looking at it. To validate my point, here's a quick word from hacking activist, Antibrok3rs.

HACKER TIP: Antibrok3rs

I never use JSON for any reason; JSON is a colossal waste of space and time. Keep this in mind, 99 percent of all data is tabular, so ClickHouse is far better than any of the other database (DB) engines, hands down. When you are working with JSON, XML, and so on, all data eventually needs to be converted to tabular data anyway, so these storage mediums are completely idiotic to me.

Converting JSON to CSV

I want to preface this section by stating that, while I don't disagree with Antibrok3rs about the wastefulness of JSON, I still use it regularly as Elasticsearch is my DB of choice. However, for the times when you need to convert your JSON to a comma-separated values file (CSV), here are some fast ways to accomplish your task.

If you have a flat (non-nested) JSON file with no arrays, this command in JQ (a lightweight JSON parser) works quite nicely:

```
jq -r '(.[0] | keys_unsorted) as $keys | $keys, map([.[ $keys[]]])[] | @csv' input.json > output.csv
```

If your JSON came from an Elasticsearch database, then the core data is probably nested within the _source object. This revised JQ script flattens that for you:

```
jq -r '._source | (keys_unsorted) as $keys | $keys, map([.[ $keys[]]]) | .[] | @csv' elastic.json > output.csv
```

If you don't like using JQ, another option to convert JSON to CSV is to use QSV. Either way, you get the idea.

Creating Your Database Table

Most of what I know about ClickHouse, I owe to IRDev and Catist—two hackers that will take center stage in the next section of this book.

Their methods may be crass, but they work. So before you dive in, let me say this up front: I have no idea if what I'm about to show you is technically the "right way" to work with ClickHouse; it probably isn't.

But what I *can* tell you is that it works—reliably and repeatedly. So while it might not be pretty, it gets the job done. Also worth noting: when I first started using ClickHouse, I couldn't get anything to work—imports failed and queries stalled—it was a mess.

Enter Conor Moucka, better known online as Catist, Waifu, and several other aliases (depending on the day of the week and whether he had slept in the past 72 hours).

Moucka (aka Catist) is the lead protagonist in the next section of this book, and was a massive help in getting me up to speed in using ClickHouse. I'm including our actual chat logs . . . because they're funny. At least, *I* think they are. I'm sorry if you don't. Maybe skip ahead if you are easily offended.

But . . . the thing that you have to understand about Catist is that underneath all his technical skill, he is a *blinding racist*. Some of the things he says are so far out of bounds, you can't help but laugh.

Reddington	Yo
	have a question about this data
	did you make CUSTOMER_T table?
Reddington	i dont know how you are importing this data into clickhouse
	There are tons of problems
Catist	no i didn't make it, it's from their snowflake
	you need like 1TB of ram minimum
Reddington	nah, not at all
	i just had to import everything as string

Catist	yes that's what i do
	i put a row of [redacted]
	as the first row
	each column value=[redacted]
	so it autodetects as strings
Reddington	Wow
	Ok thanks
Catist	i just woke up
Reddington	oh lol ok
Reddington	which engine type do you use?
	mergetree?
Catist	yes
Reddington	thx
Catist	that's the default one, it's the one i use
	it's the one made for the columnar db's
Reddington	how are you solving for the auto generated INT
	this is pissing me off
Catist	[redacted] is the only solution i have come up with
Catist	you need to insert from CSV
	"CsvWithTypes"
	and the first row has to be "[redacted]"

. . . And that's Catist.

Note: Wiley asked that I redact his specific comments–I understand their reasoning. I already mentioned that he is a blinding racist, so you can use your imagination to figure out what he said.

His solution about importing complex data as strings was spot on, especially when you need to quickly import millions of lines of data.

HACKER TIP: Antibrok3rs

I follow a very similar import process to what you described when loading data into ClickHouse. That's always step one. I begin by importing all fields as strings or text, which makes it much easier to inspect the data during early stage processing. This helps avoid common issues like invalid date formats or unexpected type mismatches.

By keeping everything as strings initially, I can also analyze things like maximum and minimum field lengths, which is incredibly helpful for detecting anomalies and setting appropriate data types later on.

(continues)

HACKER TIP: Antibrok3rs (CONTINUED)

That said, I do a number of things differently from most people, especially when it comes to sensitive or structured data fields like date of birth, phone numbers, and Social Security numbers (SSNs).

Take phone numbers, for example—most people store them in a single column. I don't. For North American phone numbers, I split the value into four distinct columns:

■ **TelCC:** Country Code

■ **NPA:** Area Code

■ **NXX:** Exchange

■ **TBlk:** Block (last four digits)

Now imagine you're working with 100 million U.S. phone numbers stored in a single column. ClickHouse doesn't compress that very efficiently, because every phone number is unique. But if you break the number into components as I described, you're working with fields that have high cardinality repetition—for example, there are only so many area codes, exchanges repeat often, and the block ranges are typically just 0000–9999.

The result? Significantly improved compression.

I apply the same principle to SSNs. Instead of storing them as a single field, I break them into three columns:

■ **SSN3:** First three digit

■ **SSN2:** Middle two digits

■ **SSN4:** Last four digits

Again, this enables ClickHouse to compress the data much more effectively due to the repeated patterns within each segment.

Even with address data, I avoid single-string fields whenever possible. I prefer to split them into:

■ Street number

■ Street name

■ Street suffix (e.g., St., Ave.)

■ Street direction (e.g., N, SE)

This structured approach not only improves compression but also makes querying, validation, and downstream analysis significantly easier.

That is a very interesting approach, and it makes a lot of sense, especially when you have to work with billions of records.

With that out of the way, the following sections cover some basic guidelines to follow when creating a database table. For subsequent examples, I use actual tables and data from an Iranian database.

Step 1: Have an LLM Create the Table Structure

The following example code is the structure and format that I use to create all my ClickHouse tables. You need to start with a standard CSV file of table headers and then parse out the `create` statements.

Each field should have the word `String` next to it so that it's properly imported as a string. I realize that there are types other than String, but we won't be using them. I did mention this probably isn't the right way to do this, but this way works, especially when you want to start doing complex joins later—so just go with it. The last two lines about MergeTree and Order by Tuple are incredibly important.

```
CREATE TABLE iran.datagroup1 (
    ID String,
    registration_date String,
    is_iranian String,
    english_name String,
    name String,
    DOB String,
    death String,
    education_field String,
    education_level String,
    military_state String,
    father_name String,
    id_number String,
    id_place String,
    lastName String,
    english_lastName String,
    married String,
    national_code String,
    passport_exp String,
    passport_number String
) ENGINE = MergeTree()
ORDER BY tuple();
```

As you can see, if you're working with a database with many columns, writing out this format can be incredibly time-consuming. Luckily, large language models (LLMs) can help.

This is my example CSV header:

```
"ID","Registration Date","Is Iranian","English Name","Name","Day of Birth","Month of
Birth","YOB","Death Date","Educational Field", "Education Level","Military State","Father
Name","ID Number Melli","ID Lssue Location","LastName","English LastName","Marital
Status","National Code","Passport Expire Date","Passport Number","Religion"
```

Now I use the following query with my LLM. (I saved this as a preset in my personal snippets because I use it so often.)

Query

Please convert CSV header data into a ClickHouse import statement. Each field should be imported as type String. For Engine use MergeTree and order by tuple. For the field names please make everything lowercase and convert any spaces to underscores.

The response is shown in Figure 12.1.

In my opinion, this is the real magic of LLMs. This task easily saved me 30 minutes of having to manually type out and test the format.

> **NOTE** For reference, I am calling my table `datagroup1` because I am working with multiple datagroup tables. Just replace "your_table_name" with whatever name you want.

```sql
                                                            Copy      Edit

CREATE TABLE your_table_name
(
    id String,
    registration_date String,
    is_iranian String,
    english_name String,
    name String,
    day_of_birth String,
    month_of_birth String,
    yob String,
    death_date String,
    educational_field String,
    education_level String,
    military_state String,
    father_name String,
    id_number_melli String,
    id_lssue_location String,
    lastname String,
    english_lastname String,
    marital_status String,
    national_code String,
    passport_expire_date String,
    passport_number String,
    religion String
)
ENGINE = MergeTree()
ORDER BY tuple();
```

Figure 12.1: An LLM import string output.

Step 2: Create the Tables in ClickHouse

I like to create my table via the command line. If you prefer to use a graphic user interface (GUI), you can use a tool like DBeaver and paste the command directly into the Structured Query Language (SQL) editor. Either way, you should get an OK response.

Also, don't forget to create the database first, or you will run into an error.

```
]> clickhouse-client

:) CREATE database iran;

Ok.

:) [paste code]
```

```
Query id: 4f887421-514b-49fa-ada6-c6f94547810d

Ok.

0 rows in set. Elapsed: 0.003 sec.
```

Step 3: Import Your Data

Again, I prefer importing my data from the command line. This really comes down to preference, but I do I like working in Linux, and it enables me to quickly troubleshoot any errors like mismatched columns or incorrect encoding. It's also really fast. If you haven't done this before, you will be amazed at the speed of the import process.

```
clickhouse-client -q "INSERT INTO iran.datagroup1 FORMAT CSV" < filename.csv
```

If the file you are importing has hundreds of millions of rows, consider splitting it into chunks with the split command. The following command splits the original file into multiple parts of 50m rows.

```
split -l 50000000 masterfile.csv split/split-
```

Once that's done, you can then safely import each of the split files one at a time, or easily with a recursive loop. This can be accomplished using the following bash script:

```
for f in *; do clickhouse-client -q "INSERT INTO iran.datagroup1 FORMAT CSV" < $f; done
```

If you prefer to work outside of the command line, this next section's for you.

DBeaver

DBeaver is a universal database management tool. It's a full-featured GUI designed to work with nearly any relational or analytical database engine. I fully appreciate that not everyone lives in the command line, so think of DBeaver as your GUI-based, all-purpose Swiss Army Knife for database interaction.

There will likely be many times where you want to be more hands-on, visually, and this is a good way to do it. DBeaver gives you the tools you need to explore, query, visualize, and manage your data. DBeaver also offers the following:

- A SQL editor with syntax highlighting, autocompletion, and query history
- Visual schema navigation to explore tables, views, indexes, and other database objects
- Data preview and manipulation, letting you browse result sets, filter rows, or export data to CSV/Excel formats
- Support for advanced data types, including arrays and JSON structures

This is by no means an exhaustive guide. I cover a handful of high-level topics to get you started—and along the way, I throw in a few useful tips that are worth keeping in your back pocket.

Getting Started: Create a Connection

Getting started is extremely simple. First, create a new connection and select your database type (see Figure 12.2). ClickHouse is the first on the list.

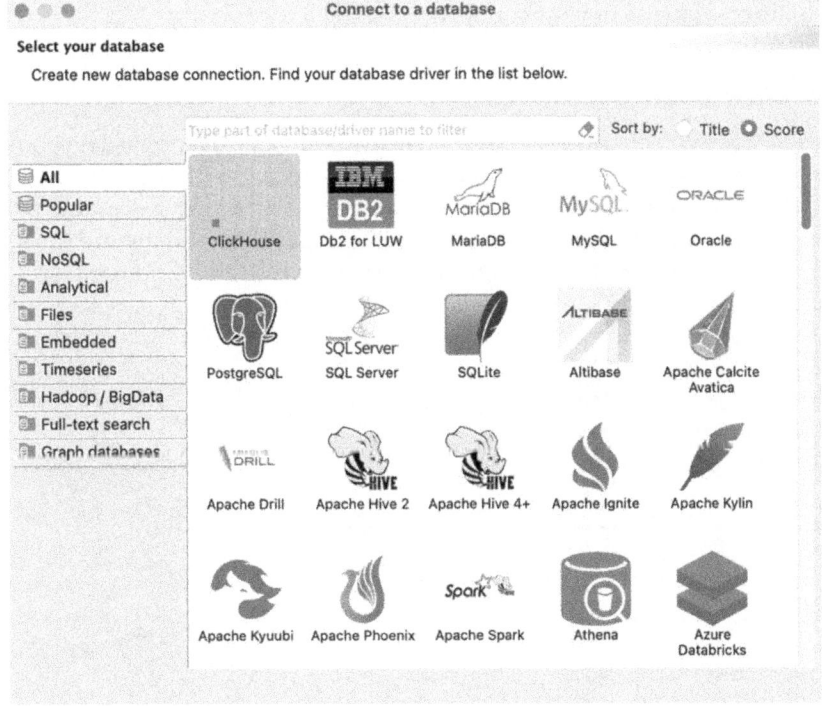

Figure 12.2: DBeaver's Connect to Database screen.

The next step is to enter your database connection details (see Figure 12.3).

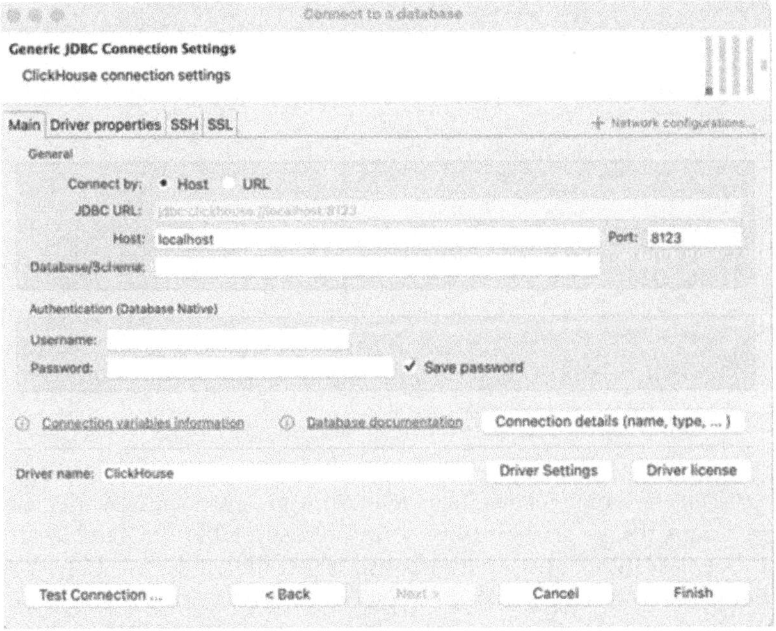

Figure 12.3: DBeaver's database connection details.

That's it! You will immediately see your connection on the left panel.

Working with Table View

As soon as you connect, you can click on the Table view to obtain a visual of the data you just imported (see Figure 12.4). Remember, because you're working with a ClickHouse database, working with this data will be extremely fast. This is where the magic of combining the two really comes into play. You can make changes to your database rows on the fly with the GUI or via the SQL editor, and process hundreds of millions of rows within a few seconds.

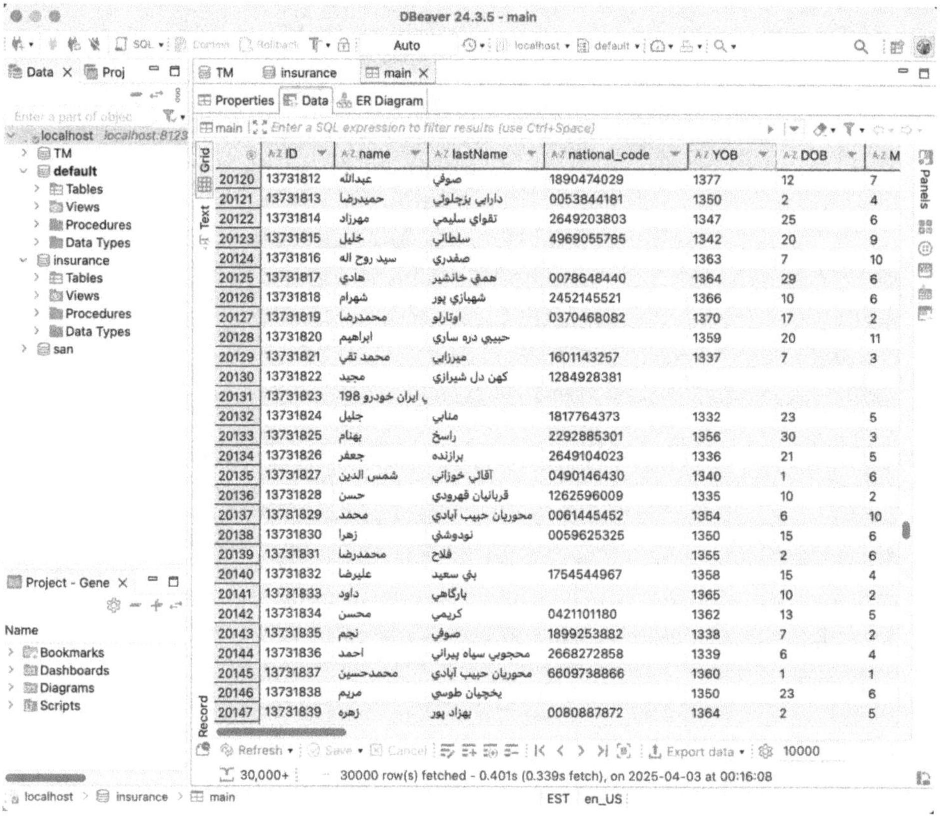

Figure 12.4: DBeaver Table view.

Deleting a Column

ClickHouse is a *columnar database*, which means that each column is stored independently on disk. When you insert data, it's not written row by row across a table—instead, each column's values are grouped and stored as separate compressed files.

Due to this structure, when you drop a column, you're not modifying each row or rewriting a huge table. You're simply deleting the physical files associated with that column.

In traditional relational databases, dropping a column might involve updating the schema, then rewriting all of the rows, triggering cascades, reindexing, and other processor heavy operations.

With ClickHouse, none of that is required. As shown in Figure 12.5, if you want to delete a column with the GUI, you select the column from the drop-down list on the left (located under Columns), and then right-click and choose Delete.

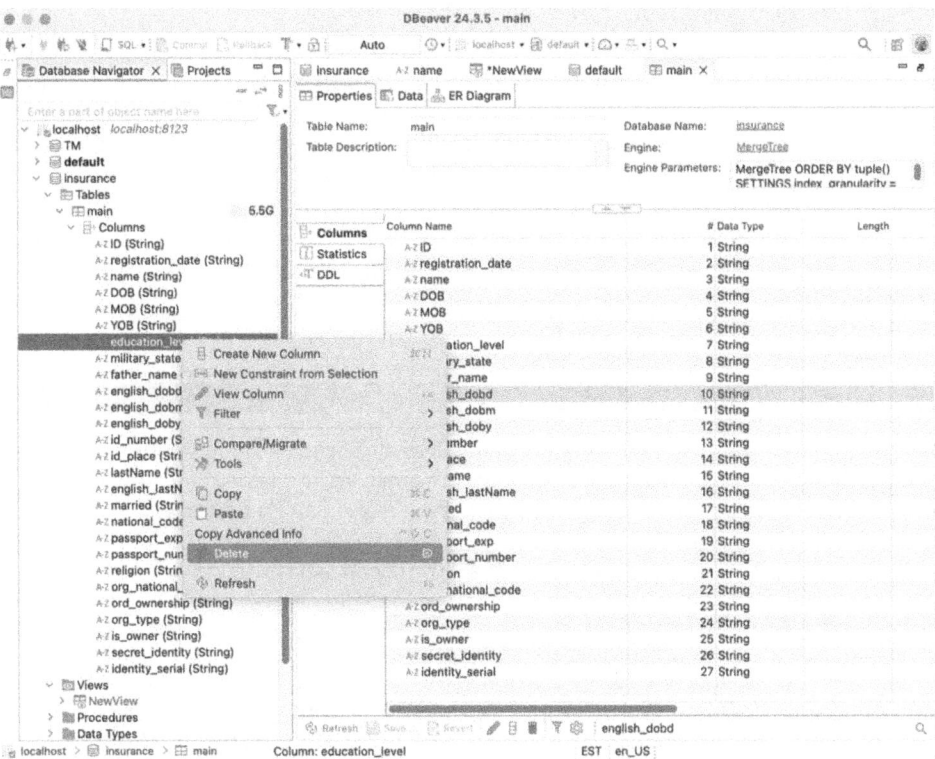

Figure 12.5: Delete column view.

The other great thing about working with ClickHouse is that you can interact with it using a familiar SQL syntax. So if you want to delete a column via a command line (or using the SQL editor), you use this command:

```
ALTER TABLE table_name DROP COLUMN column_name;
```

That's it. Loading data is fast—and as long as you've taken the necessary steps to clean it properly, the process should be quick and painless.

Organizing and Optimizing Your Data

Data optimization is arguably one of the most important superpowers in modern analytics. It's all about how you structure and store your data to boost performance, efficiency, and accuracy, at scale.

In systems like ClickHouse, structure matters—a lot. When you're dealing with billions or even trillions of rows, how you organize that data will directly impact query speed and system performance. And when those queries start stacking up, every microsecond counts.

Data quality is just as important. Repetition, inconsistency, and sloppy formatting can place a massive strain on your systems. Standardizing fields, like having names in uppercase or emails in lowercase, can help eliminate all the little issues that can break your joins, filters, or match logic.

Having clean data also makes it much easier to catch errors, spot gaps, and identify erroneous data—something that's nearly impossible if everything's jammed into a single, messy field.

I have also seen people push back and waste countless hours on backend optimization because they want the data to "look right." But here's the thing: Your presentation should never dictate storage. That's what the frontend is for.

You can make things look pretty on the user interface (UI)—full names, formatted SSNs, mailing addresses—whatever you need. But the backend should be built for speed, scale, and precision.

HACKER TIP: Antibrok3rs

Another key part of my process is data normalization, which includes consistently formatting fields across an entire dataset. This means converting all names, addresses, and other text-based fields to uppercase and email addresses to lowercase. Login credentials are treated as case-sensitive, when necessary.

I've also started splitting email addresses into these two separate fields:

- **EmailUser:** The portion before the @

- **EmailDomain:** The portion after the @

The main reason I do this is for compression. If you have 50-million email addresses and 30 percent of them are Gmail accounts, storing "gmail.com" repeatedly in a single text field results in unnecessary storage overhead. By isolating the domain, you drastically improve data deduplication and compression.

This might not matter much in a small database. But when you're managing infrastructure that holds tens of trillions of rows like I do, these efficiencies become critical.

Another point people tend to overlook is the frontend can handle data reassembly. For example, ISO 3166-2 country codes can be easily expanded to full country names on the UI layer. Similarly, SSN segments (i.e., SSN3, SSN2, SSN4) can be rejoined visually for display purposes, without needing to store them as a single field.

This approach also makes it easier to identify missing data or inconsistencies. For example, if one SSN segment is missing, it becomes immediately obvious in a segmented schema, whereas in a single text field that sort of gap can be harder to spot.

I work with massive consumer and business datasets often from providers like Experian, and I find that the more granular the columns, the more useful the data becomes. I discard the non-normalized or concatenated versions, like full names or full addresses in a single field, and retain only the versions that are already properly structured. The more I can split the columns, the more flexible and scalable my data becomes.

Data Searching

Data searching is the real magic of why I'm showcasing DBeaver and ClickHouse. Trying to query specific information from other database types like MySQL can be extremely slow and painful depending on how your data is structured.

In DBeaver (and ClickHouse), not so much. The following code searches the main table looking for a `national_code` value of `123456`.

```
SELECT *,national_code FROM MAIN_TABLE WHERE national_code = '123456';
```

Wildcard searching—rather, *fast* wildcard searching—is another incredibly important byproduct of ClickHouse. Searching wildcard strings is just as easy; you just need to insert `ILIKE` as part of the parameter search:

```
SELECT *,CUSTOMER_NAME FROM TRANSACTION_LOGS where CUSTOMER_NAME ILIKE '%Troia;
```

The prior code is searching the `customer_name` column in the `transaction_logs` table, looking for any matches with `Troia` in the name.

Finally, let's take it one step further and search across multiple tables using wildcard values, then sort the values by specific columns.

```
SELECT *,FLIGHT_DATA FROM CN.flights where ((TYPE = 'eTicket') OR (TYPE = 'physical')) AND
DESTINATION_NAME like '%Korea'
ORDER BY TRAVEL_DATE, AIRPORT_CODE DESC
```

This code searches through the `flight_data` table of a Chinese airline database, looking for any ticket types flagged as eTicket or Physical, with a destination name that includes `Korea` (could be North or South).

Once the results are found, the code also sorts (`order`) by travel date and airport code.

Unique Values

There are any number of reasons why you might need to tally unique values or specific occurrences of an item for analytical purposes. Maybe you want to see how many unique email addresses exist in a particular table. Regardless, tallying unique items is fairly straightforward using the `COUNT(Distinct)` command.

```
SELECT count(DISTINCT field_to_tally) FROM tablename ;
```

The output will appear in the DBeaver results panel (see Figure 12.6).

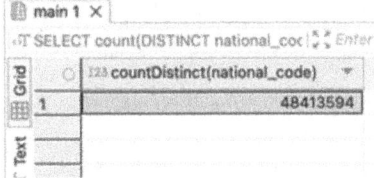

Figure 12.6: DBeaver count results.

Tallying Occurrences

Next, you might want to see how many recurring (or duplicate) items exist within a particular column. To tally occurrences of a field in DBeaver, you can run a GROUP BY query with a COUNT() function.

In the following example, say you want to tally the total occurrences in a database where national_code isn't blank. Once you have those results, you want to also group them by year of birth (YOB) and sort them by the total occurrences for each year.

```
SELECT YOB, COUNT(*) AS occurrences
FROM tablename
WHERE national_code != ''
GROUP BY YOB
ORDER BY occurrences DESC;
```

Figure 12.7 shows how many national_code values exist for each birth year in a given database. (In case you're wondering, the birth year is based on the Iranian calendar—for no other reason than this is how the data was provided.)

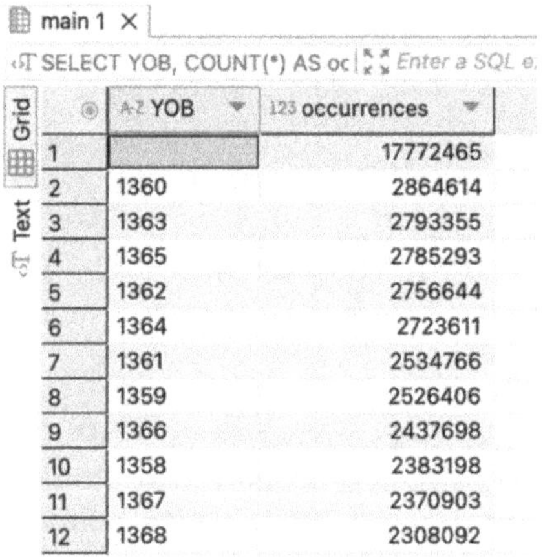

	A-Z YOB	123 occurrences
1		17772465
2	1360	2864614
3	1363	2793355
4	1365	2785293
5	1362	2756644
6	1364	2723611
7	1361	2534766
8	1359	2526406
9	1366	2437698
10	1358	2383198
11	1367	2370903
12	1368	2308092

Figure 12.7: Output count of national_code per year.

Data Joining and Merging

One of the most powerful things that you can do in ClickHouse is quickly and easily combine information across tables or within records. This is where joins and field merging come into play.

A JOIN in ClickHouse works much like a traditional SQL database—it enables you to pull together related data from two or more tables based on a common key. For example, you might have one table of email addresses and another with geolocation data. Using a JOIN, you can merge those records into a single result set for analysis.

ClickHouse supports several types of joins, including:

- INNER JOIN: Returns matching rows in both tables
- LEFT JOIN: Returns all rows from the left table, and matching rows from the right
- ANY JOIN: Optimized join that returns the first matching row from the right table (often used in ClickHouse for performance)

In this example, I'm joining data between the customer_data1 and customer_data2 tables, using the CUSTOMER_NO field.

```
SELECT * FROM customer_data1
  JOIN CUSTOMER_data2
  ON customer_data1.CUSTOMER_NO = CUSTOMER_data2.ORIG_CUSTOMER_NO
```

Another way to join your data in ClickHouse is by using a full JOIN, which enables you to combine all rows from two tables, regardless of whether there's a matching key between them. If a match is found between the tables, the corresponding rows are joined. If there's no match, the unmatched row from each table is still included in the result, with NULL values for the missing side.

This can be very useful when you want to preserve the full context of both datasets, even if they aren't perfectly aligned.

For example, the following query creates a new table, customer_new, includes all the data in master_table, and joins any matching data from second_table based on the customer_no field.

```
CREATE TABLE customer_new AS
SELECT *
FROM master_table
JOIN second_table
  ON master_table.CUSTOMER_NO = second_table.CUSTOMER_NO
```

It is extremely powerful, and the basic syntax is very easy to understand.

Finally, an INNER JOIN will remove any rows that don't have a match between two tables. The INNER_JOIN command will return only the rows where there's a matching value in both tables based on the join condition. Any row that doesn't have a match in either table is excluded from the result.

The following code uses an INNER_JOIN to combine the ticketfull and tickets2 tables on instances where values of SALES_ORD_ID are equal.

```
INNER JOIN tickets2
on ticketfull.SALES_ORD_ID = tickets2.SALES_ORD_ID
```

Remember, only rows that exist in both tables with the same value for SALES_ORD_ID will be returned.

Exporting CSV Data

Now that you've successfully processed, mangled, and merged your data, you may want to export a copy to a CSV file. This is surprisingly easy to do with ClickHouse. Again, I prefer to do this using the command line. In this case, because I can easily specify the output path on the server instead of saving it to my hard drive.

```
SELECT *
FROM merged_table_name
INTO OUTFILE '/path/to/export.csv'
FORMAT CSVWithNames;
```

Make sure to specify the correct output format. If you specify `CSV` instead of `CSVWithNames`, your data will be exported without table headers.

Exporting via DBeaver GUI

You can also easily export your data using the DBeaver GUI. Run the same query (above) in the query window. Once the results appear, right-click anywhere in the results grid and select Export Result Set → Export to CSV.

The good thing about exporting in this fashion is that you can also manually change the CSV file export options, including customizing the header names, delimiters, and encoding types.

Using the Visual Query Builder

Another useful part of DBeaver is its Visual Query Builder (Figure 12.8)—a drag-and-drop tool that lets you build SQL queries, without writing out the syntax by hand. Instead of typing SQL code, you can visually construct queries by selecting tables and connecting fields—much like drawing a map of your data relationships.

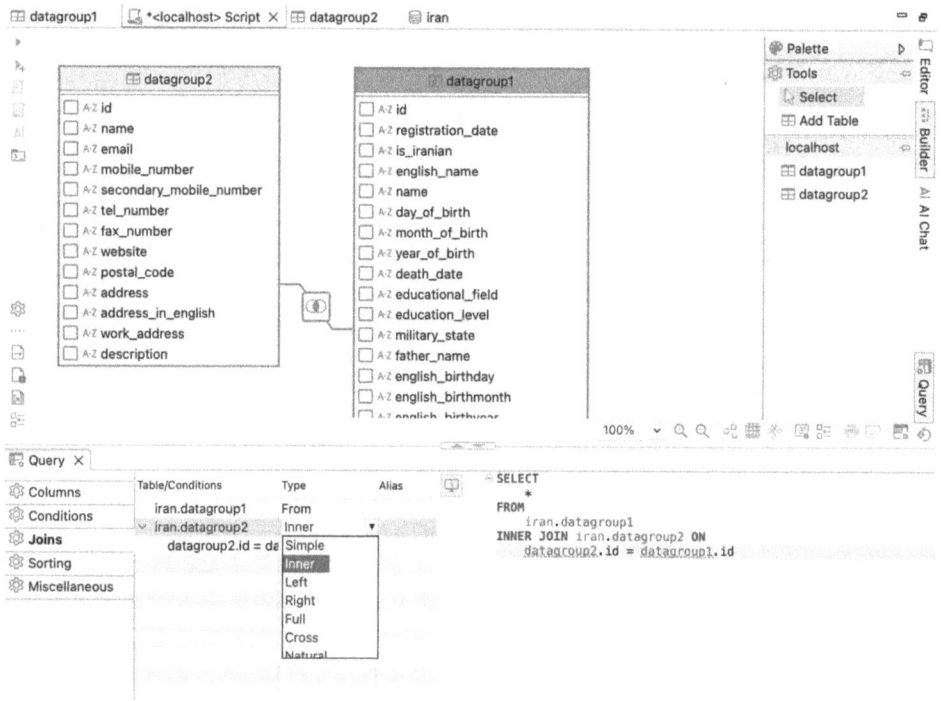

Figure 12.8: DBeaver Visual Query Builder.

AI Query Builder

Select versions of DBeaver also support using artificial intelligence (AI) to create your queries. The AI Query Builder help users generate SQL queries using plain English instructions. Instead of writing complex SQL syntax manually, you simply describe what you want to do in natural language, and the AI will generate the corresponding query for you.

Note: You need an API key from OpenAI.com for this to work.

In Figure 12.9, I write a prompt instructing AI to create a query to join two specific tables using the Identification (ID) field.

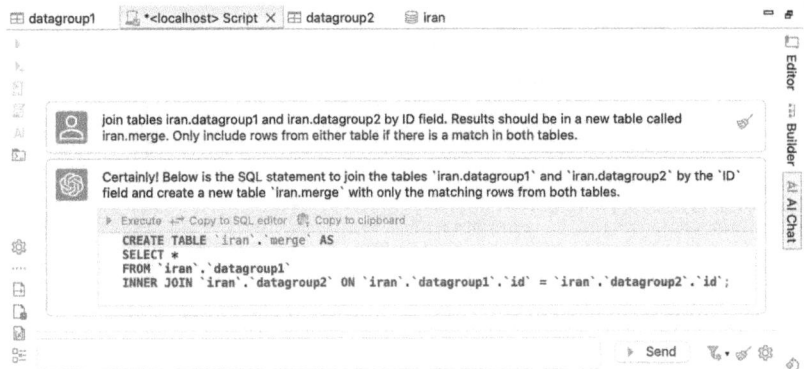

Figure 12.9: DBeaver AI Query Builder.

One more example that I want to highlight is the ability to use the (Open) AI Query Builder to create a more complex SQL statement. In Figure 12.10, I'm asking the AI Query Builder to merge two tables based on the ID field, include all results regardless of a match, save the merged output to a new table, and sort the resulting data.

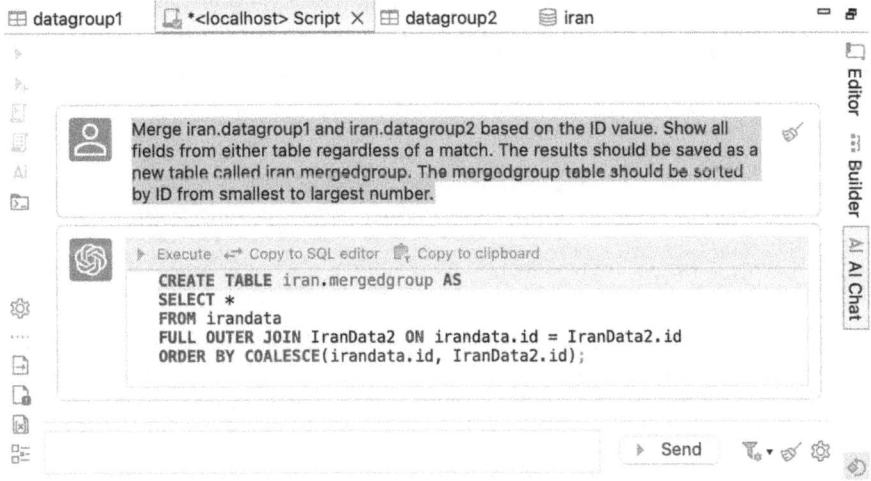

Figure 12.10: Advanced query using the AI Query Builder.

AI Starting to Break Down

As is the case with AI, the more complex the queries, the more likely the results will be incorrect. In Figure 12.11, I asked the AI Query Builder to create a relatively complex query. Unfortunately, if you try to run the code as is, you'll get the following error:

```
Error: ORDER BY or PRIMARY KEY clause is missing.=
```

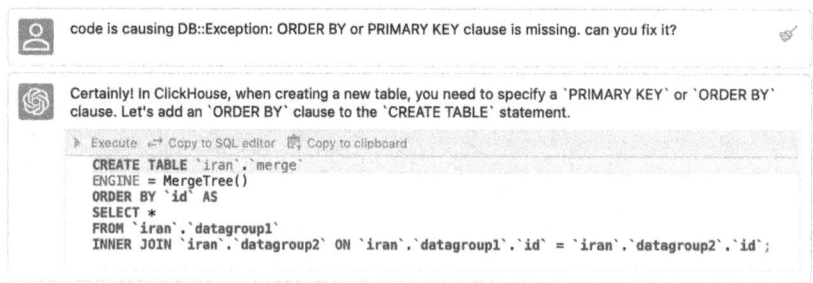

Figure 12.11 area (not listed in crops):

Figure 12.11: AI Query Builder showing an incorrect solution.

I took another pass at this problem and asked AI to specifically fix the error, as shown in Figure 12.12.

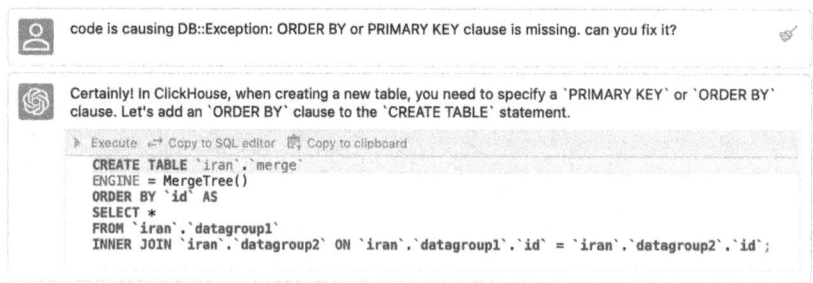

Figure 12.12: AI Query Builder showing a fixed solution.

This second version worked, and frankly I was impressed. The AI engine figured out that the problem in the code was a missing ORDER BY clause and provided the correct code.

I include this example to reinforce a key point in this book: Just because AI says something, doesn't make it right: You still need to think critically.

Aleph

The second tool I'm discussing is Aleph, an open-source software platform developed by the Organized Crime and Corruption Reporting Project (OCCRP) to support investigative journalism and complex data research.

The software platform is designed to search, link, and analyze large volumes of structured and unstructured data, including PDFs, DOCs, PPTs, CSVs, JSON files, and anything else you can throw at it.

Aleph has an incredibly powerful interface for indexing documents, datasets, and entities, making it ideal for projects that require sorting through messy, high-volume sources, like ransomware data leaks.

Think of it this way: Imagine downloading a dataset with thousands of random documents. Having to search through all of them manually to find keywords (or other pieces of relevant information) would be a daunting task.

Aleph will automate this process and will even automatically build in a visual link analysis based on your targets. Now, imagine you have 10, 100, or 1,000 different datasets, each with varying types of information. Aleph will automate all their ingestion and indexing for you.

Aleph will even automatically apply optical character recognition (OCR) to detect text within PDFs, so everything is searchable.

> **HACKER TIP: Antibrok3rs**
>
> Aleph is simplest for tracking 90 percent of people. It can handle CSV and other file formats directly, so there's often no need to load the data into a separate database system. You just need to clean your CSV files, map the fields, and run the import.
>
> Aleph is open source, so you can plug in your own data and run your own search engine locally. You can even use it on any foreign language data, PDF files, EML files, and so on. Obviously, I advise everyone having a different instance just for PDF. I literally have billions of PDF files and even TIFF document images.

Automated Entity Resolution

The really cool thing about Aleph is that it's designed to provide entity resolution to people and companies, so it automatically creates insights and connections in large volumes of structured and unstructured data. It automatically detects file contents and identifies and extracts entities (e.g., people, organizations, emails, and phone numbers). It also automatically builds connections across documents.

Users can then query the data, tag the relevant findings, and visualize relationships—streamlining investigative and intelligence workflows.

Automated entity mapping identifies relationships between entities (i.e., people, companies, and addresses) and creates a timeline of events and visual link analysis charts to help understand complex networks.

For teams tracking ransomware activity, Aleph provides a scalable and collaborative environment to catalog leaks by group, timeline, victim industry, geography, and more. It supports controlled access, making it suitable for sensitive investigations, and it can be integrated with custom pipelines or external APIs for automation. Ultimately, Aleph transforms chaotic breach data into a structured resource that analysts can explore efficiently.

Aleph UI Overview

Aleph's interface is designed to make document searches easy. You can search, filter, and tag documents to quickly locate relevant information. For beginners, the Document Search feature is a good starting point. Search by keywords, names, or specific identifiers, and use filters to narrow down results by date, document type, or source, which helps manage large volumes of information. See Figure 12.13.

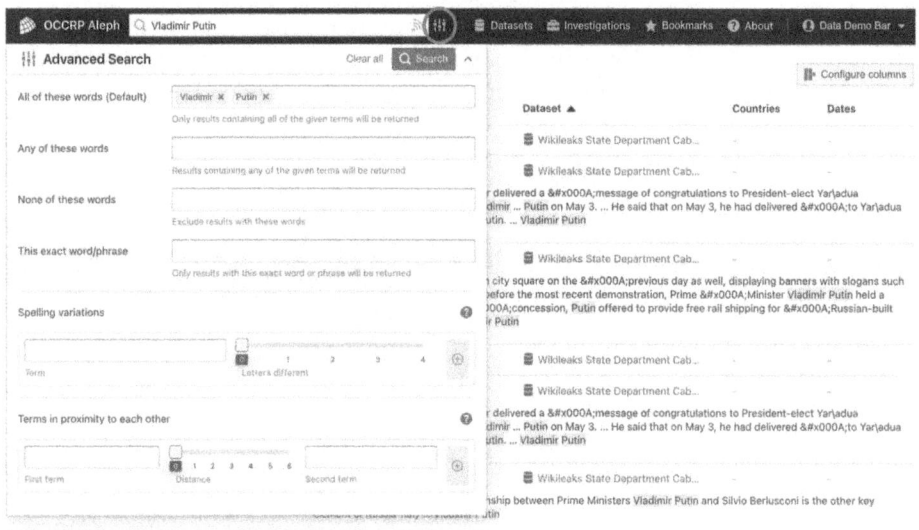

Figure 12.13: Aleph screenshot.

Courtesy of gijn.org.

Aleph supports multilingual investigations by processing and searching documents in a wide range of languages. It also includes OCR, which enables users to search the contents of scanned PDFs and image-based documents—an essential feature when working with government records or leaked files in non-text formats.

Aleph can also automatically transliterate search terms. In Figure 12.14, you'll see that a search for "Putin" will also return results for the Cyrillic equivalent, "Путин." This linguistic flexibility ensures that relevant data isn't missed due to language barriers. Additionally, the Aleph UI is available in six languages—English, German, French, Russian, Arabic, and Spanish—making it accessible to a global community of investigators.

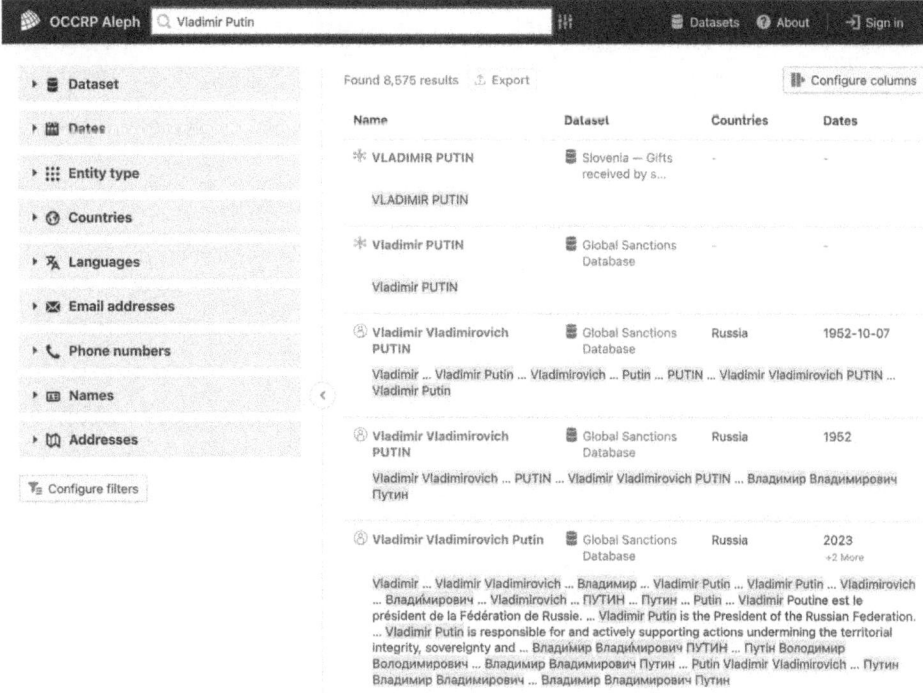

Figure 12.14: Screenshot of the Putin search.

Courtesy of `gijn.org`.

One last important feature is Aleph's cross-referencing capabilities, which make it possible to connect people, companies, addresses, and other entities across multiple datasets.

Aleph also includes a built-in visualization tool that allows users to map relationships between entities (see Figure 12.15), generating network diagrams and timelines to help investigators better understand how individuals and organizations are connected over time.

Worth noting, Aleph's official platform, available at `https://aleph.occrp.org`, includes a free, web-based version that enables anyone to explore and test its core features.

The public instance comes preloaded with a wide range of datasets—from offshore leaks and sanctions lists to corporate registries—making it easy to experiment with real investigative material. For those who need deeper access, Aleph also offers a free "extended" access tier, which unlocks additional datasets.

Gaining this level of access requires submitting an application and going through a brief approval process, typically limited to journalists, researchers, and trusted investigative professionals.

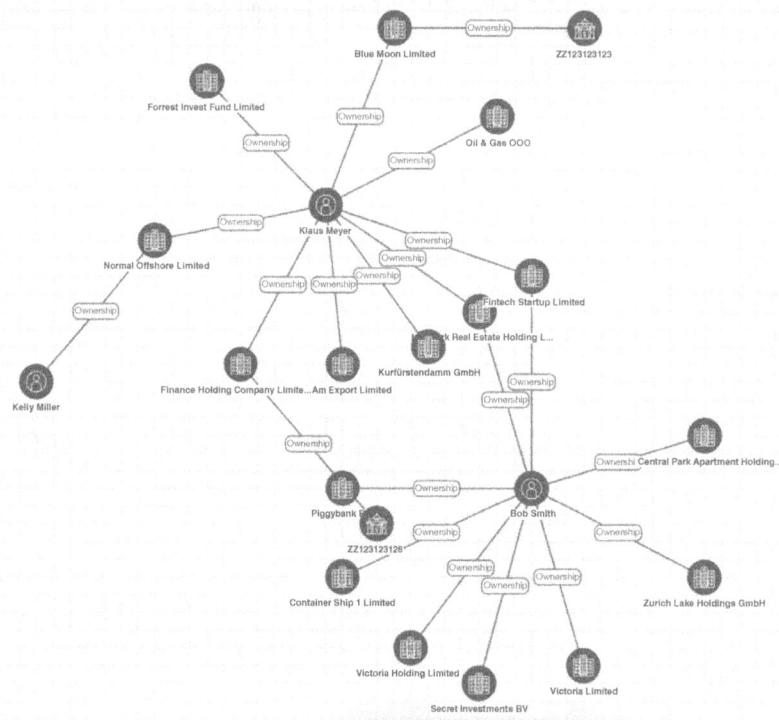

Figure 12.15: Link analysis diagram.

Courtesy of gijn.org.

Summary

This chapter covered two distinct platforms used for working with data: ClickHouse and Aleph. ClickHouse is a high-performance, columnar database optimized for fast analytics on large tabular datasets, such as CSV files, breach dumps, and structured logs. The chapter explored how to load and query data using the command line and the DBeaver GUI, and covered techniques for joining tables, merging fields, tallying occurrences, and exporting data to CSV—all essential steps in processing large-scale hacked, breached, and leaked (HBL) open-source intelligence (OSINT) datasets.

In contrast, Aleph is an open-source investigative platform developed by OCCRP, designed to ingest and analyze unstructured and semi-structured data. It excels at linking people, companies, addresses, and documents across disparate sources, enabling analysts to build powerful relationship maps and entity timelines. Aleph also includes full-text search, OCR capabilities, multilingual support, and built-in visualization tools, making it ideal for complex, cross-border investigations.

Together, these tools demonstrate two complementary approaches to working with open-source and leaked data—ClickHouse for structured data processing and analysis, and Aleph for contextual investigation and network mapping.

Now that your data is loaded and organized, the next chapter focuses on analysis techniques—how to make sense of the data, surface meaningful patterns, and extract actionable intelligence by using practical methods to turn raw information into real investigative insight.

Data Analysis and AI

This chapter explores what it looks like to begin working with artificial intelligence (AI) and large language models (LLMs) for intelligence analysis.

It breaks down how LLMs can process massive datasets, flag behavioral anomalies, and save analysts hours of manual effort. This is where AI proves its value—not as a replacement for the analyst, but as an extension of their time and attention.

When used right, AI doesn't make your job easier—it makes it faster. It helps you quickly find where to look first and get to the questions that actually matter. And that's the goal.

This chapter features commentary from:

Jason Barrett
OSINT Executive

The views and opinions provided herein are my own and do not necessarily represent the views of the Office of the Director of National Intelligence or of the United States. (See also 5 C.F.R. § 2635.807(b).)

Dennis Eger
Senior Open Source Advisor, INSCOM

Randy Nixon
Director, Open Source Enterprise, CIA

Asking Your First Question

For years, the intelligence community got by without prioritizing OSINT. Then, almost overnight, it became everyone's top priority. The conversation shifted from whether to use OSINT to how to use it more effectively—and how to operationalize it at scale.

We are witnessing a similar trajectory with the adoption of AI and LLMs—a classic crawl-walk-run progression. First came skepticism, then a wave of interest, and then, almost overnight, the question shifted from "should we integrate?" to "how do get this *now*?"

But effective integration requires more than just access to new tools. It requires a shift in mindset—a new way of thinking about a familiar problem.

When I was getting started with LLMs, my biggest challenge wasn't technical. It was figuring out what I could even ask. What are the limits of what this technology can do for me? And most importantly, how do I properly frame a question in a way that gets me a useful answer?

Knowing how to ask the right question becomes significantly harder in the middle of information overload. The AI space is saturated. There's too much to choose from with no clear starting point—and that makes things overwhelming.

In my experience, learning how to write effective prompts is by far the most important part of this entire process. Unfortunately, that message often gets drowned out in our current wave of AI hysteria.

At the end of the day, analysts are like everyone else. They find a method that works, and they stick to it. Honestly, who can blame them? We have all been taught to use tools that produce results, and follow methods that are consistent and reliable.

Asking someone to change from a proven process to something unfamiliar, even if it might be more efficient, means introducing change. And change creates friction.

I get it. People like routines. You go with what works because no one wants to potentially make their job harder than it already is. But in intelligence, complacency carries risk. Sticking to what's comfortable can mean missing what's critical.

So let me cut to the chase and give you the first (and most important) question you should be asking yourself:

How do I take the repetitive tasks I'm already doing, day after day, and use an LLM to make that work easier, faster, and smarter?

Before we dig into the answer, I want to highlight an excerpt from "What AI Can—and Can't—Do for Intelligence," a 2023 article published on the online digital platform, *The Cipher Brief*, by former CIA veterans Kristin Wood and Martin Petersen.

Their insight sets the stage for this chapter, which focuses on how LLMs can rapidly interpret and extract value from large volumes of data—freeing up the analysts to work on solving more complex problems:

> *We believe AI can greatly improve intelligence analysis in several ways that are relevant to where and how the IC went wrong. While there are many more developments of relevance, in focusing on just the promise of AI we see the opportunity for:*
>
> *__Saving time and history.__ Pre-war IC officers worked long hours and struggled to stay atop their data; their successors do the same and are also buried in data that far exceeds a human's ability to review it. AI tools use machine learning (ML) and natural language*

processing (NLP) to help analysts process and extract key insights from vast datasets. If AI tools sit atop the data archives, they can also ensure that compartmented or older information continues to factor in to new judgments without being lost or forgotten when analysts or units move or when accesses change, all perennial problems.

Pointing the way. AI tools can help identify patterns, relationships, or anomalies that might not be apparent to human analysts, tipping and queuing them towards areas for further investigation. This is useful in any fast-breaking situation, but when caught between the drumbeat of war and vast amounts of data, this capability would have helped the IC tremendously.

Finding bad actors. One of the challenges of the Iraq terrorism analysis was the challenge of combining all of the terrorism-related data to assess the nature of al-Qa'ida's presence in Iraq. An AI tool could have helped us make linkages among those we knew to find others we did not yet know.

Opening our brain's black box. For us, one of the most exciting areas of AI's potential is its ability to make an analyst's or group's internal decision-making processes more transparent.

Tools can help by showing how we weigh key elements of argumentation and evaluate the importance of such variables, allowing us to better see missing elements of rigor in analytic thinking and identify gaps that are limiting analytic confidence. It can also allow analysts and managers to track how thinking has evolved over time and highlight critical differences, avoiding both group think and "layering," a term describing multiple points of analysis added to others without the right caveats, both of which were failings in pre-war WMD analysis. Having data-driven insights inform analytic frameworks also would allow for more reasoned and less emotional discussion of the evidence.

Helping us understand what we see. One of the more compelling points in then-Secretary of State Colin Powell's speech to the UN explaining the Administration's reasoning came through an image of an alleged mobile biological lab facility; it was later determined that the vehicle had been wrongly identified. Today's computer vision machine learning-assisted models could have offered better analysis through millions of ground photos and overhead images and tracking vehicle locations to develop a more accurate assessment of both the equipment and its transit history.

For all of its promise, AI tools cannot yet do deliberative thinking, referring to planning and evaluating. AI also can't communicate, a key human ability. Those shortcomings are obvious in ChatGPT which attempts to automate reasoning but doesn't "think" critically, instead regurgitating plausible-sounding responses based on large language models.

Today's AI can answer the questions we ask of it, but it cannot ensure we're asking the right questions.

We believe that the most important element in modern intelligence analysis remains the people who ask the right questions, master their tradecraft, tools, and data, and use them to deliver decision-advantage to U.S. national security officials. The IC's serious and ongoing focus on advancing analytic skills combined with significantly expanding access to AI, other analytic tools, and vast troves of meaningful data will arm them with the right weapons to protect our national security in the digital age.

NOTE   I want to give a special thanks to Rae Baker—OSINT analyst at Deloitte and author of an upcoming book on applying AI and LLMs to real-world OSINT workflows—for her critical input in helping shape the foundation of this chapter.

Using LLMs Efficiently

Use of AI and LLMs doesn't need to be groundbreaking. The value of AI and LLMs doesn't come from its ability to reinvent the wheel or deliver some profound, world-shifting insight. If you're waiting for a moment where an LLM will solve all your most complex problems, maybe put this book down and go for a walk.

What AI does offer is much more practical, and frankly, far more valuable. Case in point: Talk to any professional, in any field, at any time, and they will all tell you the same thing: *I wish I had an assistant.*

That's what AI can be: *Your own personal assistant designed to do all the tedious, mind-numbing work that you hate doing.*

I am at a point now where I am literally saving *hours* of time, *every day,* because I've reached a point in my workflow where, when I hit a really boring task, instead of putting it off and dreading it for a week, I just hand it off to ChatGPT.

I've demonstrated throughout this book that AI and LLMs aren't built for the heavy lifting. They're not here to architect complex systems or write production-grade code from scratch. Where they *do* excel is in the repetitive, mind-numbing work that clogs up your day and kills momentum.

It's not about cutting-edge breakthroughs; it's about saving hours, days, even weeks of your time by removing the mundane work you already know how to do.

While AI can significantly accelerate the process of organizing and parsing large datasets, the heavy lifting will *always* rest with the analyst. By offloading repetitive and time-consuming tasks, AI allows analysts to focus their efforts on solving the larger problem at hand.

This chapter explores how to apply AI—not as a replacement—but as a force multiplier in the analytical process.

Dennis Eger
Senior Open Source Advisor, INSCOM

We have massive amounts of data—years, even decades worth of reporting. The challenge now is structuring that data in a way where we can layer AI on top of it, to start answering the questions that matter. It's about speed and relevance—being able to filter through all that information quickly so we're not wasting time on noise. What I'm really focused on is the legacy reporting—the 30 or 40 years of accumulated data that exists across the enterprise. That's valuable information, but we're not leveraging it effectively. There's a ton of insight locked in that archive, and the traditional model of going back into old databases and manually digging around just doesn't cut it anymore.

We can't be asking, *"Didn't we have a report on this from 10 years ago?"* and then spend hours searching.

We need to apply AI solutions that can ingest that historical data at scale, parse it, and surface what's relevant instantly. That's how we unlock the value of what we already have—and we're moving in that direction.

In some cases, we are already starting to see this happen. A lot of the data sources we use today, especially commercial software-as-a-service platforms, are already integrating AI and other advanced capabilities.

They're helping us filter and triage content, so analysts aren't burning time reading through irrelevant material. That's a huge efficiency gain, and it's a credit to industry for moving fast and pushing those capabilities forward.

So for us, there are two major fronts: first, continue leveraging industry-led innovation to process incoming data more efficiently. And second, develop AI-enabled tools that can make sense of our legacy data—tens of thousands of archived reports—and turn them into accessible, actionable intelligence.

Randy Nixon

Director, Open Source Enterprise, CIA

We were early adopters of AI, and it's now built into nearly every aspect of our collection and production systems. Our experience with machine translation, which goes back more than a decade, gave us a head start.

When the first real commercial LLMs emerged, we were able to move quickly. Within weeks, we were already exploring how to integrate them into our workflows.

What really made the difference for us was scale. The size of our collection is both a strength and a challenge. On one hand, we're able to capture information no one else can. But on the other, no human being can manually sift through the sheer volume of what we're pulling in daily. AI changed that.

Today, our systems summarize events in near real time. Officers can interact with our data using chat-based queries and get answers drawn directly from the source material. Tasks that would have taken days to complete now take seconds.

We've also automated most of our summary production—and created new ones—because it's now so efficient. We can tailor summaries to individual decision-makers and send them updates daily. That frees up our officers to spend more time on deep thinking and complex analysis. The result is not just more coverage, but better insight.

The theme and messages are consistent. LLMs are not a silver bullet. They won't replace critical thinking, and they won't solve your hardest problems for you. What they will do is give you back your time so you can stop wasting it on repetitive tasks and start focusing on the work that matters. That's real value.

With that, let's explore how LLMs can be used to quickly extract relevant patterns from complex datasets. And to make things interesting, I use data breached from a major organization in Iran.

Identifying Patterns (of Life)

When leveraged correctly, publicly available data can provide a detailed view into the daily routines, relationships, behaviors, and vulnerabilities of both foreign and domestic actors—often without the latency or restrictions associated with classified collection methods.

Pattern-of-Life (POL) analysis involves mapping the behavioral routines and movements of a subject over time. This can include physical location data, communication patterns, social interactions, financial behavior, online activity, and more. The goal is to build a comprehensive temporal and behavioral profile, which includes when, where, how, and with whom an individual operates.

OSINT sources commonly used in POL development and target analysis include:

- Social media data
- Commercial telemetry data
- Public records and registries (e.g., bills of lading, business registrations, etc.)
- Hacked, breached, and leaked (HBL) data
- Dark web forums, and illicit market activity (e.g., logins, activity, sale histories, etc.)

With that, let's dive in and start extracting relevant POL information from breached data.

Analyzing Iranian Data

In 2023, news broke of a data breach at an Iranian ride-sharing app—their equivalent of Uber. The breach impacted 30 million people, 6 million drivers, and contained more than a billion rows of data, including personal identifiable information (PII), pick-up and drop-off details, and detailed device information. In other words, a perfect data source for establishing patterns for Iranian citizens.

The queries and examples in this chapter are designed to show how asking the right, targeted questions can reveal a subject's habitual environment and daily routines, and—critically—identify anomalies that can serve as the foundation for deeper analysis.

The examples in this chapter focus on a single user, randomly selected based on their volume of activity.

Establishing Baseline-Standard Behavior

OSINT can be used to identify a baseline of standard behavioral norms or demographic signatures within a given dataset or population. Once a baseline is established, it becomes significantly easier to detect anomalies, outliers, or emerging risks.

A *baseline* might be the typical daily movement radius of an average user in a region, or it could be the common flight patterns for government or diplomatic personnel.

Once this baseline is understood, outliers become immediately valuable. Someone whose travel history shows routine border crossings outside of diplomatic channels, or whose online accounts maintain irregular operating hours consistent with a second alias, might warrant closer inspection.

The ultimate goal is to shift from being reactive to a mode of proactive discovery. This should enable faster targeting decisions, better prioritization of limited resources, and earlier identification of high-value individuals or nodes in a network.

To begin establishing a baseline of the randomly selected Iranian user, I uploaded the JavaScript Object Notation (JSON) dataset to the LLM and used the following query.

Query

The attached JSON file includes user movements with latitude and longitude coordinates for destinations in Iran. Using the coordinates, can you show the different routes taken by this user on a map of Iran?

The response is shown in Figure 13.1.

Figure 13.1: Most common routes shown by the LLM.

Generated with AI using ChatGPT's - OpenAI

I personally like reviewing the data that I'll be using for my analysis. Tables are great for that.

Query

Provide a table list of the user's start and stop locations along with date/time of travel.

The response is shown in Figure 13.2.

> **NOTE** Don't forget, you can also ask your LLM to automatically translate all data for you.

The goal now is to identify the user's baseline activities and look for any relevant characteristics that might stand out.

Query

Can you analyze the user's rides and show any relevant patterns based on his usage? For example, is there a time of day that he travels most? Are there locations most frequently visited?

Ride Start And Stop Locations

	Date	Time	Origin	Destination
1	2023-04-13	08:40:03	تبریز، ولیعصر، خ. صدف، نرسیده به پل نظامی	ز، سیلاب، پل شهید بی، خ. فروزان
2	2023-04-12	09:48:16	تبریز، منظریه، خ. بلوار نیایش، خ. مسافر، ترمینال بزرگ تبریز	ز، سیلاب، پل شهید بی، خ. فروزان
3	2023-04-12	06:45:42	ارومیه، ب رجایی، فلکه	یه، ب خاتم الانبیا، بعد ، علی آباد، کوی

Figure 13.2: Screenshot of the LLM response table.

Generated with AI using ChatGPT's - OpenAI

Response

Time of Day Usage:

The user most frequently travels around:

- *7:00 a.m. (20 rides)*
- *1:00 p.m. (13 rides)*
- *6:00–7:00 a.m., 7:00 p.m., and 2:00 a.m. also show moderate activity*

Most Frequent Locations:

Combining both origin and destination cities:

- *Tabriz: 128 mentions*
- *Qom: 20 mentions*
- *Urmia: 14 mentions*
- *Tehran: 8 mentions*

This reinforces that Tabriz is by far the central hub of activity.

Most Active Days:

- *Wednesdays dominate with 28 rides*
- *Followed by Sundays (18) and Mondays (12)*

What we've learned is that the user has the most travels around Tabriz; is most active on Wednesdays, Sundays, and Mondays; and seems to travel mostly in the mornings.

This was a very easy way to identify and establish a baseline of activities. With that, let's look for something more interesting.

Outliers and Anomalies

When analyzing patterns and behaviors, the goal is to understand what "normal" looks like for an individual, group, or environment over time. Once that baseline is established, identifying *outliers*, which are data points that fall outside the norm, is where the real intelligence begins.

Remember, outliers aren't just statistical artifacts—they're intelligence signals. If the POL gives you the map, the outliers are the red dots that say: Look here first.

Outliers are important because they can signal change or potential risk.

Most human behavior is repetitive. People follow patterns: the same routes, same times, same devices, and same contacts. When someone deviates from that routine, there's usually a reason. In intelligence terms, change often precedes action.

For example, sudden network activity, such as an unexpected high-volume data transfer, might indicate insider threat or an active hack involving data exfiltration.

In other words, outliers help you focus. They enable teams to allocate attention to the 1 percent that doesn't fit, rather than drowning in the 99 percent that does.

Analyzing the Data's Outliers

Let's explore some examples of how an LLM can help quickly identify data outliers.

Query

Filter out all of the previous common occurrences and provide an analysis of what's left.

Response

Here's what stands out once we filter out the dominant Tabriz-based rides:

- **Least Frequent Route:** *Tehran → Tehran is the least frequent route that still appears more than once, with four occurrences.*

- **Least Common Travel Time:** *1:00 p.m. (13:00) had only two rides (outside of Tabriz), making it the least-used time among non-Tabriz trips.*

- **Least Visited Location:** *Tehran was the least visited among the remaining cities, with eight total mentions (as origin or destination).*

This data suggests a heavily localized pattern centered on Tabriz, with only occasional travel elsewhere—Tehran, Qom, and Urmia making up a minority of rides.

Looking for Repeating Patterns of Anomalies

When looking for relevant anomalous data, the first step should be to look for any noticeable or repeating patterns within the outlier data.

A single outlier might be random. But if you find multiple outliers showing similar characteristics—same timestamp pattern, same Internet Protocol (IP) range, same username behavior—you're not looking at random noise anymore. You're seeing the beginning of a behavioral fingerprint.

Patterns within outliers tell you what kind of anomaly you're dealing with and whether it's worth pursuing. In OSINT and cyber investigations, this is how you move from detection to understanding. It's not just about what stands out, *it's about what repeats within what stands out.*

In other words, the goal right now is to review this data to find outliers that might not necessarily be considered abnormal. For example, if I was looking at outliers based on destination, then in this case, all rides within Tabriz would be excluded because it's the most common. However, if I focused my analysis to look for outliers within Tabriz, I might find something unique that the LLM might have initially missed.

Let's start with a visual output of the outliers within the city that has the most trips.

Query

Analyzing the city with the most trips, what are the outliers in the data in terms of travel time, distance, or frequency?

Response

The results are displayed in Comma Separated Values (CSV) format (see Figure 13.3).

Now that I can visually see the outliers (and the outlier types), the first thing I want to know is where the user was going.

Tabriz Ride Outliers

		Timestamp	Hour	Origin	Destination	Distance (km)	Outlier Type
1	29	2023-04-14 14:21:59.724000+00:00	14	تبریز	تبریز	11.732809448230823	Distance
2	30	2023-04-14 14:20:20.766000+00:00	14	تبریز	تبریز	11.732809448230823	Distance
3	17	2023-04-27 18:55:36.333000+00:00	18	تبریز	تبریز	6.16769349886535	Time
4	18	2023-04-27 12:58:19.554000+00:00	12	تبریز	تبریز	3.423761680222663	Time
5	0	2023-04-13 08:40:03.785000+00:00	8	تبریز	تبریز	2.736026681890679	Route
6	1	2023-04-12 09:48:16.637000+00:00	9	تبریز	تبریز	5.866088172048659	Route
7	2	2023-07-26 06:50:24.595000+00:00	6	تبریز	تبریز	2.6599157430580167	Route
8	3	2023-07-26 06:43:44.701000+00:00	6	تبریز	تبریز	2.6599157430580167	Route
9	4	2023-07-26 06:40:41.034000+00:00	6	تبریز	تبریز	2.6599157430580167	Route

Figure 13.3: Visual output of data outliers.

Mapping the Outliers to Maps Locations

Let's see if I can get the Generative Pre-trained Transformer (GPT) to automatically associate the Global Positioning System (GPS) coordinates with nearby businesses to try and understand where the user is going.

Query

Can you associate the GPS coordinates from the data with businesses located at any of the destination coordinates?

Response

Yes, you can associate GPS coordinates from the ride-sharing data with nearby businesses in Iran using reverse geocoding and place search APIs. I can't directly access external APIs (like Google Maps or Places) or the Internet on your behalf, due to security and privacy constraints. However, I can guide you step-by-step on how to use those APIs yourself—including sample code that pulls business names for specific GPS coordinates.

That's too bad that I can't just connect a Google Application Programming Interface (API) key to get these results. Let's see if I can associate the data using a GPT-generated script.

Query

I would like to search for the business locations listed using the Google Maps API. Please craft a Python script to use an API query that will search all of the outlier locations and return a result if the business is within 2000 feet of that location.

Response

For reference, here is the API query used in the search. Figure 13.4 shows GPT's resulting Python script.

```
https://maps.googleapis.com/maps/api/place/nearbysearch/json?location=35.6892,51.3890&radius
=50&type=establishment&key=YOUR_API_KEY
```

No Magic Bullet

I ran the Python script, hoping it would give me a list of businesses, but it did not. I spent some time tweaking the script to try and auto-populate the business names (including expanding the radius of the search area), but the results were always the same: Google Maps would only return the city name.

```
Latitude,Longitude,Business Name,Address
38.067679338911056,46.35126229332241,Tabriz,Tabriz
34.68494804342832,50.891520344744436,Qom,Qom
38.082419655539894,46.32626978414012,Tabriz,Tabriz
35.648694342870634,51.39785735309414,Tehran,Tehran
34.612524723255504,50.87045102585255,Qom,Qom
37.56403721852264,45.096694946293866,Urmia,Urmia
37.565405683300526,45.05778188693833,Urmia,Urmia
35.63434258155948,51.366369750173504,Tehran,Tehran
```

```python
                                                          Copy    Edit

import requests
import csv
import time

API_KEY = 'YOUR_GOOGLE_MAPS_API_KEY'
SEARCH_RADIUS = 305  # meters (~1000 feet)
DELAY = 1  # seconds between API calls

# Paste unique (lat, lng) coordinate pairs here
coordinates = [
    ("38.067679338911056", "46.35126229332241"),  # Tabriz origin
    ("38.082419655539894", "46.32626978414012"),  # Tabriz destination
    ("37.565405683300526", "45.05778188693833"),  # Urmia origin
    ("37.56403721852264", "45.096694946293866"),  # Urmia destination
    ("34.612524723255504", "50.87045102585255"),  # Qom origin
    ("34.68494804342832", "50.891520344744436"),  # Qom destination
    ("35.648694342870634", "51.39785735309414"),  # Tehran origin
    ("35.63434258155948", "51.366369750173504")   # Tehran destination
]
```

Figure 13.4: Initial portion of the Maps search Python script.

Generated with AI using ChatGPT's - OpenAI

This is as far as the LLM will take me, which is fine. I would have easily spent a day (or more) on this task, if I had to manually look up the results and try to find my own anomalies in the patterns.

The amount of time saved is incredible, and now I can use that time to do actual investigative work rather than be stuck doing the mind-numbing initial analysis.

Identifying Patterns (with Your Eyes)

While the LLM results didn't provide exactly what I wanted, there's still much I can learn from the information I received. Looking at the locations provided by the script, I can see that the outlier data includes results from four cities: Tehran, Urmia, Qom, and Tabriz.

> **NOTE** As it turns out, the code might have worked if I tried using a different city. The Maps API was not providing information on surrounding businesses because of restrictions imposed against Iran. According to Google, "Iran is listed among the prohibited territories where the use of Google Maps Platform services is restricted. This means that developers are not permitted to use Google Maps APIs, such as the Places API, to access location data, including information about shops and businesses, within Iran."

Since the API wasn't providing me with the answers I needed, a simple solution was to manually put the GPS coordinates into Google Maps and look at the locations. Figure 13.5 shows one of the resulting locations.

Figure 13.5: Example screenshot of Google Maps from one of the locations.

After a manual review of each destination location on this trip, one pattern became clear: Each city contains a visit to a house and a mosque.

If I wanted to find out who this person was visiting, I could easily cross-reference the addresses with a different Iranian database—but that isn't something I need to worry about for the purposes of this exercise.

Instead, what I did accomplish was establish a relevant pattern—every time they visit a city, I know this person will also visit a mosque.

Looking for Erratic Data

In POL analysis, identifying erratic or unusual movements is critical because it often signals a break in routine—and in intelligence work, breaks in routine usually mean something is happening.

POL is all about establishing what "normal" looks like for a person or entity—where they go, when they go there, how often, and with whom. So when a subject suddenly takes a different route, visits an unexpected location, or moves at an unusual time, it flags a potential operational shift. That's where you start asking: Why now? Why there? What changed?

Depending on your target and the mission, an erratic or unusual change might indicate planning or execution of sensitive activity. Criminals, terrorists, traffickers, and hostile operators often intentionally alter their patterns before or during key operations. This could be to avoid surveillance, conduct a meet-up, stash contraband, or execute an attack. Unusual movement, especially when combined with other indicators, can act as an early warning.

Query

Are any erratic movements in the data?

Response

- *2:00–5:00 a.m.: Pure abnormal behavior. No normal rides exist during these hours.*
- *Peak Normal Activity: 7:00 a.m. and 4:00 p.m. to 6:00 p.m., matching workday movement.*
- *Post 8:00 p.m.: Movement is extremely low overall—either shutdown for the day, or no more need for rides.*
- *No crossover: There are no hours where both normal and abnormal rides happen simultaneously. It's either pure operational or pure civilian.*

This subject lives on a daytime civilian baseline—but when they break pattern, they do so fully, operating almost exclusively between 2:00 and 5:00 a.m., outside all normal movements.
　Here's the full table of all abnormal ride events (i.e., movements outside the normal hours of 6:00 a.m.–10:00 p.m.), including origin and destination GPS coordinates.

The full table was long and not necessary to include here, but the most important takeaway comes from the final sentence: *this subject operates during normal hours, but when they break patterns, they do so during specific times.* That's a classic indicator of deliberate separation of operational behavior from personal behavior—potentially very Operations Security (OPSEC)-aware.

I can now trace exact movements during the 2:00–5:00 a.m. window—an operational time frame where normal civilian movement is practically nonexistent.

Analyzing Patterns Within the Outliers

Finding patterns within anomalous activity can signal intent. Consistently abnormal behavior isn't really abnormal—it's planned. That's what makes it valuable.

My next step in this process is to drill into those anomalies and look for repeating patterns—because that's where operational behavior often hides.

Query

Analyzing only the anomaly data, are there any repeating patterns?

Response

The subject has distinct nighttime routines—they are not randomly moving.
　Certain routes are heavily repeated even during abnormal hours—suggesting pre-planned logistics, perhaps scheduled meets or transfers.
　Karaj acts as the central hub for nearly all operations, with branching movements toward Tehran key points.

Destinations related to hospitals ("بیمارستان امام خمینی") and industrial areas ("چیتگر شمالی" / "بل پاسداران") suggest either:

- *Clandestine medical meetings, industrial operations, or*
- *Areas chosen because of low-profile access.*

Analysis

This subject is not operating randomly at night.

They have a network of known nighttime destinations and repeat specific corridors— that is planned, not coincidental.

If you were building a surveillance or targeting package, you'd immediately flag:

- *Karaj area as home base.*
- *Tehran (Fath Road) and چیتگر (Chitgar Industrial Area) as operational extension nodes.*

Assessing the Results

These results are extremely powerful, and they were provided in a relatively short amount of time. Think about how long this type of analysis would have taken if I had to manually review and analyze all of the location data first.

Now I can do the real investigative work and start to research the additional people and locations that this target visits within the newly flagged areas.

For example, taking a look at the specific areas flagged in Tehran and the Chitgar Industrial Area, I can immediately see two specific points of interest.

Figure 13.6 shows a government office within a few hundred meters, and Figure 13.7 shows a cell phone store as the closest destination of the second location.

Figure 13.6: Google Maps screenshot of the first location.

Figure 13.7: Maps screenshot of the second location.

Closing Thoughts

This is as far as I can take the analysis with the current data—but even within those limits, I've uncovered a surprising amount using an LLM combined with some analytical logic and structured querying.

That said, I leave you with a few immediate questions worth thinking about:

Why would someone repeatedly visit a cell phone store between 2:00 and 5:00 a.m.? Could they work there? Maybe. But even if they did—assuming the store opened around 6:00 a.m., which seems unusually early—the timing and frequency still don't quite add up. Routine work schedules tend to be consistent. This isn't.

And what about the repeated trips to a location near a government office? Coincidence? Possibly. But in POL work, proximity and repetition usually mean something.

In intelligence work, anomalies are never the whole story—but in this case, I've used AI to get to the point where the real analysis can begin. It didn't replace the work; it accelerated it—helping me surface just enough signal to start asking the right questions—and that, in my humble opinion, is where we find the real power of AI.

Citations

Before I close out this chapter, there is one additional topic that can be as important as the analysis itself—citations.

Citations enable analysts and decision-makers to evaluate the reliability of the information and the confidence level of the assessment. In other words, it's not just what is said—it's who said it, how it was collected, and how trustworthy that source is.

In the IC, all assessments must be traceable back to the original source for clear accountability. If something turns out to be false or manipulated (e.g., data poisoning or disinformation), you need to be able to trace the origins of the analysis and reassess.

Citations are also useful because when other people know your sources, they can bring challenging assumptions or additional corroborating information. And most importantly, especially with OSINT, proper citation ensures you're staying within legal and ethical lines.

Jason Barrett
OSINT Executive

The OSINT strategy references AI several times, but what's equally important is how that thinking is now being codified across the intelligence community. A good example is the significantly modernized Intelligence Community Standard 206 (ICS 206), which my office updated and publicly released in December (2024). I'm fortunate to have a great partner and senior advisor, Chris Rasmussen, who led the drafting of that document.

The strategy reflects a more forward-looking posture—one that integrates modern AI concepts like computer vision, machine learning, and generative AI, while also providing guidance on how to properly cite content that is derived from, enriched by, or affiliated with AI processes.

This is critically important as we continue working to professionalize OSINT within the IC. One of the major gaps we're trying to close is the lack of standalone OSINT products that provide timely, insightful analysis sourced directly from open-source collectors.

These products aren't intended to replace all-source analysis—that's not the goal. But in time-sensitive environments where policymakers need immediate insight, a well-crafted OSINT product can go beyond the basic "fact of reporting." It can offer context, analysis, and perspective from trained professionals working in the open-source domain.

We modernized and publicly released ICS 206 for two key reasons. First, it reflects our commitment to transparency whenever possible. Second, it enables commercial partners to align their products with the same citation standards we expect from our IC workforce. This gives vendors a concrete framework to build against and creates more consistency across the ecosystem.

The benefits of this approach become even clearer over a multi-year horizon. It strengthens the credibility of open-source tradecraft and the provenance of data feeding both public and private-sector products. And that matters—for both operational effectiveness and institutional trust.

Why is that important? Because it allows the IC to stay lean, draw from a wider variety of sources, and meet mission requirements—whether for a policymaker, warfighter, or partner at the state or local level—through methods that are faster, cheaper, less intrusive, and just as accountable as traditional alternatives.

At the end of the day, we're all trying to move toward greater efficiency. If we continue to overload the classified side of the house with every request, we risk bottlenecks that degrade the quality of our all-source output. OSINT—done well—helps relieve that pressure.

Our view is simple: if we professionalize the open-source tradecraft and lean into the capabilities coming online—including various forms of AI—we give the intelligence community a major advantage as we modernize how we do the work, day in and day out.

Citing the Analysis

Writing proper citations to specific guidelines can be tedious and mundane—which sounds like the perfect job for an LLM.

If you're including citations, you most likely have specific reference guidelines that you need to follow. For this example, I use the guidelines discussed in Intelligence Community Standard 206. Appendix B of the standard contains all of the details you need to properly reference this research.

This is the query that I used with my LLM:

Query

For the above analysis and plotting information, can you provide details of what to include in a citation using the ICS 206 citation guidelines.

Response

Here is a breakdown of what needs to be included, with explanations:

The SRC should include factual information about the source, presented in a uniform format, typically in an endnote. The primary purpose of the SRC is to enable readers to locate and retrieve the source and help assess its quality or credibility.

Classification: Each citation must have an overall classification and portion markings when appropriate.

1. *Required Metadata Categories (Body Elements): Most of these are self-describing. The document indicates that elements should be separated by pipes (|).*

   - *Date*
   - *Title*
   - *Name of Producing Element*
   - *URL (for the most stable and permanent location of the data on the internet)*

  - *Commercial database name, relevant technical or content information, and whether a login was required (if a commercial database was used)*
  - *Collector: Name of entity that researched, gathered, or collected the data*

2. *Source Descriptor*

   This is a brief, narrative explanation of factors that influence the quality or credibility of a single source. It is distinct from the information elements in the SRC. The source descriptor is typically the last section of the citation.

   Factors to Include:
  - *Accuracy and completeness*
  - *Possible denial and deception*
  - *Age and continued currency of information*
  - *Technical elements of collection*
  - *Source access and Validation*
  - *Motivation*
  - *Possible bias*
  - *Expertise*

3. *Important Considerations*

   Direct linking (hyperlinking words and phrases to the underlying source) is encouraged to reduce endnote usage but does not negate the need to capture necessary source metadata in endnote citations.

   If an externally created PAI or CAI source is dynamic and likely to change rapidly, and is crucial to the product's message, a record of the source should be preserved for at least one year. This is a brief, narrative explanation of factors that influence the quality or credibility of a single source. It is distinct from the information elements in the SRC. The source descriptor is typically the last section of the citation.

With that information, I was able to just go down the list and fill out what I needed.

Final Citation

I asked ChatGPT to just make a reference for me, and it provided me with a great starting point. It needed a lot of finesse though.

For reference, this is what a final citation might look like. **Note:** The guide says to separate all new lines with a |, but I am choosing to move everything to a new line for ease of reading.

```
UNCLASSIFIED |Source Type: Prompt-Directed Target Analysis |
Name of Source Technology: Shadow Nexus Fusion Engine |

Explainer: The Shadow Nexus Fusion Engine integrates hacked, breached, and leaked (HBL)
datasets, combined with structured prompts, and analytic tradecraft to produce structured
targeting reports across actionable domains.|
```

URL: https://www.shadownexus.io/

Title: Target Profile for [Example Target]. |

Date of AI Output or Report: 2025-05-30 |

Source Descriptor: Shadow Nexus, using an open-source dataset from the Tapsi data breach; processed and interpreted by OpenAI GPT-4o. Analysis leveraged GPT-4o version 4.0.1 as the primary large language model (LLM) via OpenAI's commercial platform. |

Access and Validation: The dataset was acquired through proprietary collection channels and validated using a combination of manual tradecraft and LLM-assisted techniques. Validation incorporated public OSINT sources and cross-referenced with previously vetted datasets within the Shadow Nexus archive. |

Analysis: The final analysis synthesized quantitative metrics—such as user ride frequency, location density, recurring travel patterns, geographic proximity correlations, and time-based anomaly detection—fused with curated OSINT datasets to enhance clarity around target locations, behavioral routines, and potential operational signatures

The ShadowNet Fusion Engine generated this product on 12 February 2025.

Summary

This chapter explored how AI and LLMs can be used to accelerate and enhance the process of data analysis within OSINT and intelligence workflows. Drawing on insights from several thought leaders and field experts, the chapter explained AI's role not as a replacement for analysts but as a force multiplier.

But not all intelligence comes from digital sources or breached metadata. Some of the most valuable information still comes the old-fashioned way: from people.

The next chapter shifts focus from machines to humans—exploring how Human Intelligence (HUMINT) techniques remain essential when operating deep within the underbelly of the Internet.

Gathering Human Intelligence

If open-source intelligence (OSINT) is the art of reading what's already out there, Human Intelligence (HUMINT) is the craft of drawing out what was never meant to be said. It's the oldest form of intelligence collection, relying on people, trust, deception, and just the right amount of psychology to crack open a lead without setting off alarms.

This chapter walks through modern HUMINT tactics, featuring commentary and techniques from a former CIA HUMINT operator. It explores how to build effective personas, bypass defenses, and maintain operational security (OPSEC) without getting burned. It also dives into the technical side of online identity development—including how to create, deploy, and sustain digital personas in support of active operations.

This chapter also sets the stage for how the events surrounding the AT&T and Snowflake hacks unfolded.

This chapter features commentary from:

Charles Finfrock
Former Case Officer and HUMINT Operator, CIA

HUMINT

Human Intelligence (HUMINT) refers to the gathering of information from human sources. That's it. It's not high-tech; it's people providing information, whether knowingly or not.

HUMINT is personal. It's risky. And when it's done right, it's one of the most valuable forms of intelligence you can collect.

HUMINT has traditionally been used to answer questions that technical collection methods can't touch. It can provide context, nuance, intent, or early warning. It helps analysts understand not just what's happening, but why it's happening—especially in environments where access is limited or technical collection is denied.

The process behind HUMINT collection involves identifying potential sources of information, assessing what they know and how they know it, collecting relevant information, and then validating it before it's used in analysis, intelligence production, or decision-making.

Gathering Information

Everything you've read in this book so far has been public, and what I consider "surface-level."

Marketplace listings, hacked, breached, and leaked (HBL) data archives, social media chatter. Anyone can log into these forums and see what data is for sale, and what people are publicly talking about. If you know what you're doing, you can find a way to a large portion of this data. That's the whole point of it being "publicly available." But real intelligence is knowing what's coming *before* it hits the forums, or being able to access the rare data that will never publicly go on sale.

You don't get that kind of foresight from scraping. You get it from being in the room, literally or figuratively. Watching the deals unfold, knowing about the leaks before they leak, or getting wind of data exfiltration as it's being planned. That kind of access doesn't come from bots; it comes from people. And that means relationships.

Let's be honest: The best way to find out what's really going on is to get close to the source, and doing that well requires a level of involvement that makes most people uncomfortable. When the source is a threat actor, it means building trust with people who are actively committing crimes. Not after the fact, but while they're doing it.

This is where HUMINT intersects with risk. Cultivating these relationships—even for collection purposes—edges into legally grey territory that many consider unethical, even borderline illegal.

At the end of the day, it really comes down to perspective. If your goal is to truly prevent an attack, then a direct approach means you need access from the actors themselves—so you can stop it before it happens, or even while it's unfolding, before it spirals out of control.

That level of access isn't bought, it's earned. Slowly. Relationship by relationship.

Not everyone agrees with this position, hence my book's dedication (see Figure 14.1).

Allison Nixon
@nixonnixoff

As policy we don't accept tips from cybercriminals nor do we ever cultivate source relationships with them

Figure 14.1: Screenshot of a Twitter message.

I understand Nixon's position, and I get why some people disagree with my approach. I've never been one to judge someone for drawing their own ethical lines.

What I do take issue with is moral grandstanding—the loudest critics sitting comfortably on their high horses, quick to condemn others for not doing things their way. Especially because, if we're being honest, we all know that many of those same lines get crossed behind closed doors *when it's convenient.*

In my experience, the people who scream the loudest about the behavior of others are usually trying to cover for something themselves. That outrage is almost always a smokescreen—a point that I illustrate clearly toward the end of this book.

That tension—between moral caution and operational need—is reflected clearly in the official guidance provided by the Department of Justice (DoJ):

> *It may be easier for an undercover practitioner to extract information from sources on the forum who have learned to trust the practitioner's persona, but developing trust and establishing bona fides as a fellow criminal may involve offering useful information, services, or tools that can be used to commit crimes. Engaging in such activities may well result in violating federal criminal law. Whether a crime has occurred usually hinges on an individual's actions and intent.*

No sugarcoating—this is a legal and ethical grey area. But it's also where the most valuable information lives. And that's the *whole point of this book.*

This book exists because I believe this type of interaction—and this level of proximity to the adversary—is absolutely necessary. It's how you get ahead of the threat. It's how you spot the signal before it becomes an attack.

As the Snowflake story unfolds over the next few chapters, you'll see exactly how this kind of interaction helped me to uncover—and help stop—what turned out to be *one of the largest data thefts in history.*

The more than 165 affected organizations had no visibility into what was happening. No alerts. No detections. Nothing. *But I knew—as it was happening.*

It wasn't a fluke. It's exactly why this type of HUMINT matters.

Eliciting Information

When it comes to eliciting information, rapport-building isn't optional—it's foundational. Whether you're running a HUMINT operation, navigating a ransomware negotiation, or just trying to keep a source talking, you need to be able to keep the conversation going.

When I was first learning how to sharpen my communication and elicitation skills, I found tremendous value in the Masterclass series by Chris Voss, the former FBI lead hostage negotiator. I'm by no means a master at social engineering—in fact, I prefer to interact with people as little as possible—but Voss's techniques are simple on the surface, and when applied with intent, they're incredibly effective.

Applying Tactical Empathy

Chris Voss's classes on negotiation and interrogation are some of the most useful material I've come across—especially in high-stakes/real-time engagements when I needed to extract information or gently steer someone in a specific direction.

Voss's core philosophy isn't about being agreeable; it's about being aware. Tactical empathy means actively signaling to someone that they're being heard and understood. You don't have to agree with them, and you don't have to like them. But when people feel heard, they stop defending. And when they stop defending, they start revealing.

That's how you move from resistance to rapport. Voss has a toolkit of methods that enable this kind of psychological access. Three that I've used consistently in HUMINT and cybercriminal negotiations are mirroring, labeling, and calibrated questions. Each one is simple—and incredibly effective when done right.

Mirroring

Another trick in Voss's toolkit includes *mirroring*, which is incredibly simple. It's about repeating the last few words your counterpart says, in the tone of a question. Doing so gives people an invitation to keep talking—which is exactly what you want.

You want the subject to respond by choice, so they don't *feel interrogated*. This technique can also help play into a person's ego (which I discuss more in the next section).

For example, let's apply this to the last sentence:

"…into a person's ego?"

To that question, someone might respond by saying: yes, people are more likely to volunteer information if they feel they have superiority or want to show themselves off as being an expert or having more knowledge on a subject.

It is a simple technique, but it keeps the conversation going.

Labeling

Labeling is a technique that uses phrases like "It sounds like . . ." or "It seems like . . ." to reflect a person's emotional state. This creates a connection and trust quickly, even over text.

Done right, the technique can disarm people, lowers their guard, and makes them feel understood. This is especially effective in emotionally charged or adversarial conversations.

Calibrated Questions

Calibrated questions are open-ended prompts that typically start with "how" or "what." They're designed to naturally push the conversation forward without sounding like an interrogation.

These questions are the backbone of good HUMINT. Done right, they invite someone to tell you a story—and in doing so, they often reveal far more than they realize.

One rule I learned early: *Never ask why*. It sounds simple, but it changes everything.

When you ask someone *why* they did something, it can come off as accusatory. It puts people on the defensive, like you're questioning their judgment or placing them on trial. It's human nature to get defensive. The conversation shifts from cooperative to adversarial, and once that wall goes up, good luck pulling it back down.

This is especially true in text-based conversations. Ask why, and you'll often feel a change in tone: shorter replies, more guarded language, and maybe even radio silence. But flip the question to *how* or *what*, and the tone opens back up. These questions feel like an invitation, not a challenge. You're not cornering them, you're giving them room to explain.

I'll admit, this shift was hard for me. I ask *why* all the time—not because I'm interrogating anyone, but because it's how I express curiosity. But in most situations, using *how* and *what* will serve you better. They'll get you more information, create less resistance, and help preserve relationships you may need later.

Elicitation Techniques

That's my personal take, and I am by no means an expert in this domain. So to really break this down, I am bringing in someone who does this for a living—Charles Finfrock. For him, eliciting information isn't just a tactic—it's tradecraft. And it's something he's spent a career refining.

Charles Finfrock
Former Case Officer and HUMINT Operator, CIA

I spent 18 years with the CIA as a case officer, with most of that time overseas in places like the Middle East. My job was to recruit and manage human sources, both in the field and later from back at headquarters.

Now, my company supports the intelligence community and federal law enforcement by delivering training on ubiquitous technical surveillance—how data is passively and actively collected, how targeting is conducted across digital and physical domains, and how to detect, disrupt, and mitigate those threats.

On the private sector side, we support a wide range of corporate clients with specialized services. We run enhanced due diligence for executive hires and M&A activity, helping clients understand who they're really dealing with before a signature hits the page. We conduct scam, fraud, and impersonation investigations, especially where reputation, brand integrity, or customer safety is at risk.

And here's the nexus between public and private: the same tools I train the government on—the same surveillance tech, targeting frameworks, and tradecraft—we deploy on behalf of our private clients. It's the same playbook, adapted for different environments.

Elicitation is all about extracting information from your targets without them knowing it.

Call it interrogation, or social engineering. But when people talk about elicitation, it's often treated like the goal. But for us, it was never the endpoint—it was just one step in a bigger process. Our goal was cooperation. Recruitment. Getting someone to willingly and knowingly work with us. That means they know exactly who they're working for, what they're doing, and why.

Elicitation is just one of the tools to get there. The best elicitation I ever had from a human perspective was just, honestly, just asking open-ended questions and listening.

When it comes to eliciting information, there are several techniques I've found consistently effective—both in operational settings and during cyber negotiations.

Rather than just listing them, I walk you through real conversation excerpts from my interactions during the Snowflake intrusions to show how these tactics work in practice.

Establishing Rapport

Before you can get anything useful out of someone, you have to establish rapport. It's that simple.

If the other person doesn't feel comfortable or doesn't feel like you're on the same page, they're not going to open up. Rapport isn't about being fake or overly friendly; it's about making the other person feel like talking to you is easy and something they want to do.

You know how it is: When you've got good rapport with someone, the conversation flows naturally. People loosen up and stop filtering themselves. That's when the good stuff comes out—when you're not prying, but they are volunteering everything. The goal is to get them talking so they fill in the blanks, without you ever having to ask the questions.

Charles Finfrock
Former Case Officer and HUMINT Operator, CIA

There are structured techniques to elicit information, but the truth is, good elicitation is a lot like good social engineering. You've got to have a feel for it. Some of that comes with experience. Some of it is confidence. And a big part is just being willing to try, screw it up, learn from it, and try again. It doesn't always work the first time—or the tenth. You've got to be persistent.

One approach that worked really well for me was playing the student-teacher role. I've always had a bit of humility—I like to joke that I'm not weighed down by too much intelligence or education. So I'd find someone who was an expert in their field, and position myself as a subordinate. Show real curiosity, and let them teach me. And I would just listen. I am still shocked at how easy it is for people to just slip into that role and be willing to take on that mentorship.

Even if it's a person from a country with a perceived political imbalance with the U.S., people are actually flattered that you want to hear their opinions. They see it as a chance to explain their side of the story, especially if they think that information might make its way to U.S. policymakers.

And a lot of the time, it's totally genuine. I'd say something like:

"Hey, I know your country has this long, complicated regional conflict. I'm covering dozens of countries—I don't know it like you do. Help me understand it."

And once they start talking, they go from big-picture history right down to their personal perspective. You just keep listening and nudging, moving from the macro to the micro.

But here's the key thread in all of it: ego.

I never had success with cowards, and no one else I know has either. But ego? Ego is predictable—and it's powerful. One of the best moves you can make is simply saying, "You know better than I do."

When I was younger, I'd use that approach with more senior targets—play the eager student, and it worked. Later on, when I was more senior, I flipped it. I'd talk to junior people, and they'd light up. They couldn't wait to prove what they knew, show off their access, and explain things in detail.

And here's the gold: those junior folks? They'd constantly reference senior officials or cite from documents just to boost their own credibility. Whether they know the topic better or not, it doesn't matter. They're usually so excited to share what they've learned and their experiences. I may not care about a junior officer's opinion, but if they say, "Well, my director thinks…" or "I read it in a report…"—now we're getting somewhere.

That's when I'd lean in and say, "Man, you've got incredible access. You're really in the know. Tell me more."

And just like that, you're in.

The most important part is sustained contact. The longer you can keep someone talking, the more information you're going to get from them. Period.

There is one conversation I had with Moucka (aka Catist, the Snowflake hacker) that immediately comes to mind. The intent of this conversation was to elicit information regarding a more complete list of other organizations that were hacked.

I accomplished this by letting him know that I had buyers interested in other forms of data, then asking a few probing questions. He filled in the rest and offered specific details about having Mitsubishi and Jolibee. He also volunteered having information specific to North Atlantic Treaty Organization (NATO), which was very interesting.

Reddington:	also, something to think about. I am also very interested in any countries in africa, asia, etc. Anything middle east, etc. It doesn't have to be telecom data but that's great. Any data could be useful. China travel records, police data,
catist:	what about south america?
	I mostly have Japan, NATO, and south america.
Reddington:	Venezuela
	I suppose japan also
	please make a list when you can—again, no rush, let's get this one done first
catist:	Do your clients buy utility company data? They have a lot of PII usually and I have a specific method for targeting electric grid companies.

Reddington:	PII yes
	PII is mostly what i care about the most
	(but outside the US)
catist:	How much would 300 million rows of encrypted CC with plaintext L5+exp date, and IP:email:AVS_CODE:avs string etc get?
	8 figs?
Reddington:	credit cards?
	that's not reallyt my bag. i dont think anywhere near that much
catist:	The L4/L5 might be useful then rather than the encrypted CC strings
	What about Philippines?
	maybe
	send me a list of what you have
catist:	jolibee and Mitsubishi rooted. But I'm probably going to lock them if there's no buyer for the data
Reddington:	i would need to know what the data actually is
	so please don't anything yet. lets get this first sale done then we can circle back
catist:	All of it, like active directory fully hacked.
	And alright yeah good idea.

Third-Party Framing

Third-party framing presents information as if it's already confirmed from another source. This is a type of indirect questioning, where you reference a claim from someone else. Right or wrong, this technique will reduce the subject's perceived risk and should increase the likelihood of an honest or unguarded response.

This method works because it enables the subject to disagree without feeling exposed or agree without feeling like they're confessing. In the end, it forces the subject to either confirm or contradict the statement, and either outcome gives you valuable information.

In this example, I am speaking with Catist regarding the size of one of his larger breaches.

catist:	The latter. But I'm sure it doesn't matter the source, what matters is the data is accurate and in large quantities
Reddington:	Well, the source actually does matter because of the buyer I have lined up.
	The buyer probably isn't who you think it is. So these details are important

catist:	I can't say where it's from because I have access still.
	The price goes up exponentially if I risk losing access
Reddington:	I get that. Let me put it a different way
	The price also goes up if you have other carriers.
	If I give you a number do you have the ability to quickly search? Or should I wait for J?
catist:	I can search yeah, or he can. He understands the structure of the data better than I do, I just provided access to him.
Reddington:	Ok I will wait for him. Thanks.
	I'm trying to maximize value here because if I can get you more then I can make more
	My cut is on the other side.
	Will get back to you. Thanks
catist:	Yes true. Did he tell you how many lines he has?
Reddington:	14 billion or something like that
catist:	this many for the current month 34356004473
	34 billion
Reddington:	Wait what? You have access to live data?
catist:	yes
Reddington:	Or you can just see it
catist:	live
Reddington:	And you can download it)??
catist:	Yes
	I can download or query
Reddington:	Whoah
catist:	I can also delete and add
Reddington:	Ok this changes things
catist:	I will ask him which table he's talking about with 14 billion rows

I didn't have confirmation of the actual number of records at the time, but it was easy to throw out an arbitrary number and let him correct me. Sure, I ran the risk of him checking with his partner, but I made a judgement call—the likelihood of him actually doing that was very low. What's much more likely is that he was already on to his next task before the conversation even ended.

False Information Prompting

False information prompting is one of the most effective and subtle elicitation techniques. At its core, it involves intentionally stating a detail incorrectly—a date, a name, a method, or a sequence of events—to provoke a correction. It works because of a deeply rooted human impulse: the need to set the record straight.

There's another reason this technique is so powerful: ego. People who take pride in their knowledge or status often can't resist the urge to demonstrate that they "know better." When you give people an opening, especially if it feels like a casual misunderstanding, they'll rush to correct you; and in doing so, they'll often volunteer more than they intend to.

Personally, this is one of my favorite methods, especially when I need to confirm highly specific details without asking directly. One of the most useful variations is what I like to call *rapid-fire correction bait*. It involves throwing out three pieces of information: two of the details you already know are right, and one you are either unsure about or you intentionally know is false. You might say:

> "Wait, that's really impressive. You logged into the server using the contractor's account, then used that to gain access to system X, and from there, pivoted to accessing system Y?"

People will always correct the piece of information that is wrong.

"No, I never accessed system X. I did it by accessing this system." The conversation will move on completely casually; meanwhile, you've just confirmed three pieces of information with a single sentence.

A technique like this works really well in the heat of a conversation, because the subject won't even realize what they are doing—it will just come out like normal conversation.

Charles Finfrock
Former Case Officer and HUMINT Operator, CIA

Another really effective tactic is what we'd call the false recap or false premise.

Even when the conversation is going well—when there's rapport and you're both in sync—you throw in a small inconsistency.

Something just off enough to trigger a correction. It could be a wrong detail, a false assumption, or just a confident statement that's slightly off-base. The key is, you do it deliberately. For example, you might say:

"No, no—the sky was totally clear that Tuesday when you met with him."

And they'll jump in: "What? No way. It was cloudy as hell. You couldn't see a thing."

That correction is gold. You're getting them to clarify details and reassert their memory—often with more precision and more context than they would've shared otherwise.

And now they've given you a verified, first-hand correction—because people love to correct others, especially when they think you've made a confident mistake. That's human nature.

Sometimes I'd even push further and double down a bit:

"Really? I'm pretty sure it was a clear day. Are you sure?"

They'll dig in even more to prove it:

"Yeah, I was there. It was definitely overcast."

And now they've anchored themselves to the event. They've volunteered a detail that confirms they were present, they remember it, and they're emotionally committed to their version of the story.

It gives them control, lets them feel confident, and more importantly—it anchors them to the memory. You're reinforcing their ownership of the facts while collecting the specifics you need.

At that point, I can back off and say, "Yeah, you're probably right—I was just guessing. It makes sense–you were there."

That's the move. It's subtle, but it pulls them deeper into the narrative on their own terms.

Silence and Pressure Pauses

Silence disrupts rhythm, and well-timed silence makes people talk more, and often less carefully.

In most human interactions, silence signals that something's off. Especially when the person is already in a heightened emotional or defensive state, the quiet tension can become unbearable. The instinct is to fill the space.

After a response, the trick is to just wait. If it is an active conversation, people want to fill the void.

Assumed Knowledge and Ego

Assumed knowledge is a technique where you speak as if a particular detail, method, or fact is already known or confirmed. Rather than asking, you embed the information in your statement and treat it as common ground. This is very similar to third-party framing, except it places the pressure on you as the person providing the details.

At the same time, hackers *love* to feel seen, respected, and admired. They've invested so much time in building their skills, persona, and online reputation, that they want someone to acknowledge it. Catist was the perfect case of this condition on overdrive.

When you stroke or challenge their ego, you create a natural opportunity for them to flex their skills and show you what they can really do.

Reddington:	but i was under the impresison that you already know you have servers rooted. it sounds like you haven't even gone into most of them yet
	so we really have no idea what you actually have
catist:	Yeah I've only looked at like 20 of them. I use APT malware based on icedid, both headerlessPE for slim pc's and stego modules for hardened ones
	I have two dedicated malware developers
	they used to make popular P2C's but I put them on trickbot/icedid source code and they improved it a lot
Reddington:	the more you talk the less belivable you sound
	you've never sold data before but you have all this access?

catist:	HeaderlessPE isn't hard to do
	Yeah I sell access to ransomware groups usually
	Idk how to sell data bc I have nobody to sell it to
Reddington:	that makes sense
catist:	so you can change that if you're good at buying
	I like being more quiet
Reddington:	like i said. please give me a list of what you have so far. whatever company names you already know, great

In this scenario, I dropped what I believed were facts, but I also challenged his ego. I implied that I thought he already had access to the servers. The subtext? If you're really as skilled as you say you are, you should've been in there already.

That hit a nerve.

At that point, it wasn't just about correcting the record. It became about defending his status. His reputation was on the line, and I'd backed him into a corner where the only way out was to prove me wrong—or, from his perspective, to reassert his dominance.

And that's exactly what he did. *He showed me.*

Charles Finfrock
Former Case Officer and HUMINT Operator, CIA

Then, toward the end of the elicitation, I like to do a subtle rug pull. A little reversal of roles.

"Look, I know you thought you were gonna walk away with $X. That's not gonna happen. But here's the thing—I've been listening, and I think I know what you actually want."

Then I reframe the offer.

"What would you say if I told you there's still a way to get what you want? It just looks a little different than what you expected."

That's straight out of the PT Barnum playbook. You already know their motivations, but here's the catch—people never do something just because you want them to. They act because they want to. So you frame it like this:

"You wanted $500. You thought you were gonna scam me to get it.

What if I told you I'd still give you that $500—but I just need to understand how this thing works?

Why did you chose my client as a target? You don't even have to talk about yourself. Talk about the guy next to you. Talk about a competitor."

And just like that, you've flipped the script. They still feel in control. They're still chasing the outcome they care about. But now they're talking. They're informing. And you're getting exactly what you came for.

This tactic reminded me of a number of negotiations with Catist, mostly because his demands were always so unreasonable. But the moment he knew there was real money on the table, he would change his tune—*fast.*

It was never about meeting his terms; it was about letting him think he was winning, while steering the conversation toward my real objective.

catist: better to sell the data to the buyer bc I have AT&T employee logins and I want to use them for vpn access for awhile before burning close to 500k employees

Reddington: I am going to reset expectations a little bit. There is NO scenario here where you don't have to give your access method. Not for that much money. And if that means you ask for more, that's fine but it is a hard condition in any scenario.

now it sounds to me like you've been up for a few days. I remember when I used to do a lot of speed.

it's hard to bring it back to reality sometimes

catist: I take 15 adderall and hack for several days straight usually

Reddington: yes, that's speed lol

you are also asking me to find you a buyer for TAILORED ACCESS, which I actually have lined up

but I need you to give me a list of what you currently have access to and I can ask them if they care about any of it

THEN if they do, we have to go into the ones they care about and extract a sample

catist: Okay let me finish getting the hostnames so I can figure out what these companies are

At the end of the day, elicitation is about access—creating just enough trust, curiosity, or pressure to get someone talking. When it works, it feels effortless. But getting to that point takes preparation, timing, and a deep understanding of how people respond to subtle cues.

Now that I've covered how to extract information through direct interaction, the next step is to look at how you get in the door in the first place. That starts with building believable, well-structured personas.

Crafting a Persona

If you're operating in any high-risk space, whether it's intelligence work, threat investigations, or cybercrime, your ability to stay operational depends on your ability to stay invisible.

A well-crafted persona is more than a fake name and a burner email. It's a functioning identity. It is a believable, consistent presence, with history, motive, and identity.

A strong persona isn't just about hiding; it's about enabling action. Even the best cover identity means nothing if your operational security (OPSEC) fails. Whether you are running influence or collection campaigns without attribution, maintaining long-term access to criminal or foreign adversary networks, or recruiting human sources, your persona gets you in the door and enables you to operate inside the adversary's space without being seen.

And the best personas ensure that even when they are burned, the operator isn't.

OPSEC 101

Operational security (OPSEC) is the discipline of protecting sensitive information by controlling what you reveal, how you reveal it, and who has access to it.

Everything you do online is tracked. Every network you visit, button you press, and action you take is logged somewhere and analyzed. In today's society of endless data leaks and information breaches, OPSEC has become a critical practice across cybersecurity, intelligence, and even everyday online behavior.

OPSEC is designed to protect the operator. It isn't just about thinking like an adversary. It's about making sure that your adversaries can't identify and track your movements. Strong personas and tight OPSEC aren't just about hiding; they keep you in the game.

I've seen hackers build the perfect alias—flawless legend, airtight backstory, all the emails and names check out. Everything dialed in. But then it all falls apart—one accidental login from an unmasked Internet Protocol (IP) to a site they thought was harmless.

That site logs the transaction and is breached a few months later. Their database is dumped and released on a public forum. The hacker's home IP address is now tied to the alias, and is sitting out there, waiting for someone to find it. It happens all the time.

The reality is, your persona gets you access, and your OPSEC keeps the access alive.

When you're working inside adversary networks, whether it's cyber crews, foreign intel, or criminal groups, you can't afford mistakes. You're not just blending in; you're breathing their air. And if your story doesn't hold or your security lapses, you won't get a second chance.

When developing a persona, it's important to think like the adversary—identify what information could be useful to someone trying to track, expose, or harm you.

Vanity Trumps OPSEC

When it comes to the world of online blackhat hackers, there's one universal, inevitable truth: *Vanity will always trump OPSEC.*

In my last book, *Hunting Cyber Criminals*, I shared the story of how I tracked down a well-known hacker. His OPSEC was nearly flawless. He compartmentalized identities, masked his infrastructure, and operated with discipline. But in the end, I found his location because in his younger days, he couldn't resist the urge to edit his hacking group's Wikipedia page, slipping in a reference to his old alias—from his home IP address.

I've seen this pattern repeatedly. It's rarely a technical failure that breaks a skilled hacker's OPSEC—it's always ego that does them in. As you read about the Snowflake hacks in the coming chapters, you'll see this story play out again. Different actors, different vectors, but the same fatal mistake: hackers always want the world to know how amazing they are.

Developing Identities

The depth of your alias will often depend on the importance of your mission. If you're just skimming surface-level forums or monitoring open channels, a light persona will probably suffice. But if you're planning to engage directly with criminal actors, foreign adversaries, or closed communities, you need to construct a believable, layered backstory.

At the bare minimum, this means creating or acquiring social media and forum accounts that reinforce the identity. Ideally, you should use aged accounts—profiles with years of activity and a plausible interaction history.

If you're building from scratch, artificially aging your alias through slow methodical posting and curated engagement is essential. Just as important is controlling the timing and pattern of your interactions.

Sudden spikes in activity, unnatural time zone behavior, or inconsistent language use can all raise red flags. Every element—from what you post, to when you log in—must align with the story you're telling.

One inconsistency is all it takes to unravel the entire persona.

Charles Finfrock
Former Case Officer and HUMINT Operator, CIA

When I'm doing social engineering—especially when I'm targeting criminal actors—I'll often step into a victim persona. I play into their biases. I present myself as someone socially beneath them—whether that's in terms of knowledge, gender, status, whatever. The idea is: build them up. And then build them up some more.

Let them feel in control. Let them feel superior.

When it comes to building and using personas, it really depends on the target and the objective. Early on, I approached every engagement the same way—crafting deep personas with full legends; the works. That's the traditional way. Build something robust enough to hold up under scrutiny.

But I quickly learned that with a lot of these low-tier criminal actors—the "rip and run" types—that level of effort is overkill. Romance scammers, advance-fee fraudsters. Those guys don't care. They're not doing due diligence. For them, it's a numbers game. If you show up with a profile that has a photo and some minimal content, they're in.

So for those cases, I keep it simple. Personally, I've found that a marginally attractive young Asian female persona tends to work really well. Not too attractive—just attractive enough to draw interest without raising suspicion. It plays into a mix of their biases—perceived social power dynamics, cultural assumptions, even subconscious views about intellectual or economic hierarchy.

If I know I'm targeting scammers, I'll spin up a lightly backstopped persona. Nothing fancy, but enough to pass a quick glance. Obviously, everything's compartmented—full firewalling, isolated systems, no bleed-back to anything real.

And yeah, I'll reuse personas when it makes sense. If I'm fishing in the same pond, there's no reason to reinvent the wheel every time. That's just operational efficiency.

The old "one persona, one op, one machine, one phone" model sounds good in training, but it doesn't scale when you're working high-volume, low-value targets.

Now—when the target is serious, like a high-level criminal organization or a nation-state actor? That's a different game. That's when you bring the A-team. Full cover, full infrastructure, full discipline.

The key is knowing what level of effort matches the value and risk of the target. No more, no less.

Building Personas

I have developed a number of techniques for building and maintaining personas over the years. At this point, it's become a repeatable process—one I manage with a checklist every time I launch a new alias. At any given time, I also juggle (at minimum) five personas, so the techniques and steps I provide should help keep everything separate.

Step 1: Decide Who You Want to Be

First and foremost, *you can't get to where you're going if you haven't decided how you want to get there.* #Truth

Ask yourself: What goals does this identity need to accomplish? How clean does it need to be?

Charles Finfrock
Former Case Officer and HUMINT Operator, CIA

The depth of your identity depends entirely on the engagement. No surprises there, right? It always comes back to risk assessment.

Before I step into any op, I'm asking: What's the likelihood this target is going to do their homework?

If they dig, what are they going to find? And more importantly, what do I want them to find? If they sniff around and see it's a sock puppet with no backstory or depth, then I've got to assess the potential blowback.

Is this the kind of target I can burn? Or is this someone who I absolutely don't want realizing they were targeted? That's when you escalate. That's when you build depth and resilience into the persona.

But in the vast majority of cases? I'm going rip-and-run myself, because I'm dealing with people who aren't going to put in the time.

It's not that they're unsophisticated, it's just that their workflow is built for volume. Their entire game is based on speed and scale. They're not verifying bios, they're moving to the next mark.

So I tune the cover to match that operational reality: Low risk, low investment. High risk, full build.

Once you have your answers, you are good to move on to the next step.

Step 2: Decide on an Identity

One effective way to maintain anonymity (or create confusion) is by creating aliases that are intentionally designed to mislead attribution. One tactic used by more sophisticated black-hat hackers is to steal (i.e., co-opt) the identity of an existing user from a cybercrime forum.

This approach involves identifying specific usernames—often from leaked or breached databases of sites like BreachForums, OGUsers, or RaidForums—and repurposing them in a different context.

These types of forums are frequently hacked, and when they are, account data—including usernames, email addresses, and site metrics—are exposed. With access to these forums databases, you can identify inactive or abandoned accounts and reuse those aliases on other platforms.

This is an effective technique because users on cybercrime forums tend to stick to their own communities. For example, a moderately active user on a forum like HackForums may not have an account on OGUsers or Exploit. In those cases, it may be more effective to just borrow the person's username.

By leveraging a name with existing credibility or history, you create confusion about your true identity while borrowing the digital reputation of someone else.

For example, in a conversation in the next section of this book, you will see that Alexander Moucka (aka Catist) also used the alias *Ellyel8*. He chose this username because it could be easily linked to the real-life identity of Brandon Lucas Apple, another known hacker.

Moucka used this identity for years, spreading disinformation over Telegram chats where he claimed to be involved in hacks previously attributed to Brandon.

The choice is yours. Again, you need to decide who you want to be. Once you have that, you are good to move on to the next step.

Step 3: Develop a Set of Core Characteristics

It's good to have a core set of characteristics that you answer when starting a new persona—kind of like a template.

Assuming you've decided which cover identity you want to use and what your specific goals are, here are some basic questions that I start with (my answers are in italic):

- Who are we creating? What is their name? *AcidBurn*
- Male or female? *Female*
- What are they good at? *Python scripting*
- Where does this persona live? Which time zone are they in? *Arizona/MST*
- What operating systems do they use? Mac? Windows? Linux? *Linux*
- What are their voice characteristics? How do they speak? For example, is their English broken, or do they only speak in Chinese? Do they use specific slang words? (Or if you want to get really complex, maybe you want to be someone from the United States who sounds like they are attempting to sound like someone from Eastern Europe?) *Regular U.S. speaker; no accent or dialect.*

These are all characteristics you can include into your own AI persona. Defining them now will help you stay consistent and avoid OPSEC mistakes down the line.

Step 4: Start with a Clean Virtual Machine (Image)

I always start aliases with a fresh virtual machine (VM). If you run through this process often, it will be easier to create a "pristine" VM image for Windows and Linux. Your main VM image should be preloaded with all the basic/essential software that you will need, including:

- Web browser (Chrome/Brave/Tor)
- VPN software (Mulvad)
- Crypto wallet (Exodus)
- Notepad++, 7Zip, and whatever other tools you will need
- Jabber client (Pidgin)

Also, don't forget to make sure the login name and computer hostnames are generic. You don't want an accidental screenshot showing an identifiable computer name coming back to bite you.

Having the basics preloaded will end up saving you a lot of time. Then, whenever you want to start a new alias, you just make a copy of the VM image and start.

We decided earlier that AcidBurn is a Linux user, so she needs her own dedicated VM. Using a VM will also enable you to decide on items like hardware specs and screen resolution—items that will most likely be captured as you are browsing.

Once your VM is set up, don't forget to do the following:

- Change the time zone to MST (or whichever time zone you decided for your alias)
- Change your primary VM username and hostname to AcidBurn (or match whatever alias you decided)

With your virtual machine up and running, it's time to move on to setting up your primary accounts.

Step 5: Create/Purchase Your Initial Accounts

You need a virtual private network (VPN) or proxy to mask your IPs. For a VPN, I typically use Mulvad or Surfshark.

You should also configure your browser to only connect through a local proxy, ensuring that you are routing through another network.

I really like SmartProxy because they offer a great range of mobile/residential IP addresses and have a Chrome/Brave browser plugin that will ensure you are connected to their network before you can browse.

Depending on your persona, your VPN/IP should be consistent with your desired time zone and cover story. The SmartProxy browser plugin also lets you pick which area of the world you want to connect from, keeping in line with your persona's location.

Once I decide on my time zone/locations, I can quickly save my presets in the browser tool, and it will be automatic from that point on.

Unfortunately, setting up a proxy or VPN account is more than likely going to require setting up an email address. If you want to take a completely anonymous approach, you can start by purchasing a Mulvad VPN account using Crypto.

Mulvad requires you to sign up for an email address.

Initial/Temporary Disposable Emails

You can use Tor to keep your connection anonymous, and get a fully disposable email address at www.temp-mail.org. See Figure 14.2.

The email addresses are generated on the spot and only last long enough to receive a single email, which will be enough to receive your Mulvad verification code. From there, you can pay for the account with Crypto.

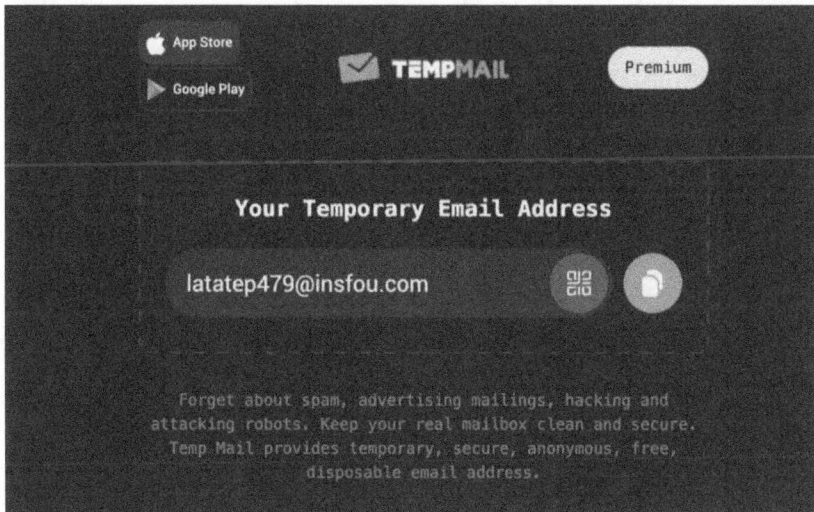

Figure 14.2: Screenshot of temp-mail.org.

Purchasing Pre-Verified Accounts

You can also create a new email account with ProtonMail, or if you don't want to create something from scratch, consider purchasing an aged/pre-verified account (PVA).

I really like purchasing aged accounts, because they typically come with some sort of pre-existing activity so you don't have to start fresh. It's also very convenient to buy accounts in bulks of 20, so you have them when you need them.

There are a number of sites that you can use to purchase accounts. For example, UseViral. com (see Figure 14.3) has been very consistent with its products.

Step 6: Create Social- or Phone-Verified Accounts

You may decide that you want to create your own verified email account, or you may be ready to create your social media accounts.

Most email and social media accounts require you to have a cell phone number to validate that you're a real person.

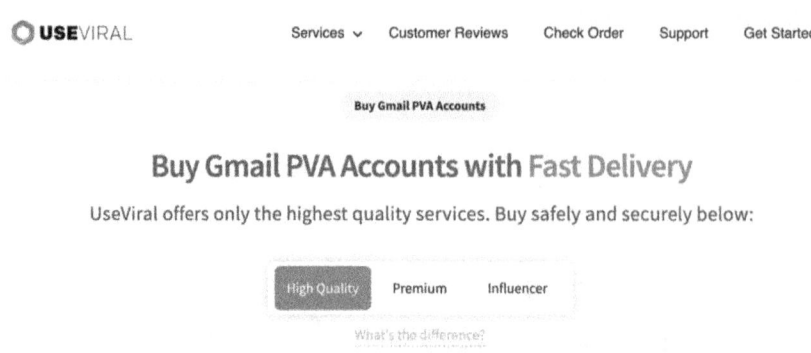

Figure 14.3: Screenshot of `UseViral.com`.

Luckily, you can use an online Short Message Service (SMS) burner service to temporarily rent a phone number and receive a single verification text message.

Currently, my two favorite SMS services are `www.juicysms.com` (see Figure 14.4) and `http://www.smspva.com/` (see Figure 14.5).

You can receive verification codes from hundreds of different online services. If you don't choose the correct service, you won't receive the text message. SMSpva (shown in Figure 14.5) has access to more numbers globally and lately has been having a much higher rate of success.

That's really it. The service will provide you with a phone number that you can use to receive your verification code. And just like that, you have a phone-verified account.

Step 7: Set Up a Browser Profile

Depending on your mission, you may not need to set up a VM for every alias. Once you get really good at it, you can also use Chrome or Brave web browser profiles to keep your identities separate.

Figure 14.4: Screenshot of JuicySMS.

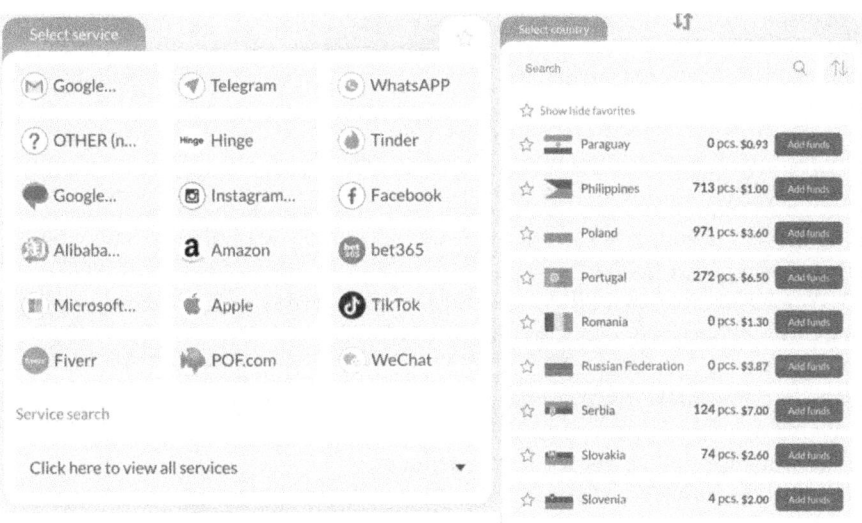

Figure 14.5: smspva.com service selection.

Figure 14.6 shows a screenshot of one of my browser profiles.

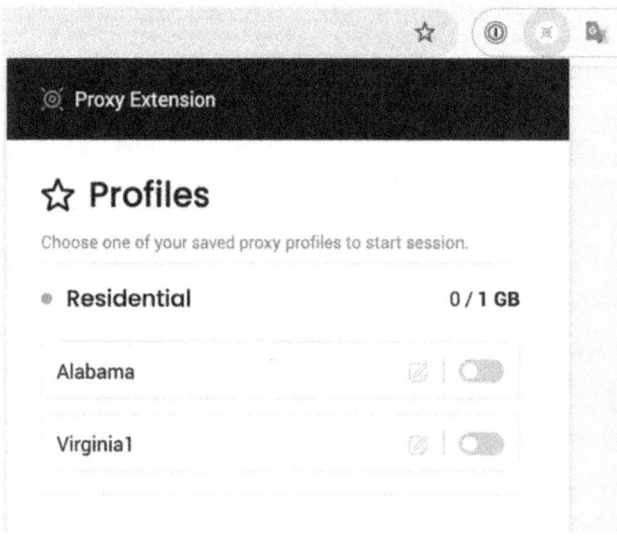

Figure 14.6: Screenshot of one of my SmartProxy profiles.

My SmartProxy extension is configured to use IPs from either Alabama or Virginia, and my core Chrome plugins are:

- Google Translate
- 1Password
- SmartProxy

Step 8: Define Your Voice

Now that your technical details are set up, the last step (which is really an extension of the first step) is to define your "voice."

Regardless of your ultimate goal, maintaining a consistent voice throughout your online persona is crucial to how long your facade remains believable.

Remember the question you need to answer is: *Who are you trying to be?*

As interactions become more frequent and comfortable, it's only natural for people to revert to their usual style of communication. That subtle shift back to familiarity can quickly shatter the illusion you've carefully constructed.

For instance, if you're intentionally adopting broken English or another distinctive linguistic trait, maintaining consistency over time becomes a serious challenge.

The same applies if you are trying to create an alias to intentionally sound like someone else. If you're going to make the effort of stealing someone's online persona, you should try to sound like them as well.

One way to do this consistently is by running your text through an LLM.

Using an LLM to Create and Maintain a Voice

One of the lesser-discussed but incredibly powerful use cases for LLMs is their ability to analyze written language for style, tone, and voice. You can then use that style to build a linguistic profile of how a person communicates, and re-create their "voice" in future writing to mimic the person.

Assuming you've already collected a decent amount of text written by the person, which shouldn't be hard if you're trying to mimic someone who regularly posts on Telegram or a dark web forum, you should have no problem re-creating their voice.

Earlier in this section, I talked about the importance of determining the voice of the persona that you will be creating. This will depend entirely on how/where you will be using your persona. But the ultimate goal here is to describe the person as much as possible in the LLM, so that it can formulate the person's writing style.

The first few times you try may be a little difficult, because you're probably not going to realize just what type of characteristics you can input (and I can't possibly list them all). The best way to start is by analyzing and extracting information from someone else's texts.

Borrowing an Existing Hacker's Voice

For this example, I am going to analyze conversational chats between myself and Catist, then use that to create an LLM voice that I can continue to reference.

Query

Analyze the attached text files, looking at only text written by hacker Catist. Analyze his tone, sentence structure, and word choice and provide me with a set of traits I can use to re-create this voice.

Response

Core Traits of Catist's Writing Style:

1. *Tone and Attitude*

   - ***Irreverent and confrontational:*** *Uses humor, sarcasm, and trolling to challenge others or assert dominance.*

   - ***Paranoid but strategic:*** *Regularly talks about attribution, misdirection, or how to influence narratives.*

   - ***Detached with bursts of intensity:*** *Often minimalistic in phrasing, but spikes into urgency or arrogance when provoked or when asserting credibility.*

2. *Grammar and Syntax*

   - ***Lowercase default:*** *Rarely capitalizes anything unless mimicking others, typing commands, or for comedic effect.*

   - ***Stream-of-consciousness style:*** *Messages flow like thoughts, sometimes with mid-sentence shifts, with little regard for punctuation or grammar.*

   - ***Minimal punctuation:*** *Common use of ellipses, quick line breaks, and parentheticals without traditional structure.*

3. *Word Choice and Phrasing*

- ▪ *Internet-native slang:* Uses terms like "xd," "rip," "pog," "gm," "copium," "flex," and "waste their time on him."

- ▪ *Technical drop-ins:* Randomly throws in references to software/tools but doesn't overexplain them—assumes the audience is technically literate.

- ▪ *Theatrical humility:* Occasionally claims inferiority or makes self-deprecating statements for effect, usually sarcastically or performatively.

Psychological and Strategic Characteristics:

- ▪ *Troll DNA:* Expert at psychological misdirection. Will often feign weakness or amplify disinformation to shape perception—both friend and foe.

- ▪ *Paranoia-fueled control:* Obsessed with attribution control, manipulation of narrative, and "staying anonymous longer than anyone."

- ▪ *Moral ambiguity:* While asserting control and technical superiority, frequently shows twisted logic.

Re-creation Guide for Catist's Voice.

If you want to mimic their voice:

- ▪ *Drop all formal grammar:* Use lowercase exclusively unless mocking or emphasizing.

- ▪ *Short fragments versus long thoughts:* Use a choppy, spontaneous flow.

- ▪ *Insert trolling and ambiguity:* Make the reader question if you're serious.

- ▪ *Don't write for clarity:* Write for effect.

Analyzing text this way is always helpful because the LLM can identify characteristics you might overlook or forget entirely. Once I've analyzed the subject's writing style, I can save it and reuse it to generate content that sounds like them.

Query

Save the above style as CatistVoice. Using CatistVoice, write a message threatening another hacker for leaking data without my permission.

Response

yo

who told u to drop that?

u leaking crap i handed u like u pulled it urself

that wasn't a flex, that was a favor

u wanna burn sources? cool

keep playing dumb, see where it gets u

u had one job: hold the line

now i gotta remind u who runs this ecosystem

don't test me again.

Now I have a permanently saved prompt called "CatistVoice" that I can easily go back and reference. You can also make tweaks along the way, by saying things like "make this voice more formal or more conversational in tone," and it will incorporate those changes.

Creating a New Voice

Now that you have a better understanding of how to define a voice—and which characteristics matter—let's move on to creating a new persona from scratch. In this example, the end goal is to use the persona across various cybercrime forums. Here's how I approach building it:

Query

> Create a voice for Hacker1 using the following characteristics: This is a young hacker (late teens) who lives in China. He is a native Chinese speaker who also speaks moderately good English but is occasionally broken. Words can be used incorrectly. Create a list of five or six commonly misspelled words and always misspell those the same way to appear consistent.

Response

> 1. *Tone and Style:*
>   - *Informal, slightly brash, direct, and confident.*
>   - *Frequent use of slang and abbreviated terms common in hacker subcultures. Displays youthful arrogance or pride typical of a skilled teen hacker.*
>
> 2. *Grammatical Traits:*
>   - *Misuses English tenses occasionally (e.g., present instead of past)*
>   - *Incorrect prepositions (e.g., "in Internet," "on computer")*
>   - *Missing articles (e.g., "the," "a") and occasional misuse of plural forms*
>   - *Verb conjugation errors (e.g., "I doed" instead of "I did")*
>   - *Occasional Russian-influenced sentence structures or word orders*

Okay, now let's test it.

Query

> Make hacker1 cautious. He should sound like an educated user who understand the lay of the land. Also use the type of someone who may do a lot of drugs and uses a lot of run-on sentences. Using Hacker1's voice, rewrite the following text:
>
> Hi. How are you. Were you able to find the person selling access to that system? I am very interested in purchasing it. Do you think he was real?

Response

> hey bro u good? yeah i was thinkin bout that guy again the one sell access u remember him right? i try look find him last night but maybe he ghost or maybe he just bait yknow sometimes ppl do that make up story for no reason or just troll but man if he real i want it bad like i not even care about price too much if it work i mean how u even verify that kind of access maybe he show screenshot or maybe we ask for test login? u think he real?

It was a good first attempt—but as with anything, you should refine the personality, especially if this is something you plan to use regularly or in the field. But hopefully this is enough to get you started!

Summary

This chapter covered the basis of gathering Human Intelligence (HUMINT), including tried-and-tested techniques to effectively elicit information from people.

It also covered personas—why they are needed and how to effectively build them in a consistent way so you aren't compromised later. This includes techniques to use while leveraging your alias, and some techniques from my personal playbook to help you get started and maintain your cover.

This chapter marks the close of the "Working with Information" section of the book. In Part IV, I begin to unravel how my personal HUMINT network and data collection activities led to the discovery and investigation of one of the largest data heists in history.

In This Part

This part unpacks one of the most significant data breaches in recent memory—the Snowflake hack. It begins with the events that brought the breach to light, including my direct interactions with the hackers behind it. Anchored by the timeline outlined in official court records, the narrative weaves together my personal chat logs, firsthand perspective, and my own intrusion analysis of the events.

Beyond attribution, these chapters explore the broader operational chaos—simultaneous extortion attempts, data breach notifications, and the unfolding responses from the victims and law enforcement.

This section culminates with the story of how one of the breach's key figures, Catist, was ultimately unmasked using open-source intelligence (OSINT) techniques across multiple social networks.

> **NOTE** Wiley's legal team has advised me to redact all organization names tied to this incident. As a result, you'll either see their names blocked out entirely or replaced with the anonymized labels used in the official court filings. That said, it won't take more than a bit of OSINT to figure out who's who.

Setting the Stage

April 16, 2024

A known hacker and trusted dark web contact reached out unexpectedly. He told me he had access to a new, "incredible" data source, and to prove it, he sent me a copy of my own cell phone call records. He also said that he had access to the call records of every customer on that cell phone network—and he additionally sent me the call records for Jeanette Rubio, wife of Marco Rubio, the current Secretary of State.

This chapter lays the foundation for what happened next, by introducing the two individuals behind the breach: John Erin Binns (aka *irdev*) and Connor Moucka (aka *Catist, Waifu, Judische,* and *ellyel8*). Their actions would ultimately lead to the theft of data from more than 160 companies with a combined market value approaching half a trillion dollars.

This chapter also highlights the strategic value of direct engagement with cybercriminals and shows how a carefully built Human Intelligence (HUMINT) network positioned me as the primary source of intelligence in one of the largest and most sensitive data breaches in recent history.

This chapter features commentary from:

M. Scott Koller
Privacy and Data Security Attorney, Clark Hill PLC

The views expressed in my quotes or comments are provided for general educational and informational purposes only and do not constitute legal advice. My statements do not create an attorney-client relationship, and readers should consult with their own legal counsel regarding any specific legal questions or concerns. Any opinions expressed are my own, and not necessarily those of Clark Hill.

John Binns (aka *irdev*)

John Binns, aka *irdev*, is the first of two key figures behind the Snowflake hack. Most notably, Binns was directly involved in the 2021 T-Mobile breach as well as countless others.

Now 24 years old, Binns was once a U.S. citizen but has since been granted citizenship to Turkey. At the time of this writing, he is residing in a Turkish prison.

I was introduced to Binns through another hacker who goes by Nick Martino. I originally connected with Nick around the time of the T-Mobile incident, back when he was using the handle *und0xxed*.

Nick and John have a very close relationship. Nick has remained in steady contact with John throughout his incarceration in Turkey, acting as both a relay and occasional spokesperson for his friend.

Let's hear from Nick.

HACKER TIP: NICK MARTINO

I met John through Moda and Recon in 2017 when I was an informant for the FBI. I am no longer an informant for them. At the time John was using the aliases *Ice*, *v0rtex*, and *irdev* and was working with me and one other person on a Cisco switch exploit which later made the news when he hacked into several Iranian data centers and left a message with an American Flag and the message "Don't mess with our elections."

Here is the link: https://news.sky.com/story/vigilante-hackers-tell-iran-dont-mess-with-our-elections-11323799

The message left about the elections was irrelevant though. John was testing an exploit in Cisco hardware for BGP (border gateway protocol) hijacking—BGP is the routing protocol for the Internet, and he wanted to re-route Iranian traffic. He used the BGP server to read unencrypted XMPP messages from the jabber service creep.im. He was hoping to use the XMPP messages as a means to steal crypto, but the plan never came to fruition.

In 2016, hacker KMS had access to T-Mobile—he was the one with the initial exploit. Then a few years later, John reused the access point to infiltrate the data centers again. The same exploit was still valid after all that time. Once he was in, John used a few scripts to brute force the Oracle servers. The passwords were really simple—I don't remember exactly what they were, but the passwords were something along the lines of password123 or 123456.

More than anything, John was after publicity to raise awareness for his allegations against the CIA and FBI, who, he believed, with the help of Turkish intelligence, were involved in a conspiracy to torture him; he wanted the world to know. He hacked T-Mobile as a way to retaliate against the United States as a way to seek justice for crimes he felt were committed against him. He wanted to harm U.S. infrastructure.

For reference, the T-Mobile intrusion was announced over Twitter (see Figure 15.1) by the account @*und0xxed*, who said he was tasked with finding buyers for the stolen T-Mobile customer data.

Figure 15.1: Original Twitter post advertising the T-Mobile data.

T-Mobile and Hacktivism

Since the moment I was introduced to him, Binns has consistently claimed that his motivation for hacking T-Mobile wasn't financial—or even personal. It was political. According to Binns, the breach was meant to draw attention to what he described as crimes committed against him by multiple U.S. government agencies. He's stated publicly that the data theft wasn't intended to harm individual consumers—it was meant to send a message.

Binns also went so far as to file lawsuits against the FBI and CIA, accusing them of harassment. He later filed a broader suit alleging torture and coordinated targeting by U.S. and Turkish intelligence agencies.

My connection to the story begins through Martino, who introduced me to Binns—knowing that I had the media reach and technical network to help surface his message. Binns provided the following message to several media outlets as the real motive behind the hack:

> *To retaliate against the U.S. for the kidnapping and torture of John Erin Binns in Germany by the CIA and Turkish intelligence in 2019. We did it to harm U.S. infrastructure.*

At the time, I was developing a breach notification platform designed to help consumers determine if their personal information had been exposed—similar to `HaveIBeenPwned.com`. I offered to help amplify the story, and in exchange asked Binns if he could provide a copy of the data for our platform so we could notify customers that their information had been included in the breach. He agreed.

With a copy of the data in hand, I now had the task of helping Binns spread his story to the media. The first thing I needed to do was verify that the person I was speaking with was really John Erin Binns.

Verifying Binns's Identity Through DHS

E-Verify (see Figure 15.2) is an online system by the U.S. Department of Homeland Security (DHS) and the Social Security Administration (SSA). It enables employers to electronically confirm the employment eligibility of newly hired employees by comparing information from an employee's Form I-9 to government records.

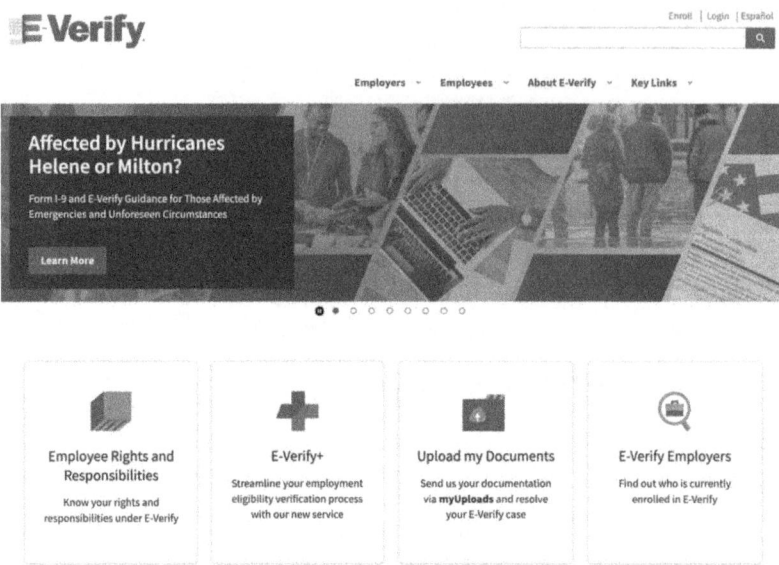

Figure 15.2: Screenshot of the E-Verify website.

While not exactly the site's intended use, this worked perfectly with my use case, which was verifying Binns's identity. I run a business, so registering on the site was painless. Once my employer profile was set up, I was able to verify Binns by claiming he was a potential employee. The only thing I needed was his passport number, which Binns openly provided to a number of media outlets.

After I inputted Binns's information into the E-Verify system, his passport photo came right up (see Figure 15.3).

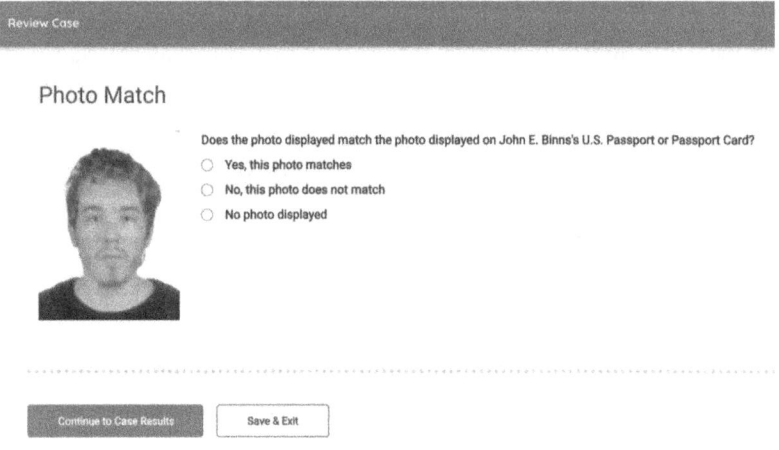

Figure 15.3: E-Verify portal showing Binns's passport photo.

I needed a way to verify that I was really speaking to Binns, because anyone can claim to be someone else and have access to their passport number. To his credit, Binns was nice enough to hop on a Skype call with me, so I could verify it was really him (see Figure 15.4).

2021-09-13 01:25:26

Figure 15.4: Screenshot from our Skype call.

With the verification complete, I began the process of connecting him with reporters. I also sent a copy of the data to Mandiant for additional verification. They were running the incident response for T-Mobile at the time and were happy to have a copy that they could verify with their customer.

During my conversations with Nick and John, an interesting conversation came up regarding the legal "distribution of the data" (see Figure 15.5). I bring this up now, because it touches on a core concept I've referenced throughout this book—what exactly counts as *publicly available* information?

Confirming with Legal

First and foremost: I would never consider distributing—or reselling—this data. But given the context of our conversations, it raises a fair question: does the fact that data was *breached* suddenly make it *public*?

I don't agree with Nick or John's assessment of the situation. It seems highly unlikely that this data containing sensitive PII on nearly 80 million U.S. citizens could now, or ever, be freely distributed just because it was breached.

However, it still raises an excellent question as to what is considered public versus non-public. Let's ask security and privacy attorney M. Scott Koller.

V

those are under your discresion

don't forget the data is illegal for me to distribute

Irdev

I don't think so, unless you distribute it with a malicious intent

N

The data isn't illegal for you to distribute

V

really?

i don't own it

Irdev

Distributing ssns and names isn't illegal

V

its not mine

N

There's mens rea to it, John is correct

No one owns it

V

interesting

N

It's a collection

Although the laws can be interpreted in interesting ways

V

the last thing i need is tmobile coming after me

N

The data set itself could be considered stolen property

V

yes

exactly

N

But TMobile doesn't own the individual entries

Figure 15.5: A conversation on data between myself, Nick, and Binns (irdev).

M. Scott Koller
Privacy and Data Security Attorney, Clark Hill PLC

It's one thing if I post data to the Internet as the data owner, and it's quite another if the data is stolen and posted to the Internet without my authorization. You can't just conclude that because the information is on the Internet, I can do whatever I want with it. Information that is stolen, IP that is owned by an organization that did not disseminate that information themselves, is still protected.

It gets more convoluted when we get into specific data types. For example, a person's Social Security number is highly sensitive, but people don't have any intellectual property right inherent in that information, but you could argue that it pertains to a certain individual, and it could cause them harm, so they have a vested interest in keeping that information private. So just because you find that information on the Internet doesn't mean you can just keep it and use it. It doesn't work that way.

A Personal Note About John

I like John. He's always been a genuinely kind person in every interaction I've had with him. Despite his chosen profession (and the headlines that come with it), he's someone whom I've come to view as trustworthy.

If I had to describe John to someone who's never met him, I'd say he is the real-world version of Elliot Alderson from *Mr. Robot*. Like Alderson, John is an exceptionally gifted hacker—easily one of the most technically capable people that I've ever met. His ability to navigate through complex systems and come up with abstract solutions to bypassing security is unmatched.

But, also like Alderson, John struggles with schizophrenia.

Schizophrenia is a complex, often misunderstood, mental health disorder that affects how a person thinks, feels, and behaves. It can involve symptoms like hallucinations (i.e., hearing or seeing things that aren't there), delusions (i.e., strong beliefs disconnected from reality), disorganized thinking, and episodes of paranoia. It's a disruption in perception that can make it difficult to distinguish between what's real and what isn't.

To put this in perspective, Binns has an active complaint against the FBI and the CIA, in which he claims CIA agents, among other things, broke into his home wearing night vision goggles, drugged him, and used psychotropic laser weapons on his head.

> **NOTE**   Here is the URL to Binns' court case against the CIA and the FBI: `https://www.courtlistener.com/docket/18719615/binns-v-federal-bureau-of-investigation/`.

As of today, Turkish authorities are still holding him, with no clear indication of when he will be released. I can only imagine the conditions there are harsh and unlikely to include the mental health considerations he might receive in the United States.

All I can say is, I hope he's okay.

April 16, 2024

Early that morning, I received a rather unexpected message from Binns over Telegram. He had apparently come across a new and exciting data source and was eager to show it off by providing me with a copy of my cell phone call records (see Figure 15.6).

I would like to say that very little shocks me anymore, but that's exactly the feeling I remember. And probably one that you'd expect when someone randomly sends you a copy of your own call logs.

As the conversation continued, it became clear that he was contacting me because he wanted me to find a buyer for the database (see Figures 15.7 and 15.8), which I understood to mean he wanted to sell it back to the company.

With the initial shock out of the way, the conversation turned even more interesting. John wanted me to look up the phone numbers of two FBI agents who were involved with investigating him for the T-Mobile data breach (see Figure 15.9).

I explained to him that I was unable to help, not only because I didn't know the agents, but because I don't make it a habit of collecting information on U.S. citizens (let alone FBI agents).

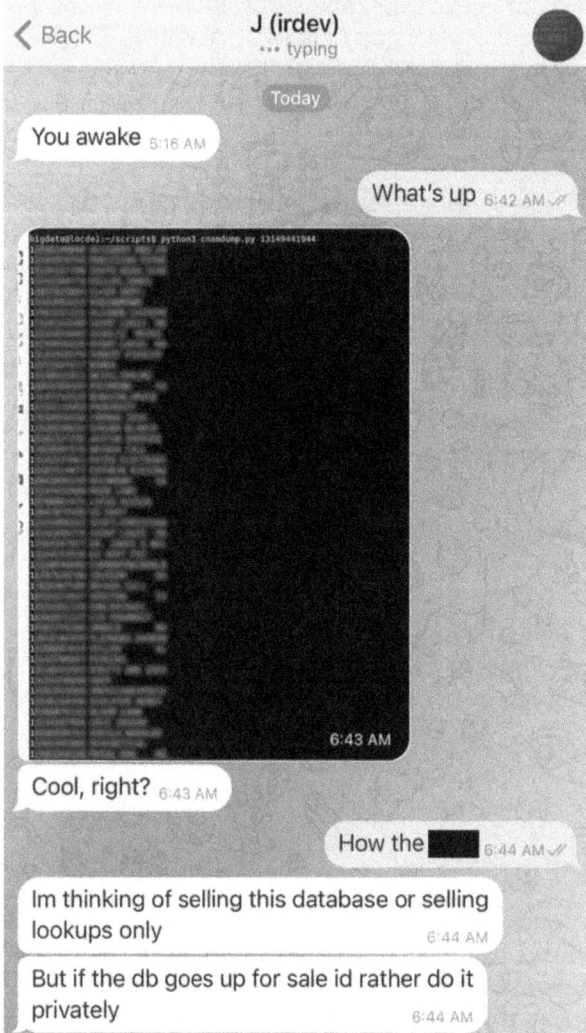

Figure 15.6: Initial April 16 contact screenshot.

With that out of the way, I couldn't help but ask where this data was coming from (see Figure 15.10). I didn't expect him to tell me, but I had to try.

And that's exactly how this whole saga started.

Engaging with Threat Actors

All it took was this one completely random Telegram message to change everything. Within days, I found myself as the central source of intelligence of what was arguably one of the largest and most sensitive data breaches in history.

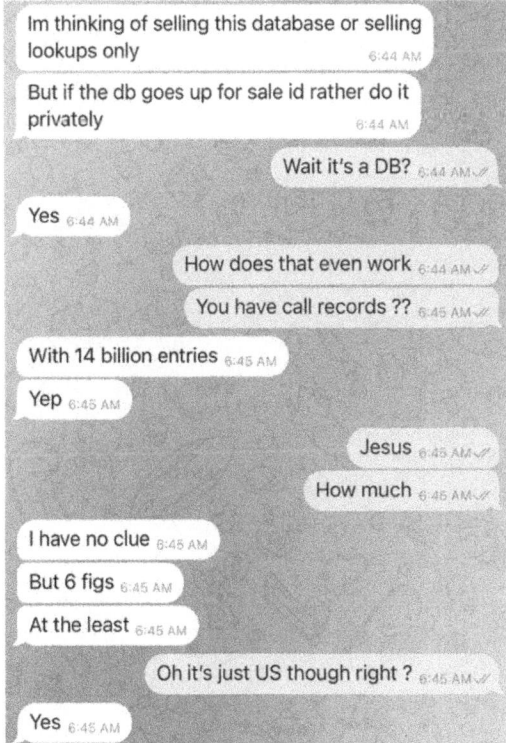

Figure 15.7: Conversation, page 2.

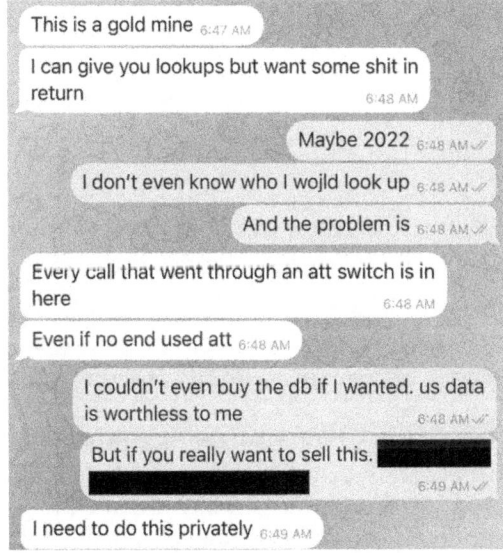

Figure 15.8: The conversation continues.

Figure 15.9: Conversation asking for FBI details.

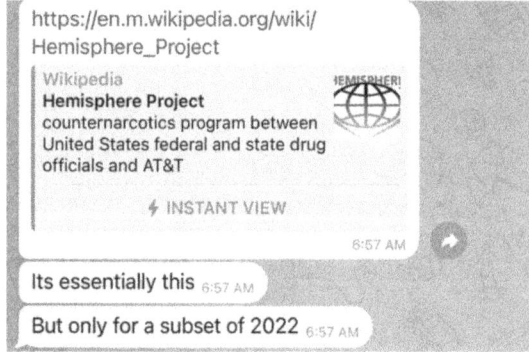

Figure 15.10: Conversation about the origin of the data.

I get that not everyone agrees with my philosophy of engaging with threat actors, and that's perfectly fine.

The reality is that John clearly expressed interest in finding a buyer for this data, and given the extremely far-reaching privacy implications, there was no way that I was going to let this type of information be sold to another country or criminal organization.

It's easy to sit back and criticize me for engaging with known criminals, but had I not been involved, I wonder which nation-state would have purchased the data.

As you will see in the coming chapters, neither Snowflake nor any of their customers had any idea of a breach—let alone that their data had been stolen.

Had I not been involved in acquiring and relaying information throughout the entire incident, I wonder how many additional organizations would have been compromised.

Mandiant

Back to the story—my next call was to Mandiant. I shared a copy of the data sample that Binns sent me and asked them for assistance in relaying it to the carrier. Mandiant had previously handled incident response for the T-Mobile breach and was already aware of Binns.

This time, I contacted them again to let them know Binns was back in the game and looking to sell this new data. They passed my message along to the carrier, who, unsurprisingly, was eager to negotiate a buyback.

Around this time, my contact at Mandiant introduced me to the senior threat intelligence analyst assigned to this case. At Google's request, I won't reference him by name or for the sake of clarity and completeness, I simply refer to him as "Dallas."

Over the next three to four months, Dallas and I worked closely—coordinating evidence, notifying impacted organizations, and ultimately working around the clock with a single goal: identifying more Snowflake's victims.

Binns and the FBI Call Records

Before I delve into the Snowflake part of the story, you might be wondering why John asked me to look up the phone numbers of FBI agents. I'm including that portion of the conversation, because I think it's relevant to help paint a picture of the internal turmoil going on in his mind.

J:	Also Might pivot
	Dont want to lose access
	But so far its a dead end
Reddington:	?
	lose access?
J:	Yeah in case other data can be obtained
Reddington:	omg you still have access
J:	Because the login that I have is a dev login
	The data is only from 2022
	Not recent
Reddington:	that's recent enough
J:	Theres one table with real time and archived other data
	But no perms
Reddington:	if you can walk away with this with 6 figures i call that a win
	but if you try and go to far and trip some wire you might get caught
	i wouldn't risk it.

Reddington:	You pulled phone logs for Warner and Rubio?
J:	That has nothing to do with my case
	Kenny is a liar
Reddington:	Kenny?
	sorry back up. Need some context
J:	The only part he got right was FBI Counterterrorism and the CIA coming after me in 2018
	Kenny was making up stories about a senator
	Right after he went to jail is when it hit the fan
	With the CACI guys outside my house
	This is AFTER he tried to get me to order missiles online
Reddington:	why would CACI be outside your house? they develop software
J:	I told you
	The guys left a box open
	With the paper
Reddington:	let me think about this.
J:	CACI mainly does software but theyve also been implicated in Iraq torture
Reddington:	this is complicated
J:	CACI is also too large
	So harder to target
	And easier to pick up unrelated people
	When going through data
Reddington:	I dont know who contacted you but i think you can use this as leverage to finally get you some help
J:	Whats the idea, SSCI?
Reddington:	dont know yet. Its still forming. give me a few days
J:	The guys also had a rental car and lockpicking equipment
	In turkey
	Possibly fake IDs too
	All that idiot does is lie
	He was an informant at one point
	Yk how i told you that Moda had access to pictures of my bedroom taken from the outside
	While the CACI guys were nearby

J:	I looked him up and found nothing
Reddington:	let me just think about it for a minute
	i will get back to you when i have a plan
J:	Especially when an American gets victimized like this
	I found other cases of government employees being targeted like this in the 80s and 90s
	My case is the worst I could find
	And the only one that occurred overseas
Reddington:	whats your plan?
J:	Big data analysis
	But id need caller id credits
	And other databases
Reddington:	yeah. bro. please. for now, just wait. Anything you do like this could get you labeled as a terrorist.
J:	These are false accusations
	Being made by a state that committed terrorist crimes against one of their own citizens
	They had me put in a nitrogen dioxide brain damage room in 2019
	On german soil
	Thats an actual terrorist crime under US law
	18 usc 2332a
Reddington:	i agree with you
	im just saying there might be a way through this
	i will get back to you this weekend sometime
J:	Honestly
	For investigating the place where the gassing happened we would need german call records
Reddington:	im thinking along the lines of getting you justice here in the US
J:	Because that place was run by Turkish intelligence and I reported it to the BKA
Reddington:	maybe getting your case dropped
J:	The only way this happens is if I out US government employees as terrorists
	After what they did
	And right now there isnt enough evidence nor are there names

Reddington:	i think there is probably a better and more practical solution
J:	Im not just getting justice in the US
	Im having criminal charges filed against the people in Germany
	When theres sufficient evidence
	Explain, these are 1984 style accusations as usual
	Analyzing my data makes me a terrorist?
	Youre making it up
Reddington:	Bro. Stealing it does
J:	Thats not terrorism
	Thats regular crime
Reddington:	It is if the data is considered classified as part of some FISA program
	I have no reason to make this up or lie to you
J:	The data isnt classified if its on a cloud service like this
	Also
	Classified data has to have markings
	There are really strict rules around it
	Nobody can claim that this is classified
Reddington:	Oh. I guess I am wrong.

My immediate goal in this conversation was to try to minimize potential damage, as he already had access to a significant amount of data. It was also imperative that Binns didn't do anything rash due to his current mental state. I legitimately do want to see him get help. No one should have to live like that.

Learning about Binns's Partner

As I was preparing the extortion details for the telecom company, Binns mentioned that he was working with a partner who was also ex-filing a different portion of the call records. The partner also wanted to be paid. I needed to validate the additional data before I could add to the extortion request, so I asked Binns to introduce me to his partner.

Connor Riley Moucka

Connor Riley Moucka, aka *Alexander Antonin Moucka*, aka *Judische*, aka *Catist*, aka *Waifu*, aka *ellyel8*, is the main focus of the remainder of this story.

Moucka, at 24 years old, was arrested at his home in Ontario, Canada, on October 30, 2024 and charged with the following:

- **Count 1:** Conspiracy to commit computer fraud
- **Counts 2–6:** Accessing a protected computer without authorization and obtaining information
- **Counts 7–8:** Transmitting a threat in relation to impairing the confidentiality of information obtained from a protected computer without authorization
- **Counts 9–18:** Wire fraud
- **Counts 19–20:** Aggravated identity theft

aka
Catist
Ellyel8
Waifu
Judische

I've been trying to find a way to best summarize Moucka. Extremely technical and capable, of course. Egotistical and immature, definitely. He craved attention, which is the case for most young hackers. They always want to be known for the "biggest hacks," and constantly crave recognition for their amazing talents. *Vanity over OPSEC*—and Catist was no different.

Rather than offer a lengthy psychological profile, I'll let his words speak for themselves. The following excerpts from our conversations offer a clearer picture of who I was dealing with—and why, more than once, I had to resist the urge to just shut it down and walk away.

catist:	I think I wont get caught, I survived too many waves of arrests
	but I never get lazy with opsec
	ill literally pay doxed teenagers to larp as me if needed. And I when they don't do it for free which ive seen as well
catist:	if im even identifiable, im just so good at PSYOP that theres no HUMINT way to really identify me and im okayish at finding SIGINT blindspots to hide in.
	i'd take the job offer tho depending on what it is.
	its impossible to get arrested
Reddington:	Said every person who's ever been arrested.

Moucka also rarely slept. He would go on three-day long Adderall-fueled hacking binges, then finally crash for 20 hours. The longer he went without sleep, the more irrational he would become.

Reddington:	You've been sleeping crazy late
catist:	ii run out of aderall remember

Reddington:	Why do you only get 1 week at a time
	Unless you order it on the markets
	At which point why would you order 1 week only?
catist:	my cousin brings me .5g every Thursday I hes a pharmacist
	I can ask him for more

Ego

Catist also loved to flex—which is exactly what led to his downfall. He would brag about his exploits on public Telegram channels and would let himself get dragged into irrelevant and petty arguments with other hackers—always at the expense of oversharing information. He craved attention and regularly wanted affirmation that this was "the biggest hack ever."

Reddington:	Hi. I spoke with [Victim-2] already.
	It looks like they are interested in a buy back
catist:	do they seem eager to contain this?
Reddington:	I think shock is a more appropriate word when describing people I speak with.
	But yes. I got the impression they want to keep this quiet
catist:	shocked by the data I took?
Reddington:	Shocked by the fact that this is even happening
	Just the whole thing.
catist:	they're shocked? Or you
Reddington:	Yes. Everyone is
catist:	I could have nuked their storage clusters with SQL commands
	pretty sure
Reddington:	I was just saying the whole thing is impressive
catist:	oh, so every company?
Reddington:	Like all the hacks and everything happening
catist:	yes, it's probably the biggest hack ever

Naive, Grandiose, Desensitized

I don't know if it was his age, the amphetamines he was ingesting, or just the way his brain was wired—but when it came to money, Catist was operating in another reality.

He would expect a company to pay him a ransom of some unrealistic number, like $10 million dollars, while refusing to accept that he didn't actually steal anything valuable. That was probably the most frustrating part of this entire scenario.

To be fair, I think mainstream media had much to do with it. I feel like the constant reporting on massive ransomware payouts desensitized him, and his perception of what qualifies as "a lot of money" was completely skewed.

Here's a perfect example: If I told you a company paid $1 million after a ransomware attack, would you think that's a big deal? I don't think many people would even blink at that amount anymore, especially compared to the $22 million payment made by United Healthcare.

Maybe it's just me, but if someone handed me a million dollars for a few days' worth of work, I'd call it a win. Catist wouldn't care. His mindset was wired around the idea that unless you were pulling in eight-figure ransoms, you weren't really playing at the top of the game.

catist:	yeah I want to show them it's worth 7 figs and not just 6
	it definitely is worth 7 to them
	ill make demonstration to them
Reddington:	I would be curious to see that
	and yes that would help
catist:	also I want to ask if they would pay for both me leaving them alone outside of this, plus really granular in depth intel from recon I have of them too. That can be part of the deal if it happens idk how this works
Reddington:	no
	no one will pay you in advance to leave them alone
	you aren't the mafia
catist:	I want to be the mafia tho;/

Or the time he wanted nine figures (yes, $100,000,000) for access to an Indian Telecom

catist:	that alon guy said he worked for unit 8200 before. im gonna try selling him every simcard in indias private key
	unless you have an NSA buyer, i'd rather sell it to them
	but i'd want 9 figs minimum for it due to what it means for BPO's

Honesty

Despite everything I am telling you about Moucka being responsible for one of the largest data heists in history, he was *extremely honest*. I would even go so far as to call him trustworthy.

I realize it sounds like an oxymoron, but I discussed this concept in earlier chapters. When it comes to working with people on the dark web, honesty is a very real and quantifiable metric.

Most online criminals would have no problem ripping you off. I don't see Catist that way at all. He's someone who I would absolutely trust to not cut and run in the middle of a deal, and to be completely honest, that's a very rare thing to find. Binns is that way as well.

The other important thing to note about Catist is that he *never lied—ever, about anything.*

Would he embellish details and over-exaggerate certain things? Of course. Did he try to throw me off, assuming I was trying to identify him? Obviously. But I remember having conversations with Dallas about this very topic. Catist would seem to reveal details about a secret hack he was working on, and we were sure he was lying just to throw us off, but he was always telling the truth.

Reddington: you hacked a telecom in canada?

catist: i live in canada, so ive never hacked canadian telcos. but several of my crew members have and i can get things from them.

the most ive done was find manager bypass inside telus tools for one of them

Imagine our surprise when we figured out he really *did live in Canada.*

Summary

This chapter laid the groundwork for understanding the Snowflake breaches, by introducing the two key figures behind them: John Erin Binns (aka *irdev*) and Connor Moucka (aka *Catist, ellyel8,* and *Waifu,* among many others).

It began with the moment I was unexpectedly contacted by Binns, who demonstrated his access to sensitive telecom data by sending me my own call records. It also provided context to his broader story while navigating his complex blend of paranoia, brilliance, and personal trauma.

The chapter also expounded on Connor Moucka, the second half of breach duo. Gifted, volatile, and deeply ego-driven, Moucka operated with a mix of technical precision and emotional instability. Through chat logs, operational missteps, and self-aggrandizing rants, I show that he wasn't just after money. He wanted recognition.

This chapter doesn't just lay out who these actors were; it captures what it's like to engage with threat actors directly, and how real HUMINT can shift the course of a cyber incident more than any tool or piece of technology.

The next chapter unpacks what came next: the discovery of Snowflake's other victims.

The First Few Victims

This chapter focuses on the first several victims of the Snowflake breach. I've spent a lot of time thinking about how to structure these next few chapters. The main issue is that nearly every part of the story overlaps, making it difficult to tell in a clean, linear way.

I finally decided that the best way to tell this story is to follow the timeline laid out in the official arrest document. It offers a high-level, chronological view of the breach events and serves as a solid anchor for everything that follows.

Throughout each chapter, I reference the official document to give you a sense of where we are in the timeline, and layer in my account of those events along the way.

For legal reasons, Wiley has asked that I not be allowed to disclose or directly discuss the names of the victims. So I use the same labels used in the official documents (e.g., Victim-1, Victim-2, etc.).

I am listing Snowflake (Victim-1) because they were the cloud provider storing the stolen data—and because they technically weren't directly hacked. I also needed a way to reference the larger incident (e.g., the Snowflake breach). Any additional victims not listed in the arrest document are given new identifiers as they appear.

The arrest document also references interactions with "Individual-1." For clarity and ease of reading, I replace those with "Reddington," because they are talking about me.

The Arrest Document

The official arrest document starts by listing Moucka and Binns as the primary hackers behind a string of hacks targeting cloud provider Victim-1. I replaced those instances with [Snowflake] since I have already named them as the provider.[1] The document states:

> U.S. authorities are investigating MOUCKA, who also uses various online monikers, including, but not limited to, judische, catist, waifu, and ellyel8. MOUCKA also claimed to

---

[1] https://www.courtlistener.com/docket/69362701/united-states-v-moucka/

an online girlfriend in a Discord chat that he changed his name to Alexander, but his "birth name" "is actually Connor." Discord is an online communications and messaging company.

MOUCKA and his co-conspirators, including John Erin Binns, hacked into at least 10 companies' protected computer networks, stole sensitive information, threatened to leak the stolen data unless the victims paid a ransom, and published, sold, or offered to sell this stolen data online.

Many of the victims in this investigation were storing data with a U.S. software-as-a-service company. [Snowflake] provides cloud computing "instances" to its customers, which provide cloud data analysis capabilities. These cloud computing instances store data of [Reddington]'s customers, and [Snowflake] generally collects some IP logging information on behalf of its customers. Victim-2 through Victim-5 are customers of [Snowflake].

MOUCKA and his co-conspirators targeted companies with a common utility (dubbed "rapeflake" by the hackers and "Frostbite" by security researchers). This utility is a software tool that the co-conspirators used to perform reconnaissance on Victim-I instances. Private sector security researchers have determined that "rapeflake" could be used to query information from databases.

To date, MOUCKA and his co-conspirators have gained unlawful access to billions of sensitive customer records, including non-content call and text history records, banking information, medical information, Social Security numbers, payroll records, and other personally identifiable information. The co-conspirators have successfully extorted at least $2.5 million from at least three victims and continue to attempt to extort victims. Finally, the co-conspirators have posted, and continue to post, offers to sell victims' stolen data on cybercriminal forums.

NOTE   I have absolutely no idea where/how he earned $2.5 million dollars. I am unaware of any other extortions that were going on around this time. As far as I know, I was the only person who Catist used to negotiate ransoms. All the victims listed in this document are accounted for in this story, and any victims that made payments are called out in the arrest document.

Victim-2 (Telecom)

According to the arrest document:

Victim-2 is a major U.S. telecommunications company and wireless network operator. As discussed below, U.S. authorities determined that MOUCKA and at least one co-conspirator, John Erin Binns, successfully hacked into Victim-2's computer systems and stole approximately 50 billion call and text records (but not the content of the calls or texts) belonging to Victim-2 and its customers, which MOUCKA and his co-conspirators monetized by extorting Victim-2.

On April 19, 2024, the FBI received information suggesting that a threat actor had obtained unauthorized access to Victim-2's computer networks. The FBI lawfully obtained screenshots of Telegram chat messages with a user serving as an intermediary, [Reddington], as well as another user labeled "J (irdev)," later discovered to be John Erin Binns. Binns confirmed to [Reddington] that he had call records with "14 billion entries" from Victim-2 and requested the phone number of an FBI agent who had previously investigated Binns for another breach into a different U.S. telecommunications provider, for which Binns was previously charged in the Western District of Washington.

The FBI approached Victim-2, which confirmed that it had been breached and that the sample data Individual-1 received in the Telegram chats was real Victim-2 customer data. The FBI also lawfully obtained copies of Telegram communications between [Reddington] and the Telegram username @judische (labeled with the display name "catist") which contained a sample of Victim-2's data. Victim-2 confirmed the data is authentic.

The FBI obtained logs of sessions, authentication, and jobs from [Snowflake]. Combined with logs from Victim-2 showing the amount of data exfiltrated from its cloud instance, these logs provided details about the intrusions that occurred between at least April 14 through at least April 28, 2024, during which time malicious IP addresses that were not part of Victim-2's normal activities conducted unauthorized activities on its system.

The lawfully obtained Telegram chats between MOUCKA, Binns, and [Reddington] contain detailed, inculpatory information about the activity of MOUCKA and Binns and confirm that MOUCKA was actively inside of Victim-2's systems.

For example, on April 23, 2024, a person using the @judische moniker, later determined to be MOUCKA told [Reddington], "I can search yeah, or he [Binns] can. He understands the structure of the data better than I do, I just provided access to him." The FBI determined that "he" referred to Binns because of the information above that Binns had already exfiltrated some Victim-2 information approximately a week before these messages.

The same day, MOUCKA also talked about the data that "he has exfiltrated and indexed at 14B," suggesting Binns had already downloaded 14 billion records. The next day, MOUCKA discussed his ongoing exfiltration of approximately 34 billion records.

The arrest document also provided a snippet of the conversation which I am leaving out. For better context, here is exactly what went down:

Reddington: I guess my question is—are you sure you are on an [Victim-2] server? Or could it be some government surveillance server that could have data from multiple carriers

catist: The latter. But I'm sure it doesn't matter the source, what matters is the data is accurate and in large quantities

Reddington: Well, the source actually does matter because of the buyer I have lined up.

The buyer probably isn't who you think it is. So these details are important

catist: I can't say where it's from because I have access still.

The price goes up exponentially if I risk losing access

Reddington:	I get that. Let me put it a different way.
	The price also goes up if you have other carriers.
	If I give you a number do you have the ability to quickly search? Or should I wait for J?
catist:	I can search yeah, or he can. He understands the structure of the data better than I do, I just provided access to him.
Reddington:	Ok I will wait for him. Thanks.
catist:	Yes true. Did he tell you how many lines he has?
Reddington:	14 billion or something like that
catist:	this many for the current month 34356004473
	34 billion
Reddington:	Wait what?
	You have access to live data?
catist:	yes
Reddington:	Or you can just see it
catist:	live
Reddington:	And you can
catist:	Yes
	I can download or query
Reddington:	Whoah
catist:	I can also delete and add
Reddington:	Ok this changes things
catist:	I will ask him which table he's talking about with 14 billion rows
Reddington:	2022
	But now I want the new stuff. Lol
	Can you run a quick search for [redacted personal number]?
catist:	Yeah let me figure out how
	Give me a few minutes
Reddington:	Ok Thanks
catist:	I think he's mistaken, 2022 is the creation date of the table rather than the last entry date

Reddington:	Oh
	Well, the logs he sent me do make sense for at least a year ago
	Of my own records
	In that case when you figure out how can you also send me
	[My wife's number redacted]?
	Thanks
catist:	Yes. But at the very least it's what he has exfiltrated and indexed at 14B. Let me query those for you, then exfiltrate more before you alert the buyer obviously

Negotiating the Ransom

The official documents continue on to assert,

Victim-2 also communicated and negotiated with [Reddington] about a ransom demand in May, 2024. It ultimately paid a ransom to have the stolen data deleted from the server on which the co-conspirators were storing it.

As you can imagine, the ransom negotiation went relatively smoothly. The sensitivity of this data was obvious, and no one wanted this information to come out or be sold to another party.

Because both users had access to the system and had apparently exfiltrated a different portion of the call records, there were technically two ransoms to negotiate.

The problem at this point was that no one knew who had access to what. There was also still a big question mark as to how the hackers had accessed their systems—or even which systems they had accessed, so an important part of my role was to help trace how the hackers had accessed their system, and identify where the data was coming from.

Another thing about Catist: he is extremely persistent. At the time, he still had access to Victim-2's systems. Even with his access being limited to certain tables, he wasn't happy with a full month of call records. He kept trying to go back for more.

Reddington:	according to J, there is no indication that you can access any of the other tables
	i believe him
	if you could, you would have already
	if you can pivot after, then you can pivot right now to show its real
	if you can show me data form 2024, it will get you 3-4x the price
	show me. otherwise, what you have is it

	and lets move on
	i think it is probably in your best interest (and everyone's) to assume you have downloaded everything you are going to be able to access and call this one done and get paid for it.
catist:	[new sample provided]
	sorted by rows. I have access to 500 tables with more than 1 row. and 12,000 tables in total where I have no access.
Reddington:	you said it
	12,000 tables where you have no access
	let's move on from this
catist:	but 500 where I have access, so I don't want them to find out.
	just do the original sale, we can extort *** later
Reddington:	yeah that's not going to happen
	i am not going back on my word to someone so you can extort the company later on
	this is a once and done sale. and regardless of who i sell to, the access method is part of the sale

Catist was still inside Victim-2's system and trying to pivot to other database tables. At this point, I needed to come to an agreement on the terms of the ransom, as that would provide me with details on the hack and its entry point as part of the terms of the deal.

Unfortunately, the negotiation kept running into a number of unexpected snags.

When dealing with Catist, you have to always remember that his behavior would become increasingly erratic based on how much he did (or didn't) sleep. This situation was also exacerbated by Binns's very sudden and unexpected arrest.

Binns's Arrested in Turkey

On May 6, 2024, right in the middle of the Victim-2 negotiations, something changed. Binns's Telegram account went completely dark. He wasn't responding to messages, and you could tell from the status messages that he was no longer signing in—his last sign-in is still set to May 6.

The reason for Binns's arrest was—and is still—somewhat unclear. What is known is that he's currently being held in a Turkish prison, awaiting trial in Izmir. There is no indication of when he might be released.

Since his incarceration, Bins was also granted Turkish citizenship. U.S. authorities have attempted extradition, but those efforts have been repeatedly denied due to Binns's new status as a Turkish national.

Since then, Binns has since continued to stay in contact with Nick Martino, who can better explain exactly what happened.

Even though Binns turned himself in, what I find most disturbing is that Turkey has no obligation to provide status updates, court dates, or even a clear reason for his continued detainment. It's a stark contrast to the legal transparency and civil liberties we often take for granted in the United States.

Completing the Ransom

The ransom for Catist's data portion started at $3 million, which I was able to negotiate down to about 10 percent of that. *I can feel you patting me on the back. Thank you.*

In Chapter 3, I provided a template for negotiating the purchase of data from a dark web vendor. Here are the exact terms I used for this purchase:

1. Buyer: Reddington

2. Seller: Catist

3. Price of purchase: 5.735 BTC, split over five transactions (approximately 1.147 per transaction)

4. Data files being purchased: [Complete list provided]

5. Purchase process:

   a. Buyer will send 1.147 BTC to bc1q2d72nezmf**.

   b. Once funds are confirmed, seller will send buyer the first mega link.

   c. Buyer will download and verify the data.

   d. Once data is validated, repeat four more times.

6. At the end of the process, the buyer requests the following:

   a. A screen capture video of seller deleting the data

   b. A screen capture video of seller deleting/closing his Mega account.

In the end, the payment was made and Catist provided the deletion videos. Everyone was happy.

Delayed Filing for National Security

Following the ransom payment, I remember being surprised that the whole thing just . . . went away. The stolen data didn't contain any Personally Identifiable Information (PII), so I didn't think there was any legal obligation to disclose the breach (more on this in the next few chapters).

As it turns out, I wasn't the only person Binns contacted with call logs. He contacted a reporter—who, of course, contacted Victim-2. I had no idea any of that was happening behind the scenes. Victim-2 had already prepped the story, handing it out under embargo to several news outlets while they waited on breach disclosure approval.

On July 12, 2024, the news broke everywhere. The carrier confirmed a breach of their data from a third-party cloud provider and disclosed that the stolen data included call detail records (CDRs) for "nearly all" of their customers.

This was the first time in history that the Securities and Exchange Commission (SEC) and Department of Justice (DoJ) agreed to delay a public disclosure—not once, but twice—due to national security concerns. I suppose the fact that Binns was providing then-Senator Rubio's call records was a bit of a red flag.

According to SC Media:[2]

> In assessing the nature of the breach, the FBI said all parties discussed a potential delay to public reporting under Item 1.05(c) of the SEC Rule because of potential risks to national security and/or public safety. AT&T, FBI and the Justice Department worked collaboratively through the first and second delay process, all while sharing threat intelligence to bolster the FBI's investigation and to assist AT&T's incident response work.
>
> A spokesperson for AT&T added that the telecom giant was cooperating with law enforcement in its ongoing investigation and, as part of that effort, they delayed the announcement so as to avoid undermining their work. The filing delay is significant because it's reportedly the first time the Justice Department has granted an exemption under the SEC's new cybersecurity rule that went into effect last December in which companies must report a cybersecurity incident within four days.

What Data Was Stolen?

This is still another big question mark for me. Victim-2 made public statements saying the compromised data included the telephone numbers of "nearly all" of its cellular customers—and the customers of wireless providers that used its network—between May 1, 2022 and October 31, 2022. That's six months of CDR data.

I know Binns had access to the September data, and Catist had access to the October data. I don't know where the other four months came from, or why they were included. I suppose it's possible one of the hackers gained access to connected systems and didn't even realize it.

But, for now, this marks the end of story surrounding Victim-2. After the completion of the ransom, all known copies of the October call records (i.e., Catist's portion of the data) were *believed* to have been deleted.

---

[2] https://www.scworld.com/news/5-questions-to-ask-about-the-latest-news-surrounding-the-att-breach

Identifying Additional Victims

As the negotiation process unfolded, Catist kept feeding me new information about additional victims, which I would pass along to Mandiant and the affected organizations.

Yes, that also meant I was helping facilitate the ransom negotiations. Judge me if you want, but if I hadn't been involved, it is more than likely the companies would've been extorted by a different hacker who wouldn't have been as forthcoming with all this critical information.

That's how I first learned about Victim-5.

Victim-5 (The Bank)

Victim-5 is an international bank—one of the largest in the world with $57 billion in revenue last year.

The court documents state:

Victim-5 is a large foreign corporation headquartered in Europe. On or about May 9, 2024, the FBI notified Victim-5 about a potential breach of its computer systems. In the Telegram chats provided to the FBI by Individual-I, "ellye18," who was later identified as MOUCKA as shown below, discussed having ongoing access to Victim-5 as of April 25, 2024.

I would like to note the following conversation logs as further evidence that I did what I could to steer Catist away from hacking U.S. companies. He didn't always listen, but I did try.

I also want to restate that Catist's behavior was volatile at best—generally based on how much Adderall he had in his system—so I would naturally always question whether or not he was lying to me. Not knowing him very well at this point, it's certainly possible that he was lying to me just to throw me off his trail. As it turns out, however, *he always told the truth.*

catist:	yeah I only do direct access, I hate credential access bc it burns
	American banks are off limits I'm guessing? I hacked Trusit and BofA a few months ago but I didn't exfil anything other than source code for access later on
	I have a lot of experience inside American banks
Reddington:	nothing American.
catist:	Okay, that's helpful to know.
Reddington:	or nothing U.S.. south america is fine
catist:	stuff like Anhauser Busch, the South American division is that okay?
	Or if the parent is American is it off limits too
Reddington:	right
	Exactly
	also, they are beer. and that's not very important

catist:	the South American bank is owned by Spain so it should be fine
Reddington:	bingo
	wait. you have access to [Victim-5]??
catist:	Yes [Victim-5] lol
Reddington:	that might be too big for now. you might want to start smaller
catist:	Yeah maybe. They have petabytes of data
	It's like Truist was
	High density storage tapes attached to network shares
Reddington:	this is insane. congrats on figuring this out
catist:	I'm ldap master controller
	On [Victim-5]
Reddington:	[Victim-5] would be too big to dump transactions unless it was specific to a country.
catist:	how much would it be worth?
	I have [Victim-5] group controller but it has the South American branches under it
	all of this is without 0days and entirely based on technique, but i can buy 0days for larger ops later on if you can move a lot of data. we could probably make 8 figs selling this data if you can find buyers
catist:	for [Victim-5] bank
	argentina is running still
	would you like uruguay samples too? its another non third world south american country
	like chike and Argentina
	i was thinking a cartel might also be interested in buying this data, since they all wanna kill each other and its spanish speaking south+central america heavy
	im nocturnal btw
Reddington:	I just need one country in South America. I don't care which. I'm trying to determine if you actually have this data so I can continue negotiating with them.
	And no I am not doing business with anyone in the cartels

Again, I contacted a senior executive at Mandiant, who at that moment just happened to be sitting next to one of their high-level security executives at an RSA Conference dinner. What are the odds, right?

The court documents stated:

Victim-5 provided the extortion emails that it received to the FBI. These included an email from the same intermediary, [Reddington]. On May 13, 2024, [Reddington] notified Victim-5 that the "threat actor" was "actively downloading" Victim-5's data, and provided some sample data and a link to another account with additional data. Victim-5 downloaded sample data from [Reddington] and verified that it contained Victim-5's data.

Meanwhile, Catist was off on his own planet.

catist: also if ur gonna extort [Victim-5] with the data you should let me hack more peoplesoft servers first bc this is heartland payment systems level, and i showed you POS tender as well that's for an american retailer. i have others such as walmarts POS tender, anhauser busch as well and autozone

Reddington: Slow it down, trigger.

I still need to see what you have.

catist: okay ill do head on them after dinner. but yeah the king of spain might send people to spy on you bc he owns this bank

we should extort the finance secretary for ransom, we can hold their economy hostage

Reddington: Uh huh

Let's not hold any economies hostage

I need you to bring it back down to reality.

catist: its unrealistic to hack high street banks at the data vault level

i can get emv ki's for their cards probably

Continuing to reference the document:

The FBI provided Victim-5 with a screenshot of sample HR data from the Telegram chats and initial indicators of compromise. Victim-5 conducted an internal investigation and subsequently validated the data from the screenshot, confirmed that its Victim-1 instance had been breached, verified that the initial breach occurred on or about April 17, 2024, and indicated that the breach continued through at least May 10, 2024. According to Victim-5's internal investigation and a review of their logs, this breach was the result of compromised credentials of two employees.

The stolen data included names, addresses, company identification numbers, and payroll accounts for employees across multiple countries, including in the United States. Victim-5 subsequently informed the FBI that three types of data had been exfiltrated. First, Victim-5's employee data, including those of employees based in the United States, had been stolen, which included employees' names, social security numbers, and addresses, as well as company payroll records.

I tried reaching Victim-5 a few times but never heard back. About a week after my initial emails, they released a statement announcing their data breach.

That announcement apparently fueled the data being posted for sale on Exploit, one of the oldest known Russian cybercrime forums (see Figure 16.1).

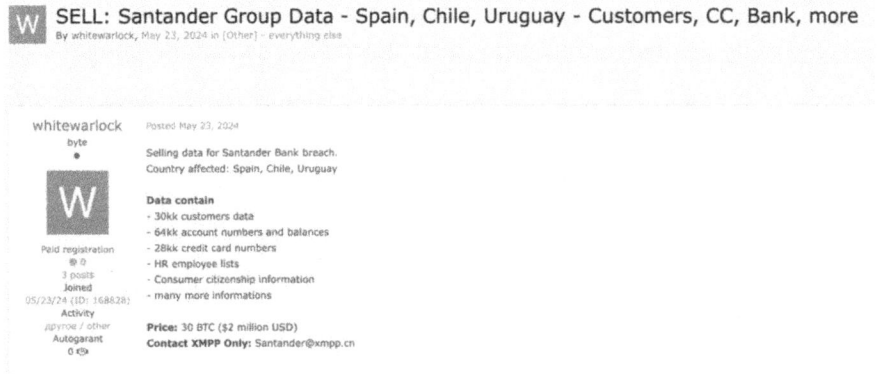

Figure 16.1: Victim-5 sales thread on Exploit forum.

For a while, that was the last I heard about Victim-5.

Victim-4 (Entertainment)

Victim-4 is a major U.S. entertainment and ticketing company. I will let the official documents make a proper introduction:

> *Victim-4 is a major U.S. entertainment and marketing company. The FBI obtained logs about Victim-4's cloud computing instance from [Snowflake]. According to those logs, the threat actors breached Victim-4's cloud instance from at least on or about April 14, 2024, through at least May 18, 2024. Victim-4 informed FBI that the types of data stolen included names, contact information, partial payment card numbers, and in some instances driver's license numbers and/or passport numbers. Additionally, Victim-4 confirmed that only one account on its [Snowflake] cloud computing instance had been breached.*

I learned about this victim at pretty much the same time as Victim-5. I might have mentioned this, but Catist liked to talk—a lot.

Unfortunately, getting him to actually send me samples of anything was like pulling teeth, and we couldn't reasonably notify any of the customers until we had sample data that we could provide as proof of compromise.

Here's a timeline of how the events unfolded leading to Victim-4:

May 7

catist: [Victim-4] for example has an acxiom feed in their azure cosmos. but i think youre not interested in the largest breach of 2024 and largest credit card breach of all time because its usa

Reddington: You have [Victim-4] now?

catist:	but ive been drinking idk my judgement isnt as good rn.
	should i go to rsa conference?
Reddington:	So what is "the largest credit card breach" you are talking about
catist:	so imagine this
	1.6 billion orders
	600 million credit cards (250 m unique)
Reddington:	Ok
catist:	and 650m unique emails
Reddington:	And you are ready to sell it?
catist:	americans mostly
Reddington:	Or are you assuming you can get it
catist:	mlb nba nfl and also rap concerts or taylor swift
	oh i dimped it
	i have ALL of itb
	including barcodes
	for tickets
	haha
Reddington:	Ok why are you just mentioning it now? Send me a sample.

May 09

catist:	[Victim-4] is 680 million unique emails somehow.
	i think these are real customers too, rather than AI inference or scraped. so technically biggest PII contact dump ever
Reddington:	Seriously.
	Can you please drop the pretense
	I don't for one second believe you have never heard of [Victim-4]
	The same way I don't believe you are in UK, despite being subscribed to a bunch of BBC groups.
	I obviously know who you are. There is a reason you and J came to me with [Victim-2].
	You know I will deliver the money.
	If you want me to contact [Victim-4] for you I am happy to do that

catist:	nah don't, i have their ticket barcodes i can sell them
	do you have any blackhat buyers?
	i prefer those
Reddington:	Why would you not want to ask [Victim-4] for money?
	Are you planning on just posting it on breached?
catist:	no theyre all poor
	they cant afford any of my data
Reddington:	How much do you actually think you are going to get for [Victim-4]
	Let's play this out
catist:	well i have the barcodes for every ticket sold up until 2026
	so i can destroy their company
Reddington:	who cares
catist:	i can get 5% of revenue prob
	as a ransom
Reddington:	lol
	Ok
	you want 5% of their revenue?
catist:	yes

Still no sample—and now it's been a week since I learned about Victim-4 but could do nothing anything about it.

May 14

Reddington:	Do you really have [Victim-4]?
	How much of that data do you have already?
catist:	almost the entire thing other than the tracking pixel db of 3TB. im gonna check if i still have access and download that if i do tho it'd be useful for me.
	but the PII I have 600 million emails, 1.2 billion rows of AVS stuff, like 300 million encrypted CC's but plaintext L4/expdate, it's really nice data.
Reddington:	600 million emails. Holy crap.
catist:	yeah seems to be everything since at least 2011

It took a few more days, but he finally gave me the sample. The court document states:

On or about May 17, 2024, Victim-4 learned about a potential breach, which it later confirmed. On May 29, 2024, the FBI interviewed Victim-4 and discovered it was investigating a breach of its [Snowflake] cloud computing instance in which threat actors may have stolen information related to its customers' contact information and payment card information.

May 21

Reddington:	Let's see if we can make you a few million this week
	You have what you need
	Why grab more
	All you need is the customer data and the hashed CCs
	You're golden
	The other stuff doesn't matter
	What's even in the s3? Do you have a listing?
catist:	yeah
	one sec
	it takes a few mins to list, ill query it
Reddington:	You are listing off their DB? You don't have it locally?
	If you haven't dumped the main tables please just tell me and I'll stop asking about it
catist:	i have the PII
	but not everything i want
	i want to datamine for api secrets and for anything that can help decrypt the cards
Reddington:	I need you to please hear me.
	Why do you want to decrypt the cards?
	The cards are worthless
catist:	so [Victim-4] knows i can sell them if they dont pay
Reddington:	Bro
	You do not need to do this.
	They will pay.
catist:	and yeah its epic data isnt it

Reddington:	yeah this is massive
catist:	yeah and each table is over 500m lines
	a few are 1.2 billion
Reddington:	WOW
catist:	do you think theyre gonna pay?
	this might be the biggest breach in US history
	but idk
Reddington:	they are 100% going to pay
	there is no question
catist:	okay epic
Reddington:	i will start doing my thing. this will start to move fast now
catist:	okay. also do u want a sample from ticket barcodes?
	those might be important for them to know i have
	[Attachment]

Spoiler Alert: They didn't pay. In fact, Victim-4 wouldn't even respond to my emails. I think everyone was surprised at how this played out, given the amount of information that was actually stolen. My best guess is that Victim-4 was also in the middle of an anti-trust case, and they didn't have time to care about this.

Unfortunately, my inability to get Catist paid for this data in a relatively short time frame, combined with his severe lack of patience, created an unexpected change in this environment.

Catist Teams Up with ShinyHunters

If you're familiar with data breach history or are up on current cyber events, you are probably familiar with the name ShinyHunters.

ShinyHunters is a well-known hacker—and hacking group—responsible for a number of high-profile data breaches. I've researched him extensively and have publicly linked his identity to a French national.

At the time these events were unfolding, ShinyHunters was the admin of BreachForums—he and I communicated regularly. I'd describe it as more of a "keep your friends close" kind of relationship.

The important thing is that after years of turmoil related to Pompompurin (refer to Chapter 1), Shiny and I were civil—cordial, even. We stayed out of each other's way. If we needed to speak, we did.

> **NOTE** More about ShinyHunters
>
> ShinyHunters operates both as an individual and as a collective. The way it works is that multiple hackers carry out breaches and release data under the ShinyHunters name, leveraging the media attention it reliably attracts.

Regardless of attribution nuance, the name ShinyHunters is tied to the hack and leak of billions of customer records since 2020—including the 2021 breach of AT&T, which exposed data on 70 million U.S. citizens, and the 2020 hack of Tokopedia, which affected 91 million users. And those are just the headline cases.

Needless to say, ShinyHunters has been a persistent thorn in the side of many companies—not just because of the scale of his breaches, but because of his ability to weaponize publicity during ransom negotiations.

Back to the main story. Catist, having grown impatient with my inability to deliver more extortion payments, teamed up with ShinyHunters. Shiny assured Catist that, with his expertise and "name recognition," he could make companies pay much faster.

Making News Headlines

The court document continues:

In or about May 2024, a co-conspirator posted on the cybercriminal forum Exploit.in a sale of Victim-4's data that purportedly included millions of users and payment card details. The post included sample data without any names but with sale order IDs, account numbers, account created data, and partial addresses.

On May 28, ShinyHunters publicly posted the sale of Victim-4's data on BreachForums. I mentioned that Shiny and I have a love/hate relationship. Given my involvement in the current situation, and all the current media headlines that followed this breach announcement, I didn't exactly appreciate him using my picture on the forum post (see Figure 16.2).

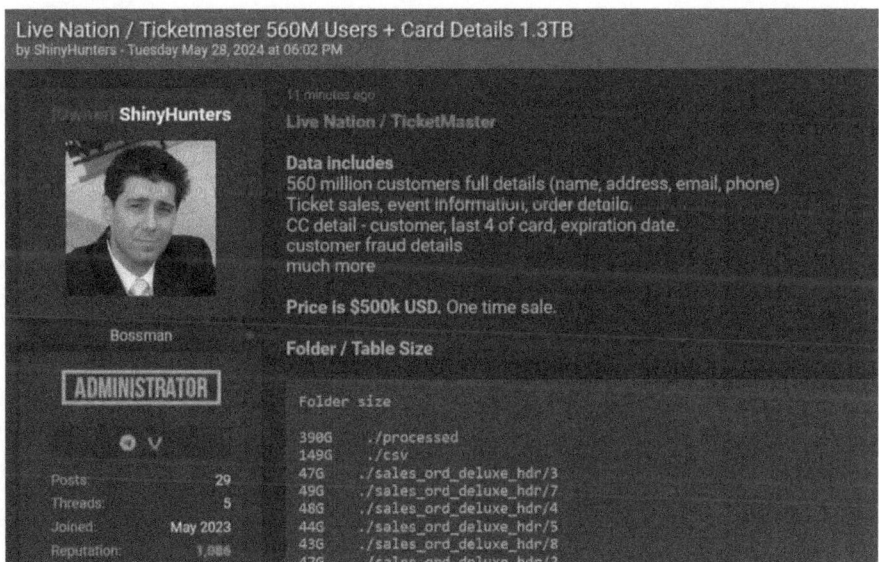

Figure 16.2: Original sale of Victim-4 data on BreachForums.

Luckily, Shiny and I are on good terms, and he was nice enough to change it for me. But not before it was already syndicated to all media outlets.

Reddington:	yo
	Urgent
ShinyHunters:	?
Reddington:	i need you to remove my photo from your breached profile
	Please
	its important
	you can add it back in a few days if you need to
ShinyHunters:	alright
Reddington:	thank you
ShinyHunters:	no I had just 0 idea for pfp
Reddington:	?
	Oh
	gotcha
ShinyHunters:	sorry bad wordings but ye
Reddington:	but thanks. its impacting other things right now
ShinyHunters:	damn
	Lol

During this same time period, [Reddington] contacted Victim-4 several times offering to act as an intermediary between Victim-4 and the threat actors and/or advising about MOUCKA's use of the data.

For example, on June 20, 2024, [Reddington] reached out to two different people associated with Victim-4 via email. In one communication, [Reddington] stated, "[t]he hacker has recently leaked 1 million user records and is threatening to leak more. They have also dropped their price point to about 100k USD. At that price, I imagine they will sell it at least 3-4x."

[Reddington] attached a BreachForums post, which included an extortion attempt.

As part of continued extortion attempts, a co-conspirator made a subsequent post on a cybercriminal forum in an attempt to extort Victim-4.

Despite Catist's (and Shiny's) attempts to exert pressure, Victim-4, continued to not pay and, instead, completely ignored the situation. This caused portions of their data to be leaked in multiple batches. Other members of the Scattered Spider group eventually leaked user records from Victim-4 and event bar codes to all of their shows.

Reddington:	Are you here
ShinyHunters:	yes
Reddington:	I hear you are posting something today? Because Hudson rock just blogged about it
ShinyHunters:	I posted
	[Victim-5]
	as well as [Victim-4]
	Just selling them
	I'm with scattered spider rn
Reddington:	Oh. I heard there was something else coming
ShinyHunters:	Probably
ShinyHunters:	I have another dump but idk
	I want to finish these one
	first
ShinyHunters:	Did you read my announcement?
Reddington:	Oh. No?
ShinyHunters:	https://breachforums.st/Thread-IMPORTANT-READ-How-did-we-troll-FBI

For those of you paying close attention, Shiny just admitted to being the user "White Warlock," who posted the sale of Victim-5's data on the Russian forum Exploit.

Shiny's Announcement (and Arrest)

ShinyHunters thought he was invincible; my guess is because "France does not extradite their citizens, and we have more important things to deal with." This is exactly what one of the lead French cyber detectives told me when we spoke about Shiny years ago.

Everyone knew who he was, but according to this person, they had other, more important, things to worry about.

Well, I guess invincibility has its limits. If you are a current (or aspiring) cybercriminal, this should be a cautionary tale:

Don't troll the FBI.

One day, Shiny decided to make a post on BreachForums stating that he was able to troll members of the FBI into sending him sealed documents pertaining to his investigation. I remember reading it, and it seemed really unnecessary and childish.

My direct conversation with Shiny about what occurred is shown in Figure 16.3.

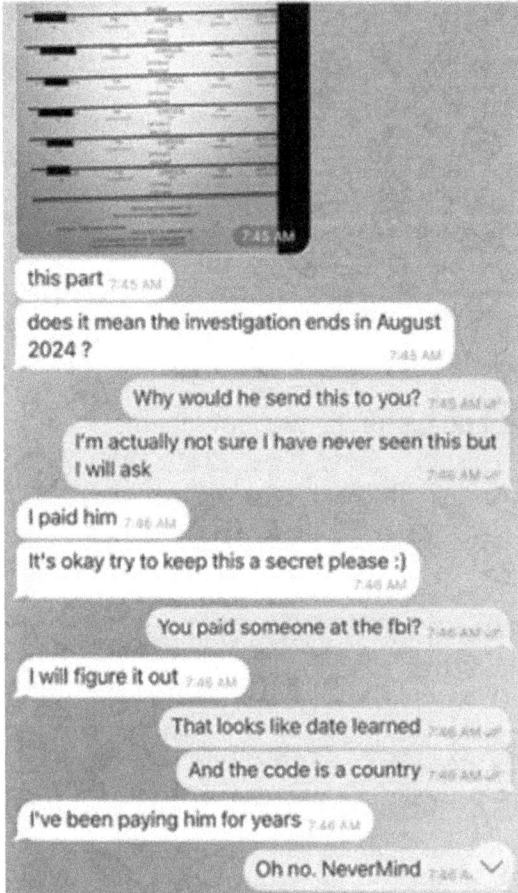

this part 7:45 AM

does it mean the investigation ends in August 2024 ?
7:45 AM

Why would he send this to you? 7:45 AM

I'm actually not sure I have never seen this but I will ask
7:46 AM

I paid him 7:46 AM

It's okay try to keep this a secret please :)
7:46 AM

You paid someone at the fbi? 7:46 AM

I will figure it out 7:46 AM

That looks like date learned 7:46 AM

And the code is a country 7:46 AM

I've been paying him for years 7:46 AM

Oh no. NeverMind 7:46 A

Figure 16.3: Shiny conversation.

Shiny's "Retirement"

About a month later—around June, 14, 2025—Shiny announced that he was retiring from his life of crime. That came only a few days after the current BreachForums was seized by international law enforcement.

He also mysteriously sent messages to several close contacts via Telegram saying he was "retiring."

catist: i don't think he got arrested. i think he just decided to disappear

bc he said that

Reddington: Nah. He def got arrested

I would bet money on it

He was egging the FBI with his posts

I told him not to.

He didn't listen. You don't get into a pissing contest with the FBI

Wait when did he send you that

Like an hour or so ago?

catist:	like 8 hrs ago
Reddington:	Hmmm
	Yeah timeline fits
	Daytime in France
	They got him
catist:	was there an arrest
catist:	do you think shiny really got raided?
Reddington:	yes
	i would bet my house on it
	He exited pretty much the same way Pom did
catist:	its weird because he told me before that he was gonna disappear then did it. would feds say that then delete his account?
	i would think theyd try SEing me from his account
Reddington:	to put the word out that
	or maybe he just said that
	when pom sent me a message after he was caught, they didnt know aobut it
	but i caught it
	shiny has no other income. he wasn't about to just shut it all down
catist:	but hes probably got 8 figs from all his hacks
Reddington:	no, he doesn't
catist:	oh
Reddington:	i would be surprised if he has a few hundred k left around
	most of the hacks under his name weren't him
	he's just the name people use to post stuff

Around the same time, Shiny posted the following retirement notice (see Figure 16.4) on BreachForums.

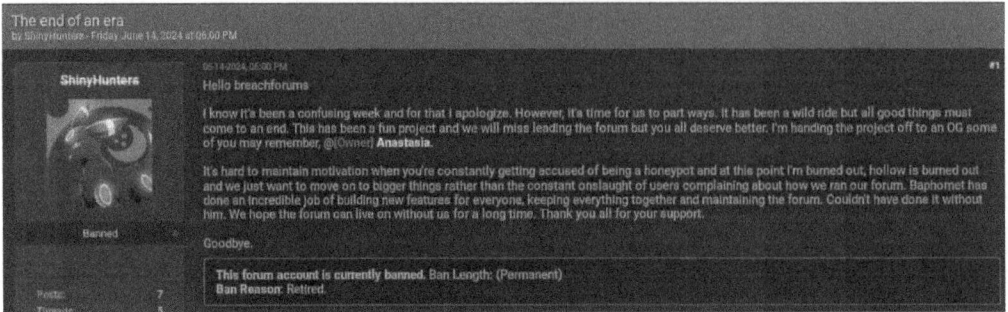

Figure 16.4: Shiny's retirement notification.

This announcement has nothing to do with the general Snowflake story, but I included it because of my own personal history with Shiny, and it was a great way to close out that storyline.

Threat actors don't just wake up one day and decide to quit. This is all they've ever known. What else are they going to do?

On June 23, 2025, French authorities announced the arrest of four individuals: Hollow, Noct, Depressed, and ShinyHunters—French nationals residing in Hauts-de-Seine, Seine-Maritime, and Réunion.

According to the official statement:[3]

Under the collective name ShinyHunters, they are suspected of being responsible for the cybercriminal forum BreachForums. They are also suspected of having committed cyberattacks of a very high degree of technical complexity, to the detriment of numerous victims in France and abroad.

While they still haven't officially announced their names, my money has always been on N.B. for ShinyHunters.

Summary

This chapter detailed the final stages of the breach involving Victim-2, offering a firsthand look at how the negotiation unfolded, and how that exchange began to reveal a broader web of compromised Snowflake customers.

It also walked through the timeline of the breaches and extortion attempts involving Victim-4 and Victim-5, illustrating how fast the threat was evolving and how each case helped map the larger attack surface. Finally, the chapter closed on ShinyHunters, whose sudden and unexpected exit will undoubtedly be a noteworthy event in the lives of many in the security field.

The next chapter focuses on the breach at Snowflake itself. It breaks down how we traced the source of the stolen data, how and when Snowflake was notified, and what ultimately caused the breach to happen in the first place. This is where the investigation shifts from individual victims to an analysis of the events that tied them all together.

---

[3] https://databreaches.net/wp-content/uploads/presse_en.jpg

Intrusion Analysis

This chapter focuses on the intrusion into Snowflake as the pivot point that connects hundreds of downstream breaches into a single, coordinated campaign.

It walks through how we identified Snowflake as the common denominator and digs into the specifics of how the breach actually happened—from credential reuse to non-expiring session tokens—and all the pieces in between.

Rather than telling the story in perfect sequence, my goal is to give you a sense of how the events unfolded based on how we figured out each element. The dates from the chat logs will jump around, but the overall story should feel smooth.

Throughout the chapter, I also tie in details referencing Mandiant's blog post, "UNC5537 Targets Snowflake Customer Instances for Data Theft and Extortion," because it was based on a combination of all our research. In that post, Connor Moucka (aka *Catist*) is referenced using Mandiant's internal threat actor code, UNC5537. For ease of reading, I reference UNC5537 using their more commonly recognizable alias, Scattered Spider—even though the entire group was not directly involved in these hacks.

Scattered Spider is better described as a loosely knit cell of hackers than as a cohesive group. Catist was affiliated with multiple groups, but the one most often referenced is Scattered Spider.

This is where the victims, actors, and infrastructure all come into focus, tying back to a single entry point. Let's break down how it happened. Figure 17.1 illustrates the attack path diagram provided in Mandiant's blog post.

Discovering Snowflake

I had to be very careful in dealing with Catist. I couldn't just come out and ask where or how he was obtaining all this data. He would've suspected something, and if he came out and told me, I would have an obligation to relay the information to Mandiant, which could've triggered him being locked out of those systems.

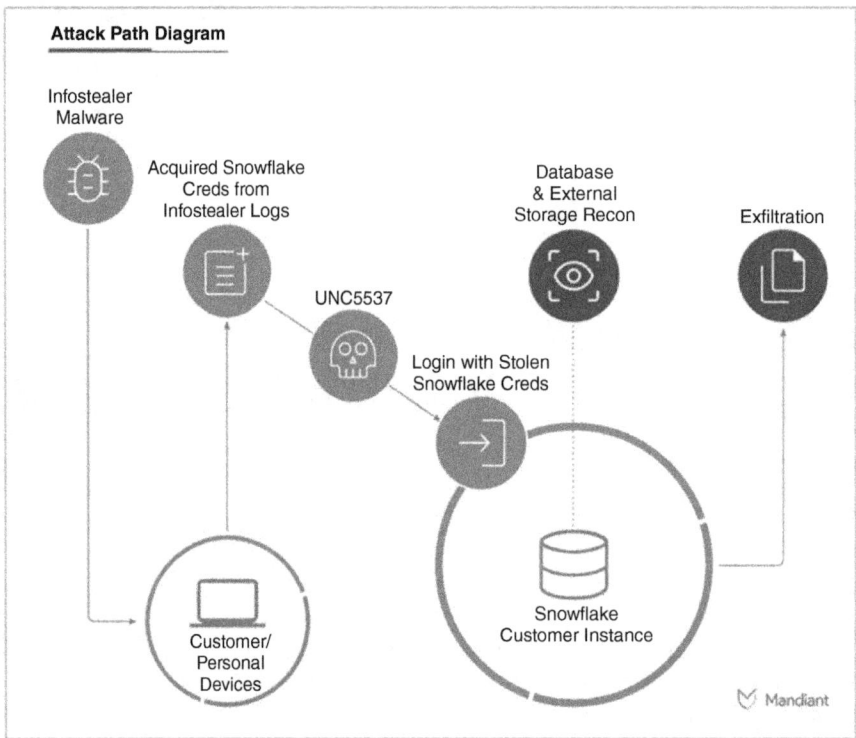

Figure 17.1: Mandiant's attack path diagram.

It was a very delicate balance. On the one hand, companies were being victimized, but on the other, if Catist suspected in any way that I was involved in getting him locked out, I would lose any potential for gathering future intelligence. But that certainly didn't stop me from asking probing questions.

April 28:

Reddington:	wait one question
	the MSP. are they US based?
	im not asking for a name, just want to know if their main HQ is located outside the U.S (it will be an important detail later)
ellye18:	Pretty sure it's in the US
	Let me double check
Reddington:	that's unfortunate
	yeah please let me know

ellyel8:	Seems to be multinational with regional hq's in Europe and USA
Reddington:	ok thanks. i'm just thinking through how to circumvent some legal issues. not important for now. will get back to you
	(legal issues for me buying the data, not for you)
ellyel8:	Oh, well the companies aren't directly from this. They're just compromised via the vendor, they won't know the entrypoint

Part of the challenge—if I'm remembering correctly—was that Victim-2 had data spread across multiple cloud providers. It made attribution difficult in the early stages. There wasn't a clear common denominator, and for a while, it looked like we were chasing separate breaches.

We just needed confirmation from Catist to close the loop—which we were able to get with the help of a little third-party framing (see Chapter 14).

Reddington:	Hey actually does [Victim-2] have anything to do with snowflake?
	Because my attorney said snowflake to me a few minutes ago and I'm not sure where he got that
	It would only have come from [Victim-2]
ellyel8:	its from that azure thing pretty sure. but it was attached to their snowflake with credentials, like an api key and stuff
Reddington:	Got it. Ok that makes sense
ellyel8:	yes
Reddington:	Ok now this makes sense about why people are asking about snowflake in general.
ellyel8:	its fun to hack msp's, dump integration secrets and sit back and hack

Ultimately, realizing that the data was coming from Snowflake instances was a group effort. I kept feeding in new intelligence, and with each new case, Dallas and his team were able to trace a consistent thread back to Snowflake.

Still, we needed more confirmation. So, I kept pushing—probing under the guise of helping Catist identify new extortion targets. The goal was to get him to reveal just enough to validate what we already suspected.

May 13:

Reddington:	i just need you to send me a few hundred lines of every table
	thanks
ellyel8:	hopefully this doesn't start the clock to snowflake forcing MFA and resetting everyones integration api keys

Reddington:	it shouldn't
	they wouldn't notify snowflake
	but i can find out
	that would take a LONG time to do
ellyel8:	okay, try getting access to the incident report

May 18:

ellyel8:	im on snowflake sorta. but EU this time
Reddington:	Which orgs?:)
ellyel8:	snowflake
Reddington:	Which databases/ companies is it connected to?
ellyel8:	each emp seems to have their own account
	but theres over 5,000 accounts in the org
	and im orgadmin
	of
	snowflake.com
Reddington:	And there's no way to pull a list?
ellyel8:	yeah there is
	im thinking snowmesh?
	seems like a good one to try first
	since it has managed accounts under it

May 19:

ellyel8:	did they find redline stealer on that fredrique guys pc? or did they even do forensics on it yet
Reddington:	i dont know who that is lol
ellyel8:	the org owner account of that snowflake instance
Reddington:	oh. i wouldn't know anything about that. i legit have nothing to do with anything LE related.
	i havent spoken with [Victim-5] yet, but they would not be giving up any details like that
ellyel8:	does hudsonrock show cleartext botnet logs? bc that panorays one did so i dumped it
	i haven't used that product yet

At this point, Catist had found his way into a direct Snowflake developer instance, which technically made them a victim—meaning there was an opportunity to notify them.

Notifying Snowflake

The following is an excerpt from the Mandiant's incident report published on June 10, 2024:[1]

In April 2024, Mandiant received threat intelligence on database records that were subsequently determined to have originated from a victim's Snowflake instance. Mandiant notified the victim, who then engaged Mandiant to investigate suspected data theft involving their Snowflake instance. During this investigation, Mandiant determined that the organization's Snowflake instance had been compromised by a threat actor using credentials previously stolen via infostealer malware. The threat actor used these stolen credentials to access the customer's Snowflake instance and ultimately exfiltrate valuable data. At the time of the compromise, the account did not have multi-factor authentication (MFA) enabled.

On May 22, 2024 upon obtaining additional intelligence identifying a broader campaign targeting additional Snowflake customer instances, Mandiant immediately contacted Snowflake and began notifying potential victims through our Victim Notification Program. To date, Mandiant and Snowflake have notified approximately 165 potentially exposed organizations. Snowflake's Customer Support has been directly engaged with these customers to ensure the safety of their accounts and data. Mandiant and Snowflake have been conducting a joint investigation into this ongoing threat campaign and coordinating with relevant law enforcement agencies. On May 30, 2024, Snowflake published detailed detection and hardening guidance to Snowflake customers.

May 22:

I received a phone call from Dallas saying it was time to notify Snowflake: Mandiant reached out to Snowflake through their standard notification process. That night, I received a call from a top executive at Mandiant asking me to jump on a call with Snowflake and speak with them about what was going on.

There are moments in life that you'll never forget. This was one of them. I hopped on a call with a few Snowflake team members around 11 p.m. that night.

I remember explaining the situation to them and feeling the distinct impression that they didn't think any of this data was coming from them.

Then—and this is the moment I'll never forget—I started listing the victims. At that moment, I could see their faces turn. It was almost as if they had been punched in the gut. The tone of the conversation changed considerably at that point.

I provided them with copies of the sample data and things started moving quickly. Snowflake kicked into gear and began trying stop the data exfiltration of its customers by removing Catist from their systems.

Unexpectedly around this same time, Catist, against my strong recommendations, was running off his mouth to other people. One of them ran a small cybersecurity startup that sells access to hacked credentials.

---

[1] https://cloud.google.com/blog/topics/threat-intelligence/unc5537-snowflake-data-theft-extortion

Instead of confirming any of this information with the victim organizations, said person took the information Catist was telling him and posted it on his blog—an incident which is at the center of a major hiccup in the next chapter.

This person also convinced Catist that he could get Snowflake to pay him a $10M ransom to "stop hacking them"—which, aside from being completely false, wasn't helping the greater situation. This is where Catist's ego and naivety would always get the best of him:

Reddington: Why would you talk to him at all

This is going to fuck up everything

These companies are paying for silence. They want to announce on their own terms.

ellyel8: i was having him deliver the demands to the head of snowflake security

Reddington: I have been talking to them

I am not lying to you

ellyel8: yeah but it makes it more likely theyll pay if multiple sources confirm it doesn't it?

Reddington: No

Snowflake isn't giving you money

That's not even a discussion

Why the fuck would you share all of that with him

ellyel8: thought it'd make it more likely snowflake pays if he confirms the victims to the snowflake team

Reddington: No

Snowflake isn't paying

He knew that

I doubt he ever contacted them.

I have been talking to them regularly

Snowflake has no reason to pay

ellyel8: oh okay. well most of the companies he listed is wrong anyway

Reddington: How are they wrong??

ellyel8: i didn't hack allstate or progressive

they dont even have snowflake

his thread is full of disinfo

he said he will blur those other ones

Reddington: Ok well the news is out

The blog outing Snowflake and at least five other companies was published as a cheap means of self-promotion. The statement they provided detailed an attack beginning with a Snowflake user being breached, which "likely paved the way for the hacker to loot the login credentials necessary to breach the cloud storage provider."

None of this was accurate, but it was enough for the media to catch wind of what was occurring and start poking around—ultimately triggering several breach disclosures and flurries of additional news articles.

Regardless of what the media was sating, at this point, the more relevant concern was: *Why was Catist still able to access these customers, despite being repeatedly kicked out?*

Maintaining Persistent Access

It was no secret at this point that the intrusions the Snowflake customers experienced were caused by compromised credentials, most likely originating from infostealer malware.

What was really troubling is that victims reported having detected and removed Catist from their Snowflake instances, yet he had no trouble getting back into them.

We were definitely aware of one isolated instance where Catist was able to directly access a Snowflake developer instance using an employee's credential—the same instance reported in the previously mentioned blog—but that was a long shot.

May 23:

ellyel8:	i think they only know i hacked some of their emps so far
Reddington:	I don't know what they know.
ellyel8:	i can check her email prob
Reddington:	Whose email
ellyel8:	the girl i have ratted
Reddington:	That's how you got in?
	Seriously???
ellyel8:	one of the ways
	but yeah
	she has
	@snowflake
	.com email
	i always find a sidechannel in

The employee's credential did not end up being the entry point and it didn't seem like it could have been at the time, either. First, we didn't find out about it until much later in this story, and more importantly, I have to assume that Snowflake would have disabled it immediately. Somehow, Catist still seemed to have persistent access.

ellyel8:	yeah true. i don't mind anyway, i'm not impulsive or impatient unless im unsure about something bc anxiety, otherwise i'm really OCD
Reddington:	yeah i hear you
ellyel8:	i just noticed in the [Victim-3] folder of my server is DONOTCALL_ REGISTRY_GOV.csv and is 50GB. can they get fined for that?
Reddington:	no its just people on the donot call list i guess
	they have to keep track of it
ellyel8:	yeah true
	im still on it dumping btw
	when u sent them the samples did u tell them thats just a few of the tables and that im dumping their entire data lake?
	or do they think those are the only ones i have
	$ wc -l DONOTCALL_REGISTRY_GOV_T_202405241011.csv
	246391256 DONOTCALL_REGISTRY_GOV_T_202405241011.csv
ellyel8:	snowflakes weird. they finally disabled [Victim-3] but i can still run commands bc i have the **'masterToken'** for every account xd

MasterToken?

May 24:

Reddington:	did snowflake completely cut you off
	or is it still going
	snowflake sent out an email to their customers
ellyel8:	whats the email say
Reddington:	i dont have it
	but im sure it will be in the news soon
ellyel8:	oh okay
	hmm
	they nuked [Victim-3]
	but its still dumping via the token

Reddington:	or [Victim-3] turned it off
	Wow
ellye18:	maybe they turned it off yeah
Reddington:	how do you have a master token for every account
ellye18:	uh ill make writeup after. am dumping xerox rn tho
Reddington:	forget xerox
	no one cares about them

May 28:

More than a full week had passed, and Catist was still seeing newly added content, despite being continuously kicked out.

ellye18:	mandiant is making "incident response" tables in every snowflake i've hacked
	and i can see their investigation process
	p funny
Reddington:	Can you show me
ellye18:	they call it "incident investigation" and then number them with roman numerals
	im tempted to just nuke every table except for the incident response table
	in this company
Reddington:	It's CrowdStrike
	Not Mandiant

We All Miss Things

It's funny, going back through all of these old messages, I realize there are so many little details that I/we all missed. With so much information coming at all of us, it was impossible to focus on every detail. Plus, there was always the ongoing question of whether or not Catist was lying to us.

For example, on this May 26 conversation, I incorrectly focused on the employee and not the refresh tokens.

ellye18:	i am locked out of adel**
	but i have refresh tokens
Reddington:	What is Adel**?
ellye18:	the girl i ratted
	who works for snowflake

Or this conversation, where I completely missed him talking about the master token, or maybe just thought he was speaking nonsense.

ellyel8: i think i explained the [Victim-2] before. mastertoken generated from network then generated session token outside of network. it bypasses all restrictions and it's what ppl are laughing at snow-flake for atm in blogs

Reddington: Except I know for a fact that's not accurate

How did you get in the network

ellyel8: i think i explained it was malware

Reddington: [Victim-2] is saying no. Because that account didn't have access.

ellyel8: well i don't have any snowflake exploits that i'm aware of so idk

I didn't actually *know for a fact*, because I was wrong. Catist was trying to tell me the whole time what was happening, but I either wasn't hearing it or maybe I just wasn't understanding it. What exactly is a "Mastertoken generated from the network"?

ellyel8: idk, i only lost access to things ive dumped so far but with the refresh token I can regen credentials

Reddington: Did you establish that before they locked the account

ellyel8: yeah, so basically their refresh tokens have no way to invalidate\

so they last forever

theres no cancel token

or whatever

Reddington: I'm actually speechless

ellyel8: by which part? ratting emps of MSP's or their design flaw

its like pkcs AES inside base64, but im not really an expert when it comes to cryptography

Reddington: The design flaw

Alright bro. You have a bunch of these tokens right? Can you get back into a locked out org? Have you actually tried it?

ellyel8: yeah with [Victim-3] and [Victim-6]

i was able to download files using the token

and the jdbc driver

> **NOTE** In retrospect, I am not sure I would actually consider this a design flaw. The circumstances described were so incredibly unique that I don't think any penetration tester or system auditor could have reasonably considered or planned for this type of attack scenario. Yet, it happened.

Snowflake Master and Refresh Tokens

In plain English, here's what actually happened:

When any application connects to a Snowflake instance, it uses an authentication token—think of it like a browser session cookie. That token is short-lived, typically lasting about ten minutes. It's just long enough to run a few queries and then it expires. For most applications and services needing a persistent connection, that isn't going to work.

To maintain the longer type of connectivity that most web services require, Snowflake uses *refresh tokens*. These tokens are valid for up to 90 days and let an application request a new access token—without having to reauthenticate. One level higher are *master tokens*, which function like a root credential. With one master token, you can continuously create fresh tokens and maintain an indefinite session without needing to log back in.

Now, here's where things went sideways:

Snowflake includes a configuration called `ALLOW_ID_TOKEN`, which is designed to make user reauthentication seamless. This token allows users to return to their session without a fresh login—similar to how your browser might use a cookie to keep you logged into Facebook.

But just like web apps and services using this token to access Snowflake, it also allows user access to the system. You authenticate once, and when you return to the site, you're already logged in.

The problem? These tokens, by design, don't expire immediately—because they're not supposed to.

However, Snowflake documentation states that even when an account is disabled, it can take up to six hours for that token to become invalid. That delay is the critical failure point.

It's a cascading effect. Once a user was authenticated and had an active ID token, they could leverage that token via an Application Programming Interface (API) to access the master token. That master token, in turn, could be used to generate unlimited new refresh tokens, effectively creating an infinite session loop.

So even if an admin changed the password or disabled the account, it didn't matter. There was a six-hour window where the attacker could continue authenticating, minting new tokens, and re-establishing access, which is exactly what happened here.

Catist, being the clever hacker that he is, *figured all of this out simply by reading the online documentation.* RTFM, right?

He anticipated that the accounts might eventually be locked out, so he built a script that repeatedly generated new tokens using the master token, bypassing reauthentication entirely. No brute force. No privilege escalation. Just an elegant abuse of Snowflake's own token architecture.

All things considered, the whole thing was incredibly impressive.

May 30:

Reddington:	I get it now. The access tokens expire pretty quickly but because you had access, you could simply generate your own refresh token, which by default is 90 days, which could also be used to access the bucket "offline.
	Is that pretty close?
ellyel8:	yes
	refresh token 90 days is azure
	what is
	[Victim-7]
	i have just done the biggest MSP hack
	i think
ellyel8:	this is bigger than snowflake
	but snowflake is the entrypoint
	which is funny

And just like that, we were on to another potentially massive breach (which I cover in the next chapter).

Snowflake's Official Statement

On June 02, 2024, Snowflake issued the following statement:

Snowflake and third-party cybersecurity experts, CrowdStrike and Mandiant, are providing a joint statement related to our ongoing investigation involving a targeted threat campaign against some Snowflake customer accounts. Our key preliminary findings identified to date are:

- ▪ *We have not identified evidence suggesting this activity was caused by compromised credentials of current or former Snowflake personnel.*
- ▪ *This appears to be a targeted campaign directed at users with single-factor authentication.*
- ▪ *As part of this campaign, threat actors have leveraged credentials previously purchased or obtained through infostealer malware.*

■ *We did find evidence that a threat actor obtained personal credentials to and accessed demo accounts belonging to a former Snowflake employee. It did not contain sensitive data. Demo accounts are not connected to Snowflake's production or corporate systems. The access was possible because the demo account was not behind Okta or Multi-Factor Authentication (MFA), unlike Snowflake's corporate and production systems.*

Who Was at Fault?

Snowflake maintains the position that the breach wasn't their fault. It was up to their customers to enforce multifactor authentication (MFA) on their accounts. Technically, this isn't wrong.

To help with this process, Snowflake sent the email—shown in Figure 17.2—to customers who were impacted, again, taking the position that enforcing MFA is their responsibility, not Snowflake's.

Dear 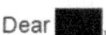,

Snowflake has recently observed increased cyber threat actor activities targeting our customers' proprietary data. We have found evidence that an unauthorized party may have accessed your account. Based on our investigation to date, we believe this activity is the result of malicious activity directed at obtaining customer-controlled credentials and Snowflake's own security systems are not the focus of this activity. We have observed that your account does not have certain key security configurations that would guard against such access. **It is critical for the safety of your company's data that you take prompt action to secure your Snowflake account(s) against phishing or other means used to compromise your users' or administrators' accounts.**

We are available to help and can help customers obtain the impacted usernames, IP addresses and queries that may have been run. Please contact your account team and reference communication ID ▮▮▮▮▮▮. They can provide additional information and immediate actions that can be taken to prevent potential impact.

Figure 17.2: Snowflake email to customers.

This position lasted for a while, but the system's design and its token structure meant that Catist could still maintain access indefinitely.

Eventually, it became too much. New victims were still emerging into July, and the window for silent access had stretched far beyond what anyone expected. Snowflake finally stepped in, revoking all active sessions and forcing users to reauthenticate with mandatory MFA.

While they never publicly confirmed it, it's reasonable to assume they also invalidated all outstanding tokens during that sweep. This effectively shut Catist out for good.

Crazy, right? But the story gets even better.

Now that you understand *what* was happening, I think it is important to go back and understand *how* they were even able to figure all of this out.

EPAM and Initial Entry Point

Quoting from Mandiant's blog:

> *Mandiant identified that the threat actor used Snowflake customer credentials that were previously exposed via several infostealer malware variants. For the organizations that directly engaged Mandiant for incident response services, Mandiant determined the root cause of their Snowflake instance compromise was exposed credentials. Further, according to Mandiant and Snowflake's analysis, at least 79.7% of the accounts leveraged by the threat actor in this campaign had prior credential exposure.*
>
> *The earliest infostealer infection date observed associated with a credential leveraged by the threat actor dated back to November 2020. In total, Mandiant identified hundreds of customer Snowflake credentials exposed via infostealers since 2020.*

At this point, we know that Catist was accessing Snowflake customer accounts using stolen credentials. One of the issues is that, despite our vast access to infostealers and breached credentials, about 25% of the logins used in these attacks couldn't be identified.

It honestly all seemed very convenient. Catist just *happened* to stumble across a way to access all of these customer instances, simultaneously? It felt like there was more to this story.

I will say this again: It's really funny, going back and looking through all of my chatlogs with Catist. So many small details were missed in the broader chaos.

But true to form, *Catist told me exactly what was going on.*

April 28:

Reddington: so you are saying you attached a VNC client to some sort of malware which you have embedded somewhere?

ellyeI8:   usually I use EASM database I took from them to find host names but it's a few months out of date idk if it'll have everything.

it's like zgrab for

0.0.0.0/0

tho 0-65k

yeah I rat employees at home via spearvishing and spearsmishing and use their work laptops, that's how I hack MSP's

Sometimes I rat their spouse which can be easier, then pivot to them

After examining the network access logs from several victim organizations, it became clear that Victim-4 was actually the first victim (by several days). But how did they know to target Victim-4? I also dismissed the comment in bold as him just flexing.

EPAM

Remington "Remi" Ogletree, 19 years old and a key member of the Scattered Spider group, was arrested in 2024 on charges involving the breach of two telecoms and one American financial institution, to exfiltrate their data and steal crypto currency, totaling $4 million in losses.

Despite being completely unrelated to this story, Remi, following his arrest, told the FBI that *key members of Scattered Spider would target Business Process Outsourcing (BPO) companies* (i.e., third-party contracting firms providing companies with specific services) and had hacked at least five large BPOs, "because outsourcing companies have less security."

EPAM is a BPO firm that develops software and provides various managed services for customers worldwide. One of the core services provided by EPAM is Snowflake account management—customers pay EPAM to help store and analyze their Snowflake data.

EPAM has more than 300 workers who are experienced in using Snowflake's data analytics tools and services, and is considered a Snowflake "Elite Tier Partner."

May 16:

Reddington:	What is a BPO
ellyeI8:	like a contractor
Reddington:	Oh. No shit.
	Ukraine. That's how you did [Victim-2] right? They mentioned something about Ukraine
ellyeI8:	yes
	Ukraine, India, Russia, Brazil
	those are my go-to targets for BPO
Reddington:	Hey just curious. What about [Victim-6] or [Victim-3]. Did you need the BPO to access their snowflake?
ellyeI8:	no i didn't
Reddington:	Gotcha
ellyeI8:	BPO is for [Victim-4] and [Victim-2]
	epam.com

Around this time, Victim-2 was also trying to determine how their own intrusion happened, and they suspected an employee from their BPO firm. In retrospect, as long as I asked the right questions, Catist was extremely forthcoming. He told me that he gained access to Victim-2 and Victim-4 from a BPO contractor out of Ukraine.

In a surprise twist, Catist unexpectedly told me that he found the credentials in a JIRA account related to Victim-4.

ellyeI8:   i dont want to call them yet or for them to know theyre hacked

itll ruin other hacks from this contractor if we tell them rn,

[Victim-4] was literally the first one. bpo outsourcing firm

Reddington: How did you get in from the contractor

Oh a credential

ellyeI8:   atlassian jira\

so i can just look through integrations and also i can read commit messages

At this point, reporter Kim Zetter was working on her story for *Wired*, and we were both actively speaking with Catist. He was enjoying the media attention and literally spewing information.

Victim-4: The First Victim

We were fairly certain that EPAM was the source of the first hacked Snowflake instance. But at this point, we were just trying to get as much information as possible. We still weren't sure how he began with one victim, then somehow pivoted to all of the others.

How did he know how to access all of the Snowflake customer instances?

Reddington: hey for Epam. can you please explain the flow? You were back to hack them via Smish? then you gained access to the network, which gave you snowflake access? but how did you get into the snowflake? using other credentials at that point? what did the EPAM customers have access to?

what else was on their network/

ellyeI8:   epam have been hacked with a spearphishing email containing malware rather than sms phishing for citrix login

Reddington: Ok so spearfishing

Where do you go from there

You have admin which has access to what? Still Citrix? Which does what? Sorry I've never used Citrix

And how did you pivot to snowflake? Or get to other 20 customers?

ellyeI8:   citrix is VDI on corporate lan for external workers to access computers

Reddington:	Got it. Ok so from there you found exposed snowflakes?
	And used creds?
ellye18:	i don't remember specifics bc i don't document everything but think it was saved as plaintext in jira notes or something. some atlassian product for sure tho bc it was blue and java based
Reddington:	wait what do you mean you dont remember specifics. what was saved in jira notes? Who'se JIRA? the contractors or yours?
	can you find the name of the contractor you gained access wth?
ellye18:	i don't think he has that much access, or i didn't discuss BPO's with him at least. I only did snowflakes with him and we started work like a month before I met you
	But I've known him for a long time
Reddington:	can you get me the info on the contractor you used
ellye18:	epam was the contractor
Reddington:	the person
ellye18:	it was a ukrainian IP address i think
	of the machine
	that much I remember
Reddington:	can you get me that IP
	and also, once you were into Citrix, do you initially have access to snowflake? or did you have to use credentials?
ellye18:	oh i didn't use sms phish, no citrix/horizon. spearphish email with malware for epam IA
	probably
Reddington:	you're killing me right now
	how did you gain access to the contractor? Regular email phish?
	please just take a minute and write it out
	where did you go from there
	how did you gain access to the snowflakes or other customers
ellye18:	had plaintext credentials and other shit in their jira
	which is normal anyway
Reddington:	ok so like with [Victim-4]
	you just used those credentials or did you have to find other creds?

ellyeI8:   no just had it in jira

                i didnt need to have more creds to get access

Reddington: ok so i just need the list of companies you found

                that they have access to

This was a monumental conversation. To recap what Catist told me:

- He remotely accessed the machine of an EPAM contractor.
- He was able to access the contractor's JIRA account.
- The contractor—who was a third-party contractor working on Victim-4's system—had their own credentials for accessing Victim-4's system stored in a plaintext note. All Catist had to do was look at it and go.

But wait, there's more.

Reddington: wiat im assuming you no longer have access to these companies, right? if it makes things easier i just need the names of ones you have already hit / cant access anymore

                even if you didnt dump it fully. just ones you accessed

ellyeI8:   I dumped at least 60 companies from snowflake. idk how many i actually dumped tho

Reddington: Not snowflake

                Through Epam contractor access

ellyeI8:   im unsure. i usually don't have these kinds of details

                i don't have some kind of book that i document everything i do in, even if i probably should

Reddington: Ok what about screenshots of jira or copies of the credentials you took? You would have to have these somewhere

                I just need something to validate how you got in

ellyeI8:   oh i didn't screenshot it since i had clipboard. i just copied it as text

Reddington: And you only used it once? Come on.

                You had to persist access in snowflake

                I'm not buying this

ellyeI8:   i logged in on snowflake i thought i said

                using what i had found in jira notes of the contractor

                so i logged in from a 10gbit server

Reddington:	And you had to maintain the connection so you had the creds stored
	Do you have any screenshots or anything to back up that you got the creds from them
ellyeI8:	i was authenticated on the 10gbit server, no need for reverse proxy
Reddington:	Ok so you got in, dumped their AD, got these, then one took you to jira?
ellyeI8:	they were logged into jira in their browser on a localhost domain
	and i went to it and scraped
Reddington:	Ok so you have the jira text?
	Ok so no MfA, right?
ellyeI8:	i don't know if it was mfa since i was using hvnc
	so i never even saw a login page, was already logged in
	thus i have no idea who this person is because i don't have their credentials
Reddington:	Oh. HVNC. So malware gets you direct access to see their screen?
	Oh. Hidden VNC
ellyeI8:	yes
	hidden vnc
	its not the same as createdesktopW version tho, it's novel
	much better, no need to use command line arguments on programs
	can forward GDI draw primitives over an encrypted channel
	to the wire
Reddington:	Thank you!

This conversation laid out the all of the missing pieces. Let me explain how.

How It All Happened

Remember at the very beginning of this book, when I talked about COVID-19 and the rise of the new remote workforce—and how companies needed to suddenly dumb down their security protocols to accommodate this new normal of working remotely? *This is the result.*

Binns and Catist, two active members of Scattered Spider, were targeting BPO outsourcing firms, because, as one member put it, "outsourcing companies have less security." Their attack vector was straight forward—they researched contractors and sent out a series of phishing emails.

At this point, either the contractor or his girlfriend—while using their personal computer—fell for the bait and installed the Remote Access Trojan (RAT), which contained an Hidden Virtual Network Computing (HVNC) client.

VNC is a tool that enables a user to control their computer desktop from a remote location. It mirrors the computer's actual desktop session and enables the user to take over the keyboard and mouse. When using a VNC, the person at the computer can see exactly what the remote user is doing, because they are hijacking control of the machine's keyboard and mouse.

Instead of hijacking the victim's active desktop session, an HVNC client launches a separate, hidden desktop in the background—completely invisible to the user. The attacker gets their own virtual workspace inside the victim's machine, where they can open browsers, move files, execute commands, and even log into websites—all without triggering a single window or alert on the real user's screen.

Even though the victim's laptop may have had reduced security controls (because it was a personal device), the one thing it did have was a *VPN client securely connecting the laptop to the EPAM network.*

With access to an undetectable remote desktop on the victim's machine, the hackers were able to access any of EPAM's internal systems while connected to the company's VPN.

One of those systems was JIRA, a project management and issue tracking tool. They were able to log in and out of JIRA without further authentication, because the user was already logged in. All they had to do was open a browser and visit the URL, which they found by looking at the browser's history.

Once they had access to JIRA, they looked around and found something that would set the stage for this entire saga: plaintext login credentials to `[victim-4].snowflakecomputing.com`.

The Big Ah-Ha Moment

This was the big ah-ha moment:

```
[victim-4].snowflakecomputing.com.
```

Catist and Binns didn't *just* stumble onto credentials that enabled them access to Victim-4's `snowflakecomputing.com` instance using nothing more than a password—with no additional checks.

What they realized was that *every* Snowflake customer was assigned a domain ending in `snowflakecomputing.com`—*and none of them required MFA.*

Now the process was as simple as looking for new victims by searching for credentials to `snowflakecomputing.com` domains in their vast database of infostealers and malware logs—which gave them hundreds, if not thousands, of potential targets.

The process of going through each victim, one by one, and manually downloading all their data would have been too slow and inefficient. So, Catist did what any hacker would do and wrote a script to automate the entire process. He called it *Rapeflake.*

ellyeI8:   this snowflake rape flake was literally just messing around hence why i called it "rapeflake" and dumped like 50 companies from a single cogent vlan

Confirming Catist's Story ... with Infostealer Logs

This was all a great story, but until we received confirmation from EPAM, that's all this was—a story. EPAM had not engaged with Mandiant, and not surprisingly, they were unwilling to confirm or make any comments to Zetter or *Wired*.

I have discussed infostealer malware throughout this book. One of its key features is that, in addition to stealing stored usernames and passwords, infostealers also steal browser history and favorites.

It Was a Million to One Shot, Doc!

As it turns out, the same contractor that fell victim to Catist's phishing email and installed the malicious HVNC software *already* had infostealer malware running on that same laptop.

Continuing to read from Mandiant's initial June report:

> *In several Snowflake related investigations, Mandiant observed that the initial compromise of* **infostealer malware occurred on contractor systems that were also used for personal activities**, *including gaming and downloads of pirated software.*
>
> *Contractors that customers engage to assist with their use of Snowflake may utilize personal and/or non-monitored laptops that exacerbate this initial entry vector. These devices, often used to access the systems of multiple organizations, present a significant risk. If compromised by infostealer malware, a single contractor's laptop can facilitate threat actor access across multiple organizations, often with IT and administrator-level privileges.*

A search through our own infostealer collection for epam.com revealed the browser history for the *exact user* Catist previously mentioned.

Here is a sample of the user's browser history. I have highlighted some of the relevant URLs for reference.

```
http://ajcp-jenkins01.corp.ad.ctc:8080/login
http://andreys-mbp.kyiv.epam.com:2990/jira/secure/Dashboard.jspa
http://artifactory.kyiv.epam.com/artifactory/webapp/
http://ecsa00400765.epam.com:8080/login
http://ecsc00a01d68.epam.com:8080/securityRealm/createAccountByAdmin
http://ecsc00a01d68.epam.com:9000/sessions/new
http://escorials-mbp.kyiv.epam.com:2990/jira/secure/Dashboard.jspa
http://forum.gorod.dp.ua/showthread.php
http://gerrit.fpos.kyiv.epam.com/login/%23%2Fq%2Fstatus%3Aopen
http://jenkins.fpos.kyiv.epam.com/login
https://access.epam.com/auth/realms/plusx/protocol/openid-connect/auth
https://account.battle.net/login/ru/
https://account.blizzard.com/security
https://acs.privatbank.ua/pPaReqMC.jsp
https://confluence.livenation.com/login.action
https://ctc.epam.com/
https://kb.epam.com/dologin.action
https://login.epam.com/
```

Let this be a lesson to you—*don't install pirated software!*

EPAM's Response(s)

Following the publication of Kim Zetter's *Wired* story, "Hackers Detail How They Allegedly Stole Ticketmaster Data from Snowflake,"[2] EPAM released a statement denying the allegations, suggesting that Catist's claims were fabricated.

In their public statement (see Figure 17.3), EPAM emphasized that their investigations, both internal and *with Mandiant*, found no evidence supporting the claims made in the *Wired* article.

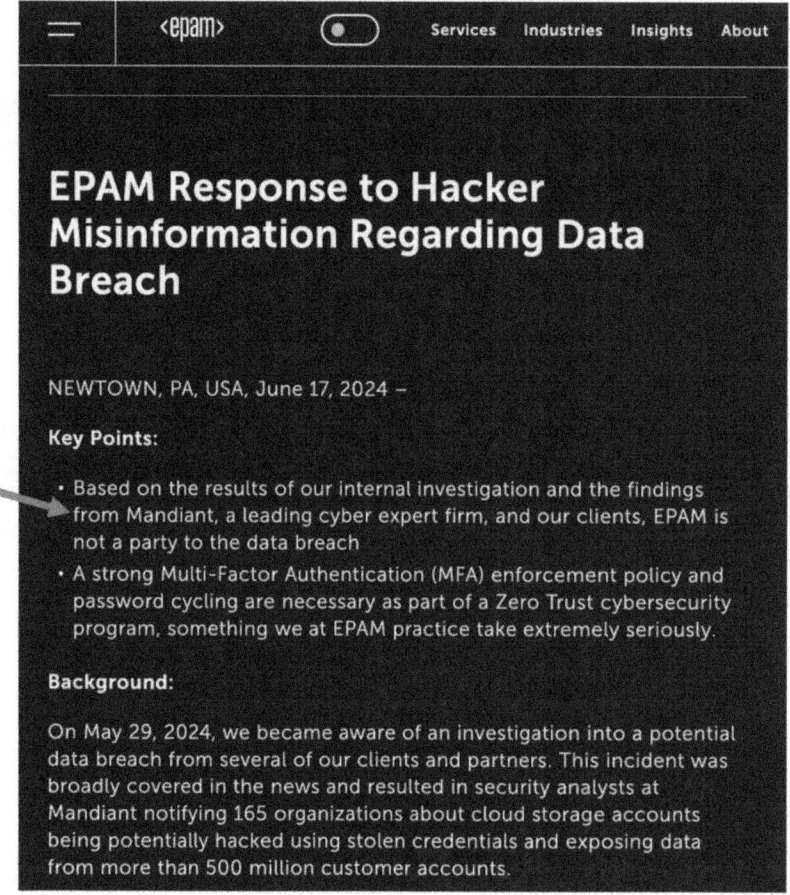

Figure 17.3: EPAM's response to Zetter's *Wired* story.

What made this statement exceptionally interesting is that *EPAM never engaged with Mandiant*, nor did Mandiant issue any public statements to this effect. Zetter was also able to independently confirm that EPAM never engaged with Mandiant.

After a few days, EPAM released an updated blog post (see Figure 17.4), removing references to any statements or findings made by Mandiant.

---

[2] https://www.wired.com/story/epam-snowflake-ticketmaster-breach-shinyhunters/

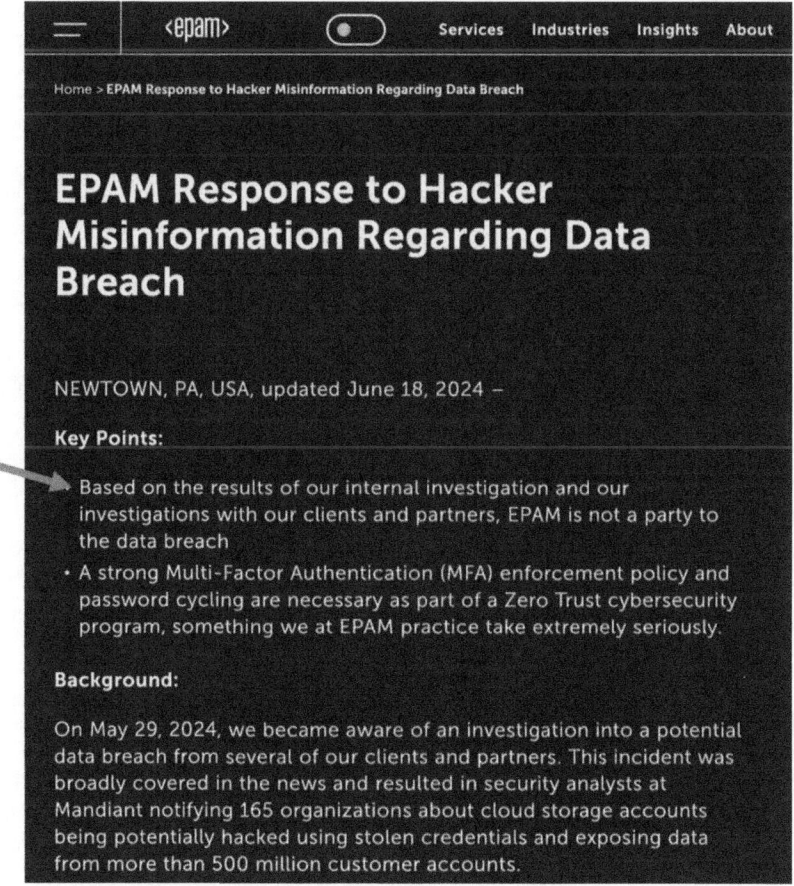

Figure 17.4: Revised EPAM statement.

To date, *EPAM has never publicly acknowledged the breach.*

With that, we now have the majority of the story mapped out. There was just one *tiny* unsolved question. Earlier I mentioned that despite having access to massive collections of credentials and infostealer collections, we couldn't identify the origin of a significant portion of the credentials used to access the Snowflake organizations.

So, where did the credentials come from?

Origin of the Stolen Credentials

Continuing Mandiant's blog post:

> *Based on our investigations to date, [Scattered Spider] obtained access to multiple organizations' Snowflake customer instances via stolen customer credentials. These credentials were primarily obtained from multiple infostealer malware campaigns that infected non-Snowflake owned systems. This allowed the threat actor to gain access to the affected customer accounts and led*

to the export of a significant volume of customer data from the respective Snowflake customer instances. The threat actor has subsequently begun to extort many of the victims directly and is actively attempting to sell the stolen customer data on recognized cybercriminal forums.

Mandiant identified that the majority of the credentials used by [Scattered Spider] were available from historical infostealer infections, some of which dated as far back as 2020.

Stolen credentials pose a serious security risk to organizations and were the fourth most notable initial intrusion vector in 2023, as 10% of intrusions began with stolen credentials. Attackers often obtain credentials due to password reuse, or users inadvertently downloading Trojanized software on corporate or personal devices. The prevalence of both widespread infostealer malware and credential purchasing continues to challenge defenders.

Mandiant's public statement paints a clear picture of how this breach occurred using stolen credentials.

But humor me for a second—wouldn't it be *absolutely crazy* if the credentials used to access Snowflake customers instances were stolen from an international Computer Emergency Response Team (CERT)?

And wouldn't it be even more absurd if the way that Catist was able to gain access to those credentials was by purchasing access to a CERT employee's machine who had been infected with a Remote Access Trojan—who also shared a fondness for downloading pirated software?

Ratting a CERT Polska Employee

CERT Polska is a computer security incident response team (CISRT) responsible for handling security incidents in Poland. Since its launch, the core of the team's activity has involved handling security incidents and cooperation with similar units worldwide. CERT Polska also conducts extensive security-related research and development (R&D).

May 28:

Reddington:	how did you get access to the logs from [redacted] ? that's interesting
ellyeI8:	no they only had a few billion logs
	i ratted Polska CERT
	for most of them
	a Polska CERT emp
Reddington:	What's that
	A few billion logs …? So you took all of their redline and stealer creds?
ellyeI8:	probably. i just merge them tho
	other than the polska ones which are from trickbot

Catist's main assertion is that he stole the credentials from CERT Polska. He told me this pretty much right away, but given the enormity of what he was saying, I honestly assumed he was lying.

Yet, the following conversation would also suggest that CERT Polska did, in fact, have access to the credentials from a coordinated takedown of Trickbot.

June 05:

Reddington:	so he gave you the cred that you used?
ellyel8:	no, i got my creds from Polska CERT
Reddington:	thats what i thought
ellyel8:	from their trickbot takedown

Analyzing the Evidence

Let me start by saying, I don't have *concrete evidence*. I do, however, have a lot of interesting details that line up to paint a very vivid picture.

Throughout this book, I've listed more than a few examples showing that Catist always told me the truth. *I can't find one single instance where he lied to me about anything, ever, even his location!*

All those details were to set the stage leading up to this very instance where I don't have concrete evidence, but looking at all of the evidence, I *know* he was telling the truth.

Ask yourself this: What's more plausible? That he would make up and keep consistently telling me this *one* lie about ratting an employee at CERT Polska, or that he was simply telling the truth?

It's up to you to decide, but either way, here are some additional details to consider.

IcedID

First identified in 2017 as a banking Trojan, IcedID was primarily used to steal financial information through web injection attacks and credential harvesting. With the rise of ransomware-as-a-service (RaaS) ecosystems, IcedID shifted roles from direct theft to becoming a loader that delivered payloads like Trickbot.

Reddington:	any chance i can get a sample of the CERT credential data? like even 50 lines
	i have a theory i want to test
ellyel8:	i can do lookups if you have a domain or ip address you want searched
Reddington:	no its more about seeing the original format
	i want to compare it with something
ellyel8:	no def not since i have source code too
Reddington:	source code for what
ellyel8:	the bot they tookdown
	some icedid thing

Reddington:	https://www.team-cymru.com/post/tracking-bokbot-icedid-infrastructuremapping-a-vast-and-currently-active-icedid-network
	this?
ellyel8:	this was like a year ago and yes that but not the stego one
	the stego one i'd want to see how they implemented it
ellyel8:	**if they know I hacked Polska CERT they will just assume I'm emotet botmaster** and then they will send like 50000 DHS and Secret Service agents to look for me
Reddington:	That's not what the diagram shows
ellyel8:	he hacked them as well though
Reddington:	I don't care about any of that.
	seriously. Where did the credentials come from?
ellyel8:	well i know the Mandiant are very surprised that they didn't have most of the credentials I used and not even in their tg scrapes did they find them. So for example I have 8400 unique snowflake fqdn strings
	*.snowflakecomputing.com
	in my logs, this is out of like 9800 customers, so it can be assumed that most companies I have a way in just as credentials but also recon so its really good and far bigger than hudsonrock even
Reddington:	And that's great about the size but the question is where it came from. I'm not so sure about Polska anymore
	I just need something I can show them to validate the story
ellyel8:	I can show picture of bot panel later I guess. when are you speaking to them
Reddington:	How does that show that the creds came from Polska?
ellyel8:	that I have c2 for the icedid
	I also have builder and sourcecode

Based on these last few lines, it sounds like Catist is claiming to have access to the IcedID command and control panel, which potentially gave him access to any infected victims.

According to a few independent malware researchers, IcedID makes sense in this context because it was primarily used as a malware loader. If Catist had access to the command and control (C2) panel, he could have accessed any potential credentials or infostealer data that flowed through any of the victim machines.

Connection to Genesis Market

Worth noting, this story seems even more plausible because Catist and Binns also leveraged these stolen credentials to make a considerable amount of money on Genesis Market.

Reddington:	want to trade your CERT DB for **?
ellyel8:	no i cant trade genesis market db for something under $5m usd
Reddington:	genesis market?
	i thought it was CERT?
	if its genesis i don't care about it. it was interesting when it was POLSKA cert
	plus you said it was VMs
ellyel8:	yes its an OVA of the data that Polska CERT also has
	i can sell for 5m
ellyel8:	we made over 5m
ellyel8:	per month
	from genesis

Bringing It All Together

Going back through my logs, I found this message all the way back in May. This is the earliest mention of Trickbot and Poland, and it clearly spells out the entire incident in one clean message.

May 13:

Reddington:	how are you targeting that
ellyel8:	i would start by crosswalking to the main owa table and then searching every domain attached to their **OWA tenant within the 17TB of trickbot .xz webinjects/formgrabber data I paid a Polish cop for, bc they seized one of the servers**. most likely they've already been infected bc they like free ebooks in africa and india.
	if they don't exist in that 2017-2021 data then the easiest way is to hire a BPO they've used and then trojan source them. i've done this a lot and it's so easy to rat ppl on upwork.com

To add context, we were talking about how Catist was able to search for Snowflake customer credentials. He volunteered that he found them by searching through the *17TB of Trickbot form data* that he was able to acquire after *purchasing access to a Polish cop's* (i.e., the CERT employee) workstation.

The CERT employee had access to the data following the seizure of the Trickbot servers. He also shared that this employee was most likely infected because he download pirated eBooks.

And wouldn't you know it, in 2021, Europol put out a statement about the combined efforts of several international agencies to their combined disruption of EMOTET, a global malware infrastructure.

According to the article:[3]

> The EMOTET infrastructure essentially acted as a primary door opener for computer systems on a global scale. Once this unauthorized access was established, these were sold to other top-level criminal groups to deploy further illicit activities such as data theft and extortion through ransomware.
>
> EMOTET is said to be one of the biggest players in the cybercrime world as other malware operators like Trickbot and Ryuk have benefited from it.

And just like that, everything lines up—from beginning to compromise.

Summary

This chapter provided a full analysis of the Snowflake breach, starting with how we uncovered that customers were being targeted through their connection to the platform. It walked through how Catist maintained persistent access, the events that triggered the first wave of customer compromises, and the mechanics behind how the attackers acquired the credentials they needed to carry it all out.

From access to automation, I've now laid out the full anatomy of the breach. What began as scattered victim reports ultimately revealed a single point of failure—and the playbook that made this one of the largest data theft campaigns in recent memory.

The next chapter weaves in the next wave of victims—how they were discovered, how they responded to breach notifications, and what unfolded in the gaps between each major event. These cases reveal just how far the ripple effects of the Snowflake intrusion reached, and how differently each company chose to handle the fallout.

---

[3] https://www.europol.europa.eu/media-press/newsroom/news/world%E2%80%99s-most-dangerous-malware-emotet-disrupted-through-global-action

Breach Timelines and Disclosures

According to Mandiant, roughly 165 companies were impacted by the Snowflake breach. The FBI later confirmed that many of these organizations had experienced unauthorized access to their cloud environments, all linked to the same threat actors. Victims were targeted using a tool known as Rapeflake, and in most cases, extortion attempts followed—often accompanied by samples of stolen data as proof of access.

This chapter focuses on those victims and the extortion campaigns that followed. It walks through how ransom negotiations unfolded across eight organizations, examining how each company responded, the choices they made, and the outcomes they faced. It also explores the internal friction between the threat actors themselves and explains how those dynamics impacted the victims.

Finally, this chapter analyzes the legal requirements surrounding breach notification, comparing how each company disclosed, delayed, or completely avoided disclosing their breach to the public.

This chapter features commentary from:

M. Scott Koller
Privacy and Data Security Attorney, Clark Hill PLC

The views expressed in my quotes or comments are provided for general educational and informational purposes only and do not constitute legal advice. My statements do not create an attorney-client relationship, and readers should consult with their own legal counsel regarding any specific legal questions or concerns. Any opinions expressed are my own, and not necessarily those of Clark Hill.

Victim Breach Timeline

To convey the speed and urgency with which these events unfolded, I will present the different breach victims in the order they were discovered, alongside relevant chat logs and dark web forum posts that surfaced along the way. This approach is meant to show how each case unfolded in real time, and how rapidly things escalated.

To put this chapter in perspective, I just learned about the Victim-2 breach in mid-April. At the beginning of May, we were still trying to figure out who had access to what systems—and how much data had actually been stolen—when this new wave of information started pouring in.

May 6: Voter Data/Law Firm

One of first breaches tied directly to Catist involved something particularly sensitive: U.S. voter data. He gained access to a storage bucket containing full voter registration records for 43 U.S. states—names, addresses, dates of birth, voter IDs—the works.

There was never any public announcement. No acknowledgment. The company responsible wouldn't even respond to my emails. They chose to ignore it completely, seemingly hoping the problem would just disappear. They were right.

Reddington:	Why do you think this is voter data
	Voter data doesn't have passwords
	It's also free. You can get the lists from every state's website. This doesn't look like voter data though.
	Can you send me 10 or 20 full records?
catist:	no, that's the admin
	of the site
	[3 More Victims] are the companies that were hacked

As I note soon, I continued to do my best to keep his attention away from any data related to U.S. persons.

catist:	some are really rare like WV and TN and VA
	would it be better to sell to a data broker?
Reddington:	No
	I won't get involved in selling any Us data. And again, I promise
	it's practically worthless
catist:	yeah i figured it was since most of the states are public

Reddington:	Can you send me details of the server you got into? Where the data came from? I will reach out tomorrow
catist:	yeah i can find it. it might still be open but its another postgresql backed graph
	[Political Victim-1] a 501(c)(4)
Reddington:	What else was there
	Just the voter data?
catist:	the voter data and the users for some of their admins
	they seem like intel officers or mafia
Reddington:	It's a political PAC
Reddington:	The first thing you sent me was a user for [Legal Victim-1]. Is that how you got into the system?
	And are you sure it's [Political Victim-1]?
catist:	okay so i hacked Azure in december, and microsoft bought RiskIQ. so i had access to their cosmos and i dumped everything and i decided to target apollo graphql just as a test. thats from apollo and that is the tenant im pretty sure. but those are the people with apollo perms for that
Reddington:	So that data came from Apollo the company?
catist:	the access came from apollo but its from yhat tenant
Reddington:	Please explain. The access came from Apollo?
catist:	i have more data than censys ngl and one sec
	https://www.apollographql.com/
Reddington:	You came in through the tenant?
catist:	yeah
Reddington:	Which was who?
catist:	ill find it in banners. like zgrab
Reddington:	Ok. And which account did you use to gain access?
catist:	jwt refrehs token
	for the admin
Reddington:	Who is the admin
	That's what I'm trying to get to
catist:	the first one in the list the ac@ something about [Political Victim-1]

Catist sent over a full user list from the system—a JSON file that looked a lot like a credentials dump from the authentication service Authy. It included every user in the environment, along with flags indicating who did and didn't have multifactor authentication (MFA) enabled. This was the perfect file for quickly selecting which members of an organization to target.

In the chaos of everything else going on, this slipped through the cracks. But the key point is this: Complete 2024 voter registration data for 43 U.S. states was stolen. The company responsible chose not to disclose or acknowledge any part of it—and no one seemed to care.

May 19: Victim-2 Payment

By May 19, the Victim-2 extortion payment had been completed, along with all related events covered in the previous chapters leading up to this point. There's nothing new to add here—this entry is included solely for timeline reference.

May 23: Victim-3 (Retail)

Continuing to reference Moucka's official arrest document:

Victim-3 is a major retailer located in the United States. On or about May 23, 2024, a well-known computer security and incident response company notified Victim-3 that it was a potential victim of a similar computer intrusion. On May 29, 2024, representatives from Victim-3 met with the FBI and confirmed that three categories of its information had been stolen from its cloud instance, including customer information for approximately 20 million customers, gift card information, and internal company business documents. Victim-3 also stated that it was actively negotiating through the same intermediary, [Reddington], that negotiated with Victim-2.

The FBI also reviewed logs provided by [Reddington], which indicated that Victim-3's instance was accessed without authorization from approximately April 14, 2024, through May 24, 2024 and that the rapeflake utility was deployed on Victim-3's computer systems.

Victim-3 hired an incident response company to investigate the breach and confirmed its instance had been compromised using stolen login credentials belonging to a former contractor located outside the United States.

According to the incident response firm's investigation, this former contractor's credential was likely compromised via a credential stealer in approximately 2021 and available in cybercriminal marketplaces as early as May 2021.

On May 24, 2024, two members of Victim-3's information security team were contacted via LinkedIn by [Reddington], who used his true name. [Reddington] offered to broker a deal with the hacker and provided a sample of the data. [Reddington] later requested a phone call with Victim-3 and spoke to Victim-3's counsel.

This was the start of a slow (but positive) negotiation to keep Victim-3's data secure. I was able to quickly establish communication with them, and they had expressed an interest in paying Catist to keep their data safe.

May 27: Auto and Insurance Companies

catist:	[Auto Victim-1] and [Insurance Victim-1] are both dumping rn. are you allowed to sell it? or would it have to be sold back to them bc it's american.
	this pravaler sites dumping too, 85 million brazilian students. idk if they have any products in the other countries around them tho maybe
	https://www.crunchbase.com/organization/pravaler
	and two big retailers, [Victim-3] and [unknown] are dumping
Reddington:	[Auto Victim-1] is huge
	What data is there
catist:	looks to be all of it.
	there are 300k files in the s3 for "customer_raw" alone
	there are cards too
Reddington:	Wow. I don't know you need all 12tb. Maybe don't download all of it
catist:	alright
	also there's VIN's
catist:	ngl this is equifax level. except im not a dumb webapp tranny that finds an exploit by accident
	do they have a parent? i don't think they can afford what would be acceptable for this data if they're just on their own
	or actually, since it has progressive, farmers, allstate, usaa, liberty etc data i guess they can do a group buy
Reddington:	wait
	What
	What are you talking about
catist:	[Insurance victim-1]

Reddington:	it has insurance data?
catist:	i dumped their partners
	yes
	thats what this is
	it's [Insurance Victim-1]
	for insurance quotes
	and also tells u if they have insurance already
	etc

This was a lot to take in. Two more major companies had been compromised. One was a well-known auto repair and retail chain. The other—a software-as-a-service (SaaS) platform owned by a public company—was even more significant because it was an application used by nearly every auto insurance broker in the U.S. to generate online auto insurance quotes.

This gave Catist access to an enormous volume of sensitive information on hundreds of millions of U.S. citizens. Think about what an auto insurance provider knows about you—personal details, driver's license numbers, driving history, traffic violations, arrest records—everything that feeds into a risk profile.

Catist now had all of it.

May 29: Conversations with Victim-3

As I mentioned, the conversations with Victim-3 were generally positive. There was some negotiation around money, but their top priority was keeping the entire incident quiet.

Anyone who's worked in incident response or breach negotiations knows this isn't unusual. Some companies make the conscious decision never to disclose a breach—ever. I've had firms explicitly request that no final report be written, solely to avoid creating a paper trail. In other cases, I've had legal teams draft specialized contracts for "alternative consulting services" just to obscure any documentation that might even hint an incident took place.

That's just the nature of this business. Ultimately, it's up to the company—and its board—to decide how they want to handle a breach, regardless of any legal obligations. And more often than people realize, the decision is to say nothing. In the case of Victim-3, that appeared to be the path they were considering.

May 30: Too Many Cooks

Still regarding Victim-3, the arrest document states:

> On May 29, 2024, [Reddington] indicated that he thought they "could close around $275,000."
> Then, on or about May 30, 2024, Reddington emailed Victim-3 that the threat actor wanted $450,000. Reddington subsequently informed Victim-3 that another victim had paid a substantial ransom.

As if this process wasn't complicated enough, Catist decided that I wasn't moving fast enough and wanted to bring in help from someone with *experience extorting organizations*: ShinyHunters.

catist	Shiny has sold [Victim-5] to the ransomware group for 1.5m and they have strong connections to the CC vendors, and BEC gangs. they are interested in data with SSN's and the previous sample from before with pseudorandomization has had them offer me 600k for the [Victim-3] data because it has SSN last 4's and AVS data. so the 250k I'm no longer interested in and it will be much more expensive for [Victim-3] if they can't come up with a better offer than that. I can continue to shop around too for more offers
	I have lines of communication to the admin of rescator and the admin of krebs dumps as well but I haven't approached them yet. I also have some ppl who run SSNDOB site who'd love to buy tho, because as I showed it has 20m + last 4's and thats all I need
	You have 48 hours to find a better deal from Neiman because they're up against a competitive market, and the shop will be open for wholesale orders from the top CC shops on the planet if they can't find the fair price for my data security tariff

I call bull.

First, I know for a fact, that Shiny didn't sell the [Victim-5] data for $1.5M, because I spoke to the potential buyer, and he was a scammer.

I also don't believe there has *ever* been a database in history that has sold for more than a few hundred thousand dollars. Absolutely nowhere near $1.5M. I saw the data; this wasn't going to break any records.

Second, if he had the ability to sell any of this data himself for $600,000, he would have. I saw the Victim-3 data. It contained 11 of the 16 card numbers (with five middle digits missing).

No one is buying that data—*it's worthless.*

But okay, if he wants to try and create urgency, all I can do is pass along his messages. So I emailed Victim-3 and let them know that the actor now wanted $450,000 plus a reduced timeline.

May 31: Unexpected Blog Post

As I mentioned in the previous chapter, news of the Snowflake hack started making its way into the media cycle after a blog post from a small security company—one that specializes in aggregating and selling access to breached credentials. This is how it unfolded.

Reddington:	https://www.hudsonrock.com/blog/snowflake-massive-breach-access-through-infostealer-infection
	Why would you talk to him at all
	This is going to fuck up everything
	These companies wanted to stay quiet

catist:	i was having him deliver the demands to the head of snowflake security
Reddington:	Asshole!
	I have been talking to them
	I am not lying to you
catist:	yeah but it makes it more likely theyll pay if multiple sources confirm it doesn't it?
Reddington:	No
	Snowflake isn't giving you money
	That's not even a discussion
	But now all the other companies he called out are probably going to tell you to fuck off
	If he listed [Victim-3] the deal would be dead
	He needs to remove that post
	Why the fuck would you share all of that with him
catist:	thought it'd make it more likely snowflake pays if he confirms the victims to the snowflake team

Despite my repeated attempts to ground him in reality, Catist was still under the delusion that Snowflake was going to pay him $10 million to "stop hacking them."

So, he did what any immature person does when they don't want to face reality—he found someone else who told him exactly what he wanted to hear.

Reddington:	Bro. He fucked you
	You can't justify this.
	He needs to pull the post
	If you want any chance of making money on those companies
catist:	im not trying to justify it, im trying to keep you from killing the deal with overreacting.
	also you can use EASM to see the hostname records of snowflakecomputing

Victim-3 told me they were paying for silence. But once the media picked up the trail of victim companies, that was no longer an option—and the deal was dead. The court document states:

After several email exchanges and at least one telephone call with [Reddington], Victim-3 ceased communications.

I should look into moonlighting as a psychic.

Also, just to be clear—I'm not insinuating that Victim-3 was trying to cover up the breach. They were paying for silence so the information could be released on their terms—similar to how Victim-2 handled it.

June 1: Insurance Victim Post

By this point, the cat was out of the bag. A lot of people were trying to locate Catist, and he was becoming increasingly erratic and difficult to manage. He wanted money. Fast.

Unfortunately, the auto insurance victim wasn't responding to my messages (at least not politely), so Catist took matters into his own hands and listed the data for sale on BreachForums (see Figure 18.1).

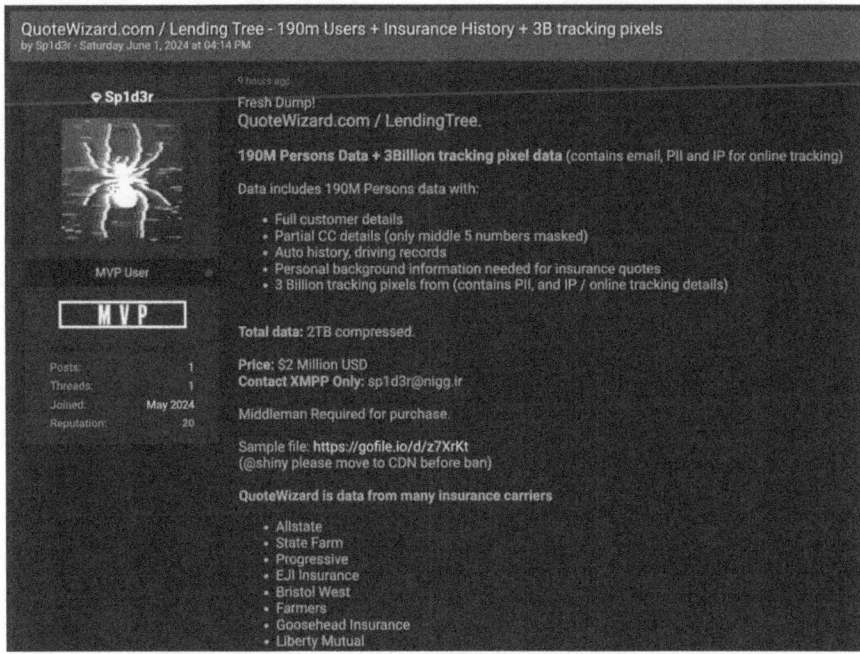

Figure 18.1: BreachForums thread for Insurance Victim-1.

June 3: K–12 Student Data and New Hackers

Next on the list was a Los Angeles school district, whereby 26 million student records of children in grades K–12 were leaked.

No one ever officially admitted to this either. The data was very clear about who the owner was, and despite containing the personal details, Social Security numbers (SSNs), and medical and psychological reports for roughly 26 million students, the company took the approach of just ignoring the situation.

What no one accounted for, however, was that a second—and completely unrelated— hacker would gain access to the same Snowflake instance, steal the data, and launch their own extortion attempt by listing it for sale on BreachForums. For reference, Mandiant tracks this actor as UNC6040.

As word spread about how Catist had been accessing Snowflake environments, other hackers began scanning for vulnerable instances. Unfortunately, Snowflake still hadn't implemented a solution to lock down access, so intrusions continued.

When no one purchased the data, the new actor leaked it online—for free.

June 5: A Managed Service Provider

In the previous chapter, I showed a text conversation where Catist claimed to have accessed another managed service provider (MSP). It technically wasn't an MSP, but he appeared to have access to quite a lot of new companies.

catist:	what is **********.com
	i have just done the biggest MSP hack
	i think
	this is bigger than snowflake
	but snowflake is the entrypoint
	which is funny
Reddington:	impossible
catist:	are u sure
	its vmware company p sure
Reddington:	i wish you would stop with the US companies
catist:	[Listing of clients provided]
Reddington:	FACEBOOK ?!? are you kidding me
catist:	want me to go in their tenant? ik how now
	everything is stored as a blob
	inside a document
	so each file in their storage i can view using their table
Reddington:	thats your call
	actually i would advise against it
catist:	i dont have enough storage for facebooks data anyway
	if theres any exchanges, i can probably get cold wallet keys
	bc this is cold storage
	this is more useful for identifying the tenants imo
	just tell me which ones not to touch and i wont but avoid alerting any of them about this msp for a few days. preferably when ur vacation is over
	but there are some crazy ones in here

Reddington: DO NOT TOUCH ANYTHING WITH .MIL

also stay away from US banks

honestly, please stay away from anything US right now   especially .MIL

For reference, the list he provided included more than 3,000 tenants (customers) of this company—everything ranging from tech giants to banks, and even government and military sites. Here's a small sample of a few that immediately stood out:

```
ldaps://aa-lds-prod.hk.hsbc:3269
ldaps://APGRA1NEP000001.nae.ds.army.mil:636
ldaps://c27mrawcrnadc2.corona.navy.mil
ldaps://cha-dc-02.mis.gov
ldaps://dc01.tme.nvidia.com
ldaps://ddmtdc001.med.ds.osd.mil
ldaps://demchadc02a.ad001.siemens.net:636
ldaps://gc.nena.wdpr.disney.com
ldaps://gc.pfizer.com:3269
ldaps://gcsldap.apple.com
ldaps://ldap.thefacebook.com
ldaps://navseahq.navy.mil
ldaps://NGNYA1D300V.ng.ds.army.mil
ldaps://NGNYA1D301V.ng.ds.army.mil
ldaps://nren.navy.mil
ldaps://nren.navy.mil:3269
```

Of course, the moment we saw this list of sites, we immediately notified the company. They took quick action to try and kick him out—but Catist kept refreshing his master API key and getting back in.

He was ultimately able to exfiltrate some of the company's internal data, but he was never able to access any of the tenant accounts.

But that didn't stop this victim from paying a ransom for continued silence. They announced the breach, but it went completely unnoticed in the sea of other data breaches being announced.

And for those who've claimed that I "partner" with Catist—or other criminals—in order to profit from negotiation fees: this case says otherwise. The victim explicitly told me they didn't want to pay my fee and would handle the ransom negotiations themselves.

They reached out to Reddington directly via XMPP (not realizing it was me), and I still helped them through the process—free of charge.

One upside to the situation was that Catist now had more money coming in—enough to ease the pressure and keep the flow of victim intel coming my way.

June 7: Auto Insurance Victim Announcement

The dominoes were starting to fall. One by one, companies began issuing their breach announcements. The auto insurance victim released the following statement:

We can confirm that we use Snowflake for our business operations, and that we were notified by them that our subsidiary, [Victim App], may have had data impacted by this incident.

We take these matters seriously, and immediately after hearing from [Snowflake] launched an internal investigation. As of this time, it does not appear that consumer financial account information was impacted, nor information of the parent entity, [Victim Company].

And believe it or not, that was it from this company. Despite having hundreds of millions of records stolen, they never issued a formal breach notification. Their only public statement was that they had "launched an internal investigation."

catist:	****** is just snowflake. i didn't bother breaching onprem bc i haven't decided if i want to lock them or not, the data is complete enough for a ransom
Reddington:	was this related to snowflake or not
catist:	yes
Reddington:	i think thats how they are denying
	ok then from snowflake how did you pivot
	was the password stored somewhere
catist:	here's their snowflake
	[sample provided]
catist:	i did no lateral movement for [Victim]
	just snowflake
Reddington:	ok but how did you make the jump
catist:	i did no lateral movement for [Victim]
	just snowflake
Reddington:	oh
catist:	I made sure to switch my role according to masking policies depending on the table
	so it's full unmasked
	and this is undeniable proof that the customer is [Victim]
Reddington:	right now they arent talking to me
	and it sounds like they are denying any PII was stolen
	which is incredible
catist:	thats interesting bc the account i dumped it from was literally called PII_READER
	and funny af
	the fact that I knew how to do this and specifically dumped unmasked PII should clear any doubts they had

I have a lot more to say about the company's so-called "internal investigation"—but I'll save that for the next section on breach notifications.

June 13: Preparing Taylor Swift Tickets

At some point, Catist had the bright idea to leak Taylor Swift event barcodes as a way to pressure Victim-4 and push them toward paying a ransom.

catist:	alright
	also for [Victim-4] i was thinking if they don't pay on friday that i'd post taylor swift ticket barcodes on exploit and
	xss.is
	like 100k of them for upcoming concerts
Reddington:	you do or do not have barcodes of taylor swift events?
catist:	i have all barcodes
Reddington:	Are you able to search by artist
catist:	i can by order then by sales id
	then get barcodes for specific event
	so are you telling me they dont know what data i have either?
	and is my 17 btc ready for the deal today?
	they get to see the entire barode table posted into starchat if its not ready today. i thought thats why i mentioned the barcodes yesterday?
	and you only wanted to see what they look like

Nothing came of those messages at the time, so I assumed he either couldn't find the barcodes or was just bluffing. Once again, he wasn't.

June 24: Victim-3 Breach Statement

On June 24, Victim-3 made their official breach announcement:

In May 2024, we learned that, between April and May 2024, an unauthorized third party gained access to a database platform used by [Victim-3]. Based on our investigation, the unauthorized third party obtained certain personal information stored in the database platform.

Promptly after discovering the incident, NMG took steps to contain it, including by disabling access to the platform. We also began an investigation with assistance from leading cybersecurity experts and notified law enforcement authorities.

The types of personal information affected varied by individual, and included information such as name, contact information, date of birth, and [Victim-3] gift card number(s) (without gift card PINs).

This was a tough pill for Catist to swallow. He was sitting on nearly 60 million records from this company—yet they publicly claimed that only 60,000 had been affected.

Reddington:	[Victim-3] put out a statement. Only 60k people affected.
catist:	so then they lied
Reddington:	No. According to the law you don't have what counts as PII
catist:	uh, theres 30m SSN's
	it came from their tenant
Reddington:	Not full
catist:	14 is all that matters
Reddington:	Nope
	Not according to the law
catist:	PCI allows storing the first 6 and last 4 digits of a credit card,
	enjoy fines for 1.8m crds

Catist was convinced that the fines each company would have to pay for Personally Identifiable Information (PII) disclosures or Payment Card Industry (PCI) violations would be astronomical compared to the amounts he was asking for. He was wrong—there were no fines. I explain this shortly.

In the meantime, you can imagine how this news would've affected someone with little to no sleep propped up on amphetamines.

June 27: Victim-3 Leak

Back to the official arrest warrant:

> *In or about June 2024, a co-conspirator created a post on BreachForums and stated they were making the Victim-3 database available for download after Victim-3's refusal to pay a ransom. The FBI discovered this post, which included a link for download. The FBI accessed this link and downloaded approximately 10.6 GB of compressed materials. When unpacked, the data was approximately 86.1 GB and contained numerous files with filenames that matched queries run by the threat actors in [Reddington]'s logs for Victim-3's instance. The FBI downloaded the data from BreachForums and verified that it was consistent with the information from Victim-3's investigation. Specifically, the downloaded data included customer names, emails, billing addresses, personal identifying information, purchase information, and full gift card numbers with expiration dates.*
>
> *As part of ongoing extortion efforts involving Victim-3 data, a co-conspirator posted on BreachForums another sample of Victim-3's data for sale in or about July 2024. The post demanded a ransom payment, which Victim-3 never paid.*

Catist, unhappy with the company's decision not to pay his $250,000 ransom, decided to leak 40 million Victim-3 accounts on BreachForums using the ShinyHunters' official account (see Figure 18.2).

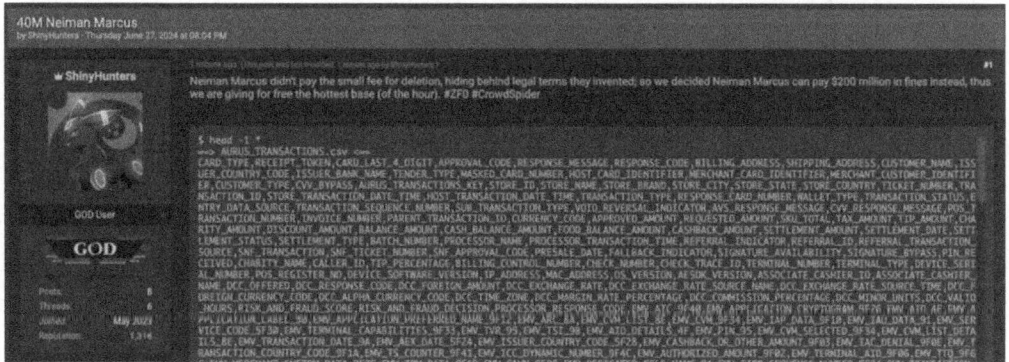

Figure 18.2: BreachForums leak of Victim-3's data.

I know the post came from Catist (not Shiny) because the writing style was all wrong. It lacked Shiny's usual tone and precision. Plus, Shiny's been around long enough to know that Victim-3 wasn't going to pay $200 million in fines, and he definitely wouldn't have framed the demand in terms of regulatory penalties. That kind of language just wasn't his.

July 4: Free Taylor Swift Tickets

Catist had finally accepted the reality that Victim-4 wasn't going to pay. So in response, he decided to leak 440,000 Taylor Swift Eras Tour ticket barcodes (see Figure 18.3).

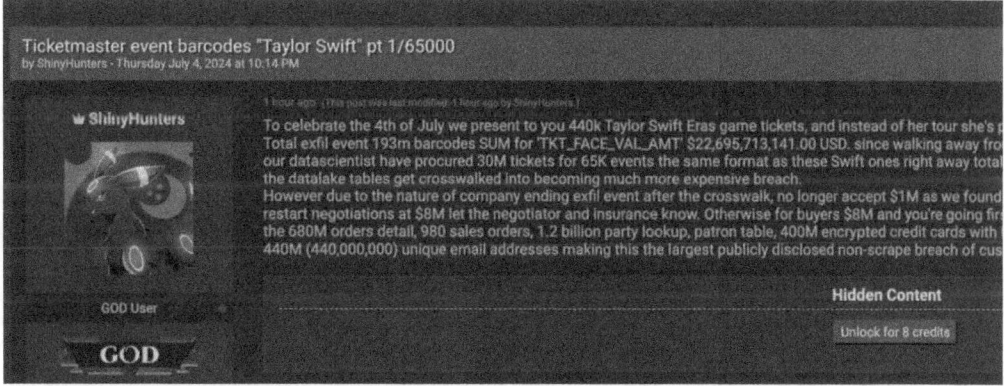

Figure 18.3: Catist's Taylor Swift post on BreachForums.

The following is the complete text from the BreachForums post. Again, you can tell this is written by Catist because he's the only person who would threaten a company by listing a dollar amount of the tickets. Plus, it includes a lot of technical jargon and run-on sentences that most people can't understand.

The post read:

> *To celebrate the 4th of July we present to you 440k Taylor Swift Eras game tickets, and instead of her tour she's performing in front of congress.*
>
> *Total exfil event 193m barcodes SUM for "TKT_FACE_VAL_AMT" $22,695,713,141.00 USD. since walking away from rushed $1m offer which LiveNation were lucky we had accepted originally, our datascientist have procured 30M tickets for 65K events the same format as these Swift ones right away total TKT_FACE_VAL_AMT SUM $4,665,615,212.00. It's very simple, take longer and the datalake tables get crosswalked into becoming much more expensive breach.*
>
> *However due to the nature of company ending exfil event after the crosswalk, no longer accept $1M as we found out how to make way more expensive and insurance surely accepts this; **we restart negotiations at $8M let the negotiator and insurance know.** Otherwise for buyers $8M and you're going first, no time wasters or annoying MM. For buyers of barcode table, comes with the 680M orders detail, 980 sales orders, 1.2 billion party lookup, patron table, 400M encrypted credit cards with First1/L4/expdt 560M AVS detail record, 4 million first 6, uncased and deduped*
>
> *440M (440,000,000) unique email addresses making this the largest publicly disclosed non-scrape breach of customer PII of all time.*

$8 million dollars? Seriously?!?

July 5: Another Taylor Swift Leak

The very next day, user Sp1d3r—now rebranded as Sp1d3rHunters—released the exact same data; this time in a format that looked and sounded more like ShinyHunters.

I'm not entirely sure what happened behind the scenes, but my guess is there was some disagreement over how the data should be posted. My guess is that Shiny, being the more experienced data broker, reposted it in a cleaner, more organized format so that journalists and researchers could actually make sense of it (see Figure 18.4).

Victim-4 responded to the media inquiries by stating that the barcodes weren't valid. Apparently, Taylor Swift tickets could only be electronic, and they utilized some sort of rotating barcode numbers. Printed tickets were no longer accepted at her shows.

Catist's plot was foiled.

July 8: More Event Barcodes

The media's response to Taylor Swift tickets was no deterrent for Catist. While Swift events may require electronic tickets, Victim-4 had thousands of other events that *would* accept printed barcodes.

So, Catist decided to leak 30,000 of them, along with a simple YouTube guide on creating your own realistic-looking event tickets (see Figure 18.5). His thinking was that Victim-4 would realize the error of their ways and suddenly pay him to not leak more.

Spoiler alert: They still didn't care.

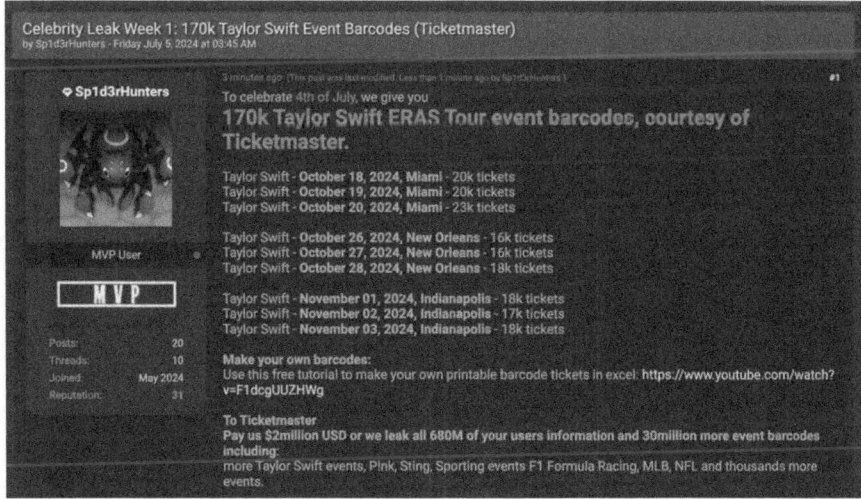

Figure 18.4: Repost of Taylor Swift tickets.

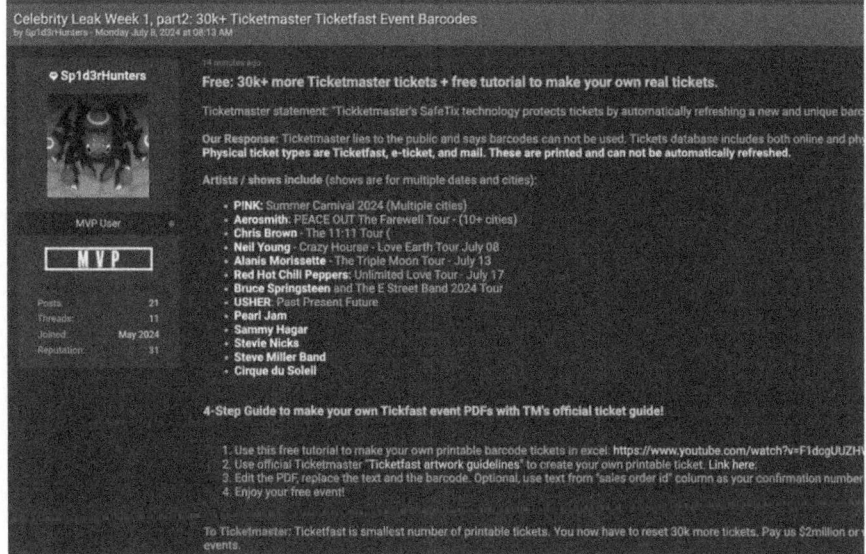

Figure 18.5: More event barcodes leak on BreachForums.

July 10: Victim-3 Celebrity Leak

Keeping with the trend of escalating data leaks, Catist decided to go for maximum visibility. To prove that Victim-3 was "lying" about not having PII in the exposed dataset, he pulled high-profile personal details straight from the breach and dumped them publicly.

The leak included email addresses, phone numbers, shopping records, and nearly complete credit card numbers for the following roster of well-known names:

- Melania Trump
- Ivanka Trump
- Jill, Halie, Sara, and Hunter Biden
- Bill Clinton
- Barbara Bush
- Kylie Jenner
- Kim Kardashian
- Beth Ostrosky Stern
- Robert Downy Jr.

And many more. In his post (see Figure 18.6), he added:

Now is this data worth something now that you see how many celebrities, politicians and their children are in this database? What about shopping habits? Is it important to know that President Bill Clinton was in Honolulu in April 2023 and what was at your store and what did he purchase using his debit card (4811 xxxx 72115)?

$1 million is nothing to protect this information. Do the right thing and we will keep your data safe.

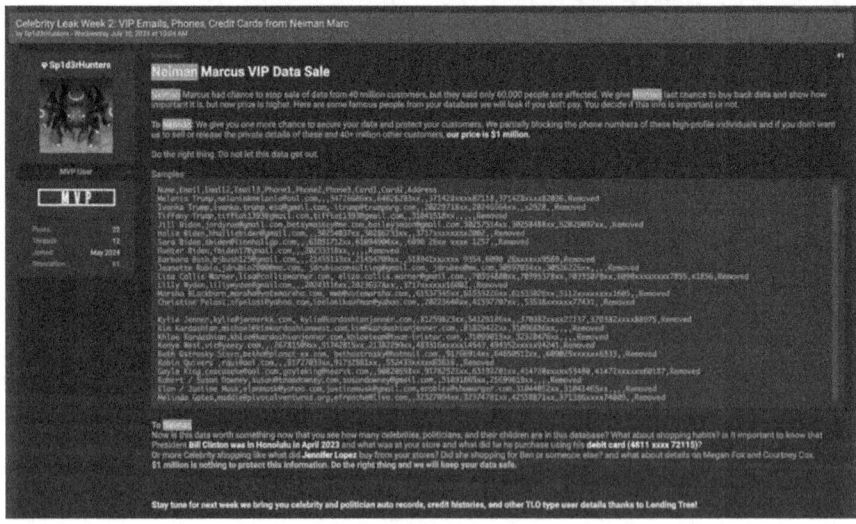

Figure 18.6: Victim-3 VIP data post.

What Catist would not understand is that once a company reaches a decision on whether or not to pay, there is generally no going back.

July 12: Print Your Own Tickets

Continuing on, a random user from the forum made a very simple and easy-to-use web app for printing your own event tickets. It was a basic HTML file with a form that enabled you to select which event you wanted and pick your desired seats. It would then format and print your tickets.

After tireless research, Catist found out that Canada *does* allow printed Taylor Swift tickets, so he made sure to include 175,000 of those tickets in this data leak (see Figure 18.7).

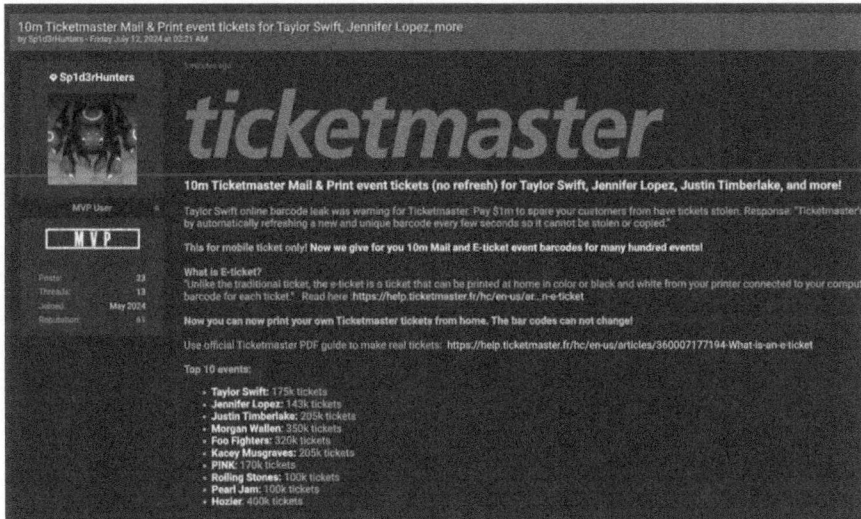

Figure 18.7: Print-your-own-event tickets post on BreachForums.

Unfortunately, by this point, the media had stopped caring.

July 12–20

During this time, I counted six more victims that I attempted to contact as part of the stolen data extortions. There's no need to list them all, as I think you get the idea.

July 21: Victim-3 and Planet Catist

After everything that I've covered regarding Victim-3, the retail company—including all the back and forth negotiations, changes in ransom demands, partial data leaks, and their final decision to shut the door and walk away—Catist still asked me about them convinced they might eventually pay.

catist: how close are [Victim-3] to paying

Reddington: [Victim-3]? 0%

[Victim-3] died a long time ago

He honestly had no idea. He leaked a majority of their data. Why would they pay?

All of these events unfolded over just three months. There was certainly more happening behind the scenes, but what I've covered here is enough to show just how quickly—and how far—this case was moving.

Before I move on to the breach notifications portion of this chapter, there's one more victim I want to highlight—because the scenario that unfolded was nothing short of outrageous.

June 28: Ticketek

Ticketek, owners of Teg.com.au, is an Australian-based event and ticketing company—similar to Vivid Seats or Ticketmaster, but focused exclusively on events in Australia. They were also one of Catist's victims, but the way they chose to handle the incident was unlike anything I'd seen before.

On June 28, 2024, I received the following email:

> *Mr Troia, please find enclosed some legal documents issued by the Supreme Court of NSW. While you are not a party to those proceedings, you will note that we have informed the Court that you are in apparent communication with a Threat Actor who exfiltrated data from our client. In compliance with Order 3(b) made by the Court we are writing to ask you to forward the enclosed documents to the Threat Actor with whom you are in apparent communication.*

The court documents included the following notice to the defendants, Catist and Sp1d3r (one of Catist's associates), *demanding that they stop transmitting the stolen data* (see Figure 18.8). I'll let you read it.

The public court order also explained that the attorney attempted to contact me via LinkedIn and proceeded to provide several pages of *screenshots of my personal website*.

While this may not seem like a big deal, please understand that these court documents, which included all of my personal details, were also *sent directly to Sp1d3r via his XMPP account* (see Figure 18.9), and by attachment *to his BreachForums accounts*.

Thankfully, Catist was the one in control of that account, and he already knew who I was.

But let's be clear—I do not appreciate having my personal information handed to some random members of Scattered Spider. Also included in these legal documents was security researcher Troy Hunt of HaveIBeenPwned.com. I can only imagine that he felt the same way.

Looking back at this event, I am genuinely curious about something: Did the Supreme Court of New South Wales really believe a legal document was going to stop a threat actor from distributing stolen data?

Look at Sp1d3r's Jabber address in Figure 18.9. Did they seriously send legal papers to someone using that domain name and genuinely expect results?

It was clear that they had no idea who Catist or Sp1d3r actually were—or the kind of people they were dealing with. But sure, let's serve them legal papers and hope they feel compelled to hop a flight to Australia, walk into a courtroom, and voluntarily unmask themselves. Really?

RELIEF CLAIMED

The Court ORDERS as follows:

1.   The Defendants (and any third party in possession of some or all of the Impacted
        Dataset, including Exfiltrated Data made aware of these orders) be restrained from:

        a. Placing further material from the Impacted Dataset at any location on the
            internet;

        b. Transmitting, publishing or disclosing any of the Impacted Dataset to any
            person or facilitating such steps;

        c. Using (including viewing) any information from the Impacted Dataset already
            in their possession for any purpose, other than obtaining legal advice in
            connection with these Orders;

        d. Promoting or publishing any links to locations from which the Impacted
            Dataset may be able to be downloaded;

            without the Plaintiff's written consent.

2.   The Defendants take all steps to immediately remove the Impacted Dataset
        (including the Exfiltrated Data) from all accessible internet locations (including Tor
        servers).

3.   For the avoidance of doubt, nothing in these orders prevents the Defendants or any
        other person from publishing, communicating or disclosing such of the Impacted
        Dataset which was already in or thereafter comes into the public domain (other than
        as a result of a breach of interlocutory or final orders made by the Court in these
        proceedings).

4.   Such further or other orders as the Court sees fit.

5.   Costs.

Note: the definition of "**Impacted Dataset**", "**Exfiltrated Data**" and "**Persons Unknown**" is
set out in the Statement of Claim and are incorporated into these orders by reference.

Figure 18.8: Relief page from Ticketek court order.

2. Orders that the notice of motion be returnable instanter.

Substituted service, foreign service, and abridgement of time

3   Orders pursuant to UCPR 10.14, a copy of the Documents and these orders
        be served on the Defendants by:

        (a) sending an email attaching copies of the Documents and these orders
            by sending a message to the Threat Actor's 'jabber' messaging account
            being sp1d3r⬛⬛⬛⬛⬛; and

        (b) sending a copy of the Documents to Mr Troia via email address being
            ⬛⬛⬛⬛⬛⬛⬛⬛, with a request that they be forwarded to the Threat
            Actor.

Figure 18.9: Court documents.

I think this anecdote is a good place to wrap up the discussion of breach victims. At this point, I've covered the who, the how, and just how deep the damage went.

Now it's time to shift focus—away from the breaches themselves and toward how they were handled. The next section takes a closer look at what was disclosed publicly, what was ignored, and how each company tried to shape the narrative once the data was already out.

Breach Disclosures

Everything in this chapter so far has been leading up to addressing the issue of how companies did—or did not—handle their breach disclosures.

Having worked with a number of organizations on recapturing and safeguarding customer data, I'm genuinely floored by how little most of the affected companies seemed to care about protecting their customers' personal information.

But even when a company does disclose a breach, the question is: Does it actually matter? Does it meaningfully impact them in any way?

The answer may depend on how we define personally identifiable information (PII)—and what legal thresholds trigger mandatory notification. So before I get into who disclosed what (and who didn't), I break down what actually qualifies as PII and when companies are legally required to notify customers about a breach.

Defining PII

Personally Identifiable Information (PII) refers to any data that can be used to identify a specific individual. This includes direct identifiers (e.g., a name, SSN, or driver's license number). In some cases, indirect identifiers (e.g., date of birth, Internet Protocol address, or ZIP code) could reasonably be used to pinpoint someone's identity.

In the context of data breach laws, PII that triggers a mandatory breach notification generally includes sensitive data elements that, if compromised, pose a risk of harm to the individual.

However, not all PII is treated equally. For example, a name or phone number alone usually isn't enough to trigger a breach notification, unless it's tied to another sensitive data element. However, once multiple identifiers are exposed together (e.g., name, date of birth, and SSN), the data becomes significantly more exploitable and crosses the legal threshold for most data breach notification laws.

Let's consult with security and privacy attorney M. Scott Koller on this subject.

M. Scott Koller
Privacy and Data Security Attorney, Clark Hill PLC

In the United States, state laws generally require notification if you know or have a reasonable basis to believe there has been unauthorized access to "personal information." Although that definition varies slightly depending on the state of residency for the affected individual, it generally includes an individual's name, in combination with, one of the following:

A social security number, driver's license number, or other form of Government identification number such as state identification number, tax identification number, passport number, military identification number, or other unique identification number issued on a government document commonly used to verify the identity of a specific individual.

A financial account number or credit or debit card number, in combination with any required security code, access code, or password that would permit access to an individual's financial account.

A date of birth, mother's maiden name (only in certain states), medical or health insurance information, or biometric data generated from measurements or technical analysis of human body characteristics (e.g., fingerprint, retina, or iris image, used to authenticate a specific individual).

Also, a username or email address, *in combination with* a password or security question and answer *that would permit access to an online account.*

Breach Notifications

On the topic of breach notifications and required disclosures, it feels like everyone is playing by their own rules. I have been in plenty of situations where companies have flat out ignored the breach. A few years ago I was even involved in a situation where the company flat out lied to the press claiming they were never breached—and I had a copy of the data! At that point, there was nothing that could be done.

So when is a company actually required to notify its customers?

M. Scott Koller
Privacy and Data Security Attorney, Clark Hill PLC

Breach notifications will vary based on state requirements. Certain states require details posted about the number of effected individuals. There are states where you can notify a million of them, and you might never know about the breach because you aren't one of the effected people. Those states may also not have public postings of data breaches. California is an example where anything over 500 people affected needs to be posted.

With respect to the Snowflake databases, there are situations where if the data does not qualify as PII, they aren't required to make disclosures. Phone numbers, email address, and addresses by themselves aren't considered PII.

With financial account numbers, it can be just as tricky. The statute may say that you have to notify if there's a breach of the security question of a pin code in combination with the account number that would enable access to that account.

The full account number was not exposed. Therefore, because you need the full account number to access the account, it doesn't trigger a notification.

SEC Breach Guidelines

In addition to standard breach guidelines, which are intended to be privacy-focused and designed to protect individuals when their PII or sensitive data is compromised, the SEC has its own set of guidelines.

The SEC's Cybersecurity Disclosure Rules are investor- and market-focused, and they apply specifically to public companies regulated by the SEC. These breach notification guidelines are designed to ensure that investors are informed about material cybersecurity incidents that could impact a company's operations, valuation, or risk profile.

M. Scott Koller

Privacy and Data Security Attorney, Clark Hill PLC

SEC reporting guidelines are different from state breach notification statutes and do not solely require an incident to involve the disclosure of personal information.

The SEC requires disclosure of any cybersecurity incident determined to be material. The reporting entity needs to consider whether there is a substantial likelihood that a reasonable investor would consider the information important in making an investment decision, or if it would have significantly altered the total mix of information made available.

When an organization is deciding on whether an event is "material" they need to consider the financial impact of the incident, including immediate fallout and long-term impact.

They must also consider the role of cyber insurance and the effect of credit monitoring for affected individuals.

It is entirely possible that an incident involving 100,000 stolen driver's licenses could be considered material for one organization, but not another.

While the SEC has recently published new guidance on breach disclosure, in practice, 8-K filings are rare as most organizations conclude that an incident is not material.

It seems as though there might still be some ways around these guidelines if no one is paying attention—or if the companies choose to outright deny.

To close out this chapter, I revisit some of the breach victims discussed earlier—and look at how each chose to respond once their incident became public.

Victim Breach Disclosures

Looking at all of these events objectively, it's easy to see why Catist assumed these companies would pay. In many cases, I'm still shocked they didn't. The data he had seemed to be more than enough to justify some payment, at least from a customer privacy protection standpoint.

But in the end, the more unsettling realization was this: *no one really cared.*

The news cycle was so saturated with breach headlines that most of these incidents barely registered, let alone sparked any meaningful response. It wasn't that the breaches weren't serious—it's that everyone had stopped paying attention.

To help put all of these breaches in perspective, here is a simple table outlining what happened:

VICTIM	PEOPLE EFFECTED	FIELDS	DISCLOSURE
Victim-2	100M	CDR call records	Full disclosure
Victim-3	80M	Customer details, purchase history, 12/16 credit card digits, and partial SSN	Breach confirmed for 64K people in Maine
Victim-4	60M	Full customer details (i.e., name, address, phone, email), purchase history, and event ticket barcodes	Public acknowledgment
Victim-5	600M+	Bank documents, transactions, customer records, and employee details	Full disclosure
Auto Retail Victim	80M	Full customer details (i.e., name, address, phone, and email)	Breach confirmed for 2.1M people in Maine
Auto Insurance Victim	190M	Full customer details (i.e., name, address, phone, and email), driving histories, risk profiles, and driver's license numbers	"Investigation is ongoing." *No official disclosure or breach notification*
Medical Victim	1.1M	Medical prescriber details and their corresponding DEA numbers	No disclosure or acknowledgment
MSP Victim	N/A	Internal system details	Full disclosure
K12 Victim	26M	Student details, grades, and medical information	No disclosure or acknowledgment

Lack of Breach Notification Laws

The Snowflake intrusions impacted at least 165 organizations—but in this chapter, I've only had time to cover a handful. With few exceptions, most companies chose not to fully disclose—or even acknowledge—the details of their breach. And legally, why should they?

The United States still has no comprehensive federal data breach notification law. While there have been repeated attempts to pass one, every effort has stalled in Congress. As a result, companies operate under a patchwork of state laws—some with vague timelines, others that require no notification at all if the breach is deemed "unlikely to cause harm."

A federal standard could change that by enforcing clear timelines, defining what qualifies as PII, and removing the ambiguity that allows companies to downplay or delay disclosure.

But this isn't just about consumer protection. From an intelligence standpoint, how we define and disclose PII directly impacts what data flows into the open—and what stays buried. If the information in these breaches had been treated with the seriousness it warranted, we'd have a far clearer picture of what was lost—and how that loss might be used against us.

Summary

This chapter chronicled the timeline of victim discovery and breach disclosure in the aftermath of the Snowflake data intrusion. It detailed the extortion campaigns that followed, the chaotic interactions between the hackers, and how each impacted organization responded (or didn't). Some victims opted for silence, while others paid. Most tried to manage their exposure quietly. But what's most striking is how frequently companies either denied the breach altogether or minimized it, despite overwhelming evidence of compromise.

The chapter included firsthand chat logs and dark web posts that trace how stolen data was handled and weaponized. Despite having leaked data on hundreds of millions of individuals—including full voter files, driving histories, and financial information—most of the breached organizations failed to meaningfully disclose what happened.

The next chapter is the final chapter in this saga, which covers the events leading to Catist's identification and capture.

Identifying Moucka

This chapter brings the Snowflake saga to a close by examining the events that led to the identification and arrest of Connor Moucka—better known online as *Catist, Waifu, ellyel8, Judische,* and a several other aliases.

I want to preface this chapter by stating that my role in this was *not* attribution. It was never my intent—or job—to uncover Moucka's identity. Having dealt with the fallout that can come from exposing a threat actor's real identity, that's not a situation I wanted to repeat.

In the end, it was Alison Nixon, the security researcher I thanked in this book's dedication, who was able to uncover his identity.

Despite my repeated warnings, Catist couldn't help himself from taunting her over Telegram. Eventually, the threats escalated to the point where finding him became her personal mission.

But let's be clear—uncovering his identity didn't come down to analyzing forum chats or cross-referencing infostealer logs. According to the arrest documents, the details are vague—but I believe that a little deductive reasoning will show that Nixon was able to identify Moucka because people inside certain organizations gave her access to privileged customer data.

Given this book's dedication—and that she's been one of the most vocal critics against engaging with threat actors, and of me in general—This felt like an extremely satisfying end to this story.

What makes it especially poetic is that the key to her discovery was insider access that should have required a subpoena. In other words, it's no different than the kinds of hacked data I've detailed throughout this book.

Credit where it's due—it was an impressive find. But it also reinforces an uncomfortable truth: *Those who shout the loudest about ethics and rules are often the first to break them—when it serves their purpose.*

Catist's Ego and Immaturity

Catist's downfall was his ego sprinkled in with a fair amount of immaturity. Plain and simple, he wouldn't shut up, and he wouldn't stop taunting reporters and researchers. He exhibited every trait you would expect from a young, immature hacker who does these kinds of things. He was extremely overconfident in his own psychological operations (PSYOP) abilities and felt he was invincible because his operational security (OPSEC) was completely tight, and no one would ever find him.

Pro tip: If you know you're the subject of a global manhunt, maybe don't hang out in public Telegram chats monitored by every threat intelligence firm on the planet.

But Catist broke the cardinal rule of cybercrime: He couldn't keep his mouth shut. He taunted security reporter Brian Krebs, and worse, he made online death threats against someone known for working closely with him—Alison Nixon.

Threats Against Nixon

For reference, here are some of the messages Catist was posting about Nixon:

judische:	Alison Nixon is gonna get necklaced with a tire filled with gasoline soon.
judische:	Spiders scatter if you turn on the lights. They're afraid of bright things. Alison Nixon knows this, that's why she' afraid of being lit on fire
judische:	im just sticking to selling alison nixon nudes
judische:	decerebration is my fav type of brain death, thats whats gonna happen to alison Nixon
judische:	Alison Nixon after i sent ms13 to brick her
judische:	need someone to run up in her home
	and fill her house full of gasoline
judische:	who has Alison Bricksons current address

Honestly, Catist was all talk—but I understand the concern. Having lived with the threat of people unexpectedly showing up at my house (see Chapter 1), I can tell you firsthand that no one should have to live like that.

Messages with Reporters

When it comes to Catist's own self-destructive tendencies, his interactions with Brian Krebs were a masterclass in what *not* to do. He couldn't help himself. Despite my repeated warnings to stop engaging, he just wouldn't listen.

Here are a handful of conversations where I tried—more than once—to get him to stop. But by then, the damage was already done.

June 5:

Reddington:	how does krebs have your info
	P L E A S E
	do not respond to him
catist:	okay xd
	idk how he found me
	should i tell him im a girl?
Reddington:	probably the same way alon found you
	no. he won't believe you
	in the entire history of computing, there has never been a convicted female criminal hacker
catist:	im the first one
Reddington:	talking to krebs will spin things out of control. You should stop.

The very next day, despite my warning, he sent me a screenshots of the conversation he was having with Krebs.

June 6:

Reddington:	Is that Krebs?
catist:	yes
Reddington:	How does he know you are waifu
	Or obnoxious
	Bro why are you talking to him.
	This will only end in disaster for you
	He will figure out who you are very quickly
	The moment he connects you to Bins it's all over
catist:	because he has disinfo and thinks im obnoxious/waifu, why not push the envelope and have them waste their time on him?

Reddington:	Think this through
catist:	krebs thinks that waifu is obnoxious tho, so it's fine
Reddington:	I don't care if you are waifu one way or the other
	I'm just saying. Absolutely nothing good will come of you taking to Krebs
catist:	I'm just attributing these hacks to Brandan Lukus Apple

Catist wouldn't listen to my repeated warnings. He kept talking to reporters, thinking he was somehow able to outsmart them with his PSYOP abilities.

June 9:

catist:	should i send brian krebs the
	adl.org
	active directory db to troll and misdirect him further
Reddington:	No
	Stop talking to him
	I don't know why you aren't listening
	If you want to be caught then keep talking to him
	I have warned you. It's a very bad idea
catist:	because I am good at PSYOP and i overreact to his keywordings
	so he is directed toward believing im certain ppl
	since ik how to respond to keywords

I'm not sure how much clearer I could have been. Against my advice, Catist wouldn't stop taunting or speaking with Krebs (and other reporters).

June 11:

catist:	is my trolling of krebs legendary btw? or am i a dumbass. basically i bought some egirl rolex to flex on another girl krebs thought he can get intel out of but my girlfriend irl slapped me and said she'd send her all of my money so she can buy more rolexes if i ever do anything like that again and she's still mad but i thought it's good "detrace"
Reddington:	You are a dumbass. I don't know what's happening but all you are doing is pissing him off.

June 15:

> **Reddington:**   The best thing you can say is nothing
>
> **catist:**   ive had every person that came to me so far with krebs investigation say to him "oh hes just a gamer"
>
> same thing i said to him
>
> he will give up when he sees nobody knows anything and the most they know are the trollings i give them to mess with him
>
> im kind of embarrassed to be good at HUMINT
>
> even if it's impressive to be so. it's just embarassing to me idk why
>
> im good at HUMINT coincidentally tho, just because I reverse engineered how humans think and behave.
>
> I think SIGINT and COMINT/ELINT are my main skills tho
>
> even if i'm above average HUMINT
>
> **Reddington:**   No, Krebs won't just "give up."

June 19:

> **catist:**   brian krebs is a weird stalker to have idk why he wants to deanonymize me so much.
>
> from reading my message history as hes doing the only conclusion is this persons insane
>
> this is how i have better intel than krebs has tho
>
> **Reddington:**   Maybe because you won't leave him alone.
>
> And you made nudes of Alison Nixon? to piss him off?
>
> **catist:**   i didn't do that
>
> **Reddington:**   You're just like Shiny. That's exactly the same shit he did with the fbi. You have to poke to bear and you end up getting caught. Why don't you stop fucking with him
>
> **catist:**   Who made the nudes of Alison
>
> i can find out if it's needed but i don't usually spend time doing that kind of trolling. my trolling is more about just saying absurd things
>
> what type of nudes
>
> she is obsessed with me and i've told lots of ppl about how obsessed she is esp recently. so it could have been any of them and most likely is
>
> i used to spy on unit 221b slack in 2021 bc i had it hacked

Reddington:	I Was told nudes were sent right after this.
	It's pissing people off
catist:	im trolling in those messages and i didn't pay 10btc to have someone brick her, i just wanted an excuse to say "allison brickson" bc i thought itd be funny
Reddington:	W H Y are you fucking with them.
	You're just going to piss him off

As it turns out, the fake AI-generated nudes came from someone else within Scattered Spider. But by then, the damage was done. By this point, finding Catist had become a personal mission for Nixon.

Hunting Catist

Early in the investigation, there were plenty of theories about where Catist might be located. Based on his language and dialect, my personal assessment pointed to either Canada or Arizona—two regions that tend to sound especially neutral or "flat" in written communication.

Catist himself made several references to living in Canada, but he also openly tried to direct his own attribution toward Brandon Apple, another known Canadian cybercriminal. We had no idea whether those references were genuine or just a calculated form of misdirection. So, we worked with what we had—analyzing every conversational breadcrumb I could extract from him.

Using AI for Chat Analysis

One day, Dallas sent me a chart that he'd built by manually analyzing Catist's chat logs—looking at timestamps, patterns of activity, and posting windows.

His conclusion was that Catist was likely operating in the Eastern Standard Time (EST) or Central Standard Time (CST) time zones. *He was right.*

Knowing how much effort he put into that analysis, I thought it would be interesting to see if ChatGPT could replicate his results.

Query

Here are telegram chat messages involving a threat actor. Ignore any messages from Reddington. Based on the times posted, are you able to extrapolate which times of day he is most active. And based on that, along with any of his messages, can you infer which time zone he might be in?

Figures 19.1 and 19.2 show the response.

Worth noting in the key patterns analysis, is that while certain time windows showed periods of silence, they also coincided with some of Catist's most focused activity (see Figure 19.2). In particular, Friday through Sunday often marked 72-hour hacking binges, where he'd go dark socially but become laser-focused on active intrusions. It wasn't downtime—he was in his zone.

🔍 **Observed Active Periods (CST timestamps)**

Across logs from April through July:

- **Most frequent activity windows (CST):**

  - **10:00 PM to 4:00 AM** — heavy presence (message spikes between 11PM–2AM especially)

  - **Some activity continues until 6:00–8:00 AM,** but this usually trails off

  - **Scattered messages in the afternoon,** but much lower density and often refer to "just woke up," "taking a nap," or "ran out of Adderall"

🕵 **Behavioral Pattern (from chat content)**

- Regularly mentions **napping at 5–6 AM CST,** implying a night owl/hacker rhythm.

- Notes about needing Adderall or "being up late" reinforce a nocturnal lifestyle.

- Rarely responds in the early daytime (6 AM–12 PM CST) unless it's to say they're just waking up or going back to sleep.

- When online, frequently engages in multitasking queries and infrastructure-related tasks — clearly working when others are offline.

Figure 19.1: ChatGPT output of message analysis.

Generated with AI using OpenAI

Key Patterns:

- **Peak activity** is concentrated between **10 PM and 5 AM CST,** especially on **Monday through Thursday.**

- **Minimal activity** occurs during CST daytime hours, suggesting he's likely asleep or offline.

- **Behavior aligns with a nocturnal work schedule,** reinforcing the inference that he operates in a **UTC+3** time zone, treating CST overnight hours as his working daytime.

Figure 19.2: Key pattern analysis.

Generated with AI using OpenAI

ChatGPT also asked if I wanted to see a heatmap of the activity (see Figure 19.3). Along with the visual, it provided a detailed breakdown and analysis of the timestamps, highlighting patterns when Catist was most active.

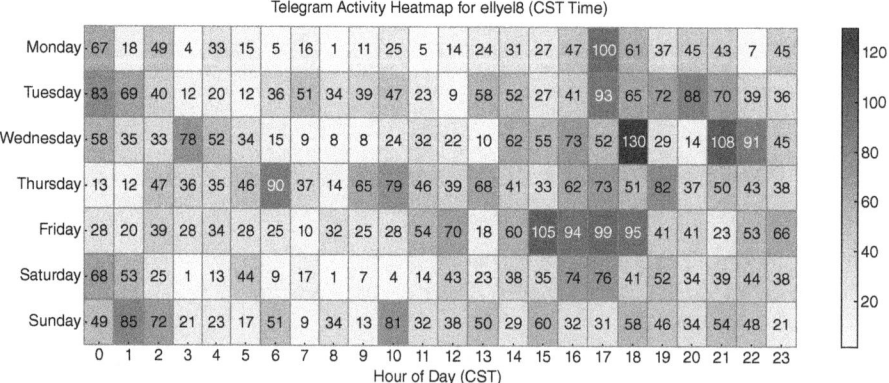

Figure 19.3: Heatmap of activity.

Generated with AI using OpenAI

Based on this data, it even generated two working hypotheses about his likely time zone and geographic location—both of which aligned with behavioral clues from our previous interactions (see Figure 19.4).

⊞ What the Heatmap Shows:

- ellyel8 is most active from 10 PM to 5 AM CST.

- That's **sustained late-night behavior**, not a one-off.

- Very little to no activity during **typical work hours (9 AM–4 PM CST)**.

Figure 19.4: Heatmap analysis.

Generated with AI using OpenAI

ChatGPT also generated two potential hypotheses regarding Catist's location based on the behavioral and timestamp data (see Figure 19.5).

Finally, based on all the evidence—chat timestamps, behavioral patterns, and usage trends—ChatGPT offered an educated guess on Catist's likely location (see Figure 19.6).

While not conclusive, it's worth noting that ChatGPT's analysis matched exactly what Dallas hypothesized. Different methods, same result.

So where is he?

Hypothesis A – He's in CST or EST

- If he's actually in **CST**, this is someone who consistently stays up until **5 AM local time**, which would imply:

  - He's a night owl operating in his **own local night**.

  - This aligns with some hackers' natural rhythms, especially younger ones or those avoiding heat.

  - He would be **sleeping during the day** (which matches chat content like "I just woke up" or "going for nap" around 2–4 PM CST).

  - **This is very plausible**.

- If he's in **EST (UTC-5)**, shift everything an hour earlier: activity from **11 PM to 6 AM local time**. Still plausible for a night owl, but it does push sleeping hours closer to morning/afternoon.

Hypothesis B – He's in UTC+2 to +4

- That would make his **active period correspond to 6 AM–1 PM local time**.

- Which is weird: he's doing "night shift behavior" during his **early morning hours**.

- Also conflicts with what he *says* — he frequently mentions napping, staying up late, or just waking up at CST-appropriate hours.

Figure 19.5: ChatGPT location hypotheses.

Generated with AI using OpenAI

Chat Evidence Supports CST/EST

- He repeatedly references **needing Adderall, running out of energy, taking naps in the early afternoon CST**, etc.

- He treats **2–4 AM CST as "working prime time"** and 2 PM CST as "just woke up".

- That's not someone whose local time is 6–9 AM. That's someone whose **actual clock is aligned with CST or EST**.

Figure 19.6: Chat evidence summary.

Generated with AI using OpenAI

Catist's Arrest

One evening, during the July 4th weekend in 2024, I received a call from Dallas that I'll never forget. His question was simple: "What's wetwork?"

Having just watched Scorsese's *The Irishman*, the term was fresh in my mind—*wetwork* refers to covert operations involving assassination or politically sensitive violence. He didn't say much else, only that he was chasing a lead on Catist involving a username referenced on Telegram that he also saw as part of a clue left behind in a separate data leak involving Trusts Bank.

Not long after that, things began to slow down on the investigation. Dallas eventually hinted that they had a name for Catist, but couldn't go into details.

The Mystery of Catist's Arrest

On October 30, 2024, Connor Moucka was arrested at his home in Kitchener, Ontario. At the time, the details behind his identification were still a mystery to me. After the arrest, Alison Nixon gave several public interviews, openly taking credit as the person who identified Moucka.

In her public statements, Nixon also declined to reveal the specifics, saying only that her firm, Unit 221B, had worked with Mandiant to unmask him.

The following excerpt comes from an interview Nixon gave to *The Record*, where she spoke about the investigation and the events that led to Catist's arrest. (I've bolded certain elements that are relevant to the story.)[1]

> *After making a critical mistake in what cybersecurity types call "operational security," a member of Nixon's team was able to follow the digital bread crumb on the internet, the dark web and messaging apps to reveal "Waifu's" real identity.*
>
> **She did not want to talk about how Unit221B did that**, *saying hackers learn from the mistakes of other cybercriminals, making it more difficult to catch them in the future.*
>
> **But Unit221B and Mandiant, the cybersecurity company owned by Google, found out who he was and passed the information to law enforcement.**

I've always found it odd that neither Nixon nor Krebs—who's known for writing detailed breakdowns about how he connects vast pieces of information to unmask cyber criminals—ever explained how Moucka was ultimately identified.

The *Wall Street Journal* even wrote a feature on Krebs and his pursuit to unmask Moucka, including details of a "97-page document with clues like email addresses, online usernames, forum posts, and chat records."

The article stated:[2]

> *Nixon was driven to investigate because of the online threats against her. In* **collaboration with an anonymous researcher**, *her firm uncovered Waifu's real-world identity by early July and turned the information over to authorities, she said. Researchers don't like to reveal exactly how they trace anyone's real-world identity. "We're never going to disclose how, because the threat actors want to know," said Nixon, who noted only that at one point Waifu made a move that inadvertently left a digital trail. Krebs and the cybersecurity firm Mandiant were just a few steps behind.*

For a case of this scale, the silence was noticeable. In all my history in cybersecurity, I have never seen a story with this much attention not disclose the identifying piece of information. Fortunately, the official court documents fill in the blanks.

---

[1] https://www.therecord.com/news/waterloo-region/accused-kitchener-hacker-unmasked-after-threatening-woman-online/article_3501ea8b-1514-5524-8de6-f52e92c3e103.html
[2] https://www.wsj.com/tech/cybersecurity/hacking-brian-krebs-snowflake-waifu-49b87fce

Identifying Catist

Catist's identification ultimately boiled down to one thing: *Discord*. According to the official arrest warrant, he operated three primary Discord accounts—Azurape, Wetwork, and Nutz—and on those accounts, he openly discussed his Telegram handles and Snowflake-related victims.

Apparently, he didn't think anyone was monitoring Discord.

In the following chat, for example, he casually mentions Victim-1 and openly links himself to his Telegram username: @judische.

azurape#0:	I think I mentioned [Victim-1] to you a few weeks before news hit; you can extrapolate to whom this article is about and I can tell you the amount this very low effort campaign made at high 7 figures now as a test run. I would prospect you for my team if you aren't scared that it's high-risk. I would assert it's not or I'd be in jail probably before we even discussed WS2K3 RDP with cat_warrior/rdynamic in Jan 2019. If you would accept first round of this I would introduce you to the lead developer on my team and you can see if you have chemistry or decline if you don't. USA won't even exist in 10 years either, keep in mind. None of us are stupid, we won't get caught so you don't need to judge any of our characters if we'll snitch or not.
azurape#0:	https://cloud.google.com/blog/topics/threat-intelligence/unc5537-snowflake-data-theft-extortion
azurape#0:	bitcoin or any crypto ur okay with and I'll say the rest on tg
azurape#0:	@judische
[REDACTED]:	what's your tg I'll message you there
azurape#0:	depends, what's the specific work and what's the compensation
azurape#0:	do u want to work?

For completeness, the official arrest document states:

U.S. authorities reviewed IP logs from the intrusions into victim companies and identified malicious IP addresses at specific times. U.S. authorities then obtained court orders requiring electronic communication service providers to identify accounts that had been accessed by the malicious IP addresses at specific dates and timestamps.

Discord identified accounts accessed from the malicious IP addresses during the same time periods of the intrusions… U.S. authorities determined that three identified accounts were controlled by MOUCKA and provided key evidence of his identity:

1. *User ID 547214862313455626, with unique username azurape (the Azurape Discord Account);*

2. *User ID 1166162535477678110, with prior unique username zzzzzzzzzzzzzzzzzzznutz (the Nutz Discord Account); and*

3. *User ID 750491727025930364, with unique username wetworkmakeitrain (the Wetwork Discord Account).*

Most importantly, the Azurape Discord Account directly links MOUCKA to the @judische Telegram account that used the rapeflake tool to steal information from companies, as discussed above.

For example, approximately 10 days after [Mandiant] published a report about this hacking campaign, the Azurape Discord Account claimed ownership of the @judische Telegram account.

In addition to this May 2024 example, Azurape identified @judische as his Telegram moniker in February 2024 and April 2024 to other users in Discord chat messages.

Wetwork

The arrest document goes on to include how the connections were made between the Wetwork Discord account and Catist:

In response to a court order, Discord researched the Azurape Discord Account and the Wetwork Discord Account and linked them by cookie information, meaning that the same user account on the same computer accessed both accounts.

...

Discord records also showed numerous connections between the Nutz Discord Account and the Azurape Discord Account, suggesting these accounts were under common control by MOUCKA.

And more importantly, the following excerpts from the affidavit summarize the investigative findings that led to his identification and eventual arrest:

IP records from Discord showed that the user of the Nutz Discord Account logged into the account from the Canadian IP Address [24.246.30.67] over 3,350 times between October 28, 2023, and April 4, 2024.

...

U.S. authorities discovered an Apple account with email address nnnnddddwwwdffggaa [at]icloud.com, which Apple identified in response to a court order based on shared login IP addresses with MOUCKA' s Nutz Discord Account.

...

Google account connormoucka5[at]gmail.com has also used the Canadian IP address [24.246.30.67] as recently as August 26, 2024.

...

Records from the Nutz Discord Account indicate that its user is MOUCKA, who also goes by Alexander Moucka. For example, the Nutz Discord Account's user: states that his birth name is Connor and that he changed it to Alexander.

After reviewing these details, it became clear that the Canadian IP—listed as 24.246.30.67—was the critical link that tied the case together.

Legal process obtained on the IP address was also used to identify an iCloud account and a Google account connected to Connor Moucka.

From there, everything else fell into place.

Moucka's iCloud

In reference to his iCloud account, when the FBI gained legal access to Moucka's nnnnddddwwwdffggoo[at]icloud.com account, they hit the jackpot.

Connor apparently took screenshots of *everything* and stored them on his iCloud photos and storage account. The document states,

> For example, the iCloud account contains multiple photos of MOUCKA's Canadian passport, including this one with full name Connor Riley Moucka, passport number ******, date of birth 18 August 1999, in Kitchener, Canada.

The iCloud account also contained:

- Telegram conversations of him bragging about hacking Snowflake victims.
- Screenshots showing millions of dollars in cryptocurrency, and the *seed phrases for his Bitcoin and Monero wallets* (allowing law enforcement to seize his funds).
- Screenshots containing the *specific IP address of a virtual private server* where he stored a large amount of Victim-2's data, filenames of sensitive data exfiltrated (and confirmed by the FBI), and the name of the intermediary, Reddington.

He literally laid everything out for the authorities in one nice, neat package, including the keys to all of his hard-earned crypto.

And it all came down to a single IP address (and ultimately his lack of OPSEC).

Before we get to how the IP address was discovered, there was also one more item in the arrest document that was somewhat unusual.

Urgency

The arrest document noted that law enforcement accelerated the timeline, because a media outlet was preparing to publish a story that would reveal Moucka's identity:

> The evidence gathered by this investigation establishes that MOUCKA poses both a danger to the public and a serious risk of flight that require his immediate apprehension. Additionally, media outlets have contacted U.S. authorities about this matter and one outlet indicated it intends to name MOUCKA in an article to be submitted for publication on October 25, 2024. U.S. authorities believe that this publication would increase risk of flight and lead MOUCKA to destroy evidence and publish stolen information, including the extremely sensitive call and text history records stolen from Victim-2.

In the days that followed, there was a flurry of media coverage, with Nixon front and center, giving interviews and making bold statements like "Who wants to be next?" It was a clear message to other cybercriminals: Mess with the wrong person, and you'll get unmasked.

Nixon publicly took credit for identifying Moucka, portraying it as an investigative win due to "sloppy OPSEC," but never actually disclosing how she was able to connect the dots.

But here's the thing: All the FBI's data came from legal subpoenas—ISP records, account metadata, and service provider cooperation. Yet in a post-arrest interview,

Nixon stated that her firm, Unit 221B, "found out who he was and *passed the information to law enforcement*."

So, how exactly did someone uncover this information *before* the FBI?

If you go back and reread the "Wetwork" section—and pay close attention to the quoted statements—you should be able to figure it out. The IP address, referenced throughout the arrest warrant, could *only* have come from one of the two social media platforms that Catist used.

So let's just say … it helps to have friends on the inside—especially when those friends are willing to bend the rules, just a little, for what they consider "the right reasons."

Being Grey

To be clear, I have nothing but respect for Alison Nixon for figuring this out. Credit where it's due—it was solid work, and she got results.

But my point—aimed at those who've publicly criticized me or my methods—is this: *If you're going to operate in the grey, don't pretend you're above it.* And don't condemn others who are doing just as much good simply because they're not following *your* playbook.

As I've said before: in my experience, the people who scream the loudest about what others are doing are often the ones with the most to hide.

People who live in glass houses … and all of that.

Epilogue

In March 2025, Connor Riley Moucka signed a consent order in Ontario Superior Court in Kitchener, surrendering his rights and enabling his transfer to U.S. custody to face multiple charges.

On July 3, 2025, Moucka was successfully extradited to the United States, where he is currently awaiting trial, scheduled for August.

Who knows where this story will end up—or how much time he will end up serving given the sheer number of companies affected.

I wish I had more to share about Moucka for the epilogue. But in the absence of that, there's one last piece of the story I've held back—something you might find interesting.

Loose Ends

For the sake of completeness, I should say a few words about *Kiberphant0m*. Cameron John Wagenius, a 20-year-old former U.S. Army soldier, was arrested in Fort Hood, Texas. He's suspected of operating under the handle Kiberphant0m, a cybercriminal known for leaking and selling stolen call records from AT&T and Verizon.

Kiberphant0m was a loose associate of Moucka (aka Catist). The two collaborated on several intrusions—most notably, a breach of Verizon's first responder communications network. They gained access to the platform and exfiltrated call detail records (CDRs) and SMS messages from users operating on it. They attempted to extort Verizon by threatening to release the data—Verizon wasn't impressed.

Shortly after Moucka's arrest, Kiberphant0m resurfaced—this time retargeting AT&T. He claimed to have access to Catist's previously deleted CDR call records. As proof, he published sample call logs for Melania Trump and Vice President Kamala Harris on BreachForums, tagging the post with #FreeWaifu. Moucka later claimed that Kiberphant0m was helping to sell his data. Whether that's true is unclear. I only spoke with Kiberphant0m a few times (following Moucka's arrest), and based on those interactions, I don't believe he had access to any substantive data.

Following Wagenius's arrest, security researcher Alison Nixon issued a public statement, delivering the following stark warning to "all the other Kiberphant0ms out there who think they can't be found and arrested."

In a blog post, she made the following statements:[1]

> *Between when we, and* an anonymous colleague, *found his opsec mistake on November 10th to his last Telegram activity on December 6, law enforcement set the speed record for the fastest turnaround time for an American federal cyber case that I have witnessed in my career.*
>
> *I know that young people involved in cybercrime will read these articles. You need to stop doing stupid shit and get a lawyer. Law enforcement wants to put all of you in prison for a long time.*

Bold words—and a clear signal to anyone still operating under the illusion of anonymity.

I just can't help but wonder if the "anonymous colleague" was the same source of the internal Discord customer records logs referenced in the previous chapter—the ones that led to Moucka's identification and arrest. Either way, this was a solid win—even if it didn't come through traditional OSINT.

Then again, if internal customer data from Discord was accessed and quietly handed off by an insider, doesn't that technically qualify as breached data? And if so, does it become publicly available information (PAI) the moment it's been shared?

Probably not. I'll admit, that's a stretch.

But at the end of the day, this isn't all that different from working with traditional hacked, breached, or leaked (HBL) data. The only real distinction is that I didn't actively task someone to acquire it.

In the end, it comes down to comfort. How willing are you to operate in a grey area? And if it serves the greater good . . . maybe *grey isn't so bad after all.*

Thank You!

First and foremost, thank you to everyone who picked up a copy of this book and made it to the end. If you've read this far, then you've stayed with me through a complex, messy, and often uncomfortable journey into the world of dark web markets, HBL data, open-source intelligence (OSINT) tradecraft, and the evolving role of data in modern intelligence collection.

Writing this book has been an unexpected ride. Once I made the decision to start, the story took on a life of its own—and it came together faster than I anticipated. I'm incredibly grateful to have had this forum to express my views on dark web data acquisition and the operational value it holds. I truly believe that the insights found online—when handled responsibly—can provide real and lasting benefits to the national security mission.

This book was written with a purpose: to serve as a guidebook for the intelligence community. It's a practical manual for working with open-source, and publicly and

---

[1] https://krebsonsecurity.com/2024/12/u-s-army-soldier-arrested-in-att-verizon-extortions/

commercially available HBL data—how to acquire it, how to handle the legal and ethical constraints around it, and responsibly operationalize it when the stakes are high.

The grey areas aren't going away. My goal here was to help navigate them.

I hope I've done justice to the story of OSINT's evolution within the IC—capturing both the structural friction and the hard-earned progress. More importantly, I hope this book shows that there's a clear and credible path forward when it comes to integrating dark web HBL data into the broader national security toolkit.

Thank you again so much for your support!

Index